STAND AND DELIVER!

STAND AND DELIVER!

40 Simple Steps to Successful Public Speaking

IAN NICHOL

Matador
9 Priory Business Park,
Wistow Road, Kibworth Beauchamp,
Leicestershire. LE8 0RX
Tel: 0116 279 2299
Email: books@troubador.co.uk
Web: www.troubador.co.uk/matador
Twitter: @matadorbooks

ISBN 978 178901 3481
British Library Cataloguing in Publication Data.

Printed and bound by CPI Group (UK) Ltd, Croydon, CR0 4YY
A catalogue record for this book is available from the British Library.

Matador is an imprint of Troubador Publishing Ltd

Contents

THE KEY PRINCIPLES

THE KEY PREPARATION

THE KEY TECHNIQUES

Acknowledgements

I wrote much of this book while commuting between Rugby and Birmingham in the Midlands. My thanks go to two rail companies, Virgin Trains and the sadly now defunct London Midland Trains. Their relaxed approach to the observation of timetables gave me more time for committing my thoughts to paper than I had any reasonable right to expect.

My deeper gratitude goes to a British journalist and politician called Spencer Leigh Hughes, often referred to simply by his initials SLH, who wrote about public speaking a century ago and is the expert I quote most often. He was said to be the cleverest after-dinner speaker of his time. His 1913 book *The Art of Public Speaking* stands out for its common sense and good humour, a surprisingly rare combination in works on the subject, and he has become my guiding mentor from afar. I hope that his spirit lives on here.

Beyond SLH, I have made many references to past and present writers on public speaking who have inspired me. If I have inadvertently infringed anyone's copyright, please let me know at ijnichol@btinternet.com, so that I can put matters right for any subsequent edition.

Thanks go to a fine teacher called John Dascombe, who adjudged me the winner of the Tiffin Boys' School Public Speaking Competition in 1968, when I was a mere thirteen years old. That changed my life.

Several writers and editors have made major contributions to this book through their constructive comments – Gary Smailes, Karin Fancett and John Paxton Sheriff. Their detailed review and encouragement were exactly what I needed during the writing process, and gave me added momentum to see my project through to publication. They could not have been more helpful.

Finally, I record appreciation beyond measure for my parents, Tom and Joan, who first encouraged me to speak in public.

Introduction

This is a book about public speaking, but it only came about thanks to a comment from my personal trainer, Katie, one Monday morning at the gym. I was complaining that my creaky sixty-something-year-old body would not do what I was politely asking of it.

"Ian," she said, and I always pay extra attention when people get my name right, "you are much fitter than most people your age." She went on to make some complimentary comments about my 'guns', 'abs' and 'pecs', which I did not quite understand.

I was pleased, since long ago at school I was the weed of the class, the boy who tried to get out of PE lessons, who never learned to swim, and whose greatest achievement in sports was to come in last but one in cross-country running, thus avoiding the wooden spoon. Forty-five years later, I'd come to have a reasonably decent body shape and level of fitness for my age. This was mainly due to great coaching from Katie, coupled with a combination of commitment, hard work and enjoyment on my part.

If I can do it, I thought, anyone can do it.

It struck me that I could equally be talking about public speaking, one of my great passions in life. Public speaking is the subject of a needless air of mystique and of unhelpful misconceptions.

There are so many destructive but pervasive myths that deter would-be speakers: that speakers are born, not made; that being nervous in anticipation is somehow a sign of failure; that success depends on some magical form of body language, or perhaps on an exhaustive understanding of how to create beautiful PowerPoint slides. That's to name just a few of the old wives' tales.

As someone who has been a mentor to novice speakers over many years, I know that the reality is utterly different. Almost anyone can become a good speaker through enthusiasm and effort, and have a lot of fun on the way.

There is no such thing as a born speaker.

Nerves and even fear should be welcomed as friends. Body language and slides are just supports, a sideshow. What matters is you, the speaker, the personality you display and the words you use. There is nothing mystical about any of this, and I aim to be a Katie of public speaking to prove it.

How this book can help you

This book will provide you with tips and techniques to make you a better speaker. In the process, it will make the act of talking to an audience more enjoyable for you, and not only for you: when you come to associate speaking in public with having a good time, it is much more likely that the people listening to you will relish the experience as well.

I will set out what a speaking career of nearly fifty years has taught me, the things that would have made my own learning curve smoother. Over those years I may not have read every book ever written on public speaking, but it felt like it. And I found that the traditional textbook approach is strong on things like rhetorical devices and voice projection; but it is less impressive on what to do when your brain is not working, or most of the audience are drunk, or hardly anyone turns up, or your listeners know the subject better than you.

This book is the practical manual I wish I had possessed when I started out.

What's the catch?

To be honest, no book alone is going to turn you into an invariably outstanding speaker. Indeed, I'm not sure there ever was such a being: even Winston Churchill and Martin Luther King Jr had their off days, as Barack Obama does now. There are simply too many factors that can go wrong on any particular occasion: a bolshie audience, terrible acoustics, malevolent slides, a lifeless auditorium or an utterly dull subject.

I reckon, however, that the pragmatic approach adopted by this book can help people to perform dependably in the top 20% of speakers. It will not necessarily make you the best in the world, or even in your town, but it should be all you need for personal satisfaction and contentment for a job well done, not to mention audience approval and job success.

Public speaking truly can be fun

I subscribe to the theory that we all have an exhibitionist gene within us. Admittedly, we may have stifled it since the days of childhood, but public speaking gives us the chance to regain that youthful enthusiasm, to rekindle the fire while also communicating our enjoyment to a contented audience. We can engage with each member of the gallery, change their outlook for the better and cheer up their day.

I can honestly say that speaking in public has been the finest thing that ever happened to my self-esteem, and a successful talk will keep me bubbling for days or weeks afterwards. Apart from anything else, as a speaker you get to dominate a captive audience for periods of up to an hour or more at a time. You do not get that chance very often in life. Younger readers may be less likely to mourn its loss, but for older ones who are married it can be an unmissable opportunity.

How hard can it be?

Nothing in this book will be rocket science.

Quite simply, public speaking is just about talking to people. No more, no less. Ray Keeslar Immel, a distinguished American teacher of practical oratory, summed it up in his book *The Delivery of a Speech*.

"The purpose of a speech," he wrote, "is to *communicate ideas*. It is of the greatest importance that the speaker, at the very outset, get the idea firmly in mind that he is *talking to people*. This would seem to be too simple to dwell upon, but a little observation will make clear that the one thing that the student finds hardest is to get this attitude. He should rid himself of the idea, so false in its usual connotation, that he is 'making a speech'. He is not 'making a speech', he is not repeating sentences before people, he is not talking *at* people. He is talking *to* people. He is communicating his ideas to them."

It is all quite straightforward. That's not to say it doesn't require hard work, which is an entirely different matter. If you put in that work and prepare thoroughly, and if you can accept that nerves at the start of your performance are precisely what you ought to be experiencing, you will do fine.

The audience will recognise in you the essential qualities of a successful speaker:

- A genuine, honest approach.
- Displaying good knowledge of your subject.
- Using straightforward, natural, direct language.
- Showing energy and commitment in the process.

Chris Anderson is the man who directs the global TED talks, probably the most famous speaking events on the planet. (The name TED comes from the themes of Technology, Entertainment and Design with which these conferences began.) His experience confirms that you do not need to be a mastermind to achieve speaking eminence. "There is no one way to success, no rules, no formula for a great talk," he says. There are tools to help you, and we will be examining those tools.

What is crucial is that you should have something you think is worth saying, no matter how mundane the subject, and then find your personal way of saying it. In that process, remember that no one else has the same life experience as you or the same unique mix of ideas. No other speaker can compare with you because no other speaker is you.

Will this book work for you?

The approach set out in this book has succeeded for everyone I have coached in public speaking, but you should still treat people who produce instruction manuals like this with caution.

Would-be advice givers take upon themselves an abundance of boldness and presumption. I am the man who, on the first day of writing this book, took an apple fizz drink from the refrigerator and downed it in a single gulp, only then to notice that it was an elegantly packaged bottle of Waitrose washing-up liquid. I was in a very frothy mood afterwards.

Beware the writer of a self-help book who tells you 'this is how you should do it' when they mean 'this is how *I* do it'. No one has the right to treat his or her life as the model for how you should live yours. Beware, in particular, the writer of a self-help book on public speaking.

"Much has been written, and spoken, by the experts on the

art of public speaking," say Chris Steward and Mike Wilkinson in their splendid *Bluffer's Guide to Public Speaking.* "Remember that these people take the whole thing far too seriously for their own good."

Not only that, but speaking styles differ from person to person. What works for one individual may not work for another. Tom Bennett, a teacher and educationist, puts it well. "People are slippery fish, driven by demons and angels of almost inscrutable origin, and we're all different."

A simple example is that modern research, which I will talk about in Chapter 27, suggests that telling yourself, 'I am excited', gets better results for a speaker than trying to calm yourself. That may be true in general, but some people, particularly if they have introverted personalities, may still feel they will be better off by trying to settle themselves down. There is no single way to achieve a strong public speaking performance.

Accordingly, while the overall approach I describe has been tried and tested, please do come to each new hint or recommendation in a critical spirit.

The judgement of what is an accomplished talk varies from audience to audience, from time to time, from place to place. For example, Americans tend to overstate, while the British understate: what goes down a storm in New York might be seen as hopelessly bombastic in York. (I write from personal experience.) Remember, again, that every rule has its exceptions. I will be talking about mindsets in Chapter 2 and lauding the value of commitment and perseverance, but there are limits. Beware the point where dogged persistence turns into flogging a dead horse.

As you read on, a practical question to ask yourself every so often is: how might this particular proposal or principle actually, if at all, work out for you, given your characteristics and personality? My job is to suggest some approaches that you could try out: yours is to see what succeeds for you and then apply it in practice.

What gives me the right?

If I want to gain credibility when I speak to an audience, I need to make sure early on that they know what my credentials are for talking about my topic. Similarly, it seems only reasonable that I should demonstrate my qualifications for writing this book.

Otherwise, why should you trust anything I say?

I have taken part in my fair share of debating contests and speaking competitions, and emerged with my fair share of medals and trophies. I have made presentations to convicted rapists and murderers serving life sentences in prison, setting out encouragingly how they might appeal against their convictions without concealing from them their statistically small chance of success. I have explained the intricacies of value added tax within the European Community to leaders of industry, a talk that will become even more convoluted after Brexit. I have given keynote speeches at business conferences, motivational talks at school prize days and celebratory eulogies at a regrettably large number of funerals. After dinner, I have entertained, or tried to entertain, people whose blood alcohol levels gave them no reasonable right to be conscious, let alone laughing at the jokes. I have also coached other people to do these things.

In short, I have been around a bit as a public speaker and as a guide to public speakers. Most importantly, I have encountered the things that can go wrong, and I have learned, often through bitter experience, how to put them right.

What a difference public speaking can make

In November 1988, I moved from London to join an accountancy firm in Southampton called Spicer & Oppenheim, as a tax partner. I was going through a rough time. I had left my previous company in acrimony, having come back two hours late from a boozy lunch with my personal assistant, who to complicate matters was also my girlfriend. We'd drunk a very pleasant claret, I seem to remember, not that I am recommending any of this as grown-up behaviour. We had both been given half an hour to clear our desks and get out of the building.

The move to Southampton was meant to start a new life with my girlfriend in the house we had bought together, except that within a month she quite understandably left me. Perhaps the drink and the sackings had not been the finest basis for a long-term relationship. I felt as though I was possessed by demons. In February 1989, my father, who suffered from multiple sclerosis, developed an infection and died a week later. My new appointment was also misfiring. I started drinking even more than I had in London: in those days Sainsbury's produced a serviceable red wine in plastic bottles of a litre and a half, and I could not get enough of it. The new job foundered even faster, and it was difficult to imagine how I could recover.

In the midst of my torment, the government announced the date of the annual tax budget as 20 March 1989. In the 1980s, the budget evening was the major public relations event of the year for many accountants, and the firm of Spicer & Oppenheim was no exception. The Southampton office had already committed itself to producing an exceptional budget night seminar for its clients, with all the bells and whistles. For better or worse, I was to be the principal attraction. It would be my first real exposure to many of the most prestigious clients. I had done so badly in the role so far that it was going to be my one chance of redemption, not only with the clients but more particularly with members of staff who had come to regard me as a complete waste of space.

So it came about that I played the Hilton Hotel, Southampton, from 7pm to 9pm on Tuesday, 20 March 1989. I had prepared and rehearsed at great length. I compered the evening, and performed in a playlet giving jolly tax advice to my imaginary clients, the Ninja Turtle Brothers; topicality has always been a stronger point with me than sophistication. I produced slides that, though I say it myself, were funny and informative. I passed over tax planning ideas that were practical and relevant to the clients, and quite simply I wowed them.

That night was a turning point in my tax career. I came in from the cold and started on a consistent run of success at work.

I have told this story often, not (I hope) as an act of masochism in the first part or triumphalism in the second, but to make the point that speaking in public can be a uniquely valuable skill in people's lives. It is relevant to everyone at every stage of their careers. It can be the reason why the school-leaver gets his or her first employment. It is why Winston Churchill is a British national hero and Clement Attlee, though he led the greatest reforming government of the twentieth century, isn't. It can explain why we advance in our life's work, or why we do not. It is one of the reasons why Barack Obama became American president, while John McCain and Mitt Romney and Hillary Clinton didn't.

This stuff is vital and of universal significance. More than that, and this is the great news, it is very, very simple to get a lot better at it. Yes, it involves hard work; but when the rewards are so great, I firmly believe it is worth devoting that effort.

How this book is arranged

The book is divided into three sections, each containing thirteen simple steps to successful public speaking:

1. The Key Principles – the fundamental attitudes and approaches that will bring us success in public speaking (Chapters 1–13).
2. The Key Preparation – the things we need to plan and anticipate before we ever stand up to speak (Chapters 14–26).
3. The Key Techniques – the tricks of the trade that will make our performance polished and professional, regardless of the butterflies in our stomachs (Chapters 27–39).

After my personal version of *The Thirty-Nine Steps*, there is then a fortieth chapter to draw my themes together and put what we have been talking about in context. A variety of supplementary notes comes after most chapters.

Each chapter is designed to be largely self-contained, so that you can dip in and out of the book as you see fit. I hope you find it useful.

Notes

When I talk about 'public speaking' or indeed 'speaking in public' in this book, I mean instances of an individual giving a speech, reading or presentation in person to a live and present audience in an organised, considered way, usually but not always with the object of informing, influencing or entertaining them.

All the quotations from Ray K Immel in this book are taken from his classic 1921 text, *The Delivery of a Speech*. The Chris Anderson comment came from a talk he gave at the Royal Institution in London in May 2016, and the Tom Bennett quote is from a *New Teachers* supplement of the educational magazine *TES*.

THE KEY PRINCIPLES

CHAPTER I

If you can drive a car, you can speak in public

Introduction

In this opening chapter, I want to set you free from the hang-ups that can prevent you from getting started as a speaker in the first place.

We will confront the wrong-headed belief that public speaking is an ability given only to a chosen few people: that speakers are born, not made. We will see that, quite to the contrary, it is an ability that almost anyone can develop, in the same way that almost anyone can learn to drive a car. In the process, I'll address an opposite argument from the distinguished, but not always very sensible, ancient orator, Cicero.

I think you'll find, as I did long ago, that making the comparison with learning to drive (or, for younger readers, to ride a bike) is a great way to get rid of the ridiculous mystique that surrounds public speaking. It puts us in a much better position to absorb the positive ideas and practices that will follow in later chapters on our road to speaking success.

Let's start with some excellent news.

Great news is at hand

There are glad tidings for anyone who is thinking of speaking in public. Most potentially good performers never speak at all because they wrongly believe it is too difficult or too frightening. The majority of the people who do speak are not good at it because they fail to prepare correctly. In reality, since there is such little opposition, it is easy to become a highly rated speaker.

What Cicero said

Admittedly, Marcus Tullius Cicero, the Roman politician and lawyer who was one of the finest orators of ancient times, would not have agreed with me. A key passage from his work *De Oratore* (On the Nature of the Public Speaker) goes like this:

> "A speaker ought to have the sharpness of a master of logic, the wisdom of a philosopher, the lyricism of a poet, the powers of retention of a lawyer, the elocution and physical presence of the finest actor. This is the reason why nothing in the world is as rare as a model speaker; the skills which virtuosos in other fields are commended for acquiring to a moderate degree, each in his own specialism, will not be praised in the speaker unless they are all combined in him to the greatest possible level of excellence."

The particular qualities Cicero looks for in an orator include, but are not limited to, all of these:

- The highest standards of humour, wit, culture, delicacy and refinement of manner.
- Complete emotional awareness and discipline.

- Great body language combined with top-class vocal control.
- Full knowledge of the widest possible range of topics, not least a thorough grasp of history and law.
- A brilliant memory to store all that knowledge.

You do not need a degree in psychology, or indeed the wisdom of a philosopher, to work out what Cicero is trying to do here. He is signifying how brilliant he himself is as an orator, compared to anyone else of his time, or indeed any budding speaker of the future.

I find the practical effect of his words unexpectedly reassuring. I know I can never match the awesome majesty of his model speaker. There is no point in even trying to compete, so I can settle for doing one of two things: either giving up, as most people do, or aiming for something more realistic. I prefer the latter route, doing the modest but wholly practical and achievable things that make anyone a more than adequate modern speaker. I hope you will do the same.

In line with what I said in the Introduction, I take 'more than adequate' to mean 'in the top 20%'. Under the 80/20 rule (also known as the Pareto Principle), the top 20% of speakers should produce roughly 80% of the decent speeches ever made. That seems a good enough target to me, even if it fails to meet Cicero's high demands.

It's tricky at first

None of what I have said so far is to deny that speaking in public is an uncomfortable experience at first. It is very different from talking casually to friends or relatives. You are under more pressure. You have to get used to holding eye contact with people for longer than in ordinary conversation, while everyone is looking at you. Beyond that, there is an implied obligation to say something amusing or interesting or important, and to do so in a coherent way using a logical structure.

Compare this with normal conversation with its constituent grunts and groans, 'ums' and 'ahs', pauses and hesitations, deviations and repetitions. At one level all this is blindingly obvious, yet novice speakers tend to play down the inevitable consequences of the difficulty of the challenge, and then give themselves an undeserved dressing-down when things go wrong.

Instead, they need just to allow themselves time.

The way to perform well at public speaking is to take it seriously, do as much of it as possible, get better with practice, and obtain focused feedback. Just as you would not expect to execute a dazzlingly good rumba after your opening lessons at dancing classes, so it would be a miracle if your first few excursions as a speaker produced rapturous feedback.

The way forward is to build up your skills over time.

It's like driving a car

This chapter is based on one of the great maxims of public speaking, coined by a Scottish journalist and editor, Sir William Robertson Nicoll (no relation):

> "Learning to speak in public is like learning to swim or to skate, or to ride a bicycle. No amount of previous theoretical instruction will enable one to overcome the initial difficulties without actual experiment."

For older readers who have forgotten how it felt to learn to swim, skate or cycle, I think the more useful comparison is with learning to drive: public speaking is as easy as driving a car.

When you have your first driving lesson, everything is difficult. You have to get the thing started, control the gears and the clutch, steer and manoeuvre while watching out for traffic, and do it all at the same time. Everything feels too much to cope with – particularly the gears and the clutch, I seem to remember. Before long, you come to take it all in your stride and carry out the driving manoeuvres subconsciously with ease, even if (as in my wife's case) it takes five attempts to pass the actual test. But to begin with, it involves constant mental and physical concentration and strain.

There is a clear and close parallel with public speaking. When you set out as a speaker you need to remember to do all of this:

- Breathe.
- Say something audible and relevant to your audience, while maintaining eye contact.
- Develop a logical and consistent stream of thought.
- Carry on in the same fashion for a period that will seem interminable, even though in real time it may last no more than a few minutes.

Doing all the distinct actions that constitute driving a car (and, indeed, doing them without conscious thought) becomes natural within the first few hours of practice. You quickly come to drive safely, in a relaxed but attentive style that allows you to concentrate on the road ahead. Similarly, provided you get stuck in and do the work, the basic techniques of public speaking become imbued in you. You attain that level of unconscious competence that allows you to focus on getting your message over to the audience in an informative and helpful way.

Let's extend the analogy a little. You can learn to drive the easier way in an automatic model, which avoids the need for the fiddly gear changes imposed on you by a manual car. The speaking equivalent to an automatic is a straightforward talk to an audience, a simple, direct interaction between you and your listeners.

The harder route to passing your driving test is to learn with a manual gearbox. This is tougher going, but with the promise of greater precision, mastery and control if you can work the gearshifts out. The equivalent of the manual model in speaking terms might be a presentation supported by all kinds of technical wizardry, lots of audio-visual input and a set of all-singing, all-dancing PowerPoint slides that will do everything short of washing up afterwards.

The important point here is that either approach can work brilliantly – an automatic or a manual gearbox, the uncomplicated talk or the pyrotechnic display of technology. Frequently the circumstances of a particular presentation will determine which route you should go down, but equally as often it will be a matter of personal choice.

For most of this book, I'll recommend the simpler approach to speaking, on the basis that greater complexity brings added stresses and strains to a talk at a time when you are already under pressure – but then I would say that: I have always preferred a nice, straightforward automatic gearbox to a manual.

You can't skip the learning process

"All the great speakers were bad speakers at first," said the poet, lecturer and essayist Ralph Waldo Emerson.

Emerson's comment echoes through time. When the great Greek orator Demosthenes first spoke in public, his audience mocked him for his strange, oafish style. The novelist Charles Dickens, a contemporary of Emerson's and a hugely successful public speaker, had a lisp that he worked long and hard to eliminate.

In modern times, the American business magnate Warren Buffett has said that he was completely unable to speak in public before the age of twenty; the very thought of it made him ill. He signed on for a Dale Carnegie speaking course and managed to stay with it. He then went on to teach a class himself, and so became a proficient public speaker.

Similarly, the man who before his untimely death came to stand out as perhaps the world's best business presenter, Steve Jobs, was not naturally gifted as a speaker. He became good because he worked supremely hard at it over a long period.

Conclusion

Just for the record, Cicero's practice often did not match his lofty ideals. As a practising lawyer, he seems to have been entirely prepared to carry on acting in a case where he knew that both parties had bribed the court. He would deliberately waste the court's time when it suited his purpose. He remarked that an advocate might need to base his argument on points that only roughly corresponded with the truth, rather than the truth itself. In one case, he was reputed to have boasted that he threw sand in the eye of the judge.

In any event, experience suggests an approach that is rather more practically based than Cicero's. It derives from the fundamental truth that public speaking is as easy as driving a car. As you set off on your speaking adventure, like learner drivers on their first lessons, you will probably feel all over the place, but you may be startled at how quickly things come together. Provided you are committed to take the time to practise, you are on your way to speaking confidently and effectively.

Points to take from this chapter

- Be aware that there is no magic in any of this.
- The comparison with learning to drive helps you develop that awareness. I bet you don't often look at other motorists and say, "What a great driver! I could never reach that standard myself."
- Be prepared for public speaking to be tough at first, just like any other human endeavour.
- Stay with it, and you will be surprised by the speed at which your skills develop.
- Work through this book thoroughly, and you should easily end up in the top 20% of speakers.

In the next chapter, we'll learn the very straightforward mental approach that will speed you even faster on your way to public speaking success.

Notes

The comparison with learning to swim, skate or cycle was made by Sir William Robertson Nicoll in a piece on *The Art of Oratory* for Volume V of the 1913 *Book of Public Speaking*, edited by Arthur Fox-Davies. The quotation from Emerson comes from *Power* in his 1860 essay collection, *The Conduct of Life*. The story of Warren Buffett and public speaking is told in *Getting There: A Book of Mentors* by Gillian Zoe Segal, Abrams Image, 2015.

CHAPTER 2

Have a positive mindset

Introduction

In the last chapter, we saw that there is nothing magical or mysterious about achieving success as a speaker. It's all about putting in the routine effort day by day to improve our skills. Now I'm going to describe the mental approach that can drive us forward to get the best results from that effort. We'll see the value of adopting a positive mindset, and examine some practical ways to achieve it. As a result, we will gain the grit and determination that can help us thrive as speakers.

To get us going on this, I want to warn you against the unintended negativity that surrounds much of people's thinking about public speaking.

Let's eliminate the negative

Lots of books about public speaking have scary titles. Here are some examples:

- *Handbook for the Terrified Speaker.*
- *Presentation Skills for Quivering Wrecks.*

- *I'd Rather Die Than Give a Speech!*
- *Would You Really Rather Die Than Give a Talk?*
- *What to Say When… You're Dying on the Platform.*

These are all good books, but in a sense their titles reinforce the unhelpful stereotype of public speaking as a sinister and chilling experience. It's not surprising that so many people go on to approach it in a negative way. By contrast, I am here to encourage you to think positively.

I don't believe many individuals start out in life with a fear of speaking up.

Babies do it, or an approximation of it, all the time to get attention. When we are very young, every challenge seems a brilliant opportunity. Offer a young child the chance to hold a room in thrall, and he or she will leap at it. Then, after a few years, something goes wrong. Perhaps it is the dulling effect of encounters with authority, or simply the effect that older people have on the psyches of the young.

I have a potent memory of a teacher remonstrating with me at infant school: "I leave you in charge, Tym, for just five minutes, and what happens?"

What the exact circumstances were, why the teacher called me Tym when my name is Ian, why she spelt the wrong name in such a grandiose style, and how I could ever have known how she spelt it: all that is lost in the mists of time. I went into a shell from that day on, and did not come out of it, and start to speak up again, until I was in my teens.

At least I did come out of my shell: positivity finally took hold and worked its magic on me. I believe it can do the same for any other would-be speaker.

Patrick Campbell shows the way

My favourite example of the triumph of positivity in public speaking is Patrick Campbell, an Irish comic writer who spoke with one of the most severe stammers you could imagine. He was witty, wise and knowledgeable, and developed into an excellent speaker. He came to be a major television personality and was one of the team captains on the word game *Call My Bluff* during the 1970s. His commitment and enthusiasm carried him through, showing the transformative effect of a positive mindset.

Here is a fine example of the Campbell approach.

He was facing the stress of preparing for his first major public performance on television. Though he was sick with anticipation, he tells us that suddenly he got "the most extraordinary feeling of euphoria". It didn't stop his tension, but he couldn't wait to try to get the audience laughing. "I felt they were warm and friendly and on my side," he later wrote.

I reckon that that is the perfect attitude from a novice speaker. He may or may not have stammered, but that was not the point. What mattered was that the audience should laugh as he had hoped: and they did just that.

Patrick Campbell realised that you don't need to be impeccably fluent, or anything like it, to be a skilled communicator. Conveying the belief that you have something worthwhile or entertaining to say is vastly more important.

Fixed and growth mindsets

Modern psychologists have had a field day studying the role of mindsets. The results of their researches have begun to have a significant influence on educational policy, and are spreading into the business and commercial world. Most famously, Carol

Dweck, a professor of psychology at Stanford University, published her book *Mindset: How You Can Fulfil Your Potential* in 2006.

Carol Dweck's argument goes like this:

In broad terms, we can divide people into two groups: those with a fixed mindset, and those with a growth mindset. Men and women with a fixed mindset believe that your talents and abilities are carved in stone and cannot develop further. They attribute any success they get in life to luck, talent or intelligence, and they believe these are fixed traits. These individuals are not necessarily lazy: they just think that effort won't make a difference. On the other hand, those who have a growth mindset believe that you can consistently develop your talents and abilities, that hard work and perseverance will lead to success.

The researches of a number of contemporary neuroscientists and psychologists support their view. Brains and talent are just the starting point. What is essential for great achievements is a continuing love of learning and development, coupled with resilience and persistence in the face of setbacks.

If you allow a fixed mindset to become your outlook on life, the likelihood is that you will avoid challenge. You will tend to give up quickly because you believe that success comes from innate talent or just luck. By contrast, an approach to life and work using the growth mindset model seems to offer greater potential for personal fulfilment.

A practical example

Let me give an everyday example where the growth mindset has worked for me.

I mentioned my regular sessions at the gym in the Introduction. By contrast, when I was younger, my self-image in physical terms was always that of a useless fat slob. I was the boy who would never pick up a discus or a javelin because of the danger to humanity if I ever let go of the infernal things. It is said that pictures of an obese thirteen-year-old Ian at a school sports day still exist. I will pay good money for the negatives.

In my fifties, I became aware of the mindset principle, and the idea that I did not have to be incapable any longer, that I could improve physically if I worked at it and persevered.

Here is what I say in my presentations when I discuss what happened next:

"I went to the gym and it was all very confusing at first, but I stuck with it and kept it simple.

The arm extension machine worked my triceps.

The pectoral fly worked my pecs.

The abs machine worked my abominables, as I call them.

Three machines, and a lot of hard work.

After much persevering I grew my first ever muscle, an ab to be precise.

Later on, I got a rhomboid muscle. It sounds like a mixture of geometry and piles, but it's awfully good for you.

Before long, I was inviting members of staff at work to feel my new muscles. Indeed, it was only last week we settled the disciplinary proceedings that followed."

I ended up as the over-fifties rowing champion at my gym, and I regularly run, or at least plod, ten-kilometre races. There has been a positive consequence for my public speaking. Whenever I am going to give a presentation later in the day, I go to the gym in the morning to release some of the extra nervous energy that the talk is likely to produce.

I came to realise that it is easy to think of abandoning your participation in any field by saying you haven't got the innate talent, you haven't got the skills, but you would almost always be deceiving yourself.

Public speaking is a classic example of this. I don't want to sound like one of those terrifying American motivational speakers, but successful public speakers really are those who possess or have developed a positive mindset to fuel their long-term consistency and commitment.

Embrace failure

A critical factor in all this is to recognise the value of failure, giving yourself permission to screw up on the way to victory. Anyone who speaks in public will find failures scattered among their successes, and that is the key to learning and improving. The actor David Harewood puts it well: "Contrary to what you might think," he says, "failure isn't the opposite of success, it's a fundamental part of the creative process."

When the tennis player Stanislas Wawrinka beat Rafael Nadal to win his first Grand Slam title at the 2014 Australian Open, it was his thirty-sixth attempt at winning a major championship. After his triumph, many people commented on Wawrinka's tattoo. He has a quotation from Samuel Beckett tattooed on his left arm. It says: 'Ever tried. Ever failed. No matter. Try again. Fail again. Fail better.'

Stan talked about his tattoo:

> "It was part of my life, how I see life, and especially how I see tennis life… When you lose, it's tough to take a positive from a defeat, from failing at a tournament. In general, that's how I see my career. I always go back to the court. I always go back to practise, to try to improve myself and to give myself the best chances to beat the best players in the world."

For me, Stan's tattoo is a clue to the essence of success. Your luck will come and go, but a positive attitude, hard work and persistence will pay off in the end. It applies to public speaking as much as to tennis. You will inevitably make mistakes: the crucial thing is to pick yourself up and learn from them.

Applying a positive mindset to public speaking

Here are some ideas for developing a positive mindset:

- Don't be afraid to ask the basic questions. How do you see yourself? Are you flexible, changeable and trainable, or fixed, unchangeable and untrainable? Do you say to yourself that your brain and your body simply don't do, can't do, public speaking? If you don't believe that you can make an improvement, what sort of effort will you make? What harm would a bit of optimism do?
- Don't assume at the outset that you have an accurate view of how good you can be as a public speaker. In my experience, people who are initially scared of talking to an audience hugely underestimate how well they can perform with training and practice. Get out there and do it. What you can achieve will surprise you.
- The way you perceive a future event helps determine how successful it will be. See it as a challenge rather than a threat, and you will be much better placed to plan for it, control your emotions and work to your full potential.
- Be prepared to take risks. Modern education often encourages children to be risk averse and conservative, to keep their heads down. Sadly, this

attitude has spilt over into adult life. Let's fight back and take sensible risks for their own sake, as a necessary stepping stone on the road to victory.

- Positivity does not imply mindless optimism. We need to do the groundwork to ensure we have a realistic understanding of what is involved in achieving the goals we set for ourselves. This book will help in that process.

- While you are practising or performing, don't stop to agonise over what you perceive to be errors on your part. There are exceptions, of course: if an audience is walking out on you in large numbers, a certain degree of soul-searching suddenly becomes appropriate. In all normal circumstances, just stay in the moment, and do the best you can right now.

- Act as if you are confident in your performance and your success. We will talk more about the concept of 'acting *as if*' when we talk about enjoying yourself as a speaker. The key point is that it works. By behaving as though you are confident and assured, not only will you appear that way to the audience, but you will indeed become more confident and assured within yourself.

- Remember that it is not always obvious when a talk has gone well. An audience that is undemonstrative by nature tends to remain so even when it approves sincerely of what the speaker is saying.

- There is a good argument for cultivating a degree of selective amnesia about your speaking performances. After you have spoken, review what went wrong along with what worked well, so that you absorb the learning points for future talks. Don't then dwell on your mistakes: accentuate the positive and move confidently on. Champion athletes are said to possess a short-term memory for failure but a long-term memory for success: speakers can learn from their example.

Conclusion

You don't have to be a disciple of Carol Dweck to believe that a positive approach to public speaking will produce better talks that give more enjoyment to both speaker and audience. By adopting an attitude that allows you to believe you can become a better speaker, you lay the path for achieving it.

I like the comment attributed to Michelangelo: "If people knew how hard I had to work to gain my mastery, it would not seem so wonderful at all."

Points to take from this chapter

- Accept that you will have frustrations and disappointments as your speaking progresses. Take them in your stride and learn from them: they are an essential component of your long-term success.
- Never underestimate the tremendous benefits that come from training and practice.
- View public speaking as a challenge, not a danger.
- If a genius like Michelangelo found that the road was often uphill, then you and I have full permission to do the same. We just need to keep on going.
- When you find yourself thinking, 'I'm just not any good at this', try replacing that thought with 'I'm not good at it *yet*'.

In the next chapter, I want to transform any negative views you may have on the nerves that accompany public speaking. We will see that, in reality, they are a wonderfully positive force in ensuring your success.

Notes

Patrick Campbell's story comes from his entertaining autobiography *My Life and Easy Times*, Anthony Blond Ltd, 1967. The David Harewood quotation is from a 2016 Sky Arts television programme, *David Harewood's F Word*; F standing for failure, of course. The comments from Stanislas Wawrinka come from an article by Paul Newman in *The Independent* for 26 January 2014.

CHAPTER 3

Welcome the fear

Introduction

In Chapter 2, we talked about the benefits of positivity in our approach to public speaking. Now we'll see that a positive attitude doesn't require us to abandon realism or normal human feelings as we step up to the podium. For millions of years, people have been nervous and fearful before significant events in their lives; and giving a speech is, without a doubt, a significant event.

This chapter will give us full permission to experience feelings of fear in public speaking without suffering embarrassment or guilt in the process. We'll see that the nerves and the fear are ingrained in our natures, and they are there to help us. We should actively welcome the fear because it spurs us on to much higher levels of performance. By the end of the chapter, I hope you'll feel a lot more comfortable in your skin when you stand up to speak and the butterflies strike.

What this chapter is not about

This chapter needs a caveat. It is not intended for people with deep-seated anxiety issues, a condition that can be truly debilitating.

I do not mean in any way to belittle the suffering they go through, which may benefit from medical advice and treatment. I can recommend the American journalist Scott Stossel's unsparing account, *My Age of Anxiety*, to anyone who would like to know more on the subject. In Scott Stossel's case, public speaking is one of numerous situations that have caused him extreme performance anxiety, and we will see how he deals with it in Chapter 25.

This chapter, by contrast, is for the individual with otherwise normal levels of fears and apprehensions, who simply gets alarmed by the thought of speaking in public. And understandably so, because it is undeniably scary.

Why it is perfectly reasonable to be nervous

Oratory has always had its perils. The Roman historian Suetonius tells us in his *Life of Caligula* that the Emperor Caligula held oratory competitions at Lugdunum (now Lyon in France). Participants who displeased him had to erase their speeches with a sponge or with their tongues, or else face either a whipping or being thrown into the nearby River Rhône.

Sheer common or garden nerves are a more typical problem. In his book *Press, Platform and Parliament*, Spencer Leigh Hughes tells this story:

"Lord Guildford, a son of Lord North [the eighteenth-century UK prime minister who managed to lose the American colonies in the War of Independence], rose to

> make a maiden speech, gasped with sudden stage fright, and sat down when he had said, 'Sir', which is probably the shortest Parliamentary speech on record. Moreover, he was so thoroughly scared that he applied for the Chiltern Hundreds, and left the House for ever."

That may be extreme, and, of course, it wouldn't have happened if he'd had this book to help him. But the logic behind Lord Guildford's behaviour was set out magnificently by the American astronomer (yes, honestly) Garrett P Serviss in his 1912 book *Eloquence – Counsel on the Art of Public Speaking*:

> "There is possibly no moment in human experience not attended by actual physical danger which puts so severe a strain upon a man's courage as this… You must seize the attention of that multitude of minds before you and hold it – control it. You have pledged yourself to interest them, to please them, to instruct them, or to convince them. You have nobody but yourself to rely upon. You must have all your resources well in hand. Your hearers may be indifferent, then you must overcome that indifference; they may be hostile, then you must conquer them and win them to your side. Some of the greatest and most experienced orators have acknowledged that they never rise to begin a formal discourse without hearing their hearts beating in their ears and feeling their nerves tingling with an inward panic."

Only in recent times, when stress has become a dirty word, has the pressure that public speaking induces been seen as anything other than an obvious commonplace, a self-evident truth.

It is perfectly reasonable for anyone to suffer from speech anxiety. The technical term for the fear of public speaking is glossophobia, from the Greek *glossa,* meaning tongue, and *phobos*, fear or dread.

The question is, do you suffer from glossophobia?

I very much hope so because, as we shall see, it will significantly improve the quality of your performance.

On other occasions, such as watching ghost or horror films, we positively welcome feelings of fear. They bring us alive. So why is there such concern about the nerves caused by public speaking? I think it's because people are embarrassed and slightly ashamed of the fear.

Much of this comes about because of the approach of the conventional teaching on the subject. The textbooks are inordinately concerned with making you less fearful of giving a speech. By contrast, I am not particularly bothered about how fearful you are. If, say, a hundred people have come to listen to you for sixty minutes, it seems entirely reasonable to me that you should be nervous about the prospect of being responsible for the quality of a hundred hours of other people's lives.

Public speaking makes me apprehensive, and I don't see why you should be any different. Our concern here is to ensure you give an effective talk – an entirely different matter from the state of your nerves.

I was thirteen when I first spoke formally in public. It was a speaking competition at school. I was nervous almost beyond words beforehand. It felt like my stomach was being not so much attacked by butterflies as invaded by a horde of aliens, like the ones in the *Alien* films but less good-looking. That was 1968. I still love public speaking, and I still get as nervous as hell at the start. And that's a good thing because the adrenaline fuels my performance.

My experience is typical. In an entertaining book called *The Joys and Terrors of Public Speaking*, David Scott, a newspaper editor and media consultant, describes his feelings after a lifetime of speaking. "The nerves are still there to a greater or lesser degree," he writes. "I console myself that is a good state to be in because it means I will give my best and not take any audience for granted."

The actress Dame Judi Dench, acknowledging the enormous energy that nerves add to a performance, said during an appearance on Radio 4's *Desert Island Discs*: "And [performing] is more frightening the longer you do it because at the beginning you are not so aware of what the pitfalls are. It's only later, after doing so much, that more is expected of you."

That makes me feel even better about still experiencing the nerves.

No one ever died from public speaking

I admit that, if you are arguing literally, this point may be debatable. In 1841, William Henry Harrison, the newly elected ninth president of the United States, gave his inaugural address in the open on a cold and wet day, wearing neither overcoat nor hat. It took him nearly two hours to read, thereby becoming the longest ever inaugural address. He caught a cold and quickly developed pneumonia, dying exactly a month later despite the treatments of opium, brandy, castor oil, leeches and Virginia snakeweed that he received. He thus became the shortest-serving US president. It is a dramatic tale, but I think it tells us more about the value of staying warm than the perils of public speaking. The medics now suggest that his death was due to typhoid and had nothing to do with his inaugural speech, but I prefer the more romantic version.

Never forget that we cannot stay safe from everything. Death gets us all in the end. The journalist and former sportsman Matthew Syed put it brilliantly in *The Times*: "Even those who lead lives of extreme caution, staying indoors, avoiding human contact and sleeping in oxygen tents eventually die, if only of boredom."

Why it actively helps to be nervous

Look at it this way: nerves come from your fear of failure to stop you failing, and that must be good.

As you move to the podium to begin speaking, your nerves and your excitement merge to become the driving force that will produce the best in you. As they say, it's not about getting rid of the butterflies, but getting them to fly in formation.

Which leads me on to the rather grandly named Yerkes-Dodson law.

This is a principle which was developed by two American psychologists, Robert M Yerkes and John D Dodson, in 1908. It describes the relationship between arousal and performance. The law states that, up to a point, performance increases with physiological or mental arousal; then it starts to decrease as levels of arousal become too high.

It can be illustrated graphically as a bell-shaped curve (the 'stress curve'), which increases and then finally decreases with higher levels of arousal. I love talking about the Yerkes-Dodson law in presentations: it is scientifically respectable, it is eminently sensible and easy to understand, and it gives me a framework for discussing the state of my own nerves as I give the talk.

To put it in simple terms:

- Yerkes and Dodson argued that, as your level of arousal goes up, so does your performance.
- That ceases to apply once the stress curve reaches its peak.
- Then there comes a period of diminishing returns, as the curve goes down.

In the context of a presentation:

- Your level of arousal will go up before an important talk.
- In other words, you will become nervous.
- Your heart rate will increase, and so will your blood pressure.
- As your arousal level rises, so will your performance improve.
- At a certain point, your level of arousal becomes higher than optimal, and your performance starts to diminish.

Should you pass out as a result of all the nervous energy you are producing, you can fairly assume that your level of arousal is indeed too high. To be fair, I have never personally seen that happen to a speaker, though I can imagine it might if, say, you used a six-pack of Carlsberg Special Brew to prepare for your talk.

The Yerkes-Dodson law confirms that, without a doubt, it is appropriate to get nervous before a talk to improve your performance. I do not recommend searching particularly hard to find your ideal level of nerves, given that so much trial and error are necessarily involved. The fundamental point in my experience is that you can become very substantially nervous before any serious reduction in your performance takes effect. (We will talk in Chapter 27 about practical ways of controlling your nerves to ensure you do not stray too far beyond the point where diminishing returns set in.)

Take comfort in the fact that you need your nerves to spark and your adrenaline to flow if you are to perform well. The author and academic AC Benson noted that a speaker who faced an audience with serenity was likely to fail, "for the simple reason that nervousness is a sign of an emotional desire to do one's best and to affect one's audience."

Far and away the worst presentations I have attended were given by nerveless senior executives and politicians who never moved up the stress curve. Their lifeless performances gave public speaking a bad name. They knew their subject, or thought they did, but they had taken no trouble to research their audiences, and they certainly had not prepared their presentations. Because they had no nerves, they felt able to wing it. The results were calamitous. They talked without energy or passion. They offered no variety of pace, wit or enthusiasm. They had not bothered to time their speeches in rehearsal, and so they overran. The audiences ended up bored or asleep or annoyed, or some combination of these. Your listeners will forgive you for many things, but not for treating them with contempt.

One of my favourite quotations comes from Emma Bunton, formerly Baby Spice of the Spice Girls, when she appeared on the fear-inducing television reality show *Strictly Come Dancing*. "I'm going to be really, really nervous," she said. "I know I will be, but I just can't wait to get out there again."

If stars like Laurence Olivier and Judi Dench, like Barbra Streisand and Adele, can endure the fear before performances, so can we.

"Hello Wembley, I've never been so fucking scared in my whole life," said Adele to a record-breaking crowd at the start of a concert at Wembley Stadium in June 2017. "I'm shitting myself." She then immediately moved into a brilliant, barnstorming performance that had the audience in raptures.

In public speaking, Harold Macmillan, who in 1960 gave one of the most famous speeches of the twentieth century on the 'Wind of Change' blowing through Africa, was often physically sick before speaking. I am not suggesting you should go that far, but it certainly did not affect his performance.

Bring on the nerves, I say.

Where the nerves come from

The amygdalae are small, almond-shaped parts of the brain that are thought to play a vital role in the way we respond to stimuli, spotting danger based on our previous experiences and the innate knowledge that evolution has given us. They are a fundamental part of the process that starts our adrenaline flow and speeds our reactions whenever we come upon a sabre-toothed cat or the threat of a public speaking experience.

There is a plausible theory that public speaking anxiety is indeed all about our primal instincts. Our biological responses have been handed down to us from ancient times, when it was not good to be the centre of attention: attention meant danger. When our ancestors were being looked at intently, it often meant they were being tracked by a wild animal which was rather keen on eating them. This, not unnaturally, raised their stress levels and gave them an eager desire to be somewhere else.

There is, sadly, no evidence that a sabre-toothed cat was ever placated from eating anyone by way of a PowerPoint presentation. Running away worked a lot better. None of this is particularly relevant to our lives today, but the primeval part of us is a bit slow on the uptake.

In 2014, when the director Michael Bay walked out of a press conference less than a minute into his presentation, an unfortunate event that we will return to, he was simply following the ancient urges of our ancestors. The fight or flight response may sometimes be annoying in a public speaking context, but it helps to know that it is with you for a historically sound reason.

The departure of predators like the sabre-toothed cat brought no more than marginal relief. Simply being surrounded by a group of humans could itself be a highly alarming experience, particularly if they were powerful and came in numbers; in other words, if they resembled a modern-day audience at a speech or presentation. Even today, setting aside any perceived physical threat, giving a talk involves exposing ourselves intellectually and emotionally to other people, and so adds to our feelings of discomfort.

In summary, we should never feel the need to explain the anxiety that comes from being on stage. The right approach to the fear is to recognise and acknowledge it, to accept its presence and its entitlement to be there.

You don't look nearly as nervous as you feel

I'm not just saying this: you really do not look as nervous as you feel.

When speakers I coach have finished their presentations, I ask how anxious they felt on a scale of one to ten, where ten represents blind panic. The usual response is somewhere between seven and nine. People who have watched the presentation typically give it a nervousness score of two or three.

This is quite logical when you think about it. Audience members do not feel what you are feeling, and they are not mind readers. Your heart may be racing: they won't know. Your mouth may be dry: they won't know. Your voice may strain: unless they are intimately acquainted with you, so that they can compare it to your usual tone, they won't know. And even if they do notice a difference, experience confirms it will be a very slight one.

If you don't believe me, make a video of your performance and compare how you felt with what it looks like in reality. You need to watch the video with a constructive but independent third party, who can comment on the reality of what they see untainted by your interpretation. Most speakers are pleasantly surprised by what they see, or rather by what they do not see. Whatever you felt internally while you were speaking is not reflected in the video, because the video does not have magical powers of telepathy.

If even now you don't believe me, I can tell you that researchers have confirmed these findings in scientific studies. You can relax in the knowledge that your emotions will not 'leak out' to the audience, who will quite simply be unaware of the extent of your trepidation.

And that's not all: the mere possession of this knowledge will make you a better speaker, because being conscious that your nerves are mostly hidden is a real help in controlling your remaining anxiety.

I have lost count of the number of people who tell me I am an exceptionally relaxed speaker. I am not: I have always been a nervous performer. However, the knowledge that the audience cannot see it is an immense help to me in achieving a strong performance. It removes a whole area of concern about my speech.

Now, repeat after me, as often as necessary until it sinks in, and in block capitals: I DON'T LOOK NEARLY AS NERVOUS AS I FEEL.

Conclusion

Experiencing fear as a public speaker is an entirely natural process. For a functioning human being the concept of nerveless oratory is a contradiction in terms.

I don't care whether you're scared: I just want you to give a good talk. The two things are different, and I think that's comforting.

Points to take from this chapter

- There is nothing abnormal about becoming nervous

or fearful before speaking in public. It's what sensible people do.

- People who tell you they are not nervous are mostly lying.
- The nerves are extremely unlikely to do you any harm.
- They have been embedded in our psyches since the dawn of human life. You won't get anywhere by fighting against them.
- Indeed, you need the nerves and the adrenaline that comes with them. They raise our performance, so we operate at our finest when we speak in public.
- You won't look anywhere near as nervous to the audience as you feel.

In the next chapter, we will move on to focus on the vital importance of zooming in early on the goals you want to achieve for your talk. We'll then discuss easy ways to accomplish this, and look at some great practical examples from distinguished speakers.

Notes

The quotation from Matthew Syed is from a comment column in *The Times* for 30 September 2015. The comment from AC Benson comes, like other material in this book from him, from a piece on *The art of lecturing* in Volume IV of *The Book of Public Speaking*. You can watch Michael Bay's awful experience at https://www.youtube.com/watch?v=R4rMy1iA268.

The research confirming that speakers don't look as nervous as they feel was reported in a helpful paper by Kenneth Savitsky and Thomas Gilovich, published in 2003 in the *Journal of Experimental Social Psychology* and called *The illusion of transparency and the alleviation of speech anxiety.* The 'illusion of transparency' is the technical description given to our feeling that our nervous thoughts and emotions are more obvious to an audience than they are in reality.

CHAPTER 4

Focus on what you want to achieve

Introduction

In this chapter, we are going to look at another fundamental principle of public speaking. We'll see that it is vital, before you do anything else, to identify what you aim to achieve from your talk. If you don't clarify what your purpose is, how on earth will either you or the audience know what point there is in attending your presentation?

We will discuss a number of straightforward, helpful methods by which you can establish compelling goals for your talk, and review some notable historical examples of how distinguished speakers went about satisfying their own objectives.

Start with the end in mind

Here are two fine writers on oratory discussing the importance of our objectives as speakers. We met the great Ray Keeslar

Immel in the introduction to this book, and here he is again, setting out his pragmatic approach:

> "Public speaking implies a purpose. It has an end to which it itself is but the means… What [the speaker] properly says is: 'I wish to raise five hundred dollars for the YMCA' or 'I wish to help elect John Jones'… Then he makes a speech to reach the desired end… He must have a desire to accomplish specific things, to achieve definite results. Then he uses the art of speechmaking to reach his goal, just as a carpenter uses his art to build a house."

Secondly, we have an equally forceful comment from a writer on oratory called Clark Mills Brink, who was professor of English Literature at Kansas State University:

> "The most distinctive characteristic of oratory is persuasion… The speaker must never lose sight of the fact that he aims to induce his hearers to do something… That is why he must choose an *object* rather than a *subject* for an oration. The orator is a speaker with a mission."

Setting specific objectives right at the start will help you focus your efforts on what matters in all that follows. On occasion, you may find that the very process of determining your goals leads you to the conclusion that you shouldn't be doing the talk in the first place, an issue we'll cover in Chapter 26.

A speaker can, of course, have all kinds of objectives. For example, some of my aims for past presentations have been:

- To get a job offer.
- To win a five million pound contract.
- To score an average of at least eight out of ten in the

marking sheets completed by attendees at a training course, so that the conference company would invite me back again.

- To get a standing ovation – this was my final talk to a group of people who knew me well, so it was a realistic (if challenging) target, and thankfully I did achieve it.
- To make mourners at my mother's funeral smile in celebration of her unique personality and qualities.

Here are the three objectives I set myself for a twenty-minute school prize-giving speech, in order of priority:

- To honour the achievements of the young people in the hall, so that they and their parents would go away with a sense of fulfilment.
- To give those who were about to leave the school a heightened sense of purpose for the future.
- At a more humdrum level, to entertain the audience and make them laugh.

To my mind, the best presentations focus on a small number of critical objectives; typically, no more than three. Longer lists can lead to a loss of focus, so that what you are trying to achieve becomes indistinct. When you have several goals, I always recommend identifying which is your number one issue and giving it priority treatment.

Once you have determined what you want to achieve:

- Do whatever you can in your talk to attain that goal or goals.
- Do nothing, and include nothing, that might distract you or the audience from them.

It often helps to tell the audience what your objectives are – again, I would suggest no more than a maximum of three – at the outset of your talk.

The audience has its objectives too

In setting your goals, take into account your best guess of what the audience's objectives will be; they may not be the same as yours. For example, you may wish to drive home a key learning point, while the audience just wants to have a good time. Your job is to meet both sets of objectives as far as you reasonably can.

A successful talk results when a speaker:

- Has thought carefully about both sets of goals.
- Recognises that there may well be a clash between his or her objectives and those of the audience.
- Produces a speech that represents a decent compromise between both.

Here's another point that can be tricky.

In working out what's in it for your listeners, and what they want to achieve, remember that their wants and their needs are not necessarily the same thing.

As an example, audience members will often be hopelessly unrealistic in what they expect to derive from the experience, given how little people remember of what they hear in a talk. (We will look at the problem of stickability, the issue of how much our memories can retain, in Chapter 11 when we discuss keeping things simple and forceful.)

While your listeners may seek high-level skills and detailed knowledge of a subject, the most practical and realistic approach for you, the speaker, will often be to give no more than a firm grounding in the core principles, making the key points and reinforcing them by repetition. We should never ignore the realities of how much an audience can absorb.

In all this, beware of substituting your personal view of what the audience needs to learn in place of what your audience research, a vital subject we'll come to in Chapter 14, informs you they really, really want. Otherwise, be prepared for the horrible feedback you'll get after your presentation.

It helps to pinpoint what you want to happen afterwards

In working out your objectives, remember to take into account not just the hoped-for smiling faces of the audience as you give the talk, but the outcome, the new things you want your listeners to learn, and in particular the actions you want them to take afterwards.

This isn't an easy challenge, but it's well worth attempting. When you ask yourself what you want the audience to do after they have listened to you, try to be as precise as you can.

Some questions to ask yourself in this process are:

- What new things will they know?
- How will I know they know?
- What new attitudes will they have?
- What good things will they be able to do that they couldn't do before?
- How can I help ensure they do those things?

I find that the answers to these questions are particularly useful in planning the detailed content of the presentation.

Further hints for setting your objectives

I recommend reasonably challenging targets. Aims like 'not being booed' or 'getting out alive' are not usually appropriate. Having said that, I found that not being booed was a largely unattainable objective for presentations I gave to mining union representatives in the wake of the UK miners' strike of 1984–85. And I would hope that staying alive is high on the agenda in, say, hostage negotiations.

Remember that your aims can fall into a wide variety of categories. The word PIETISM, the state of being pious, gives a useful mnemonic to cover most of the things a devout speaker might want to do:

Persuade
Inform
Entertain
Teach
Inspire
Sell
Motivate

Your objectives must suit the context. The journalist Daniel Finkelstein described the reaction he received for a speech he had written for William Hague, the politician:

> "He said I had drafted for him an oration perfect for delivery from the steps of the Lincoln Memorial as the million man march arrived from the Capitol. Then he would remind me that he was, in fact, addressing the Christmas club supper of Durham Conservative Association."

When you read speeches in the media, ask yourself what the speaker was trying to achieve, and how well they did that. Working through their thought processes, and seeing how they exercised them in the detailed delivery of their words, can be a real help in preparing your own future talks.

Let's now look at some practical examples from actual speeches and presentations.

The Abraham Lincoln example

One renowned occasion where a clash must have arisen between the speaker's and the audience's objectives was the speech given by Abraham Lincoln at the dedication of the Soldiers' National Cemetery in Gettysburg, Pennsylvania, on 19 November 1863. Earlier that year, the Union forces had defeated the Confederates at Gettysburg in a bloody battle that was a turning point in the American Civil War.

Edward Everett was the main speaker, with Lincoln's part as the US president being to pronounce the formal words of dedication after him. Abraham Lincoln's Gettysburg Address follows in full:

> "Four score and seven years ago our fathers brought forth on this continent, a new nation, conceived in liberty, and dedicated to the proposition that all men are created equal. Now we are engaged in a great civil war, testing whether that nation, or any nation so conceived and so dedicated, can long endure. We are met on a great battlefield of that war. We have come to dedicate a portion of that field, as a final resting place for those who here gave their lives that that nation might live. It is altogether fitting and proper that we should do this.

But, in a larger sense, we can not dedicate – we can not consecrate – we can not hallow – this ground. The brave men, living and dead, who struggled here, have consecrated it, far above our poor power to add or detract. The world will little note, nor long remember what we say here, but it can never forget what they did here. It is for us the living, rather, to be dedicated here to the unfinished work which they who fought here have thus far so nobly advanced. It is rather for us to be here dedicated to the great task remaining before us – that from these honoured dead we take increased devotion to that cause for which they gave the last full measure of devotion – that we here highly resolve that these dead shall not have died in vain – that this nation, under God, shall have a new birth of freedom – and that government of the people, by the people, for the people, shall not perish from the earth."

Lincoln's words have gone down in history as one of the finest speeches of all time, if not the very finest. The solemnity of the speech, its tough but positive message, its heightened poetical language, its rhythm and its startling brevity, have all won widespread approval.

However, if you were in the crowd at Gettysburg, might you not have been looking for a rather more fulsome tribute to those who had died? Had your son been killed in the war? How long had it taken you to get to the ceremony? How tired were you feeling? How much were you grieving? What did the event symbolise for you? How would *you* have regarded the elevated, indeed, almost cold and clinical, tone of the speech and its extreme brevity?

As we shall see later, the speech was not nearly as well received in its immediate aftermath as it has been by posterity, and perhaps some of these questions give clues as to why that was the case. It was a speech performed at a cemetery for listeners who had lost their loved ones in a horrific war, yet Lincoln puts little emphasis on glorious death for a winning cause.

But Lincoln knew what he was doing, and he was pursuing a noble objective.

It is important to set his speech at Gettysburg in context. He was not even the main speaker: that was Edward Everett. Everett, a highly popular orator of the day, had spoken expansively, as was the custom of the times, for two hours, and he had dealt in detail with the history of the battle. Everett's speech was the one to satisfy the bulk of the crowd who had come to hear tributes to the dead of Gettysburg. Meanwhile, Lincoln met his own objective of speaking to the wider world and to history, while keeping his speech short enough to ensure it would be recorded in full in the newspapers.

Both men succeeded equally in their aims. The irony is that Everett had single-handedly done the spadework to ensure that Lincoln's short piece was appropriate in the circumstances: yet it is Everett who has been relegated to stand as a footnote in history.

The CCRC example

Sometimes your objectives may initially seem at odds with each other. One of my hardest tasks in public speaking was talking to prisoners on behalf of the Criminal Cases Review Commission (CCRC). The CCRC is the independent government agency set up to investigate suspected miscarriages of justice in criminal cases; it assesses whether convictions or sentences should be sent back to a court of appeal for a further hearing.

I had some very different objectives to reconcile in my talks:

- To impress the prisoners about the work of the CCRC.

- To make them keen to apply to have their cases reviewed if they thought their convictions were wrong.
- To let them know that, if they did apply, their chances of success were just one in twenty-five – a 4% possibility.

This implies a really hard task: to enthuse the prisoners while reducing their expectation of success. The central principle in such circumstances is, quite simply, to be honest. I knew that if any one organisation could help them, it was the CCRC. That was the truth of the matter, and it simplified my task to focus on the overwhelming goal of conveying that single message: *if any one organisation could help them, it was the CCRC.*

The Tim Collins example

One of the most celebrated speeches by a Briton in this century was made by Colonel Tim Collins to the soldiers of the 1st Battalion of the Royal Irish Regiment in 2003, on the eve of the invasion of Iraq.

Here are some extracts:

"There are some who are alive at this moment who will not be alive shortly.

… If you are ferocious in battle, remember to be magnanimous in victory. Iraq is steeped in history. It is the site of the Garden of Eden, of the Great Flood, and the birthplace of Abraham. Tread lightly there.

… There may be people among us who will not see the end of this campaign. We will put them in their sleeping bags and send them back. There will be no time for sorrow. The enemy should be in no doubt that we are his nemesis and that we are bringing about his rightful destruction.

> … I know of men who have taken life needlessly in other conflicts. I can assure you they live with the mark of Cain upon them."

This speech captured the imagination of the world, and it seems that a copy of it hung in the Oval Office at the White House. The speech made me feel uneasy, despite, or perhaps because of, the poetic language and all those cultural references, but I could not quite justify my concerns at the time.

Then Captain Doug Beattie, Collins' regimental sergeant major, wrote a fiery book about his wartime experiences. He commented that Tim Collins "had left the men somewhere they shouldn't have been: thinking about home, wondering if they would ever return there again, fearful of the dangers that faced them in the hours, days and weeks ahead." It took "a string of barely separated profanities" on Beattie's part to kick his soldiers back into life, he said.

I have to take Doug Beattie's side on this.

The objective should surely have been to send men off to win the war: the ultimate in motivational talks. (We will look at an all-time model for such speeches in Chapter 7, when General George S Patton addresses his troops during the Second World War.) By that criterion, I think Tim Collins' speech does not quite hit the mark. A subsequent article in *The Times* made this point only too clearly: its heading was *There may be some who will not survive*, emphasising the negative side of the speech.

The problem may, at least in part, have arisen from the circumstances in which Tim Collins made his speech. A journalist from *The Mail on Sunday* was embedded with the British troops; she noted down the speech, and it was in the national newspapers the following day. My feeling is that, rather like Abraham Lincoln, Tim Collins took the opportunity to speak to posterity. Unfortunately, this was an occasion when posterity should have been left to go to hell. What mattered was to urge the troops who were there on the ground into action for their own sake and for the sake of their country.

Since that day in 2003, factors completely outside Tim Collins' control have affected the reputation of his speech, factors which have nothing to do with whether it met its objectives. Much has been written about the dubious legality of the war that was the backdrop to his words. Many have questioned the motives of the Western political leaders who took their countries into the Iraq War. The Tim Collins example, even more than Abraham Lincoln's speech at Gettysburg, is a salutary reminder that it is almost impossible to judge the quality of a speech objectively and for all time. The modern reader will judge by different criteria from the original audience.

The education example

Teachers have a more mundane, but still highly challenging, setting in which to determine their objectives. It can sometimes be difficult for those in education to establish goals that are both constructive and achievable.

Here is AC Benson, who as Master of Magdalene College, Cambridge, knew quite a bit about teaching, with what I think are the best guidelines on the subject:

> "I hold that the real object of lecturing is not to communicate information, but to try to plant germinal ideas in the mind, and to arouse curiosity, not to satisfy it. A lecture ought not to be the handing over of coined thoughts to be stored away in mental strongboxes; that is the work of the teacher, if indeed it is or ought to be any one's work at all. But what one desires to do in a lecture is to make a subject appear

charming and interesting; to tempt one's hearers to look into it themselves; to sweep away the dreary tissue of unnecessary and useless knowledge in which many books involve a subject, and to present, if one can, ideas in an attractive form.

… One wants to persuade people, if possible, to have a view of life – not to adopt a lecturer's preferences, but to have preferences of their own. Lecturing is really an attempt to kindle emotion and curiosity, to unveil in a desirable manner the motives which lie behind effective action… It is an attempt to summarise and suggest lines of thought, to set the mental current moving, and to rescue people from what is the cause of many of our worst troubles, the curse of muddled thinking and the confusion of similar ideas.

… If to all this a lecturer adds the conviction… that his work is not the mere imparting of information, but analysis and synthesis, a clear defining of ideas, a bid for the universal attractiveness of the subject, if only that subject be understood, he may reach a high level of effectiveness; for the purpose of it all, as I have said, is to persuade, and to start other minds on excursions of their own. A lecturer succeeds if his audience departs saying, 'I must look into that; there is more in it than I thought!' He fails if they go away with a sense of relief that they know all that is worth knowing on a particular subject, and firmly persuaded that it needs no further elucidation."

I found these words exceptionally helpful to me during the days I spent as a course leader. I would argue that AC Benson's words describe the role of a teacher just as much as that of a lecturer. I think it sad that modern government policy, with its overemphasis on examination results, takes a different view.

More generally, I believe that Benson's aims and precepts are of value to any public speaker. If you can kindle emotion and curiosity, if you can send your listeners off saying, 'I must look into that; there is more in it than I thought', then you will have done very good work indeed.

The Thekla Hultin masterclass

What follows is one of my favourite speeches of the twentieth century.

Dr Thekla Hultin was a member of the Finnish Parliament (the Diet) who campaigned for women's suffrage – votes for women. She had been the first woman ever to gain a PhD in Finland, and the second to qualify as a doctor.

In January 1909, Hultin was the principal speaker at a meeting of the Women's Freedom League at the Queen's Hall in London. She gave her speech in excellent English, which was all the more impressive as she had learned the language with the sole purpose of delivering the speech. Dr Hultin aimed to encourage the women's movement in Britain while reassuring the population as a whole that they had nothing to fear from votes for women. See just how well she achieved those deeply felt objectives, and note the way in which she uses considered, and largely unemotional, language to secure them:

"Women of England, I have come here to assure you that experience in Finland has shown that there is nothing to fear from woman suffrage, while much is to be won in the sphere of social development. When in 1907 the Finnish women were privileged to take part for the first time in the elections, we were anxious as to whether the generality of them would use their right of voting. It would hardly have been surprising had they not done so, for the majority of them were uneducated women of the lower class who had taken little interest in political matters. For this reason, we addressed ourselves especially to the women at the meetings and urged that the right of voting was one of the greatest and most precious privileges of citizenship, and that great privileges always involved great obligations. We told them that if they did not now use the right they had obtained it would be said both in Finland and in other countries that the women of Finland did not understand the value of what they had received. The Finnish women did their duty as unanimously as the men. [Cheers.] The question as to how they vote cannot be based on statistical reports, for the ballot is secret; but I can say that they vote on the whole on exactly the same principles as the men. That is to say, they are influenced by the same ideas, hopes, and prejudices as men. How could it be otherwise? Men and women are human beings first of all and are impressed by the ideas of their generation. Woman suffrage there has been attacked on practical grounds by some, the fear being that women would join their opponents. Conservatives believed that they would lean towards Socialism, while in Liberal and Radical camps it was thought that because of her greater religious feelings a woman would be led to vote Conservative. These fears have not been realised. Women have joined the organisations in the same proportion as the men. It has been said that the Socialistic success in Finland is due to the women, but that is not really the case; the Socialistic success was chiefly due to universal suffrage being extended to the poorer classes. The granting of woman suffrage has caused no change in the strength of the respective political parties. Every citizen in Finland who is entitled to vote is also eligible for membership of the Diet. There has been no rivalry between the men and women candidates; they recognise that both are there for common ends.

The women members of the Diet have followed their parties on party questions, but have joined on women's questions for humanitarian ends. We have presented petitions for the raising of the marriageable age from fifteen to seventeen, the exemption of women from their husbands' guardianship, the reception of government employment on the same grounds as men, and on the subject of the prevention of cruelty to children and animals. These have all been accepted by the Diet.

The enfranchisement of the Finnish women was no Imperial act of grace, but was part of the fundamental law of Finland; that a wave of public opinion brought it about did not detract from that position. If the law should be altered and enfranchisement taken away from women the world should know that one of the fundamental laws had been violated. Our autonomy is threatened by Russia, but we cherish a hope that we shall have the sympathy of the whole civilised world. We take the keenest interest in the movement in England, and, while I can pass no opinion on your methods, I believe that my sisters here will soon gain their end."

[Cheers.]

It seems almost miraculous that something this good could be produced by a non-native, who was delivering a speech in formal English for the first time. It is an astonishing performance by Dr Hultin.

Conclusion

Never forget that it's good to have goals because, in the immortal words of the baseball star Yogi Berra, "If you don't know where you're going, you might not get there."

Points to take from this chapter

- Ask the question, 'What am I trying to achieve?' and then answer it clearly, before you do any further work on a talk.
- Consider also what your audience wants to achieve from your talk.
- In particular, focus on objectives for what the audience should do *after* you have spoken.
- Don't be afraid to set yourself challenging targets.
- If in doubt, use the mnemonic PIETISM to review the various objectives available to you.

Once we are clear on what we are aiming to achieve, we can move on to the careful and detailed preparation we need to do for any talk. We'll be looking at the crucial importance of this in the next chapter. Yes, it involves hard work, but we will be reassured to find there is nothing complicated or difficult about that preparation process.

Notes

Extracts in this book from Clark Mills Brink derive from his 1913 work, *The Making of an Oration*. The quotation from Daniel Finkelstein comes from his article for *The Times* on 5 December 2015. Doug Beattie's commentary on the Tim Collins

Iraq speech is from his book *An Ordinary Soldier*, written with Philip Gomm, Simon & Schuster Ltd, 2008. Thekla Hultin's speech appears in Volume II of *The Book of Public Speaking*. The Yogi Berra quotation is from *When You Come to a Fork in the Road, Take It!: Inspiration and Wisdom from One of Baseball's Greatest Heroes*, Hyperion, 2002.

CHAPTER 5

Prepare, prepare, prepare

Introduction

This chapter looks at the overwhelming importance of preparation in making a speech successful. We'll see, rather reassuringly, that no one is excepted from this rule. All the great speakers had to toil hard to achieve their eminence: they were not great at the outset. We'll learn that the people who make it look easy do so because of the industry and effort that underlie their performance. Even at their peak, they risk disaster if they begin to feel they can wing it or play it by ear.

We'll move on to examine why all the preparation is so very worthwhile, and review a number of practical tips to maximise its effectiveness. A case study in Hungarian will then demonstrate how the most unpromising subject can be made to work successfully in a presentation, thanks to thoughtful preparation.

If Obama can do it...

As I write, many people regard Barack Obama as the greatest English-speaking orator in the world; but if you had said this to his audiences in the first years of the century they might well have laughed at you.

In his earlier days as a politician, he and his style were variously described as 'stiff and professorial', 'not real comfortable or confident', 'stiff and monotonous', and he spoke like a... pedantic lecturer'.

It was only through rigorous preparation and self-development that he became the speaker we recognise today; he, just like anyone else, had to work at it. He was following in a very distinguished tradition.

It all goes back to Demosthenes

As a boy, Demosthenes, who was to become the greatest orator of ancient Athens, had an inarticulate, stammering voice. We are told that he had a weakness of "a perplexed and indistinct utterance and a shortness of breath, which, by breaking and disjointing his sentences, much obscured his sense and meaning." He underwent a disciplined programme of studies and exercises to overcome this and improve his speech. He worked on his diction, voice and gestures, and his dedication and commitment passed into legend. He practised speaking with pebbles in his mouth, and recited verses while running along the seashore over the roar of the waves.

Unsurprisingly, we cannot be sure of the exact truth of the claims made for Demosthenes by later writers. It isn't clear whether they meant them literally or were exaggerating to emphasise the lengths to which he would go to develop himself as an orator. To be entirely clear on the point, I couldn't honestly advise you to go off and practise speaking with pebbles in your mouth. Nevertheless, there is no doubt that Demosthenes set the example for all that followed.

Charles Dickens and Mark Twain

Two thousand years later, the finest praise for a speech in Victorian times was to say that it 'smelt of the lamp'. This was an allusion to that man Demosthenes again, referring to a story that he lived in an underground cave lighted by a lamp so that he would have no distractions from his intense studies of speechmaking.

One of the greatest public performers among the Victorians, Charles Dickens, was himself a man in Demosthenes' image. He once made a throwaway comment – "half-weariedly, yet half-laughingly" – about a piece he had prepared for one of his famous readings from his works: "There! If I have gone through that already to myself once, I have gone through it two hundred times!"

In America, meanwhile, the great humourist Mark Twain was developing his skills as one of the finest speechmakers of his era. Here, a writer called William Dean Howells comments on Twain's methods, noting the hard work and effort an outstanding orator devotes to making it all look natural and spontaneous:

> "He knew that from the beginning of oratory the orator's spontaneity was for the silence and solitude of the closet where he mused his words to an imaginary audience; that this was the use of orators from Demosthenes and Cicero up and down. He studied every word and syllable. He studied every tone and gesture, and he forecast the result with the real audience from its result on the imagined audience. Therefore it was beautiful to see him and to hear him. He

> rejoiced in the pleasure he gave, and in the blows of surprise
> he dealt, and, because he had his end in mind, he knew
> where to stop."

Winston Churchill

Winston Churchill matches Martin Luther King Jr as one of the few speakers in modern history who can genuinely be said to have helped change the world with their oratory; in Churchill's case, by his speeches during the Second World War.

Churchill loved the English language with a passion and was committed to making the most of it when he spoke in public. He had an extraordinary memory, though there came a point when he relied upon it too much, as we will see shortly. He prepared for his speeches with meticulous thoroughness, a habit that he never lost. It was that thoroughness which set him apart, not least in wartime. Even then, he was prepared to devote very long hours to speech composition. If at times he tried to make it look easy, it certainly was not.

It was said of him that "Winston has spent the best years of his life composing his impromptu speeches." In 1955, at the age of eighty, he was still willing to spend twenty hours preparing his last major speech to the House of Commons, all of which he dictated himself.

The story comes up to date

I like the acronym, said to have originated with the military during the Second World War, PPPPPP. It stands for Proper Preparation Prevents Piss-Poor Performance. Despite all the pressures and distractions of the modern world, I believe it is still possible to achieve proper preparation within a manageable period of time.

Here is a simple but effective system used by the American comedian and writer Jerry Seinfeld, who later on will give us the world's best joke about public speaking nerves. He has used his 'don't break the chain' system to ensure that he keeps writing comic material every day. The method involves just crossing off a day on a calendar when a task is completed. Days with an X struck through them create a chain, and, particularly once you have got through the opening weeks to establish a habit, you find your momentum keeps you going on a daily basis to avoid breaking the chain.

As you would expect, apps are now available on your smartphone to take away the need for manual crossing out, not that that seemed too much of a burden in the first place. In my experience, the commitment and consistency of the Seinfeld method work well for people who are preparing for public speaking engagements.

How much preparation is enough?

An American writer, Harry Bower Bradbury, noted in 1915 the traditional view of what was expected from a public speaker. It had come down from ancient times to the start of the twentieth century:

> "[Writers on public speaking] are practically unanimous in stating that the speaker should have clearly in mind the framework of the speech and also his principal arguments. They all insist that he must also be complete master of his subject. They advise that he should have mapped out the general trend of the introduction, have clearly in mind the facts which he must state to make the speech understood and the proposition which he is to advance. He must consider the

> order in which he is to present his principal and subsidiary arguments. These should all be worked out in his mind beforehand, and it is very helpful to make a rough diagram. This process will be an immense aid to the memory, and the speech will have the force which necessarily follows an orderly presentation of a topic. Moreover, it will leave the speaker free to throw into his effort that *abandon* which is the very soul of true eloquence."

A hundred years further on, little has changed in what is expected of the top speakers.

In May 2016, Shana Lebowitz, writing on the *Business Insider* website, explained the role of preparation in the extraordinary success of the global TED talks: "Those scintillating talks are the product of an often gruelling rehearsal process; every single speaker that takes to the stage practises until their delivery is impeccable."

In the same month that Shana Lebowitz wrote those words, I heard Chris Anderson, the curator of the TED talks, speak in London. He expressed his amazement at how many people still try to wing their way through public talks. For him, preparation and rehearsal represent "the difference between owning a talk and being owned by it". That is a striking way to make the point. Similarly, Tom Peters, the management guru, explained in *MT* (*Management Today*) magazine his continuing success at presenting in terms of out-preparing the competition. "I've got a good line and nobody reacts," he said, "so the next time I tell the story I adjust it, and I adjust it twenty-three times, until the twenty-fourth time I get the connection I was looking for. It only comes from hard work and repetition."

Exactly how much preparation time will you need for any particular talk?

It may be a cop-out to say so, but it all depends. One of

the statistics commonly quoted is that you need ten minutes' preparation time for each minute of your talk. However, if I am developing a new presentation from scratch, I would expect to spend about an hour's preparation for every minute of the talk. If I am tweaking an existing presentation, I clearly need less preparatory time. On the other hand, a short talk may demand exceptionally precise and detailed development that you might be able to avoid for a longer, more diffuse presentation.

Grenville Kleiser, a prolific North American author on oratory, made this point elegantly in his work *The Art of Public Speaking*:

> "A man should take ample time in which properly to prepare his speech. 'How long do you wish me to speak?' asked a man who was invited by a society to attend its annual dinner. 'Why do you ask?' inquired the Secretary. 'Because,' said the orator, 'if you want me to give a ten-minute address I must have at least two weeks in which to prepare myself, but if you want me to talk for an hour or more, I am ready.'"

Why it's worth all the preparation

The most successful speakers down the ages, from Demosthenes and Cicero to Lincoln and Churchill, evidently felt that their preparation time was fully justified. Noting the lesson of the TED talks, Shana Lebowitz suggests the bottom line is this: "Rehearsal is stressful, and annoying, and time-consuming. But it's totally worth the feeling of walking off stage knowing you killed it, leaving your audience in awe of your magical powers."

In line with the general rule that you get what you pay for, the rewards for any speaker will match the effort they put in. By failing to prepare, you do indeed prepare to fail. I work on the basis that

80% to 90% of my success or failure at any speaking engagement will be determined by the thought and commitment I put into the preparation process, long before I ever stand up to talk. The more work I do, and the earlier I start, the more good ideas will come to me as I go along, to improve not only that particular presentation but also the ones I will deliver in the future.

It's certainly true that the best things in any speech, the sudden inspirations and flashes of insight, frequently arise on the spur of the moment. It is equally true, in my experience, that the more you have prepared beforehand, the more often those great moments will come.

I firmly believe that self-interest alone should drive us to do the necessary preparation. However, if that doesn't convince you, there is a useful exercise you can carry out that looks at things from an audience's point of view.

Work out how much time the audience are going to devote to your talk, including the time they will spend organising themselves for the event and journeying to and from the venue. If you are presenting to thirty people for half an hour, and on average they spend twenty minutes on travel, you are responsible as the speaker for 1,500 minutes or twenty-five hours of audience involvement. I calculated that one of my bigger talks involved 3,500 man and woman hours of audience time, that's to say over twenty (wo)man weeks in total. If your presentation is using up that amount of human life, you darn well owe it to your listeners to prepare properly.

Key pointers for your preparation

There are some fundamental questions to ask as you prepare:

- How do you want the lives of your audience to change as a result of hearing your talk, and how can you make that a reality by what you say? If you are a world leader, this can be a noble and awe-inspiring challenge. At a more down-to-earth level, you might simply aim to send the audience away happier than when they sat down, in which case your task is likely to relate to being enthusiastic and entertaining.

- What are the key aspects of your subject that the audience currently knows little or nothing about, or where what they know is wrong? These will be particularly productive areas to cover.

- How does each part of your talk fit in with your overall theme? Have you worked your theme into the talk clearly enough to show the consistency and coherence of that dominant idea throughout what you will say?

- Given the nature of your subject matter, what might you do to bring extra spice and variety into your talk? In particular, what stories might you tell or what examples might you use?

- What could be the problem areas? Think as widely as you can here so that you review not only the content of your talk, but also the context in which it will be given and the nature of the audience and the auditorium. How can you minimise the potential pitfalls? You will often do well to share this discussion with people whose opinions you respect, and invite their constructive criticisms and suggestions. That way you bring a wider range of points of view into your decision-making. As a simple example, first-class material translates into a lousy talk if you can't be heard because of problems with the acoustics, in which case you would benefit from consulting a sound expert early on.

- Do you have a fall-back plan? This is crucial, and it deserves our special attention.

Always have a fall-back plan

A vital part of a speaker's ammunition is to have a worst-case plan.

Assume that anything that *can* go wrong *will* go wrong. The most obvious examples of this are the technology for your talk failing utterly, or your memory doing the same. Always be ready to present a version of your speech that:

- Involves no hardware, software, slides or other technology.
- Gives you a backup for memory failure.

You will be impressed by the added confidence you can gain from having an ultimate fall-back presentation available. I have had to use it only two or three times, but each time it has brought me victory from the jaws of disaster.

One of the most famous demonstrations of the need for a fall-back plan concerned, surprisingly, Winston Churchill.

For the early years of his career, Churchill flirted with danger in his public speaking, always relying on memorisation of his script. On 22 April 1904, he dried up during a speech in a packed House of Commons. After he had been speaking for forty-five minutes without notes, his memory failed him. "There I stood, searching for the missing word. It never came," he said afterwards. Indeed, *Hansard* records that: 'the hon Member here faltered in the conclusion of his speech, and, amid sympathetic cheers, resumed his seat, after thanking the House for having listened to him.' He took full notes for his speeches with him for the rest of his life.

One person who did not learn the lesson in time was Ed Miliband, then the UK Labour Party leader. (To be fair, he later became an outstanding radio broadcaster.) He made the mistake of attempting to memorise a sixty-five-minute speech to his party conference in September 2014, had no apparent backup with him, and duly forgot to say anything about how he would tackle the sizeable budget deficit or deal with concerns on immigration – two of the biggest issues facing the country. He went on to lose the following year's general election. I can't help thinking that the time he spent trying to learn his script would have been much better devoted to improving the speech and rehearsing it thoroughly.

Above all, I can't overemphasise the need for a fall-back plan.

The Csikszentmihalyi case study

Here's a small example of how straightforward, careful preparation can make a big difference to any talk.

You work in management development, and you have been asked to give a seminar on the subject of flow theory – the idea that people are happiest and most productive when completely concentrated on, and absorbed in, the task at hand. The subject itself is not at all obscure, but you face a major problem. The academic who proposed the concept of flow theory is a US psychology professor, originally from Hungary, called Mihaly Csikszentmihalyi. I shall call him Mr C for short.

You know what's coming. There are going to be two fundamental issues in making this talk a success: the relatively straightforward one of speaking intelligently about flow theory, and the highly stressful one of saying Mr C's full name out loud in public.

In an early rehearsal, you make a valiant attempt at the pronunciation of his name. If you are like me, you may just about get through the first four or five syllables, but then you lose the plot. You have another go, and then another, but by this time you resemble a showjumper after the first couple of refusals. You're never going to jump the fence. The name just won't come. You have a problem.

You consider not mentioning the man's name at all during your talk, but you reluctantly decide that this is not a viable way forward. It seemed too extreme an avoidance tactic, even for me, when I gave the presentation. It would be like giving a talk on Hamlet without naming Shakespeare as the author. However, it occurs to you that, if all else fails, you could just put his full name up on a big slide and subsequently refer to him as Mr C – or possibly as MC, the Master of Ceremonies for flow theory.

The next step is to go on to the Internet. What can you learn here? At the outset, everyone agrees that Mr C is noted for his notoriously difficult name as well as for his achievements in happiness and creativity studies. "Just pronouncing his name is a learning adventure," says one commentator. All this is more helpful than you might first think, because it gives you a possible way forward in your talk – to play humorously on the audience's sympathy, on the basis that getting Mr C's name right in a public presentation is the Everest of pronunciation challenges.

You soon also learn that he is known as the 'Godfather of Flow', so that gives you another title you might use for him. You find a video on YouTube of a native speaker of Hungarian pronouncing his name rather sweetly. You then also discover some useful transcriptions, telling you that Csikszentmihalyi can be pronounced Cheek-Sent-Me-High-ee or Cheek-Sent-Me-High. You also find a suggestion for the entire name: 'Me high. Chick sent me high', which has an elegant symmetry to it, if nothing else.

You are pleased to find that the man himself seems relaxed

about the pronunciation of his name, saying that his students "can just call me Mike. I keep forgetting how to pronounce it well myself." You decide to use that line in the actual talk, guessing that it will get you an impressive laugh or at least lots of smiles from the audience. (Trust me, it does.) You even think about maximising audience involvement by holding a quick competition to see who can pronounce the name most impressively. By now, the level of your preparation has got you to the point where you are confident that Mihaly Csikszentmihalyi's name can be a positive factor in the success of your talk.

There is, of course, no single correct or final answer on how you should exploit the results of your preparation. When Rob Yeung, the co-author of *Public Speaking and Presentations for Dummies*, had to do a presentation involving Csikszentmihalyi's work, he decided after much practising to err on the side of caution and simply insert his name into the appendices of his visual aids rather than be obliged to say it out loud.

My own solution was to show Mr C's full name in large letters on a slide and say to the audience: "This is pronounced [long pause]… Here goes [further pause]… *Me high. Chick sent me high.*" It produced a round of applause which, though I say it myself, was thoroughly deserved. The reality is that, unless you have an unusually large number of demanding Hungarians in the audience, any decent attempt at the name, made with apparent confidence, will go down very nicely. Later in the talk, I confined myself to calling him Mr C, or MC, or Mike. That was not so much reluctance to go up to the high wire again without a net, as a recognition that frequent repetition of a long name like Csikszentmihalyi takes up time that would be better spent on flow theory itself.

The moral here is that many problems arising in a presentation can be solved by anticipating and thinking about them in a relaxed way. The earlier you start, the longer you give yourself to review the issues creatively and to seek appropriate help and advice. With this kind of forethought, problems often shift into opportunities.

Obama wobbles

The minute you start thinking, 'I can wing this', or, 'I'm good, so I don't need to prepare', you're in trouble. And that applies even to the very finest speakers. At the first US presidential debate in 2012, Mitt Romney for the Republicans flattened Barack Obama, the sitting Democratic president. Romney performed very much better than had been expected, but Obama was awful. Joe Klein, writing for *Time Magazine,* noted that: "Mitt Romney won this debate. Barack Obama lost it. I mean, he got his butt kicked. It was, in fact, one of the most inept performances I've ever seen by a sitting president." A Republican strategist commented that Obama had been "too arrogant to prepare", and most people agreed. Obama hated this kind of ordeal by television and looked down on the whole exercise. He came over as ill-equipped and unready for the encounter, and the voters could not fail to notice it.

However, Obama learned his lesson: he put in the work and came back strongly for the further two presidential debates. He went on to defeat Romney comfortably in the 2012 presidential election. But the moral is clear: if even Barack Obama can't get away without thorough preparation, neither can the rest of us.

Conclusion

I like the quotation, attributed to Abraham Lincoln (though for no obvious reason), which goes: "If I had six hours to chop down a tree, I'd spend the first four sharpening the axe." Always give the preparation of your talk the time it needs.

Why do so many speakers fail to prepare?

I think it goes back to the completely wrong-headed belief that good speakers are born, not made. It is not until you recognise the folly of this position and become aware that presenting is a trade, a craft – not a God-given talent reserved only for the special few – that success in public speaking becomes possible for you. You begin to accept that you can get much better at it by everyday activities like planning, preparation and working hard.

Dorothy Parker wisely noted that: "Time doth flit; oh shit." Following on from that, researchers on motivation tell us that the top motivator of performance is, very simply, achieving progress. Once you feel that you are making headway in a task and overcoming difficulties, your commitment will be at its greatest and your attitude at its most positive. The final performance will be correspondingly more relaxed and confident. Preparation really does make a huge difference.

Points to take from this chapter

- Start preparing early to raise your motivation and commitment levels, and to give yourself more time to come up with great ideas.
- Get into a routine: do your preparation on a regular and methodical basis, and you will find your momentum keeps you going.
- Focus particularly on the potential problem areas.
- Always have a worst-case plan.
- The minute you stop taking your preparation seriously, you are in trouble. Barack Obama can confirm this.
- The feeling you get when your talk goes well more than compensates for all the work you have put into it.

This chapter has looked at the hard graft involved in preparing a good presentation. It makes public speaking a challenge, but that shouldn't stop it being enjoyable. In the next chapter, I'm going to develop the theme of enjoyment as a key element of a speaker's success, one that also brings many consequential benefits for the audience.

Notes

The descriptions of the younger Barack Obama's speaking style come from an article by Olivia Mitchell, *You can learn to be a better presenter*, on the excellent *Speaking about Presenting* website, www.speakingaboutpresenting.com. The description of Demosthenes is in Plutarch's *Life of Demosthenes*. The quotations by and about Charles Dickens in this book are from a fascinating 1872 work recording his style and techniques as a speaker, *Charles Dickens as a Reader* by Charles Kent. The comments of William Dean Howells on Mark Twain derive from a 1912 work, *Extemporaneous Speaking* by Paul M Pearson and Philip M Hicks. The jibe about Winston Churchill's impromptu speeches came from his friend FE Smith: the story is told by Nicholas Soames in *Eminent Parliamentarians: The Speaker's Lectures*, edited by Philip Norton, Biteback Publishing Ltd, 2012. The story of the Jerry Seinfeld productivity secret was told by Brad Isaac in 2007 at https://lifehacker.com/281626/jerry-seinfelds-productivity-secret. The extract from Harry Bower Bradbury comes from his work *The structure of an effective public speech*. The Shana Lebowitz piece is from http://uk.businessinsider.com/ted-chris-anderson-people-dont-practice-2016-5. Hansard records the generous reception given to Winston Churchill after his 1904 failure at http://hansard.millbanksystems.com/commons/1904/apr/22/trade-unions-and-trades-disputes-bill. Ed Miliband's 2014 conference speech can be found online if you are a glutton for punishment, but I'm too concerned for your wellbeing to make it easy for you. Joe Klein's comments on Barack Obama can be seen at http://swampland.time.com/2012/10/03/the-debate/. The actual debate is at https://www.youtube.com/watch?v=dkrwUU_YApE.

CHAPTER 6

Enjoy yourself!

Introduction

I strongly believe that it helps any speaker to start their performance with the deliberate intention of enjoying the experience fixed firmly in mind. Speaking in public doesn't have to be a dismal event: it really is possible to have a fine time. In this chapter, we will examine the importance of this, and look at a variety of straightforward ways to achieve it.

The paramount importance of enjoying yourself

Nick Morgan, a great American speaking coach and author, has written in his blog about the most important rule for speaking success. He says: "It's a complex process, an art form, involving lots of moving parts. But if I'm pressed for one rule only, it would be this: *have fun.*"

I'm with Nick Morgan on this.

He points out that the audience wants the speaker to succeed: otherwise, the experience will be a waste of their time. The single most significant thing a speaker can do is to indicate to the audience that he or she is having a good time. It is tantamount to telling them they are in safe hands. They can relax and enjoy themselves. Nick Morgan comments: "That creates a virtuous circle – happy audience, happy speaker – and those good vibes go a long way toward creating a good experience for all."

Trainee teachers learn that children mirror their emotions, that by putting a smile on their own face they have a much better chance of making their pupils smile. In scientific studies, the subject of mirror neurons – nerve cells in one animal that 'mirror' the behaviour of another animal – has generated fierce debate in recent years. The research is far from conclusive, and indeed most of it has been done on monkeys rather than humans. Even so, I cannot be alone among speakers to have noticed that an audience can be quick to catch your mood as you take the platform, and also quick to match it.

It would be dangerous to ignore the potential power of mirror neurons to contribute to speaker success. And, anyway, going out on stage feeling positive beats a sulky and miserable mood any day.

We will now see one of the greatest exponents of this principle in action.

The great model: Charles Dickens

The Victorian literary giant Charles Dickens, whose dedicated approach to public speaking I have already mentioned, undertook a series of extraordinarily popular tours, reading from his works in both England and America. In doing so, he became one of the leading speakers of his age. Here is his friend Charles Kent's account of Dickens starting a reading from *A Christmas Carol*:

"There was... a sense of exhilaration in the very manner with which Dickens commenced the reading of one of his stories, and which was always especially noticeable in the instance of this particular ghost story of his about Christmas. The opening sentences were always given in those cheery, comfortable tones, indicative of a double relish on the part of a narrator – to wit, his own enjoyment of the tale he is going to relate, and his anticipation of the enjoyment of it by those who are giving him their attention. Occasionally, at any rate during the last few years, his voice was husky just at the commencement, but as he warmed to his work, with him at all times a genuine labour of love, everything of that kind disappeared almost at the first turn of the leaf. The genial inflections of the voice, curiously rising, in those first moments of the reading, at the end of every sentence, there was simply no resisting."

A modern example: Donald Trump

The next quotation may surprise you, given what happened to the speaking style of its author afterwards. Here is Donald Trump, sharing his approach to public speaking at a time when he was a mere American businessman and television personality: "Have a good time. It's contagious. If your audience believes you are enjoying what you are doing, they'll enjoy being in your company."

Trump's comment here is in direct contrast to many modern speakers, who give the impression of fervently wishing they were somewhere, anywhere, else. Sadly, his own style changed once he had made a serious move into the political arena, when anger and bitterness came to characterise his speeches too often.

There are exceptions to the Donald Trump 'have a good time' approach. There have been some splendid deadpan speakers for whom an expression of enthusiasm would be a betrayal of their essence as a performer – the comedian Jack Dee, for example, and in an earlier generation the droll Scottish entertainer Chic Murray, one of my heroes. But the poker-faced approach of challenging the audience to enjoy themselves is one of the hardest tricks to pull off, and requires an outstanding speaker if it is to succeed. The simple act of obviously enjoying yourself works best for most speakers.

Enjoying yourself in business settings

It can be particularly difficult to enjoy yourself in a business presentation, which is why it is all the more important to try.

Jo Owen, an expert on leadership, writes: "Sadly, in many organisations, enthusiasm is regarded as a certifiable mental disorder. Put this to your advantage. Audiences that are not used to enthusiasm will enjoy the difference."

In my own field of tax lecturing, I like to think that what distinguished me from most speakers was that I conveyed a sense of being keen on the subject and eager to talk about it because I found it all so interesting. A common piece of feedback was that "you really seemed to be enjoying yourself on the podium," stated in a positive way. Well, I hope it was said positively. Beyond the note of appreciation, there was also a sense of slight incredulity that anyone could actually take pleasure from the grim subject of tax. In any event, it helped set me apart from the competition.

By contrast, if a speaker mounts the platform in the belief that their subject truly is dull or unteachable, they will come over very poorly to the audience. If you find it's just impossible to enjoy the topic you have been asked to talk on, then turn down the engagement if you possibly can. I soon learned that if I was not enthusiastic about a project – lecturing on development land tax comes readily to mind – I simply should not speak about it in public.

How to enjoy yourself

It's all very well me telling you to go out and enjoy yourself, but how in reality do you give yourself the greatest chance of doing so?

The best way to achieve joyful public speaking is to go on stage with the confidence and self-assurance that come from having prepared and rehearsed thoroughly for a talk.

That is the most obvious route to enjoyment, but here are some additional useful approaches:

- First, please do accept that public speaking is not only for the audience; it's there for your benefit as the speaker too. To have a talk go well can be one of the finest pleasures of life.
- Donald Trump, again writing as a business magnate, suggests that we should remind ourselves as speakers before we take the floor that it is not going to be an earth-shattering event. We shouldn't have the weight of the world on us. If your self-respect is dependent on the outcome of a presentation, you're taking it too seriously. "It's merely a speech," Trump writes, "not an earthquake or a war. You'll have a better time and be a better speaker if you keep it all in perspective."
- Aim to bring into your talk those things that you personally find humorous, interesting or moving.
- Being at one with the audience and your surroundings helps greatly. You feel more comfortable and less under pressure. That sense of integration comes

from such obvious things as having arrived early enough to get to know the organisers of the event, the layout of the room and the atmosphere among the audience. Meeting as many of the attendees beforehand, talking to people over coffee breaks, listening to the speakers who are on before you: all these details can make a positive difference.

- Just keep going. Almost every public speaker finds that, the longer they stick with the experience, the more pleasure they get from it. I like this quote from an unidentified blog contributor: "I'm not a natural presenter, but I do enjoy it when I get into it. You've just got to get stuck into it. If you're comfortable with it, then it does show." This sums up the experience of many speakers, though I would deny the existence of such a thing as a 'natural presenter'. What looks like natural talent is the result of a whole lot of hard work.

If in doubt, fake it

If you can't enjoy yourself to start with, then pretend to do so and reality may well catch up with you. This may sound like a pie in the sky statement, but there is now scientific evidence to back it up. The key principle here comes from the work of the Victorian philosopher and psychologist William James, who gave us what has been termed the *As If* Principle.

His message was: if you want a quality, act *as if* you already have it.

Here, James sets out his approach:

> "The sovereign voluntary path to cheerfulness... is to sit up cheerfully, to look round cheerfully, and to act and speak as

if cheerfulness were already there. If such conduct does not make you soon feel cheerful, nothing else on that occasion can... To wrestle with a bad feeling only pins our attention on it, and keeps it still fastened in the mind: whereas, if we act as if from some better feeling, the old bad feeling soon folds its tent... and silently steals away."

James argues that, whereas normal common sense suggests that feeling happy makes us smile, it works the other way around as well: smiling causes us to feel happy.

Richard Wiseman, a leading experimental psychologist, explains the research that has been done to demonstrate the validity of James's theory, both in the area of enjoyment and in numerous other aspects of our emotional lives, in his 2012 book, *Rip It Up*.

In tests, participants felt significantly happier when they forced their faces into smiles (and also significantly angrier when they frowned). It seems that your behaviour genuinely does influence how you feel: so, if you go into a presentation looking as though you are enjoying yourself, there is a much better chance that you honestly will.

Richard Wiseman sums it up like this: "The message... is clear – rather than trying to cheer yourself up by thinking happy thoughts, it is far quicker and more effective to simply behave as if you are having a good time."

Take time out before the presentation

It helps your enjoyment if you can finish your preparation for the talk early, and then put it out of your mind until the time comes to perform. Some excellent nineteenth-century advice from Thomas Wentworth Higginson, an American minister, author and soldier, is helpful here:

"Do not torment yourself up to the last moment about your speech, but give your mind a rest before it. To combine ample preparation with a state of mental clearness and freshness – that is the [challenge]. It is not the public speaking that wears upon a man, it is the waiting for it. Look at the faces of the after dinner speakers at a public dinner: how woe-begone till their time comes! How cheerful afterwards! To make your speeches successful, therefore, learn the art of completing your preparation beforehand; and then indulging in entire rest – newspapers, Mark Twain, exercise, anything you please until the important moment comes."

That seems very sensible to me, and it explains why you will usually find me attempting, and failing at, a killer sudoku in the period before a talk.

Conclusion

One of my favourite entertainers, the late comedian Ken Dodd, always conveyed a tremendous sense of his own enjoyment and enthusiasm to his audiences, coupled with the conviction that he would beat them into submission if they didn't join in the experience. This approach carried all before him, even though some of his material might not be as strong as that of other leading comics.

I'm sure many of us will remember the teachers who got us involved in their subjects at school. Memories of Mr Ansell and Mr Ayres for Mathematics, and Mr Ditchfield and Mr Dodgeon for Latin and Greek, will always be with me. They led me to a lifelong interest in the subjects they taught, and much of that came from the sheer enthusiasm and enjoyment they took in their work. That kind of joy is infectious, and I hope you too can come to have it in your public speaking.

Look as though you want to be there; look like you're enjoying yourself. If enjoying it isn't your style, then fake it: smile at your audience and feign good humour. You will be surprised by how often you end up having a good time despite yourself. And, of course, the audience will be a lot happier if *you* look happy. That way, everyone wins.

Points to take from this chapter

- An audience is quick to catch your mood.
- If you show them you are having a good time, they can relax and enjoy themselves in turn.
- Business audiences love enthusiastic speakers, not least because of their rarity value.
- Thorough preparation gives you the best chance to enjoy yourself on stage.
- Keep things in perspective: it's a talk, not a matter of life or death.
- Try to talk about subjects that you personally enjoy.
- Arrive in plenty of time to avoid putting yourself under pressure.
- If in doubt, pretend to enjoy yourself: the real thing should follow.
- Take time out to relax before the presentation.

In the next chapter, we'll move beyond the speaker's sense of enjoyment to look at the broader issue of emotion in speechmaking. We will see that the emotional feeling you inject into your talks and presentations is a crucial element in their success, and we'll go on to review some great examples of how to achieve that.

Notes

The quotations from Nick Morgan come from a blog entry on his *Public Words* website, www.publicwords.com, for 15 March 2012, entitled *What's the single most important secret for good public speaking?* The Donald Trump extracts come from *How to Get Rich* by Donald J Trump with Meredith McIver, Random House, 2004. Trump enthusiasts may wish to obtain the edition that comes with a dollar sign charm included. Jo Owen's comment was made in his great book *Management Stripped Bare – What they don't teach you at business school*, Kogan Page Ltd, 2012. William James set out his approach in a talk entitled *The Gospel of Relaxation* (published as part of his work *Talks to Teachers on Psychology: and to Students on Some of Life's Ideals*). The advice from Thomas Wentworth Higginson is abridged from a short essay, *Hints on Speechmaking*, which first appeared in *Harper's Magazine* for November 1886.

CHAPTER 7

It's all about emotion

Introduction

In the last chapter, we saw how much public performances can gain from a simple, straightforward expression of emotion in the form of the speaker's enjoyment of the event. I now want to develop that theme to consider the benefits of emotion in a wider sense, showing the value of communicating to our listeners the feelings and passions that add flavour and character to any talk.

We will see that it is nearly always the emotional commitment of the speaker, rather than the pure logic of their words, that will win over audiences. A variety of orators in full flow will show us how they accomplished this, and we'll review some simple pointers to make the most of the psychological flavouring we can add to any talk.

The role of emotion in public speaking

Over 2,300 years ago the ancient Greek philosopher Aristotle told the world that the three essential foundations of a successful speaker are ethos, logos and pathos. Ethos refers to the credibility or authority of the speaker: the audience must regard you as believable if they are to accept what you say. Logos is the logical attraction of your argument. Pathos is the appeal you make to the audience's emotions, and the terms sympathy, pathetic and empathy derive from it.

Aristotle saw logos as the most important of the three mainstays of persuasion; but then he was a logician and scientist by trade, so he would have been letting the side down if he'd taken any other position.

For me, pathos, or emotion, is the most critical element of the three. We like to think of ourselves as rational individuals, but the work of modern psychologists and behavioural economists gives the lie to that. I am convinced that, in the world of presentations, the emotions hold sway.

In general, people make their decisions based on emotion (pathos) and only then justify them with intellectual argument and facts (logos). We like to come up with some logical justification for our choices to make ourselves comfortable, but it is the emotion that is crucial.

The word *emotion* comes into English from Latin by way of an Old French word *emouvoir,* meaning 'to stir up', and stirring up is exactly what a good presentation should be doing to its audience.

Hugh Blair, an eighteenth-century Scottish theologian who was one of the first great writers on oratory in English, noted that:

"Almost every man, in passion, is eloquent. Then he is at no loss for words and arguments. He transmits to others, by a sort of contagious sympathy, the warm sentiments which he feels... All high eloquence flows from passion... hence the universally acknowledged effect of enthusiasm, or warmth of any kind, in public speakers, for affecting their audience."

How do we achieve the emotional connection that pathos requires? There are, of course, many ways, not least telling stories and personal anecdotes, and showing passion in the delivery of the speech. In this chapter, we'll look at some examples of oratory that, using these techniques, demonstrate the power of emotion to defeat any old logic; but first, I want to mention an example of how not to do it.

The air steward

I was flying to Alicante on my way to Benidorm: well, someone has to. At the start of the flight, the air steward launched into his safety talk. He talked very quickly and at times barely intelligibly, gushing the words forth in a flat voice without variety. It must be a tough job, being an air steward, especially when you have people like me as your passengers. Saying the same words that you have said so many times before to people who mostly look as though they don't want to hear them is not one of life's easier speaking engagements.

Even so, a bit more emotional commitment on his part would not have gone amiss. If you give the impression that you attach no value to what you say, then neither will your audience. There was no passion. He could have been recruiting for Al-Qaeda, and you still wouldn't have noticed. As a safety announcement, it wasn't likely to do much for anyone's safety. It is this lack of emotional commitment, this apparent willingness to do no more than go through the motions, that ruins so much public speaking.

Whatever you say in public, please mean it.

Health and safety

In the light of the air steward's announcement, could anything be duller than health and safety? In fact, hardly any subject is inherently boring unless the speaker chooses to make it so. This applies even to air safety: an Internet search on 'best air safety videos' reveals some brilliant examples of engaging the attention of passengers. Air New Zealand produces some particularly eye-catching material, with its Men in Black rap announcement being my personal favourite.

The leadership expert Kevin Murray takes us further on this subject. He tells an extraordinarily moving story about the safety director of a house building company, where members of a construction crew had failed to safeguard a site correctly:

> "A boy had strayed onto one of his sites. He had managed to get through a gap in the fence after everyone had gone home, fallen into a deep pit excavated for foundations and had been severely injured. In pain, bleeding profusely, he died alone in the night."

Kevin Murray wisely advised the director to go out and tell this story throughout the organisation without embellishment. The positive effect on the business was profound. The story is simple, true and harrowing, and it compels its audience to reflect deeply and honestly on their own approach to safety. As such, it is extraordinarily effective in changing people's behaviour for the better.

Let's now hear from some distinguished speakers at the peak of their emotional form.

Lloyd George gets angry

Anger is a difficult emotion to express successfully on a stage because it is so challenging for the speaker to rise to the occasion and maintain self-control. However, if it is done well, the effect can be gripping.

Here we have David Lloyd George, the great Liberal politician, speaking on what was to become the Welsh Church Act of 1914, disestablishing the Church of England in Wales. The Duke of Devonshire had claimed that the proposed law amounted to the robbery of God. Lloyd George replied that the wealth of the Duke and other landowners was itself 'laid deep in sacrilege' from the era of the break-up of the monasteries:

> "They robbed the Church. They robbed the monasteries. They robbed the altars. They robbed the almshouses. They robbed the poor. They robbed the dead. Then they come here when we are trying… to recover some of this pillaged property for the poor to whom it was originally given, with hands dripping with the fat of sacrilege, to accuse us of robbery of God."

What an impressive use of invective this is – an exceptionally potent attack that makes a speaker like Donald Trump look like an absolute beginner in the use of polemics. It also shows how powerful simple repetition can be in a speech.

George Patton goes to war

The next passage comes from an inspirational speech given by General George S Patton to the troops of the United States Third Army at the start of June 1944, just before the Allied invasion of France in the Second World War:

> "Be seated. Men, all this stuff you hear about America not wanting to fight, wanting to stay out of the war, is a lot of bullshit. Americans love to fight. All real Americans love the sting and clash of battle. When you were kids, you all

admired the champion marble shooter, the fastest runner, the big-league ball players and the toughest boxers. Americans love a winner and will not tolerate a loser. Americans play to win all the time. That's why Americans have never lost and will never lose a war. The very thought of losing is hateful to Americans. Battle is the most significant competition in which a man can indulge. It brings out all that is best, and it removes all that is base.

You are not all going to die. Only two per cent of you right here today would be killed in a major battle. Every man is scared in his first action. If he says he's not, he's a goddamn liar. But the real hero is the man who fights even though he's scared. Some men will get over their fright in a minute under fire, some take an hour, and for some it takes days. But the real man never lets his fear of death overpower his honour, his sense of duty to his country, and his innate manhood.

All through your army career you men have bitched about what you call 'this chicken-shit drilling'. That is all for a purpose – to ensure instant obedience to orders and to create constant alertness. This must be bred into every soldier. I don't give a fuck for a man who is not always on his toes. But the drilling has made veterans of all you men. You are ready! A man has to be alert all the time if he expects to keep on breathing. If not, some German son-of-a-bitch will sneak up behind him and beat him to death with a sock full of shit. There are four hundred neatly marked graves in Sicily, all because one man went to sleep on the job – but they are German graves, because we caught the bastard asleep before his officer did.

An army is a team. It lives, eats, sleeps, and fights as a team.

> This individual hero stuff is bullshit. The bilious bastards who write that stuff for the Saturday Evening Post don't know any more about real battle than they do about fucking. And we have the best team – we have the finest food and equipment, the best spirit and the best men in the world. Why, by God, I actually pity these poor bastards we're going up against…"

I love this speech, with its mixture of inspiration and realism, great patriotism, crude humour and simple reassurance. It's not surprising that it has been acclaimed as one of the finest motivational talks of all time. Another glorious quotation from General Patton is: "No bastard ever won a war by dying for his country. You won it by making the other poor dumb bastard die for his country."

I have never been asked to go into battle, but if I were, this is the man I would want as my leader.

Kennedy goes to the moon

Here is an extract from President John F Kennedy's famous speech in September 1962 to a large crowd in Houston, Texas about the American space effort. It has come to be known as the *We choose to go to the Moon* speech:

> "We choose to go to the moon. We choose to go to the moon in this decade and do the other things, not because they are easy, but because they are hard, because that goal will serve to organise and measure the best of our energies and skills, because that challenge is one that we are willing to accept, one we are unwilling to postpone, and one which we intend to win, and the others, too."

From one point of view, this barely makes sense. He does not tell us what he means by 'do the other things'. And why should you do things just because they are hard? What if they are hard and stupid, as opposed to easy and sensible? How will going to the moon measure the best of our energies, and what would be the point of that anyway? When Kennedy says that we choose to go to the moon because it's a challenge we are willing to accept, isn't that just saying that we choose to go because we choose to go? At an intellectual level, you might conclude that what he says here is, on the whole, rather silly.

Yet President Kennedy's speech was well received for its emotional drive. It was front-page news around America, praised for its soaring rhetoric.

We talked earlier about the importance of focusing on your objective, and this speech certainly met that test. By the end of the decade, the United States had indeed gone to the moon. For all I know, it had done 'the other things' as well, whatever they might have been.

This speech is a prime example of the rule that an emotional appeal, driven home with enthusiasm and commitment, will often defeat a rational argument hands down.

Michael Dukakis stays in control

In the second televised debate in the 1988 US presidential election, Michael Dukakis, for the Democratic Party, was having a rough time, not helped by the fact that he was suffering from the flu. The reporter Bernard Shaw asked him, as a long-standing opponent of the death sentence, whether he would support the death penalty if his wife, Kitty, were to be raped and murdered. It was a startling question, and arguably it was unfair and offensive, but you could understand the reasoning behind asking it of a man who could at times come over as cold and unduly cerebral. Michael Dukakis replied:

> "No, I don't, Bernard, and I think you know that I've opposed the death penalty during all of my life. I don't see any evidence that it's a deterrent and I think there are better and more effective ways to deal with violent crime."

While eminently rational, this highbrow approach was not the way to win over the hearts of the voters. Commentators noted that Dukakis had answered the question almost abstractly, showing no emotion and without mentioning his wife's name. The answer cemented his reputation as dispassionate and remote. George HW Bush won the debate for the Republicans and went on to win the election itself by a hefty margin.

Speakers dismiss the power of emotion at their peril.

Tom Duane gets very, very angry

You can't beat genuine passion, strongly expressed.

Here, in the early hours of the morning on 17 July 2009, is New York State Senator Tom Duane, gay and HIV-positive, a man even angrier than Lloyd George. His comments come during a spellbinding, highly emotional twenty-one-minute speech, at times more of a tirade, on the Senate floor. It is the end of a marathon session on a bill which would prevent people who receive public assistance while living with HIV or AIDS from having to pay more than 30% of their monthly income on rent.

Tom Duane describes living through the beginnings of the AIDS pandemic, watching friends decline rapidly and die, and suffering with them the prejudice that came from ignorance about the illness:

"Visiting friends in hospitals. We'd go in. We'd go in one night, in the morning they'd be dead. I'd bring them food. My family, bring them food. My friends, bring someone food. But whoever was in the bed would be dead before they could eat it. We'd leave it – maybe the nurses would take it home. No! They wouldn't eat it! 'Cause it's contaminated. Contaminated! Wouldn't touch it. Wouldn't go into the room. Wearing masks. Gloves! Gowns! Someone gets sick in the afternoon. They'd be dead the next day. Dead! And that went on for months, and then years. Dead! Dead! You think if you got sick and your friends were dying that I would sit there and do nothing? No. But that's what happened. That's what happened. Every cold. Every virus. Every temperature. I thought I'd be dead, and so did so many people that I knew. Dead! You think you scare me? You think you can make me back off? Nothing scares me."

Duane demands that the Senate remember the hysteria and callousness that surrounded the people who were among the first to die from AIDS. He does nothing to hide his frustration with his colleagues, and at times his voice is nearly a scream.

He finishes:

"Defeat the bill: it's on you. Have a good time, have a big laugh. Go ahead, do it tonight. But I'm coming back, and you can't stop me."

Duane wins the vote by fifty-two to one. This is an astonishingly impressive demonstration of the power of authentic emotion, truthfully stated.

The Obamas as the virtuosos of emotion

Not many people handle emotion as well as Barack Obama. To see him at his very finest, I suggest watching his eulogy in June 2015 in Charleston, South Carolina to the Rev Clementa Pinckney, who was among nine people gunned down at an evening Bible study at his church. Obama calls him "a man who believed in things not seen, a man who believed there were better days ahead, off in the distance. A man of service who persevered," he was "wise beyond his years... He encouraged progress not by pushing his ideas alone, but by seeking out your ideas, partnering with you to make things happen."

Towards the end of an extraordinary performance, Obama breaks into a rendition of *Amazing Grace*, and the crowd soon joins in. If you watch the video, you will see how he maintains exactly the right emotional tone through the whole eulogy – sorrow and sadness, yes, but with an appropriate undertow of anger. Funeral speeches have been a primary element of oratory throughout history, and this is an outstanding example.

One person who does match Barack Obama for effectively controlled emotion is his wife, Michelle. Here, at the Democratic National Convention in Philadelphia in 2016, she is on the (ultimately unsuccessful) campaign trail for Hillary Clinton to succeed her husband as president. She tells an emotional story with passion, and it leads to a suitably optimistic conclusion:

"That is the story of this country, the story that has brought me to this stage tonight, the story of generations of people who felt the lash of bondage, the shame of servitude, the sting of segregation, but who kept on striving and hoping and doing what needed to be done, so that today I wake up every morning in a house that was built by slaves – [applause] – and I watch my daughters – two beautiful, intelligent, black young women – playing with their dogs on the White House lawn. [Applause.] And because of Hillary Clinton, my daughters – and all our sons and daughters – now take for granted that a woman can be president of the United States." [Applause.]

The Sarah Palin experience

One of my favourite guilty pleasures is the oratory of the American politician Sarah Palin, who is always willing to wear her heart on her sleeve, whatever the effect might be on the logic of her argument. Here, at a speech in Iowa in January 2016, she endorses Donald Trump for president:

"Trump's candidacy, it has exposed not just that tragic ramifications of that betrayal of the transformation of our country, but too, he has exposed the complicity on both sides of the aisle that has enabled it, okay? Well, Trump, what he's been able to do, which is really ticking people off, which I'm glad about, he's going rogue left and right, man, that's why he's doing so well. He's been able to tear the veil off this idea of the system."

No, I'm not sure I understand a great deal of that either, but with Sarah Palin you just have to go with the flow. And when she described the people she and Trump represented as "right-winging, bitter-clinging, proud clingers of our guns, our God, and our religion, and our constitution", I admired the rhyming of right-winging and bitter-clinging and the fiery language, even if I had no real idea what she was talking about. If you can manage the emotion while still making logical sense, as the Obamas do, that is the safer road to take. But give me Sarah Palin any day over the modern brand of politician who makes his communications a desert of feeling.

The Donald Trump factor

The Sarah Palin example leads me on to the issue of The Donald himself. Why did Donald Trump beat Hillary Clinton in the 2016 US presidential election?

History will decide that question at its leisure, but one factor not to be underestimated was the emotional engagement of Trump's speeches. They were not great speeches by most ordinary standards, but they did show passionate commitment on the part of the speaker. The emotion was not always pretty – rage and frustration often seemed to be the dominant themes – but there was a rawness about it that made Trump's audiences warm to the genuineness of his approach, if not to the factual correctness of what he was saying. This may help explain the comment of a Trump voter: "He may be a horrible, racist, misogynist idiot, but he is our kind of idiot."

His impatient, aggressive style was variously compared to that of a Mafia boss, a New York cab driver, a used-car salesman and the drunken uncle we all avoid at family reunions. The underlying emotion was there for all to marvel at or loathe.

Even those who strongly disliked the substance of Trump's rhetoric, as I did, had to acknowledge his openness. He spoke his mind, even if it contradicted the way he had spoken it that morning; and, whether you liked it or not, you could not fail to grasp his meaning.

He called ObamaCare, Barack Obama's overhaul of the US healthcare system, a "total disaster" and termed Obama himself the "worst president" in American history. Speakers don't get much more to the point than that.

By contrast, Hillary Clinton appeared a speaker on autopilot, guarded and unforthcoming. Her restrained, controlled style meant that her language was often seen as dry and her statements as vague and abstract. She was left floundering in her rather limited attempts to make direct emotional contact with the American people.

The journalist and television presenter Andrew Marr has commented on the importance of the way people speak in politics: "Another problem is the rise and rise of the full-time professional politician who's done nothing else. A lot of them don't speak human. You need a few speakers of fluent human…"

Maybe that explains something about the advancement of Donald Trump:

- He does not speak like other politicians.
- He goes out of his way to sound as though he is talking to the average man on the street (if less so to the average woman).
- He gives the impression of meaning what he says, which is remarkably uncommon in politicians.
- His approach is simple, albeit that critics would interpret this as 'simplistic'.

It is no coincidence that in 2016, the year when Donald Trump came to political power, Oxford Dictionaries announced that 'post-truth' was its international word of the year. Post-truth is defined as 'relating to or denoting circumstances in which objective facts are less influential in shaping public opinion than appeals to emotion and personal belief'. For better or worse, we live in an age of emotion.

It is irresistibly tempting to compare Donald Trump with the current British prime minister, Theresa May, who is just about clinging on to power as I write. A substantial part of May's problems with the electorate seems to derive from her refusal to reveal herself emotionally to the people. She is said to have an excellent, dry sense of humour, but she does not show it. Adjectives commonly used of her speaking style are: bland, closed, formulaic, robotic, unfeeling. It is as though she regards any display of emotion as an unfortunate sign of weakness.

This, I imagine, was why she simply did not have the words to rise to the occasion when she was called upon to comment on a tragic event of hugely distressing force – the Grenfell Tower fire in London in June 2017.

Going back to Donald Trump, I still disagree with most of what he says, not that that would bother him. But his critics consistently underestimate the importance of the emotional style in which he says it.

The role of emotion in technical and business subjects

This is all very well, you may be thinking, *but how does this stuff about emotion apply to my presentation to the board next week?*

I firmly believe that, whether your task is to talk about sales forecasts, budget allocations, regulatory issues, or any other business subject, emotion still has an important role to play.

You know that a professional audience tends to be analytical, logical and orderly. Even so, do not let that seduce you into trying to speak in a detached, dry style – the so-called double-D approach. The aim might be to appear competent and objective, but in my experience the result is that the speaker often sounds stilted, unfriendly and overly formal. I know of no better way of addressing this problem than by being enthusiastic about the subject, so that your energy creates a talk with an engaging emotional content that wins over the audience.

I remember listening to a talk by a criminal lawyer called Yewa Holiday on Article 31 of the 1951 Refugee Convention and the prosecution of asylum seekers. Initially, it sounds an arid subject. But she brought it to life by describing the plight of refugees coming to Britain from Eritrea, "one of the most repressive places on earth".

Yewa Holiday understood the essence of a presentation: that it works best when it influences attitudes and emotions rather than simply distributing information. (If your aim is just to pass on quantities of facts, put it all in writing and forget about presenting.) So, when you take the stage for a technical address, identify no more than a handful of essential points, and drive them home with feeling.

The power of emotion in business is particularly relevant for individuals in management positions who want to carry their people with them. Steve Denning, a leadership specialist with a particular interest in organisational storytelling, puts it this way:

> "You aren't likely to lead people through wrenching change if they don't trust you. And if they're to trust you, they have to know you: who you are, where you've come from, and why you hold the views you do."

It's all about establishing an emotional connection.

Practical questions to ask

When you are preparing a speech, try to make the most of its emotional content. I'm not talking about fake, unrealistic emotions: just go with what feels right and appropriate for you. Focusing your thoughts on these questions may be helpful:

- What are the emotional triggers and issues for you on this subject?
- What are they for the audience? What are their expectations, their hopes and fears?
- How can you implicitly or explicitly recognise those feelings in your audience?

- Do you want to confirm and support them in those feelings, or do you want to move them to a different emotional place?
- How would you feel if you were sitting in the audience and hearing the words you now plan to say?

Conclusion

John Hilton, a distinguished broadcaster and academic, received a letter from a radio listener that started like this: "Dear Sir, My little nine-year-old daughter doesn't mind being quiet for you because, she says, you talk as though you mean it, and as though you're alive."

That, to me, is the essence of emotion. It is also a good, short definition of a great speaker.

Points to take from this chapter

- In public speaking, emotions are paramount.
- Tell your own stories and anecdotes to maximise the emotional effect.
- Never be afraid to show passion.
- You can make almost any subject interesting if you are enthusiastic about it.
- Use your energy and passion to give uplift to a business talk.
- Ask what the emotional triggers are for you and your audience on your topic.
- Ask how you would feel if you were an audience member listening to your speech.

In the next chapter, we will look at a magical ingredient for public speaking success that few people fully appreciate – just being yourself.

Notes

You can find Aristotle's views in his *Art of Rhetoric*. Be warned, though: the book is essentially a collection of lecture notes, and accordingly is hard going. I recommend that you work on the basis that I have read it so you don't need to. The extract from Hugh Blair is from his *Lectures on Rhetoric and Belles Lettres*. You can see the Air New Zealand safety videos at https://www.airnewzealand.co.uk/safety-videos. Kevin Murray's story comes from his highly recommended book *The Language of Leaders: How Top CEOs Communicate to Inspire, Influence and Achieve Results*, Kogan Page Ltd, 2013. The story of Lloyd George's astonishing speech is told by Kenneth O Morgan (Baron Morgan) in *Eminent Parliamentarians: The Speaker's Lectures*, edited by Philip Norton, Biteback Publishing Ltd, 2012. You can see President Kennedy's moon speech at https://www.youtube.com/watch?v=ouRbkBAOGEw. Michael Dukakis's considered response to the death penalty question, and an interesting analysis of it, can be found at https://www.youtube.com/watch?v=DQNVICr9nMo. For Tom Duane's tirade, see https://www.youtube.com/watch?v=yyP9eLrvcAA. Barack Obama's tribute to the Rev Clementa Pinckney can be viewed at https://www.youtube.com/watch?v=x9IGyidtfGI. Michelle Obama's speech at the 2016 Democratic National Convention is at https://www.youtube.com/watch?v=4ZNWYqDU948. Sarah Palin speaks in Iowa at https://www.youtube.com/watch?v=Mvlm3LKSlpU. (Even more fun is Tina Fey's parody of the speech at https://www.youtube.com/watch?v=0pinZNYxQeo.) The words of the Donald Trump supporter are taken from a piece by Simon Jenkins in *The Guardian* for 10 November 2016. Andrew Marr's comment comes from an interview with Bill Hagerty in the *British Journalism Review* for March 2010. The quotation from Steve Denning is from an article, *Telling Tales*, in the May 2004 edition of the *Harvard Business Review*. John Hilton's story appears in *This and That: the broadcast talks of John Hilton*, George Allen & Unwin Ltd, 1938, as do other extracts from him in this book.

CHAPTER 8

You are special, so be yourself

Introduction

In this chapter, I'm going to urge you to be yourself when you speak in public, rather than some counterfeit version. It's not as easy as it initially sounds, particularly for people who are starting out on their speaking careers, but it's very much worth the effort. We will see how some distinguished speakers employed their personalities to maximise their success on the platform. By using myself as an example, I'll then show the kind of assessment we can make of our inherent qualities so as to bring them out fully when we speak in public.

The fundamental principle

Performers of any kind must be faithful to themselves – it's what makes them different, makes them interesting. "Be you, and be relentlessly you," says Lady Gaga, the American singer-songwriter. "That's the stuff of champions."

A speaker is no exception to the rule. It is imperative to be yourself when you speak in public.

I have not yet met a human being who did not have a unique quality or attribute in their personality or some striking, unusual way of expression. You cannot show those characteristics if you pretend to be some contrived version of yourself or try to be a walking model of PowerPoint. Your challenge is to present your uniqueness to the world when you speak: the real you, still fully identifiable as such in front of an audience.

I know it goes against nearly all the self-help books you will ever read, but most people most of the time are rather splendid as they are, unadulterated. I want your personality to come through strongly when you speak. It is great to learn from other people's speeches, but highly dangerous to try to copy them. I don't want your impression of Barack Obama, Winston Churchill, Margaret Thatcher or Steve Jobs.

At the end of the twentieth century, when Tony Blair was in his pomp as British prime minister, a number of public figures rather embarrassingly attempted to reproduce his style. It didn't work well, even at the time, and now it looks sadly dated. Pretending to be someone else never succeeds for long: you always get found out.

A maxim attributed to Judy Garland, the American singer, sums up the best approach perfectly: "Always be a first-rate version of yourself, instead of a second-rate version of somebody else."

Speakers being themselves

Judy Garland's motto has invariably been true for speakers. Abraham Lincoln became one of the finest orators of the nineteenth century, not least because of his willingness to reveal his personality to his audiences. The British author GR Benson, Lord Charnwood, put it this way in his biography of Lincoln: "It is not to be thought that he was ordinarily what could be called

eloquent; some of his speeches are commonplace enough...
But the greatest gift of the orator he did possess; the personality
behind the words was felt."

One of the finest speakers in British politics today is Jacob
Rees-Mogg, the Conservative MP for North East Somerset.
Beyond his eloquent oratory (seek him out on YouTube – he
is a joy), one of the attractions about him, whatever you might
think of his views, is that he is completely true to himself. He is
an unabashedly old-style upper-class figure who has been called
'the Honourable Member for the early twentieth century'. Jacob
Rees-Mogg is the man who, when accused of campaigning
for Parliament from the back of a Bentley, replied: "It was a
Mercedes. A Bentley would be most unsuitable for canvassing."
He is constantly himself, which means unending good manners
and cut-glass vowels, not to mention a great sense of humour. He
set a record with the use of the word *floccinaucinihilipilification*
(the action of describing or regarding something as unimportant
or worthless) in the House of Commons, thereby making it, for
a while, the longest word in *Hansard* and, for ever, the longest
in this book.

If you have a clear view of yourself and stay true to it, there is
much less chance that your talk will fail by trying to be all things
to all men and women. If there is such a thing as charisma, the
charm that inspires devotion in others, it has much to do with
the willingness to be different – doing what you think is the right
thing to do, rather than what other people expect. This is at the
heart of being special, being yourself, and succeeding.

Avoid problems with SSL

I will admit that it's not quite enough for me simply to say, "Be
yourself."

Novice speakers often find they are anything but themselves.

People who are gregarious, funny and outgoing in normal life can seem to shrivel up when they start talking in a formal situation. Ordinarily animated and engaging individuals become dull and predictable and speak in a monotone. In my presentations, I refer to this as the SSL. Technologically minded readers may have experienced SSL in the form of the Secure Sockets Layer (I have no idea what that means), but to me it stands for Starting Speaker's Lurgy.

The dreaded SSL manifests itself in a wide variety of symptoms, all of which can make the speaker appear a lesser version of their usual self.

An example is given by the journalist Gavanndra Hodge in an excellent article for *Tatler* magazine. "What surprises me," she writes, "is that even though I am a 41-year-old woman with a job, a family and a mortgage, on camera I somehow manage to look like a 14-year-old schoolgirl hatching a devilish plan at the back of a classroom. I am hunched, my arms are crossed, my back is wedged into the corner of the chair."

The great news is that SSL is easily combated and defeated by the use of the techniques and tips recommended in this book as a whole. The current chapter, meanwhile, focuses on a deeper, more fundamental issue – the value of presenting your true self to the audience when you stand up on stage.

The Ronald Reagan masterclass

In the US presidential election of 1984, Ronald Reagan was the Republican candidate seeking a second term in office, and his challenger was the significantly younger Walter Mondale for the Democrats.

Reagan, who was seventy-three, was already the oldest president ever, and there were many doubts about his ability to cope with more years in office. He had performed poorly in his first television debate with Mr Mondale, at times appearing tired and confused. In the second debate, however, Reagan had a stroke of genius. He joked: "I will not make age an issue of this campaign. I am not going to exploit, for political purposes, my opponent's youth and inexperience."

Walter Mondale himself laughed at this, and later he candidly agreed that Reagan had eliminated the issue of his age. "I knew he had gotten me there," he said. "That was really the end of my campaign that night, I think. [I told my wife] the campaign was over, and it was."

This story is a focal point of one of the best books on communication centred on the speaker as a unique individual, *You are the Message* by the late Roger Ailes, himself a controversial character in American life. Roger Ailes was acting as a speech coach to Mr Reagan at the time of the second debate. He writes: "The public had the reassurance they were looking for, and Reagan had the election won." It was a classic moment in political discourse: an older man addressing his age straight on, making the most of it, and indeed milking his senior status for all it was worth. The whole statement was pure Ronald Reagan at his finest: charm, humour, positivity, directness. You can do no better than to be yourself at your best.

Heighten your performance

Do please note the significance of the words 'at your best' in what I have just written. They are the reason why it is never quite that easy just to be yourself. If, say, you are an international terrorist or simply a common or garden mass murderer, there are aspects of your personality I'd rather you didn't display in a public talk.

The approach I recommend is to attempt a heightened version of your usual self – a somewhat enhanced, improved model. The mantra of 'be yourself plus 10%' can be useful, because the public platform loves larger than life, or at least larger than conventional nine-to-five, characters. Paul Merton, the comedian, is a typical example of this, saying: "My [television] personality comes out of the person I am anyway, but it's a rather amplified version of me, a more confident version."

Research confirms that the more successful people in public speaking tend to be the more energetic ones, if only because they communicate that energy to the audience and so get their message over better. It is, in essence, an assertive or even aggressive art, which is why speakers talk about 'getting them by the throat' or indeed 'killing the audience'.

So, be that bit more alert and lively and extrovert, smile rather more. And when in the public limelight, try to set aside the annoying habits and tics you display in everyday life. To know what these are, ask trusted friends or family, watch yourself in the mirror when you practise your talk, or record your rehearsals and performances and watch them through with an open mind afterwards.

This approach will safeguard you from some of your less attractive mannerisms during a public presentation. The most obvious benefit will be in eliminating many of the hesitations and deviations, the ummings and ahings, from your speech. There will be other foibles that you can avoid too.

For the sake of full disclosure, I had better tell you my own most questionable behaviours that I try to eliminate when speaking in public, as examples of the problems you can avert:

- Holding my arm or my hand, or indeed both arms and hands, over my mouth. This quirk tends to make any attempt to project my voice rather pointless.
- Waving my arms about excessively – this can be potentially life-threatening to the person chairing the event if I am standing too close to them.

- Thumb sucking, nail biting and hand chewing.
- Rhinotillexomania – all right, nose-picking if you must know.
- Having dirty glasses, so that those annoying little patches of fungal mould and mildew start to obscure my vision (and, presumably, the audience's view of me).
- And I can 'um' and 'ah' and 'erm' with the best of them if I forget to monitor my performance in rehearsals. I was once clocked at 186 uses of 'um' and 'erm' in a seventy-five-minute presentation, which is pretty impressive by any standard.

Only when you are consciously aware of your dodgy habits can you take effective action to eradicate them. I once worked with a man called Bertram (not his real name – his real name was Brian) who used to grope his genitals when speaking in public. Honestly. Bertram is a salutary reminder that we are often unaware of our habits; he genuinely did not know of his tendency for fondling himself until it was pointed out to him, and then in an instant he stopped altogether.

Complete honesty is not needed

'Being yourself plus 10%' involves showing your positive qualities off to their best effect. It does not require you to be constantly honest and truthful, the value of which can be much overstated.

Adam Grant, an author and professor of management and psychology, has written: "If I can be authentic for a moment: nobody wants to see your true self. We all have thoughts and feelings that we believe are fundamental to our lives, but that are better left unspoken."

Adam Grant refers to the story of the American journalist and author AJ Jacobs, who experimented by adopting the approach of a movement rather scarily called Radical Honesty. In other words, he spent some time trying to be totally authentic. In his book *My Experimental Life,* a great read, Jacobs sets out his experiences. A friend's five-year-old daughter shows him her new pet beetle and tells him that it's napping. "It's not napping," he replies, "it's dead." He tells another friend that he resents not being invited to his wedding, though he didn't, in reality, want to go because of the travel involved. He informs his in-laws that he didn't like the birthday present they gave him. He calls a friend to say he fantasises about the friend's wife. He tells his nanny that she is stunning and that, if his wife left him, he would ask her out on a date. It goes on and on like this. But the thrill of not having to think before you speak soon wears off. "A life of Radical Honesty," he concludes, "is filled with a hundred confrontations every day. They're small, but relentless."

Similarly, 'being yourself plus 10%' as a public speaker doesn't involve trying to change your natural style, but simply aiming for a modicum of enhancement. I don't necessarily want you warts and all, but I do want the essence of what makes you special, and I encourage you to radiate that essence out to your audience.

Honour your eccentricities

Beyond points of detail such as keeping your body under control, I want you to retain the attributes that make you exclusively you when you give a presentation.

I once worked with a senior manager who pronounced the word 'well' – as in 'well, I'm not sure about that' – like no one else in the world. He started it with a whooshing sound that managed to convey doubt, hesitation and questioning all in one go. He followed that up with a succession of 'el' sounds (think of several repetitions of the word Llanelli without the A, N and I) that gave abundant reinforcements of the doubt and hesitation. The els grew in volume and then slowly died away. 'Well' in the hands of the master seemed to last as long as I would take to say 'antidisestablishmentarianism', but much more intriguingly. Something profound but gently humorous was being said about the human condition. (Yes, I know it's pretentious, but you had to be there.) It would have been sacrilege to ask this man to speak that word in ordinary English. The great comedian Jack Benny used an exasperated expression of 'Well!' as one of his trademarks, but it was my man who perfected the art.

Dr Magnus Pyke was a media star of the 1970s. He was a distinguished scientist who achieved what most distinguished scientists do not: he came to national prominence and gained a reputation for conveying his subject brilliantly to a lay audience. Indeed, he was *Multi-Coloured Swap Shop's* Expert of the Year in 1978: you can't do much better than that. His success came in no small part from his natural eccentricities. He may well have been aware of the advantages of the mad scientist archetype, but the windmill effect of his dramatic arm-waving as he spoke arose from his natural enthusiasm. It won over his audiences without fail. It would have been unnatural and counter-productive to ask him to tone down his natural style.

The former government minister Chris Patten describes his experience of the performances of highly effective politicians: "watching President Clinton work a room or a crowd... admiring the urbane sweep of Roy Jenkins and the intellectual thuggishness of Denis Healey... watching Margaret Thatcher slaughter and pillage her way through a meeting, teasing some curious half-baked statistic in a footnote to the official paper under discussion into the rhetorical equivalent of Semtex."

These highly effective, but very different, speakers each

had their individual, very different angle on the craft of public speaking.

At the more commonplace level of personal appearance, the comedian Ronnie Corbett tells a lovely story in his autobiography. His fellow comic Jimmy Tarbuck had commented on the fact that Ronnie did not wear his glasses when performing. Corbett had not previously realised the contribution that the spectacles made to his image. He writes:

> "After that simple bit of advice from Jimmy Tarbuck, I kept them on wherever I appeared. It also meant I could find my way round the stage more easily and stop mistaking the microphone for a very thin member of the chorus."

Your quirks do not even need to be lovable. The comedian and after-dinner speaker Bob Monkhouse makes this point when writing about fellow comics. He comments: "In Hollywood, WC Fields exploited his appalling traits of drunkenness mingled with mean-spirited self-interest and rang true as a flawed man who was achingly funny." Monkhouse gives Jack Dee and Paul Merton as examples of modern performers who don't exactly go out of their way to be affable. He concludes: "We like that honesty, recognising a kind of integrity in their grumpy comedy."

So always beware when people tell you of characteristics or idiosyncrasies you should iron out. Could they in truth be an essential part of what makes you succeed as an individual and potentially as a speaker?

A practical strategy

Here are some ways in which you can show your individuality on the platform:

- First, and quite simply, recognise that to be successful your speaking style has to fit with your beliefs and personality. Don't try to be someone else. Paris Hilton (the socialite, not the French hotel) puts it neatly: "Life is too short to blend in."

- Never, ever think there's some stereotype of the ideal professional speaker that you should attempt to copy. There isn't.

- If you can accept these general principles, then that will help you to get down to the detail in terms of knowing yourself and what works for you. Identify your potential skills and attributes in a public speaking context by summarising yourself in five or six adjectives or short phrases. Prepare your speeches and presentations accordingly, being true to the qualities you have identified. What is it that makes them your personal talks, unlike anyone else's? What are your strongest characteristics, the unique selling points that you can take advantage of? In a minute I will show you how I have done this exercise for myself.

- Make your wording sound natural – 'I'm' rather than 'I am', 'I'll' rather than 'I will', and so on, unless you deliberately intend to emphasise the word in question.

- Use stories, examples and anecdotes that come from your personal experiences. If some of those experiences are ones that your audience has shared in, that will be even better. By all means, use other people's stories, but adapt them to make them your own. Take the basic idea and rework it to suit your purposes.

- Don't do things you are not comfortable with. For example, although I put a lot of humour into my talks in the form of asides and one-liners, I would never attempt a long joke with a punchline at the end. In daily life, my jokes always peter out, and I fluff the punchline; I know I would not be any different in giving a talk.

The writer as an example

These are the major characteristics I have identified in terms of my own speaking style:

- Enthusiastic
- Self-effacing
- Prepared
- Perplexed
- Tense

Enthusiastic: As a speaker I am undeniably passionate, and it seems to carry over to the audience. Enthusiasm comes from being genuinely interested in the subject I am talking about, and I think the urge to show off helps. Basil Boothroyd, an English humorous writer who was also one of the best after-dinner speakers I have heard, invented an organisation called GADSKIS – the Guild of After Dinner Speakers and Kindred Insufferable Show-Offs. I should like to have joined.

Self-effacing: My self-effacing style, particularly in after-dinner speeches, is in the tradition of – well, stolen from – entertainers like the magician David Nixon and the comedian Barry Cryer. My therapist says I am not, in fact, self-effacing, but just have a very realistic sense of self-worth.

Prepared: The essence of my public speaking is that I take it seriously and spend a lot of time working on the script. I can improvise and make ad-lib remarks reasonably well, but I need a solid base to operate from. After nearly fifty years of public performances, the thought of speaking impromptu still fills me with the screaming habdabs.

Perplexed: I find life as a whole challenging, so an attitude of perplexity suits me well. I spoke on tax topics from the point of view of a man trapped in tax, confused by the complexity of it all and desperately seeking to understand what was going on. In after-dinner speaking, this perplexity translates into a dithering style which seems to go down well with audiences. I have also had a genuine lifelong mystification and bewilderment in the area of technological literacy, going back to my first ZX Spectrum computer in the 1980s. In practice, this means that I address the issues arising from advanced audio-visual equipment by not using it in the first place.

Tense: I have never stopped being tense before a talk, but it gives me the nervous energy to perform. I love the 1960s nightclub performances of Woody Allen, perhaps the ultimate tense performer: to my mind he never did anything better. He has talked openly about the nerves he suffered in the process, but his highly-strung style produced hilarious results and is a great model for me.

I can't deny that some of my attributes seem oddly matched. How can tension and enthusiasm coexist? How can you be a self-effacing show-off? All I can say is that the mixture seems to work in practice. These are all natural aspects of my personality, and audience feedback suggests that on the rostrum they mostly combine well. It's another example of the benefit of just being yourself.

Conclusion

Be yourself, they rightly say, because everyone else is already taken. I believe that the strategy set out in this chapter allows you to be honest in your public persona and still succeed in front of an audience.

If you're not the real you, you'll be found out. The scientists have shown that it's pretty impossible to fake or fabricate your intentions in front of intelligent listeners. The message from your body language will be different to the message from your words, and at a subconscious level you will be seen as a fraud. If you're not being true to yourself, they'll know it.

The last word goes to Lord Chesterfield, a British statesman who will be appearing at greater length in the next chapter. "There is nothing truer," he wrote, "than the trite observation 'that people are never ridiculous for being what they really are, but for affecting what they really are not.'"

Points to take from this chapter

- To perform at your best, you need your personality to shine through when you speak. Show the world your unique qualities.
- Never try to be all things to everyone: it doesn't work.
- When you start out as a speaker, you may well appear something less than your usual self. Don't worry: it passes quickly.
- It is a sensible practical aim to be yourself plus 10%.

- Record yourself, to identify and eliminate your annoying habits.
- Identify up to half a dozen key attributes in yourself, and then prepare your speeches to match them.

You've now arrived at the point where you're going to be fully yourself when you take to the stage. That's you sorted as a personality but, in addition to your personal style, you probably feel you need to know something about the subject you'll be talking about. In the next chapter, I want to give you a realistic view of how much knowledge you need: it's almost certainly not as great as you think.

Notes

The comment from Lady Gaga comes from the 20 February 2017 edition of *Hello!* magazine, so it must be right. You can hear Jacob Rees-Mogg say *that* word at https://www.youtube.com/watch?v=GmXQOJhd0_0. Gavanndra Hodge's article, *How to give the speech of your life*, appeared in *Tatler* for June 2017. You can see the online version at http://www.tatler.com/news/articles/may-2017/public-speaking-advice. Ronald Reagan's spectacular one-liner in the debate with Walter Mondale can be found at https://www.youtube.com/watch?v=5YsUT2u38ag. Mondale's comments on the significance of Reagan's masterstroke come in an interview from 1990; the text can be found at http://www.pbs.org/newshour/spc/debatingourdestiny/interviews/mondale.html. The book *You are the Message*, Doubleday, 1989 by Roger Ailes was written with Jon Kraushar. The quotation from Paul Merton is from a fascinating book of interviews with comedy writers, *Now That's Funny* by David Bradbury and Joe McGrath, Methuen Publishing Ltd, 1998. Adam Grant's comment comes from the *New York Times* International Edition

for 4–5 June 2016; it can be found online at https://www.
nytimes.com/2016/06/05/opinion/sunday/unless-youre-oprah-
be-yourself-is-terrible-advice.html. You can see Magnus Pyke
in all his glory at https://www.youtube.com/watch?v=OL1kT3-
BPuo. The Chris Patten quote comes from his engaging book
East and West, Macmillan, 1998. Ronnie Corbett's story is
from his autobiography *High Hopes*, Ebury Press, 2001. Bob
Monkhouse's comments come from his book *Over the Limit:
My Secret Diaries 1993–98*, Century, 1998. Paris Hilton was
writing in *Confessions of an Heiress*, Simon & Schuster Inc,
2004. The GADSKIS organisation appears in Basil Boothroyd's
outstanding book about his speaking experiences, *Accustomed
as I am: The Loneliness of the Long-distance Speaker*, Allen &
Unwin, 1975.

CHAPTER 9

Know your subject reasonably well

Introduction

I have never been convinced that you need to be particularly erudite on a subject before you can talk about it well in public.

In this chapter, I want to eliminate your fears that you might be found out as a fraud or a phoney, a sham performer, for not knowing enough about your topic. We'll look at some historical examples to demonstrate that what you understand already is almost certainly enough for success as a speaker, and probably much more than you need. We will see that the essential issue is not what you know, but rather the way you use that knowledge when you go on stage; and we'll learn the fundamental ways in which you can maximise its value for the audience.

Lord Chesterfield leads the way

Confirmation of my belief that you don't need to know all that much as a speaker comes from Philip Dormer Stanhope, the 4th Earl of Chesterfield, a statesman, orator and man of letters.

In the middle of the eighteenth century, Lord Chesterfield distinguished himself in the debates on establishing a definitive calendar for Britain and its realms. What I find fascinating is the way he achieved this.

Here he is, writing to his son on the matter in March 1751. His letters were not originally intended for publication, which makes it all the more likely that he was telling the truth as he saw it:

"I... brought a bill into the House of Lords for correcting and reforming our present calendar, which is the Julian, and for adopting the Gregorian... It was notorious that the Julian calendar was erroneous, and had overcharged the solar year with eleven days... But then my difficulty began: I was to bring in this bill, which was necessarily composed of law jargon and astronomical calculations, to both which I am an utter stranger. However, it was absolutely necessary to make the House of Lords think that I knew something of the matter; and also to make them believe that they knew something of it themselves, which they do not.

For my own part, I could just as soon have talked Celtic or Sclavonian to them, as astronomy, and they would have understood me full as well: so I resolved to do better than speak to the purpose, and to please instead of informing them. I gave them, therefore, only an historical account of calendars, from the Egyptian down to the Gregorian, amusing them now and then with little episodes; but I was particularly attentive to the choice of my words, to the harmony and roundness of my periods, to my elocution, to my action.

This succeeded, and ever will succeed; they thought I informed, because I pleased them: and many of them said

> that I had made the whole very clear to them when, God knows, I had not even attempted it. Lord Macclesfield, who had the greatest share in forming the bill, and who is one of the greatest mathematicians and astronomers in Europe, spoke afterwards with infinite knowledge, and all the clearness that so intricate a matter would admit of; but as his words, his periods, and his utterance were not near so good as mine, the preference was most unanimously, though most unjustly, given to me. This will ever be the case..."

Lord Chesterfield evidently did not find his limited knowledge of the subject a hindrance. With the Calendar (New Style) Act 1750, he successfully established the Gregorian calendar, with a calendar year that begins on the first of January. His role in the process was so significant that the act came to be known as Chesterfield's Act. To achieve the calendar change, the first day after 2 September in 1752 was 14 September; as you would expect from the British, the immediate consequence was not satisfaction at a much improved system, but rather protests calling for the 'missing' eleven days to be restored.

Dr Fox

Two centuries later, in 1970, American researchers showed that a pretence of knowledge still went a long way when they gave the world the wonderful Dr Fox lecture.

They designed an experiment to find out whether a brilliant delivery technique could fool a group of experts to the point where they overlooked the fact that the content of a talk was nonsensical. The answer was: yes, they were fooled.

The researchers coached a skilled actor to play the part of

Dr Fox. He went on to deliver a meaningless presentation on 'Mathematical Game Theory as Applied to Physician Education', involving 'an excessive use of double talk, neologisms, non sequiturs, and contradictory statements'. "In short," one of the researchers noted, Dr Fox "gave a very enjoyable lecture in which he offered little or nothing of substance."

Three separate audiences composed of highly qualified professionals gave Dr Fox's lecture extremely positive feedback, both in numerical scores and in specific comments praising him for 'excellent presentation' with 'good analysis of [the] subject', 'good flow', 'lively examples' and a 'warm manner'.

Some personal experience

My restricted knowledge of the tax system was enough to support a lucrative career as a tax lecturer for nearly twenty years. That is why my advice not to worry too much about knowing your subject comes from the heart: limited awareness never stopped me. To be fair, I never went so far as to base a talk on what I had read the night before the seminar; most times, I managed to go through the textbook at least a couple of days in advance. What worked well for me was that at an early stage I branched out into the line of training which has come to be regarded as 'infotainment' – passing over some knowledge and information, with the occasional morsel of skills and attitudes training thrown in, but primarily focusing on an entertaining style of delivery. My highest achievement in this genre was an hour's talk on the Finance Act 1997, which from memory contained three actual pieces of information:

- One was of dubious validity.
- One was irrelevant.
- One was made redundant by amending legislation two months later.

I exaggerate, but by much less than you might imagine.

Beware the dangers of knowing too much

I don't want to suggest that in normal life it is a disadvantage to understand what you are talking about. On the other hand, you shouldn't go to the opposite extreme from Messrs Chesterfield and Fox, implying that you know all about your subject and your listeners know nothing.

There is a delightful quotation from Princess Marie Louise, Queen Victoria's granddaughter, comparing two formidable Victorian statesmen: "After sitting next to Mr Gladstone, I thought he was the cleverest man in England. But after sitting next to Mr Disraeli, I thought I was the cleverest woman in England."

In public speaking, it's better to be a Disraeli figure. Spencer Leigh Hughes argues the case this way:

> "Most audiences dislike the style suggested by the phrase, 'I'm telling you', and I have noticed that some really great men, who have the right to lay down the law on almost anything, never dogmatise, but suggest this, or submit that, to the consideration of their hearers. Audiences like such a method – it gives them a feeling of being consulted by the distinguished speaker."

Principles for making the most of your knowledge

My suggestion is that you should focus on maximising the knowledge you currently possess. Here is an approach that has worked well for the people I have coached:

- Recognise that a speech is primarily concerned with the human interactions and the presentation skills discussed in this book, not the display of technical mastery.

- Be aware that you almost certainly won't get put in the position of presenting unless you know enough about the subject to be convincing.
- Research your audience well in advance, so that you can be sure to speak at their level. We will talk further in a minute about the challenging situation of dealing with an expert audience.
- Never underestimate the value and importance of your practical, on-the-job, knowledge of the subject in question. Use it to the maximum in your talk.
- Confine yourself to speaking on what you know about, and never try to bluff about the rest. I'm aware that that's never quite as easy as it sounds. The novelist Samuel Butler commented: "I was nearly forty before I felt how stupid it was to pretend to know things that I did not know and I still often catch myself doing so. Not one of my schoolmasters taught me this."
- Remember that speakers do not normally go wrong due to limited knowledge of their subject. Instead, where they fall short lies in failing to think through how to present that knowledge to the audience: that is what ultimately matters.
- Aim to communicate no more than a handful of the most important points, or maybe a general strategy or philosophy, forcefully and coherently. Gyles Brandreth, the writer and broadcaster, puts it well: "A speech isn't an essay or an article. It's an opportunity for human contact, a chance to convey a mood, a feeling and, at most, one message or two."

- Throughout all this, focus on the eventual result: what do you want people to do as a consequence of your presentation?

- Don't sacrifice accuracy for the sake of clarity. Keep your message as simple as you can to ensure that you will be properly understood, but not to the point where you oversimplify and mislead the audience. Not every argument can be summarised in a single sentence or even a single group of sentences. Tom Whipple, writing in *The Times* in September 2008, noted, as a major problem caused by the era of the soundbite, our preference "for cartoonish half-truths over complex reality". There will always be a certain amount of information that you need to pass over, without which no one will be able to follow you. I like the comment made by Brian Cox, the physicist and presenter of science programmes: "You can explain anything in ten minutes, but you can't explain anything in two minutes. Take what you want to explain, do it well, then build the rest around that." A quotation attributed to Albert Einstein summarises the point helpfully: "Everything should be made as simple as possible, but no simpler." What he actually said, in a lecture at Oxford in 1933 *On the Method of Theoretical Physics*, was: "It can scarcely be denied that the supreme goal of all theory is to make the irreducible basic elements as simple and as few as possible without having to surrender the adequate representation of a single datum of experience." I leave it to you to decide whether the shorter version sacrifices accuracy for the sake of clarity.

- Don't overcomplicate either. Be careful about introducing new concepts that are not central to your argument. At the same time, if a fresh point is essential to your theme, explain it for as long and in as much detail as it takes for that point to be understood. Take difficult points particularly slowly.

- Don't overestimate people's ability to see the direction you are taking. Never hesitate to use signposts to where you are going and reviews of where you have been. Whenever you move from one major point to another, consider using a brief summary to state succinctly what you have just covered.

- If you feel you really must mention something that isn't fundamental to your argument, let the audience know that they are not required to understand it, so they can put it to one side if they want to.

- Remember that no group of people is homogeneous. There will always be those who find you too hard and those who find you too easy. If about 10% of the audience finds your talk too complicated and 10% finds it simplistic, you are getting the balance about right.

Speaking to an audience of experts

What happens if you are speaking to an audience that knows the subject better than you?

In this situation, it can be easy to lose all your confidence and give a woeful performance. The key is to treat your talk as a team effort and work with the experts in the room, rather than see them as a challenge to your ego. The presence of a specialist, knowledgeable audience gives you the chance to lead a debate of high quality and so create a thoroughly compelling session.

Here are some suggestions for dealing with a very knowledgeable audience:

- Treat them as very knowledgeable.
- Be prepared to compliment and indulge them where appropriate, so long as you don't belittle your own skills in the process.
- Actively invite their comments (and even their corrections), their experiences and their examples on the subject. This will add breadth and depth to the presentation.
- Never try to wing it, and never pretend that your knowledge is greater than it is.

It helps to accept that you are now more a facilitator than a solitary speaker, more the conductor of the orchestra than the guest soloist. This reduces the pressure on you rather than increasing it: you can take pleasure in the fact that you are surrounded by well-informed, bright people.

Joe McLeod, a communications specialist, is an expert on dealing with experts. He helpfully emphasises the way in which you should feel genuine confidence in this role. "Remember," he writes, "your confidence is not based on your superior knowledge of the subject but rather in your ability to lead, facilitate and ultimately produce a worthwhile experience for the group."

Conclusion

Writing in *The Bluffer's Guide to Public Speaking*, Chris Steward and Mike Wilkinson note that: "As soon as you stand up to speak, the very act of doing so has 70% of the audience believing that you are an authority on whatever it is you are supposed to speak about."

Following on from that, it has been suggested that the secret of presenting is either successful bluffing or appearing to have known all your life what you learned this afternoon. In the history of oratory, there has been no shortage of successful speakers who made it up as they went along.

A hundred years ago Spencer Leigh Hughes wrote this:

> "I have presumed that the man who makes a speech happens to understand his subject – and that sometimes does occur in real life. But there are other cases when, though he may think he does, he does not, and also cases in which he knows he does not. It is in these circumstances that true art is often shown in concealing ignorance, and I have known men triumphantly successful in that direction."

You need not be quite as cynical as SLH or me to agree that it is not what you know that matters in a speech, but what you do with it – how you convey it to the audience. You don't need esoteric knowledge, but you do need to have established very clearly in your mind what you aim to achieve with the material you have. That way lies success as a speaker.

Points to take from this chapter

- Focus on making the most of the knowledge you currently possess.
- A speech is about interactions between human beings, not technical prowess.
- Research your audience to ensure you speak at their level.
- Make the most of your own practical, on-the-job knowledge.
- Speak only of things you know about, and never bluff.
- Concentrate on getting the key points over, with an emphasis on what you want the audience to do afterwards.

- Actively involve any experts among your listeners.

In the next chapter, we will move on to the wider subject of getting an audience onside, and review some easy ways to ensure they are rooting for you from the start to the very end of your speech.

Notes

Lord Chesterfield's Letters are highly recommended. The passage quoted comes from Letter 65 in the Oxford World's Classics edition. The story of the Dr Fox experiment is told by Deborah J Merritt, professor of law at the Ohio State University, in an excellent 2008 article called *Bias, the Brain, and Student Evaluations of Teaching* in the *St. John's Law Review*: Vol. 82: Iss. 1, Article 6. The article can be seen at http://scholarship.law.stjohns.edu/lawreview/vol82/iss1/6/. You can see Dr Fox himself in action (though the video quality is not great) at https://www.youtube.com/watch?v=Rcr6UJwaPlQ&t=1507s. The quotation from Princess Marie Louise appears in *A Gentleman Publisher's Commonplace Book* by John G Murray, John Murray, 1996. The Spencer Leigh Hughes extracts here (and in the rest of this book, unless otherwise stated) are from his 1913 work *The Art of Public Speaking.* The Samuel Butler quotation comes from his essay *On Knowing what Gives us Pleasure.* The Gyles Brandreth comment is from a classic piece for the *Sunday Telegraph* called *Tony Blair at the WI*, collected in *Brief Encounters: Meetings with Remarkable People*, Politico's Publishing, 2003. The Brian Cox comment is taken from an article entitled *Make Complex Science Accessible* in *Wired* magazine for October 2011. Joe McLeod's advice can be found at http://www.fpratampabay.org/3-tips-for-speaking-to-an-audience-of-experts/.

CHAPTER 10

Get the audience on your side

Introduction

No two audiences are the same. But most audiences, if not quite all of them, want the speaker to do well.

In this chapter, I want to recognise the truth of those statements, together with the occasional unpredictability they can create. Having done that, I will consider in detail the good news, the tried and tested ways of getting an audience to take your side and support you as the speaker. By the end of the chapter, I hope you will agree with me that the good news very much outweighs the bad. Moreover, it is all very, very straightforward.

The nature of an audience

It's obvious, but still worth emphasising, that the audience nearly always wants you to succeed. They have come to hear you, and their pleasure and enjoyment depend on your doing well. If you have a good time, it will help them do the same.

All that goes almost without saying, but, as usual, there are caveats. There is a rare exception to the general rule when an audience is present under sufferance; we will look at the issues arising from a captive or hostile audience when we talk in Chapter 37 about surviving the speaking engagement from hell. Beyond that, an audience is a more complex beast than a straightforward collection of individuals. Jonathan Lynn, the comedy writer and director, explains this: "An audience is a thing unto itself, a specific type of crowd. Crowd psychology is different from individual psychology. This particular crowd needs to be made into a single and cooperative unit." He goes on to explain that this is why speakers often start with a joke or two: they are trying to organise a bunch of disparate individuals into one single group, one audience.

An audience is an entity in its own right, with its own personality and characteristics. It responds, within reason, to being flirted with and having its tummy tickled, but it can also get collectively annoyed and cross. We ignore the need to manage the individual character of each separate audience at our peril. The author and agony aunt Virginia Ironside has written about the approach that a sensible speaker will take. "You get on stage," she says, "to face an audience that's rather like a blank lump of dough and, by using charm and emotional trickery, you knead away at their emotions until they are, if you're lucky, eating out of your hand."

She also gives a salutary reminder that, however hard a speaker works to win over the audience on the day, there is no guarantee of success: "In South Shields, I had one of the happiest gigs of my life. But in Helmsley, a little farther south, faced with stony-faced farmers' wives, I died."

So, when we aim for a fruitful romance with our particular audience, we need to remember that it has its characteristics and spirit just as if it were an individual human being. Even so, there is an assortment of powerful yet straightforward things that we can do to win people over, and we'll now examine these.

Arrive early and meet people

If you turn up early at the venue, you will have more time to get acclimatised and sort out any problems, and you will impress audience members by being there when they arrive. I try to greet people as they enter the hall where I will be speaking, preferably on an individual basis. Logistics will, of course, be a key factor: if you are going to be speaking to a gathering of hundreds or thousands, personal welcomes will not be practical. The experts on influence recommend that you employ a strong, purposeful handshake while saying your hellos, using good eye contact as you do so. Handshakes may, however, be a step too far for people who have either a limp handshake or (like me) sweaty palms at this stage of their preparation for the talk.

Make sure you are properly introduced

Audiences respond better to a speaker they regard as an authority. It helps, therefore, if they are aware of your qualifications and expertise at the outset of your talk.

How can this best be achieved, given that you want to avoid accusations of boasting?

It is always better if there is someone else to tell the audience how wonderful you are, rather than for you to do it yourself. Expectation moulds reality: you can start to win over your audience before you say anything yourself if you have a strong, positive introduction from the chair. Your listeners will go into your talk with the genuine belief that you will indeed be good, and this will actively feed their perception of how effective a speaker you are.

As long ago as 1906, Walter Dill Scott, a leading American psychologist, noted the force of this approach:

> "In order that a speaker may have a maximum effect upon
> his audience, his coming should be well heralded in advance.
> He should be looked upon as the man who is leading his
> fellows in the subject upon which he is to speak. Formality
> also has a part in spreading the mantle of authority over
> a speaker... The speaker usually finds that his words have
> more power when he is introduced to his audience in a
> dignified way."

In short, being introduced works much better than starting straight into one's talk. Even a mediocre introduction should at least quieten the audience, so they are ready to pay attention when the speaker gets going.

This is not an area for subtlety.

If I have not previously met the person who is going to introduce me, I will talk to them in advance about what I would like them to say in the introduction. If, after that process, they still seem uncertain, I will give them a typed version of the opening words I'd like to hear from them. Assuming that they follow instructions, this will avoid the problem of the chair stealing the witty opening you had planned and leaving you with a great big hole in the first five minutes of your talk. At the very least, make sure you are consulted about what they will say on your behalf.

Once they have said their words, make a point of shaking the hand of your introducer. Do this regardless of whether your handshake is limp or sweaty: the audience won't notice. It can be easy to forget this detail as you nervously move up to begin your talk, but a warm handshake and acknowledgement immediately imprint you as agreeable in the audience's mind. They also help remove some of the natural tension you feel at the start of the talk.

If you simply can't be introduced – and I recognise that if you are talking, for example, to workmates, an introduction might seem extreme – then be sure the audience knows in advance your qualifications to speak about your topic. You could, for example, include this material in the background information they receive in advance of the event.

If it is you who is introducing a speaker, these are the key rules:

- Be brief. The audience has come to hear the speaker, not you.
- Do not alter or misquote the title the speaker is using for the talk in any way whatsoever. The speaker should not be obliged to spend the first few minutes correcting your misunderstanding of the subject they are going to discuss.
- Avoid the temptation to talk in any detail on the speaker's subject or to anticipate any points they might make. There is no better way to reduce the effect of the presentation.
- Tell the audience something about the speaker's background, their achievements and their present role. Your essential job is to demonstrate how well qualified the speaker is to discuss the topic.
- Be positive. Tell the audience that the speaker's talk *will* be absorbing, not that it *should* be. Try to whet their appetites. When I was lecturing on tax, the people introducing me could refer to the subject as complex, technical and dull, or as fascinating, thought-provoking and hugely relevant to the state of people's finances. You can imagine which approach I preferred.
- Don't over-egg the pudding. If you tell the audience that this will be the best talk on cookery they have ever heard, you are setting the speaker up for failure.

- An effective introduction often ends with the speaker's name. Here's a great example from the trainer and author Simon Raybould in his highly rated book *Presentation Genius*: "'So, it gives me great, great pleasure to welcome our expert speaker for today, Dr Simon Raybould.' Cue loud applause." It may sound corny, but this rather blatant approach truly does work.

Keep to the timings

Staying on time is a fundamental aspect of keeping an audience onside, as well as being simple good manners. Work out your timings in detail while you are rehearsing, so that you know how long each section of the presentation, and the presentation overall, is going to take. It's important to stay flexible by identifying beforehand parts which, if you had to, you could shorten or leave out; that way you can compensate for unexpected overruns elsewhere in your talk.

Start your talk on time, with all the technology working.

Be precise about when you want people back from lunch or coffee or toilet breaks. Many seminar attendees interpret 'ten minutes or so' as twenty minutes. Remember also that the slowest moving 10% of your audience will dictate the time at which you start again. My approach is to say something like: "We will start again at 11.13 prompt according to that clock on the wall." Participants take more notice of an odd time like this than 11.10 or 'a quarter past eleven'. It may not be logical, but it works. Beware, incidentally, the havoc that wrong or mismatching clocks in an auditorium can cause.

Finish on time or, even better, a minute or two early. Do not overrun. That's not to say, of course, that you shouldn't stay around once your talk is formally over. Plan your schedule so that you allow plenty of time for people to approach you afterwards with further questions and points for discussion. It's an astute way of winning over audience members even more.

Act as though you are full of confidence

The 'act confidently' rule is another example of the 'act *as if*' principle that we looked at in Chapter 6. Audiences will react to your show of authority and confidence as though you are indeed the real deal, regardless of any tremors you may be experiencing internally.

Treat the audience with respect

In 2009, Nick Morgan held a contest on his blog to determine the 'Worst Conference Experience Ever'. The stand-out winner was a speaker who read from the tax code for 'several hours with minimal commentary'. This is an extreme example of disrespecting the audience, but the problem arises all too often at a more mundane but still significant level.

A single glance down at his watch may have cost George HW Bush the 1992 US presidential election.

At a debate with Bill Clinton and Ross Perot in Richmond, Virginia, President Bush, impatient for a second term in office, checked the time to see how long there was to go in an encounter he wasn't enjoying. Meanwhile, Bill Clinton charmed the audience and showed his sympathy for their sufferings in the 1992 recession. Clinton seized the initiative from Bush, and the rest is history.

These things are important: never allow the audience to think that you are in a hurry to finish. It cannot harm your cause to demonstrate continuing respect for your listeners.

By showing such respect, the best speakers exude the sense

that they are *giving* themselves to the audience. Here, Ray Keeslar Immel puts the point strongly:

"Make a conscious effort to adapt yourself to the audience. Try now to make them understand and feel the idea. Get forward toward them. Reach out after them. Project the voice to them… Focus the eyes on the people in the audience and talk to them. Give them your idea as though you really wanted them to get it. Watch their faces and adapt yourself to them as in animated conversation."

One area where speakers can go inadvertently wrong is in failing to respect the cultural differences between audiences. In her jolly book *A Field Guide to the English*, also published as *A Field Guide to the British* for those who can't tell the difference, Sarah Lyall, an American journalist who moved to London and married an English writer, gives us a salutary lesson on this, comparing American and British speeches at weddings: "At American weddings, there are heartfelt, sloppy tributes to the couple's benign excellence. 'He's one of the best people… on the planet!'… In Britain, they have acerbic, hyper-articulate speeches attacking the groom in as offensive a manner as possible."

We have been warned! As they say, the British and the Americans are two peoples divided by a common language.

A further way of showing respect is to follow the codes that the audience members themselves have adopted for the day. Most obviously, it is natural politeness to follow the dress code for an event where you are presenting. This, of course, necessitates finding out in advance what it is. I did once give an address in a lounge suit to a black-tie gathering: I just about got away with it by mocking myself cruelly. Even that was not as bad as the day when, having turned up as guest speaker in what I thought was a rather pleasant dark suit and starched white shirt,

I spent the first hour and a half being mistaken for a waiter.

Remember, by the way, that there's no harm in turning up slightly smarter than the average person in the auditorium. All the research evidence shows that audiences respond positively to physical attractiveness. You don't need to go down the plastic surgery route on that account, but arriving neat and well-groomed for your presentation seems a reasonable concession to people's underlying prejudices.

Be likeable

It helps a lot that you be liked, in presentations as in other areas of life. One obvious way of achieving this is to smile and demonstrate a positive approach – a commonplace point to make, but many speakers forget to do it.

Remember, too, that a little flattering of the audience for their qualities or actions does no harm. In the words of a quotation attributed to Benjamin Disraeli, "Talk to a man about himself, and he will listen for hours." Along the same lines, research has suggested that the single most persuasive word in English is 'you'. So, frequent use of the words 'you' and 'yours' in a talk is unlikely to damage an audience's opinion of a speaker. At the most basic level, I still find that comments like "You've been a great audience" work well. However, do it within reason: if they are hissing or booing you, telling them how fantastic they are is not going to solve your problem.

Try a touch of self-effacement

Used in moderation, I have found that self-effacement can work wonders for an audience's opinion of you. Skilled after-dinner speakers can make a good living from a vein of sustained self-parody.

The ultimate master was Ronald Reagan. A couple of his best lines were:

- "They say hard work never killed anyone. I figured, why take that chance?"
- "I guess you fellows can see now that I've really been burning the midday oil."

As with any speaking technique, however, it is best not to indulge your self-effacement too far. Spencer Leigh Hughes writes:

"There is a danger in overdoing the modest and self-deprecatory style, as in the first place everyone knows that one does not really mean these professions, and in the next place one may receive some startling confirmation from the audience. I remember hearing a man who, while smiling with easy confidence, began a speech in this way: 'I make no pretence to be one of the clever fellows – I am only a plain, blunt man – indeed I dare say some would call me a duffer.' At this point another plain, blunt man said in a plain, blunt voice: 'You look it, guv'nor.'"

Stay calm

Different emotions will fit different presentations, but remaining composed is usually a reasonably safe position from which to operate.

In the 2008 US presidential campaign, the impression Barack Obama created, that he was competent and calm, a man without burning anger, helped him greatly. Justin Webb, the journalist and specialist on American affairs, noted that Obama radiated the comforting sense that he would not make white Americans pay for the sins of their fathers.

Twenty-eight years earlier, in another pivotal moment in US politics, an earlier would-be president, that man Ronald Reagan again, similarly demonstrated the power of staying calm. In the 1980 presidential debate with Jimmy Carter, probably the greatest ever presidential debate in its impact on the outcome of the race, the nation saw his style and was put at ease. His opponents had portrayed him as a wild man, a danger to world stability. Up to this point, the opinion polls suggested that the public agreed. Reagan's calmness and composure destroyed this image. He was warm and reassuring, deflecting the charges against him with good humour. Jimmy Carter was later to write, rather disparagingly, in his *White House Diary* that: "Reagan was 'Aw, shucks'... this and that... 'I'm a grandfather, and I would never get this nation in a war'... and 'I love peace...' He has his memorised tapes. He pushes a button, and they come out." But it worked for Reagan, and he won the election.

Maintain eye contact

We will be talking about body language in detail in Chapter 12, but for the meantime it's enough to note that maintaining eye contact with the audience during your presentation is essential to keep them with you. This is one of the very few indispensable requirements of a successful speaker.

Don't use natural shyness as an excuse to avoid eye contact: if you do, the audience will feel ignored. Fortunately, there is a great trick available for speakers who really can't stand direct eye contact. If you look at the tips of people's noses, or at their foreheads, then – as long as your audience is more than a few metres away from you, which will normally be the case for a public speaker – they won't know the difference. They will think you are looking directly into their eyes.

I can recommend an excellent, brief (about seven minutes)

video on the subject of eye contact by Jimmy Naraine, an online entrepreneur and coach, which you will find on YouTube. He makes the additional important point that your eyes need to move around the various sections of the audience. In other words, you need to work all areas of the room. If you can't manage a little bit of eye contact all around, your audience will think that you are not showing them the appropriate courtesy. It can be easy to forget this point when you are tiring towards the end of a presentation, so I like to write the occasional reminder saying *Move eyes* into my notes or script to jog my memory.

Add value

Remember that a crucial issue for your listeners is going to be, "What's in it for me?" People pay attention to things they think will benefit them. It makes sense consistently to ask yourself, "How is my talk going to add value for members of the audience?"

You can do this in a variety of ways:

- Educate – teach them things they didn't know before, or remind them of things they had long forgotten.
- Entertain – the more enjoyable you make the process, the more they will remember.
- Illustrate – this is about showing, not telling, and about using stories and illustrations to drive your points home.
- Inspire – this is where a bit of passion makes a huge difference.
- Change – how, even in the most trivial way, can you use this talk to make a positive difference to their lives?

It often helps to tell the audience what's going to be in it for them right at the start of your talk, so as to maximise their interest and focus. Try to go for an early win, covering something important at the outset. At the end, give them something extra to take away with them.

Conclusion

This chapter has examined some great ways of getting the audience to look favourably upon you, the speaker, but there remains another aspect for us to consider. Dale Carnegie, the great champion of self-improvement, argued strongly for a further way to gain popularity – to express a genuine interest in others, in those around you. His reasoning has a major consequence for speakers. We should focus not only on trying to be interesting to our audience, but equally as much (or more) on being interested in them. This leads us on to the important issue of finding out about our audience and getting to know them well in advance. We will be looking at this in Chapter 14.

Points to take from this chapter

- Arrive early and meet people.
- Ensure you are introduced well: failing that, make certain the audience knows your qualifications in advance.
- Keep to the timings.
- Always show respect for the audience.
- Smile and demonstrate a positive approach.
- Maintain eye contact all around the room.
- Focus on the five ways of adding value – educate, entertain, illustrate, inspire, change.

In the next chapter – now that we have got the audience onside – we are going to examine another uncomplicated but highly powerful principle: the need to keep our approach simple but vigorous when we speak in public.

Notes

The quotation from Jonathan Lynn comes from his comedy masterclass *Comedy Rules*, Faber and Faber Ltd, 2011: I believe his point can be applied to all kinds of presentations. Virginia Ironside was writing about what she calls her 'granny stand-ups' in *The Oldie* magazine for August 2015. Extracts from Walter Dill Scott in this book are taken from his rather splendid work *The Psychology of Public Speaking*. You can see the results of Nick Morgan's contest at http://www.publicwords. com/2009/06/29/announcing-the-winners-of-the-worst-conference-contest/. George HW Bush checks his watch at https://www.youtube.com/watch?v=hBrW2Pz9Iiw&t=38s. The Reagan and Carter debate can be found at https://www.youtube. com/watch?v=_8YxFc_1b_0&t=26s. The Jimmy Naraine video is at https://www.youtube.com/watch?v=EvB8mkOBTPE.

CHAPTER 11

Keep it simple and forceful

Introduction

In this chapter, we are going to look at the importance of making only a limited number of points in any speech or presentation, but doing so with such force and emphasis that the audience can properly absorb and retain them. We will learn the most helpful ways of avoiding information overload for your listeners, and we'll consider some excellent practical examples of the power of repetition to drive your message home.

How many points should we make?

When I talk about making only a limited number of points in a speech, I mean it.

One is an excellent number; only the best speakers can get away with more than three or four; and we flirt with disaster if we aim for more than half a dozen. Bill Clinton commented that it was a miracle if people walked away from your speech with four or five points. Coming from an outstanding speaker, that represents a major warning for the rest of us.

To appreciate fully the requirement to restrict the points we make, we need to understand the limitations of speechmaking as a medium, and the problem of stickability.

The limitations of a speech

The literary critic William Hazlitt noted that: "An orator can hardly get beyond commonplaces: if he does, he gets beyond his hearers." Sir Edgar Rees Jones, a Welsh barrister and politician, wrote:

"Speakers begin with the details – details that are very valuable, that are intrinsically of great interest to the audience. They pile them on, one after the other, until the attention of the audience is entirely lost, and a speech which has cost months of hard and clever original work has a most disappointing effect."

The after-dinner speaker and songwriter Mitch Murray sums it up brilliantly in his book *One-liners for Business: And How to Use Them in Your Speech:*

"Speechmaking – whether social, political or corporate – can only ever be an exercise in superficiality. It simply isn't a medium which allows you unlimited expansion and embellishment of your thoughts."

He goes on, incidentally, to note that the average audience nowadays has the attention span of a stick of broccoli.

This is a world where a speaker should aim to get over no more than a handful of essential points, and do it with such force that the message stays clearly in the minds of the listeners.

The problem of stickability

An important note of caution for all speakers comes in a thought-provoking book called *Made to Stick: Why some ideas take hold and others come unstuck* by Chip Heath and Dan Heath, who are specialists in organisational behaviour and entrepreneurship. They tell us about the stickability of presentations in our memory, or rather the lack of it.

In an interesting exercise, students at Stanford University, undeniably intelligent people, are asked to write down each idea that they remember from a series of brief speeches that have ended ten minutes previously. They do not have a significant volume of information to cope with; at most, they have heard eight one-minute speeches.

The Heath brothers write:

> "The students are flabbergasted at how little they remember... [They] are lucky to recall one or two ideas from each speaker's presentation. Many draw a complete blank on some speeches – unable to remember a single concept."

The most worrying point here is that, by any reasonable standard, the talks the students are trying to remember have been perfectly good ones. Chip and Dan Heath note that Stanford students are quick thinkers and good communicators: none of them ever gives a poor speech. The implications for anyone trying to convey a message that the audience can take away and work with are truly scary. It is no wonder that the physicist and noted science lecturer Sir Lawrence Bragg said: "One must constantly think of what will be retained in the audience's memory, not of what can be crammed into the lecture." Our powers of retention of what we hear on stage are, in general, dismally poor.

This does not mean that public speaking is a waste of time, but it reminds us that we need to be rigorous in expressing ourselves in a style and form that gives the best possible chance of the audience comprehending what we have said and taking it into their longer-term memory. The Heaths identify three different ways by which the students can become 'stars of stickiness'.

They are:

- Tapping into emotion.
- Telling stories.
- Stressing a single point rather than ten.

We looked at the power of emotion in Chapter 7, and we will be reviewing the importance of storytelling for a speaker in Chapter 31. For now, I'm going to concentrate on the third element of stickiness – making a single point (or at least no more than a handful) and driving the message home into the minds of the listeners.

Avoid information overload

The natural tendency for a speaker is to go into overdrive in terms of making points and passing information to the audience. The speaker will usually know a lot more about their subject than their listeners, and will want to transmit as much of it as possible. Alternatively, the speaker may be trying to stay safe by addressing numerous minor points of detail with which they feel comfortable. A third potential pitfall is that, if you have laboured at detailed fact-finding and research for a talk, it can be difficult to resist the temptation to get value for the time you have invested by offloading all your new discoveries onto the audience.

You must resist: your preparation time is a sunk cost and

is no justification for overloading hapless listeners with more information than they need. Herbert A Simon, an American political scientist, put it this way: "What information consumes is rather obvious: it consumes the attention of its recipients. Hence a wealth of information creates a poverty of attention."

These are the guidelines I find most helpful for avoiding information overload:

- In Lawrence Bragg's words: "As in a picture, so in a lecture" – and, I would add, even more so in a non-academic talk – "the force of the impression depends upon a ruthless sacrifice of unnecessary detail." Brutal editing is the order of the day.
- By presenting information simultaneously in written form (words on a slide) and in oral form (you talking to the audience), you make it harder, not easier, for people to take in what you are saying. John Sweller, an influential Australian educational psychologist, explains it like this: "It is effective to speak to a diagram, because it presents information in a different form. But it is not effective to speak the same words that are written, because it is putting too much load on the mind and decreases your ability to understand what is being presented." Don't do it!
- If your subject involves lots of figures, go for graphs and charts as visual aids rather than tables of numbers: numbers are very off-putting to many people.
- Never complicate matters unnecessarily. If in doubt, talk about ideas and principles, not the minute detail. (It seems particularly common for scientists, and those in management and administration, to wonder if they have put enough figures, information

and data into their presentations. Believe me, they have, and frequently more than enough.) I am not denying there may be anoraks in the audience, obsessive people seeking the smallest particulars of knowledge. If you encounter them, be ready to tell them where they can locate that information, but don't inflict the details on the rest of the audience. Otherwise, everyone will start suffering from anoraknophobia.

Don't overestimate what they already know

There is a further obstacle to overcome before the audience can assimilate what the speaker is saying to them. We tend to overestimate what other people will know or understand about a subject to start with. Steven Pinker, the cognitive scientist and author, makes this point in his book *The Sense of Style*: "Adults are particularly accursed when they try to estimate other people's knowledge and skills… The better you know something, the less you remember about how hard it was to learn."

The risk that what you have to say will pass over the heads of your listeners is a real one. But there are helpful ways to reduce or avoid it:

- Find out as much as you can about your audience in advance. We will deal with this in Chapter 14. Remember that they will tend to know much less about your topic than you assume.
- Beware the use of acronyms, technical language and jargon. Always explain a term in non-specialist language when you first bring it in.
- Use concrete language with lots of examples to make your explanations more intelligible. Visual images,

in particular, can have a powerful, memorable effect on your listeners.

- When in doubt, remember that it's always better to run the risk of seeming to condescend to your audience than to confuse them. It takes an unduly sensitive audience member to feel momentarily patronised by an honest explanation from a speaker, whereas a bewildered listener can be lost forever.

- None of this is to suggest dumbing down your approach. What we are saying is that speakers would produce better talks by assuming less initial knowledge on the part of their listeners, and starting more often with explanations from first principles. In this process, they should assume that the audience is as intelligent and keen to learn as they are themselves.

- When we discuss rehearsals in Chapter 22, we will talk about the importance of testing out your material on a trial audience. One of the huge benefits of that approach is that you can get honest feedback on whether people can genuinely follow what you are saying. That is the point when, as a speaker, I find out that what is obvious to me may not be at all obvious to other people. It is far better to make that discovery at the rehearsal stage rather than in front of a full auditorium. I like the approach of this unidentified blogger:

"The hardest part about public speaking for me has always been ensuring that the audience is on the same pace as you when you go through complicated info. Try to keep in mind what your audience already knows about your topic, and

> more importantly, what they don't know. I always use my mother as a guinea pig to explain my super crazy research projects before I present at conferences. I know if I can make it comprehensible to her, anyone in the audience should be able to get it."

Get your best stuff in early

How to Master the Art of Selling by Tom Hopkins is the best book ever written on sales and salesmanship. I know that because the front cover of my copy tells me so. In the book, the author informs us that the limit of maximum audience concentration is seventeen minutes. He therefore instructs us to give the entire body of our presentation, by which he is effectively referring to all the strong selling points, in less than the first seventeen minutes: "You want to make your basic presentation within seventeen minutes and then shift into your closing sequences," he says. Presumably, after the first seventeen minutes the audience has started to think about driving home, planning their evening meals, making mad passionate love, and phoning their spouses to tell them about the mad passionate love they have been making. But Tom Hopkins' point is a valid one: get your best stuff in early! We will say more about this in Chapter 21 when we focus on the first few minutes of a talk.

How long should you speak for?

The audience will be only too aware of the length of your speech. "I do not object to people looking at their watches when I am speaking," said Lord Birkett, a British barrister and judge. "But I strongly object when they start shaking them to make sure they are still going." One of the best lines attributed to John Major as prime minister was about the leader of the opposition: "Neil Kinnock's speeches go on for so long because he has nothing to say and so he has no way of knowing when he's finished saying it."

It is certainly rare to hear from members of an audience that the speaker stopped too early. Henry Labouchère, a nineteenth-century English politician, was responsible for one of the best public speaking hints: "Make sure of your first sentence, and make quite sure of your last sentence, and then bring them close together."

How close together should that be?

One of the most famous speeches of all time, Abraham Lincoln's Gettysburg Address in 1863, was less than three hundred words long, and so cannot have lasted more than about three minutes. Albert J Beveridge, an American politician and historian, who was himself a biographer of Lincoln, noted in his 1924 book *The Art of Public Speaking* that:

> "All enduring speeches have been comparatively short. None of the sermons of Jesus could, by any possibility, have occupied three-quarters of an hour, and most of them must have been less than half as long… Except under extraordinary circumstances, attention begins to lag after three-quarters of an hour – this even with the young, fresh, eager minds of students."

Nearly a century later, with attention spans much shorter, it would be a brave speaker who spoke for over forty-five minutes other than in a purely academic lecture, or perhaps at a show event like a party political conference. In the words attributed to Winston Churchill, "The head cannot take in more than the seat can endure." The most memorable speeches of the past seventy years tend to have been comfortably under twenty minutes long; this applies, for example, to John F Kennedy's inaugural address, Martin Luther King Jr's 'I have a dream' speech and Barack Obama's breakthrough at the 2004 Democratic National Convention. (I use American examples because there has been an embarrassing shortage of great British political speeches since the Second World War.)

The modern trend is in line with the advice given by President Franklin D Roosevelt to his son James on how to make a public speech: "Be sincere, be brief, be seated." At the TED conferences, speakers are limited to eighteen minutes – long enough to develop a point, but short enough to hold everyone's attention. The TED length of speech seems a good model for the majority of speakers in normal circumstances.

To be fair, I know of one exception to the rule that people rarely complain when conferences or seminars or speeches underrun. There were complaints about an after-dinner speech given by the presenter and comedy writer Clive Anderson which (from memory) lasted eleven minutes. The audience was left wanting more, which is good, but the organisers were left wanting their money back, which is less good. I cannot help feeling that the problem here was not the length of the speech but the size of the fee.

More than ever before, the message for the speaker is: don't overstay your welcome. This is the age of soundbites and ever briefer communications. For maximum effect, under-stay your welcome by a couple of minutes. If you are due to finish at 11.30, finish at 11.28 instead. Don't go over the top and stop so early that the chair has to deal with an embarrassing ten-minute gap before the next speaker. In general, though, it is the overrun that is hated by organisers and delegates alike.

Always try to be fully involved in determining the length of your speech. Even if the decision has initially been made by the event organiser, there may still be room for negotiation. If I am allotted an hour's session, I would be reluctant to give a speech of more than thirty minutes or so: I would want to leave plenty of time for discussion by way of questions and answers. The new age is one of audience participation rather than soliloquies.

To sum it up, going on too long earns you a wholly disproportionate penalty in the feedback you'll get. Speakers are the guests in the house, and if they stay too long the audience will take it personally.

Stop when you are through

An essential element of achieving the right length for a talk is to quit while you are still winning. Here is Spencer Leigh Hughes on the subject:

"There are men who will really prove their case in an admirable manner, and will then go on to add a series of ragged, ill-arranged addenda, until people forget that the argument was really finished some time before; indeed, they forget all about it. After all, when a man is in earnest, and wants to establish some case, the beginning and the end of wisdom is to know when to leave off… I may say that for one speech that has been weakened by the omission of good things forgotten when it was delivered, ten have been spoilt by the passion men have for trying to add what they regard as good things as they go on… One is reminded of the poet's lines, slightly altered –
'Men may come and men may go,
But he goes on for ever.'"

The power of repetition: hammer it home

There is a big qualification to the emphasis on brevity in this chapter. Don't let it stop you repeating key points to get your message over. This is not a contradiction: what we are saying is that we should use our limited time to communicate just our core points, but strike those points home to ensure they are fully understood and retained by the audience.

Here, doing just that, is William Pitt the Elder, 1st Earl of Chatham, who was perhaps the most highly regarded orator of the eighteenth century. In a speech in 1775 *On removing His Majesty's troops from Boston,* he shows the power of repetition, while demonstrating that it does not need to be a subtle art (the emphases are mine):

> "But it is not *repealing* this Act of Parliament, or that Act of Parliament, it is not *repealing* a piece of parchment, that can restore America to your bosom. You must *repeal* her fears and her resentments, and you may then hope for her love and gratitude.
> ... We shall be forced ultimately to retract, whilst we can, not when we must. I say we must necessarily undo these violent and oppressive acts. They must be *repealed.* You will *repeal* them: I pledge myself for it, you will in the end *repeal* them. I stake my reputation on it. I will consent to be taken for an idiot if they are not finally *repealed.*"

Yes, I think we probably all took that point about repealing.

Modern research confirms that repetition works well in the business world, where managers who use 'redundant communication', repeating the same message time and again to their teams, make faster progress on their projects than those who do not. It works for speakers too. Make key points early in your presentation, and then return to them with equal or greater force later. The old advice that has come down all the way from Aristotle – "Tell them what you are going to tell them, tell them, then tell them what you have told them" – has life in it yet.

The underlying theory was set out by Walter Dill Scott when he wrote about the power of repetition to secure suggestibility in the audience, the quality of being inclined to accept and act on the suggestions of the speaker:

> "An idea which upon its first presentation does not meet with acceptance may be more acceptable upon its second and third presentation… In public speaking there are many ideas which have to be repeated over and over again before they attain their maximum effect."

Those words lead nicely to a great quotation about emphasising the essential points in a speech, attributed to Winston Churchill in giving advice to the future King Edward VIII: "If you have an important point to make," he said, "don't try to be subtle or clever. Use a pile driver. Hit the point once. Then come back and hit it again. Then hit it a third time – a tremendous whack." That is a hugely valuable principle, and I have often employed the same tactic in writing this book, using repetition and reinforcement to drive a point home.

An effective example of Churchill's maxim is the politician Nick Clegg's speech to the Liberal Democrat Conference in December 2011. He had been justifying his party's and his own role in the ruling coalition government: "This country would be in deep trouble today if we had not gone into government." He had already mentioned his key theme – 'not easy, but right' – in exactly those words on seven separate occasions in his speech, particularly in the context of the prospects for the nation's children.

He then ended his speech:

"After the summer riots, message boards sprang up. They became known as 'peace walls'.
And on the peace wall in Peckham there was a note that simply read: 'Our home. Our children. Our future.'
Six words that say more than six hundred speeches. Our home. Our children. Our future.
Britain is our home. We will make it safe and strong. These are our children. We will tear down every barrier they face. And this is our future. We start building it today."

You could say that Clegg's approach here takes repetition, and the use of exceptionally short sentences, to an extreme, almost silly, level. In the space of less than fifty words, each of 'home', 'children' and 'future' comes up three times, and that's not to mention the nine appearances of 'our' to suggest that 'we're all in this together'. This tactic would not work in a written text, where it might well be regarded as utterly babyish. But this was a highly charged speech, not an extract from a book. Mr Clegg's rhetorical style went down brilliantly with his audience and brought him tremendous applause.

In practice, you don't have to use exactly the same words when you employ repetition. Using different forms of expression with variety in your language allows you to express different shades of meaning – in the words of Clark Mills Brink, "turning [a thought] this way and holding it that way so as to let the hearers view it in its various aspects". The aim of this approach is that "each repetition not only repeats the idea but adds something to the idea, so that its meaning and significance, with every step, becomes more definite and more luminous."

Conclusion

There was a one-word impression of Herbert Hoover, one of the less effective American presidents, which went: "Eighteenthly…" Whereas some speakers electrify their listeners, the Hoover tendency would be to gas them. A comprehensive approach is not suitable for public speakers, let alone major politicians.

One of the many upsides of speaking to the point is that it reduces the demand for material. A speaker going at 150 words a minute will require only 3,000 words for a twenty-minute presentation. There is a big reward for keeping things simple in a speech – you won't need to do nearly so much writing!

Points to take from this chapter

- You cannot convey more than a handful of essential points.
- Focus on your primary messages, and make them clear, consistent, simple and strong.
- Sacrifice all unnecessary detail.
- Don't overestimate what they already know.
- Use concrete language with plenty of examples.
- Test out your material on a trial audience.
- If in doubt, keep it out: leave them wanting more.
- Make the key points as often as you need, remembering the power of repetition, then sit down.

I hope that this chapter will help you to prepare talks that are punchy and to the point.

But even if they meet that test, could all your good work be ruined by the way in which you will present and comport yourself – in other words, by your body language – when you come to deliver those talks?

The short answer, thank heavens, is "No": life, fortunately, does not work that way.

In the next chapter, I want to demolish your concerns about body language and remove any fears you may have about its potential adverse effects when you speak in public.

Notes

The quotation from William Hazlitt comes from an essay entitled *On the difference between writing and speaking*, written about 1825. Sir Edgar Rees Jones was writing in his book *The Art of the Orator*. Sir Lawrence Bragg's comments in this book come from *Advice to Lecturers: An Anthology Taken from the Writings of Michael Faraday and Lawrence Bragg*, The Royal Institution, 1974. Search 'Lawrence Bragg lecture' on YouTube for some good material showing him in action. The Herbert A Simon quotation is from *Computers, Communications and the Public Interest: Conference Proceedings*, The Johns Hopkins Press, 1971. John Sweller's words come from *The Sydney Morning Herald* on 4 April 2007: the article can be seen at http://www. smh.com.au/news/technology/powerpoint-presentations-a-dis aster/2007/04/03/1175366240499.html. The extract from Lord Birkett comes from Robert Andrews, *Famous Lines: a Columbia dictionary of familiar quotations* (1997), citing a quotation in *The Observer* for 30 October 1960. The Henry Labouchère quotation is given by Spencer Leigh Hughes in *The Art of Public Speaking*. President Roosevelt's advice to his son is quoted from *Basic Public Speaking* by Paul L Soper, Oxford University Press, 1963.

CHAPTER 12

Don't worry about your body language

Introduction

In this chapter, I want to unravel the arcane mysteries of body language by showing that there is, in fact, no mystery whatsoever about it in the first place. We will put the subject in its proper subordinate place as an element of public speaking, and then identify some sensible and utterly straightforward ways to avoid problems arising.

What the experts say

To support my view that the importance of body language in all kinds of human interactions can often be overstated, I'll start with the traditional view of how it applies to public speaking.

Here is a prolific author on oratory, Edwin Gordon Lawrence, writing in 1913 in his book *How to Master the Spoken Word*:

"Gesticulation, even more than speech, should be characteristic of the speaker, and entirely free from parade or pretence. Any gesticulation that calls attention to itself, and not to the thought it is intended to express, is wrong and should not be made. The aim of gesture should be to amplify, illustrate, or strengthen the spoken word, and it should only be employed in the furtherance of these objects…
All gestures that come without effort it is safe to consider natural, for if they feel easy to you, they are likely to look natural and to be effective."

The classics professor, writer and presenter Mary Beard spoke in the same sensible vein when asked about her television performances. She confirmed the importance of being your natural self: "I don't always feel 100% pleased, but I recognise myself, and I think that is terribly important. People say, 'You wave your hands around', and it's true, I do. Sorry, that's me."

"But," I hear you respond, "that must all be wrong because I've been told that modern research shows that body language is the most important element in what we say."

What is going on here?

The body language myth

In fact, the modern theory, or rather the modern myth, comes from a misunderstanding of the research findings of an American psychology professor, Albert Mehrabian. Professor Mehrabian suggested that meaning in speech is conveyed in these proportions:

- Body language accounts for 55% of meaning.
- Tone of voice accounts for 38%.
- The actual words account for just 7%.

You will find these statistics in many publications on public speaking. They are often referred to as the 7%–38%–55% Rule, or more simply the 7% Rule. The natural conclusion from them would be that you need not spend much time in preparation for a speech because your success will depend almost entirely on how you look and sound on the day. Indeed, if you pursue the argument to its limits, you could take a chance that miming or jabbering might be enough to get you understood.

Well, it would not be surprising if success as a speaker involved a little bit more than the words we use. Language among humans is relatively new: it may be no more than 50,000 years old. For a very long time before that, we had to survive together and make sense of each other without language, so you might not be surprised that non-verbal communication signals still have some significance.

We need to be careful about going much beyond that. In fact, Albert Mehrabian was focusing on those situations where *what* an individual says is incongruent or inconsistent with *how* he says it. It is in those circumstances that body language takes on prime importance. If, for example, someone says "I love you" in a bored tone while looking at the ground, in that special situation the non-verbal expressions are the ones that truly matter.

The author and communications expert Max Atkinson, writing in his book *Lend Me Your Ears,* has some compelling things to say about the immoderate claims made for the importance of body language. He makes the reasonable point that: "It would have made more sense for Shakespeare to have had Mark Antony say, 'Lend me your eyes,'" and indeed for the same correction to be made to the title of his own book. He counters the body language myth of public speaking with points like these:

- How is it that we can have totally adequate conversations in the dark?
- Why have telephones and radio been so successful?
- Why do people struggle so much to learn foreign languages?

To my mind, there are two key reasons why we should reject the body language myth as unhelpful and indeed positively destructive:

- It suggests that there is some magic ingredient that is overwhelmingly crucial to a successful talk, and thereby puts many people off from having a go in the first place.
- It distracts us from our fundamental task – the hard but rewarding work of preparing the words we're going to say and getting them right.

That's the nub of the issue. Professor Mehrabian's findings give us no excuse for avoiding the detailed preparation that is needed to make our speeches successful. At the same time, they should not make us feel unnatural pressure about the delivery of our words. If we put together good material and then we deliver it audibly and without gabbling, we will convey our message perfectly well to the audience.

This book will continue to focus on content rather than body language, because it's what we say that matters. No surprises there, but it can be puzzling how many otherwise reputable sources dispute it.

Spencer Leigh Hughes on the practical approach

For me, the most helpful advice on body language comes from Spencer Leigh Hughes, writing in the same year as Edwin Gordon Lawrence. This is so good that I will quote it at length:

"It is very undesirable to give the impression that you have been... practising oratorical deportment before a looking-glass... There is such a thing as appropriate gesture, of course, but nothing is added to the effect, indeed, the effect is lessened, if the hearer gets the impression that the speaker has been told to smite his chest at a certain time, to pass his hand across his brow, as if to still the throbbing brain, to stamp his foot, or to wave his arms about. ... Of course, all men agree that the best style of delivery is the natural manner, but directly a man begins to make conscious efforts at being natural he becomes artificial. There are things which a man can do better by not thinking of what he is doing than by devoting close attention to them. Let us suppose, for instance, that a man is running quickly down a flight of stairs. So long as he does this as by instinct all will be well, but if he begins to think about the necessity of putting one foot in front of the other, and to make quite sure that he is doing this in the right order, he will almost certainly fall. It is often said by those who would instruct speakers that many do not know what to do with their hands, and the most elaborate directions are given concerning hand management. The pupil or victim is warned against [such things as] plunging his hands down into his trousers pockets...
Such advice is, no doubt, sound, but I think it better for the man not to think about his hands at all. What is 'the natural manner'? I think one may take the following definition of the phrase: 'The manner which one naturally falls into who

is really speaking in earnest and with a mind exclusively intent on what he has to say.' You cannot have your mind exclusively intent on the subject of the speech if you are worrying about what should be done with your hands...
It is the man who is for ever wondering what he looks like from the point of view of the audience who indulges in awkward mannerisms of what is called deportment. In regard to natural action or gesture, it has been well said that: 'An emotion struggling for utterance produces a tendency to a bodily gesture to express that emotion more quickly than words can be framed – the words follow, as soon as they can be spoken.' Nothing is more futile than to express the emotion in words, and then to follow them up by some studied gesture. It looks as if you knew your language had not conveyed the meaning, and you were then trying to explain it by signs.

... It may be assumed that when a man makes a speech he wishes to convey some meaning by his spoken words, and in order to do this he should first know what it is he wishes to tell his hearers, arrange his thoughts in their proper order, put them in plain language, and take care that the audience can hear him. When he has mastered these preliminaries, he will probably find that all the elaborate directions as to what to do with his hands, how to stand, when to gesticulate, and so on, are unnecessary, as all that part of the business will have been learnt unconsciously."

Try some power posing beforehand

There is, however, one aspect of body language that you can use profitably *in advance of* your performance – to go in for some power posing in the minutes before you take the stage. This is an idea that has become prominent in recent years, having been popularised among others by Amy Cuddy, a leading expert in non-verbal behaviour. Her TED talk on the subject has had over forty-five million views at the time of writing, so she may be on to something.

Power poses or stances are open and expansive body postures that we would associate with success and confidence.

Typical aspects of a power stance could include:

- Lifting your chin.
- Opening your mouth.
- Throwing your arms up in the air and expanding outwards.
- Spreading your fingers apart when you talk.

Here, then, are some examples of the poses you might take up for two minutes or so before you go onstage for your talk:

- Put your hands on your hips and stand tall, broad-chested and with your feet apart, contemplating the world before you. Two minutes of standing like Superman or Wonder Woman before you speak can work marvels for your confidence.
- Raise your arms in the shape of a V, like a victorious athlete.
- Admire yourself in the mirror as you maintain your power pose. When you walk, swagger.
- If you are really in the mood, move as though you were one of a group performing the haka, the traditional Māori tribal dance, with its strong and expressive movements. "The message to yourself," says Amy Cuddy, "is that you are so confident that you don't have to protect yourself, that you can

expose yourself to the world." You will find some striking, and indeed rather frightening, examples of the haka on YouTube.

- Yoga enthusiasts could consider Amy Cuddy's recommendation of taking up the cobra pose. (I hope that this is less scary than it sounds.)

Experience suggests that in daily life women may be less likely or willing to use expansive poses than men, and so they may benefit particularly from using power posing techniques.

Before you write all this off as mumbo jumbo, you should know that it has a scientific basis. The traditional role of power poses has been to change positively the way *other people* view us, but the modern research suggests that posing in this way can also significantly improve the way *we* view ourselves and our level of self-confidence. Taking up such stances makes us feel more powerful and self-controlled, more 'in the moment', so that our speech gets off to a strong start. Amy Cuddy argues that, once you are powerful, you see challenges as opportunities, not threats: "High power poses before your talk will give you faith in your message to the audience, help you show confidence without arrogance, and help you communicate smoothly." A feeling of power also means that you need not be on your guard, so you can bring the true, authentic nature of your personality to your presentation.

I heard Amy Cuddy speak when she came to London at the start of 2016. Her talk was interesting and challenging, and was well received by the audience. Significantly, I remember nothing whatsoever about her own use of body language during the talk. Edwin Gordon Lawrence, with his views on "gesticulation that calls attention to itself", would rightly have been proud of her.

The first major paper on power posing from Amy Cuddy and her colleagues came out in 2010. Since then, the results of that study have been widely questioned and debated. All I can say is that the approach works for me before public speaking events, and it also works for the people I have coached. Our experience is that, if you can prepare beforehand with big poses in private, you're more likely to carry out the presentation itself with a good, open posture.

Whenever it is practical to do so, I now go into a power pose for several minutes before a presentation. Many people use the technique before similarly stressful occasions, such as job interviews. To avoid misunderstandings and possible police call-outs, I recommend that speakers do their pre-speech power posing on their own in a quiet side room or, if all else fails, a nearby toilet cubicle. Otherwise, if you do it more publicly, you may well face an audience that is initially perplexed, if not downright fearful, at the prospect of seeing you in action.

We can summarise Amy Cuddy's approach as 'Fake it until you become it'. William James's principle that we talked about in Chapter 6 on enjoying yourself – if you want a quality, act *as if* you already have it – appears to apply equally to posture and power. Faking victory seems to work because it tricks your brain into thinking you have already won.

Some further suggestions

Once you have performed your power poses before the presentation, what else should you do about your body language?

Following the advice of Edwin Gordon Lawrence and Spencer Leigh Hughes, I believe that 'do what comes naturally' is far and away the best advice to give to a would-be speaker.

Beyond that, there are a few guidelines about body language for speakers that even I would accept as being helpful – or, at the very least, they cannot do much harm.

Here they are:

- When you rehearse, for at least some of the time do so in front of a mirror. It will feel awkward at first, but it will give you a greater awareness of how your body language will appear to others.
- Make lots of eye contact with the audience during the presentation, and look like you're enjoying yourself when you do it. We reviewed how to make eye contact in Chapter 10. It is particularly important at the start of your talk, at times when you are making key points, and for your conclusion.
- Keep your head up as you address the audience. This can be a challenge if you are using notes or a script, but the answer is simply to stop speaking when you move your head down to refresh your memory. You then do not resume talking until you raise your head up again. We will look at this in more detail in Chapter 18 when we discuss using the right speaking aids.
- If you want to make gestures to the audience, use outstretched arms with open palms. There seems to be an evolutionary basis for this: our ancestors used open palms to signal to people they met that they held nothing with which to harm them.
- Avoid holding a pen or pencil in your hands. It involves too great a risk that you will start playing or fidgeting with it and distract the audience from your talk; and, of course, pens leak.
- If, in spite of what has been said, you worry about what to do with your arms, try to practise with them hanging down by your side. This should make you look more confident and will, in any event, take some of the tension away from your shoulders.
- Having done your power posing before the talk, you

might reasonably consider taking a few high-power stances at crucial points during the presentation itself to increase your confidence and your feeling of being in control.

- So that you can be seen to communicate energy and enthusiasm, I recommend that you should normally stand up when speaking in public, other than in a meeting, regardless of what other speakers may do. If you feel that doing so might betray your nerves, remember that those nerves will be vastly less apparent to the audience than to you.
- Go further than that and, quite simply, take control of the room by moving around within it. I don't care if some of your movements might seem inelegant at times – it's the energy you are displaying that counts for most.

Conclusion

Let's all be sceptical about body language. The focus on it is one of the most unhelpful pieces of mythology about speaking in public. It complicates the speaker's task and, in general, would be far better ignored. The important thing in a presentation is what you say in it. The key to public speaking success is the same as for the past two and a half thousand years – decent material prepared carefully and delivered with conviction. When you forget about your body and just get on with presenting, so too will the audience forget about your body.

Spencer Leigh Hughes gave us a salutary warning for people who get too concerned about their gestures. Here's one more for the road – *The Centipede's Dilemma*, set out in a poem attributed to a nineteenth-century writer called Katherine Craster:

"A centipede was happy – quite!
Until a toad in fun
Said, 'Pray, which leg moves after which?'
This raised her doubts to such a pitch,
She fell exhausted in the ditch
Not knowing how to run."

Points to take from this chapter

- Much of what you hear about body language comes from a misunderstanding of the research.
- It thereby vastly overestimates the importance of the subject.
- Our focus should be on getting our words right and delivering them audibly.
- Power posing before we speak can add to our confidence.
- Check what you look like in the mirror during rehearsals.
- Make eye contact with the audience, and keep your head up.
- Stand up when speaking, and be prepared to move around.
- Otherwise, just forget about your body and get on with presenting.

In the next chapter, we will address another area which concerns speakers unduly – the inevitable errors that we will make in the course of a speech. We'll see that if we don't worry about our mistakes then neither will our audience.

Notes

Mary Beard was quoted in *Radio Times* magazine for 2–8 July 2016. Amy Cuddy's TED talk can be seen at https://www.ted.com/talks/amy_cuddy_your_body_language_shapes_who_you_are. Her comments in this chapter come from a lecture she gave, *Have Presence, and be Self-Assured in Moments of Pressure*, in London in February 2016.

CHAPTER 13

Be relaxed about your mistakes

Introduction

In this chapter, we'll see that every speaker will make mistakes in every talk. So what? It arises from the essential nature of human speech.

We will find that too smooth a delivery can be unhelpful anyway, and we'll go on to learn how to ignore or make light of our errors so that the audience does the same. I'll encourage you to go easy on yourself if things do go wrong, as inevitably they will on occasion, and do everything in my power to prevent you from making unmerited apologies from the stage.

The result of all this will be satisfied audiences and a much happier you.

There's no escaping your mistakes

At the beginning of their speaking careers, many people worry too much about their perceived mistakes. In fact, audiences can be put off by slick, over-polished speakers. Richard Gerver, an expert on change and leadership, puts the point well:

> "When I give people advice about speaking in public, the first thing that I tell them is not to be too polished, not to worry if they make a mistake or stumble over a word. It is a sign of honesty and helps people identify with you on a human level… Make mistakes, it's fine; people will warm to you, to your authenticity."

The reality is that you will always make several mistakes, and usually a lot more, in any talk you give. A leading text on our linguistic errors is a highly entertaining and informative book by Michael Erard called *Um – Slips, Stumbles, and Verbal Blunders, and What They Mean.*

He says:

> "Our ordinary speech is notoriously fragmented, and all sorts of verbal blunders swim through our sentences like bubbles in champagne. They occur on average once every ten words, by some accounts."

That's just speaking ordinarily. The high-pressure environment of public speaking adds further challenges.

One of the best stories of verbal infelicity concerns the actress Diana Dors, Britain's answer to Marilyn Monroe and Jayne Mansfield in the 1950s, who was born as Diana Fluck. She was opening a church fête in her home town of Swindon. The vicar who introduced her was keen to stress her local connection while avoiding embarrassment from the mispronunciation of her real surname. He said to the audience:

> "Ladies and gentlemen, it gives me great pleasure to introduce our star guest, especially as she is our local girl. I therefore feel it right to introduce her by her real name. Please welcome the lovely Miss Diana Clunt."

You might feel that reading out a speech will cut down on your error rate. That is not always true, and there is a particular danger of going into autopilot.

In a pre-election speech in 2015, David Cameron, then the prime minister, was talking about his admiration for "Britain's amazing carers". These were "the people who are up early and up late", he said. "Giving their loved ones medication. Washing them. Cooking them." The audience considered the implied change to Conservative Party policy, with its innovative approach to cannibalism, in silent surprise. "Cooking *for* them," he quickly clarified. It is so easy to sleepwalk into trouble in the course of your talk.

There are some speakers whose reputation for verbal blunders stands way out beyond the rest. The British politician John Prescott, and the Americans George W Bush and Sarah Palin, come quickly to mind. Here is a brief masterpiece from Palin, taken from an extraordinary speech in 2009 as she stepped down as governor of Alaska: "It is as throughout all Alaska that big wild good life teeming along the road that is north to the future." It takes a particular talent to produce a short sentence that is as utterly incomprehensible as that one.

Even the greatest speakers have their off days. Winston Churchill, for example, in June 1945 delivered his infamous 'Gestapo' speech, which involved vitriolic abuse of his Labour Party opponents in the run-up to the approaching general election. He said:

> "No socialist government conducting the entire life and industry of the country could afford to allow free, sharp, or violently worded expressions of public discontent. They would have to fall back on some form of Gestapo, no doubt very humanely directed in the first instance. And this would nip opinion in the bud; it would stop criticism as it reared its

> head, and it would gather all the power to the supreme party and the party leaders, rising like stately pinnacles above their vast bureaucracies of civil servants, no longer servants and no longer civil."

This passage may be elegantly crafted, but it represents a dreadful error of judgement. Churchill spoke as prime minister at a time when the horrific war crimes of Gestapo officers were receiving extensive publicity throughout Europe. To compare his political rivals at home in Britain to the Gestapo was deeply offensive and unjustifiable. Clement Attlee, the Labour leader, replied by ironically thanking Winston Churchill for showing the difference between Churchill as a great wartime leader and Churchill as peacetime politician. The Labour Party went on to take a landslide victory in the 1945 general election.

Audiences tend not to notice

We've been looking at some horrible, wince-inducing blunders, but they are the exceptions. The great thing about the huge majority of mistakes is that the audience does not notice them. On several occasions I have missed out ten minutes or so of content from my talk without anyone catching on.

Audience members will normally be less alert, and a lot less critical, than you as the speaker, and the errors will pass them by. That assumes, of course, that you don't jump up and down about your mistakes or adopt a facial expression that says, "I have cocked up on a grand scale." Mark Twain noted this point over a century ago, saying:

> "It is really very curious to see what a man can do on the platform without the audience suspecting anything to be wrong. A case in point occurred in Paris a year ago... I

began telling [an] anecdote, but I found when halfway that my memory regarding it had gone. So I switched on to another line, and was soon leaving the half-told anecdote far behind. My wife and daughter were present, and I afterwards asked them whether they remembered the breakdown. They replied in the negative. I then asked whether they heard the finish of the anecdote with which I had begun my remarks, and they at once replied they had not... If anyone would be likely to discover a flaw, it would be my wife or my daughter, and when I found that they were unaware of the defect, I was quite satisfied that the audience in general knew nothing about it."

The way to respond to your mistakes

The key thing with mistakes is simply to accept that you will make them, quite often, and then carry on regardless.

In 1882, the anonymous author of *Beeton's Art of Public Speaking* noted the importance of keeping going and not making a fuss:

"Another of the common misfortunes of the young speaker will be to land in the middle of a sentence and find himself unable to get grammatically to the end. What must he do in such a case? He may do one of two things: he may go back to the beginning again, or he may go boldly ahead in defiance of grammar, and finish the sentence as best he can. Of these two courses, the latter is the preferable. The public are more tolerant of bad grammar than of hesitation and uncertainty."

In other words, the mistake is in the past, and you need to live in the present. Focus on the current moment, and move on.

Remember that, as Richard Gerver noted, mistakes make the speaker appear more human to the audience, and consequently easier to relate to.

In a twenty-minute talk, I would expect at least three to four slips of the tongue, together with one or two moments where it takes what feels like an excruciatingly long time to find the right word for something. As we have seen, the listeners usually won't even notice. If you act as though the mistake doesn't mean much to you, then it will not mean much to your audience either. It's only when you become uncomfortable at a slip or a gaffe that your listeners start to mirror your behaviour.

The popular speaker Scott Berkun expresses it nicely in his great book *Confessions of a Public Speaker*:

> "Know that your response to a mistake defines the audience's response. If I respond to spilling water on my pants as if it were the sinking of the *Titanic*, the audience will see it, and me, as a tragedy. But if I'm cool or, better yet, find it funny, the audience will do the same."

Some practical examples

Even if, in your mind, you make a real howler, the audience probably won't regard it in the same way. If in doubt, laughing at yourself or otherwise making a joke of it can be a great recovery mechanism and put them at their ease. Something as basic as "I knew I shouldn't have gone drinking at lunchtime" works well. If a piece of humour falls completely flat, I say: "Do you know, that was the one joke that *[name the organiser or chair of the event or the person who introduced you]* gave me for today, and I understand now why they wanted to give it away."

There are some cunning ways to deal with memory lapses.

Some speakers drink from the glass of water they have with them on stage until their memory returns. Others find it helpful to carry with them a few record cards containing interesting material – statistics, say, or humorous quotations – relevant to the subject they are discussing. When they have a memory lapse, they take out one of the cards and say something like: "By the way, you might like this…" While they read from the card, they free up brain space for the recall of what they were supposed to be talking about in the first place.

In his fascinating book *Let Me Play the Lion Too: How to be an Actor*, the distinguished actor and director Michael Pennington sets out some principles for actors to follow when they forget their lines. His approach, in a section headed *D is for Drying*, can be equally helpful to us as speakers. Reminding us that drying up is not the end of the world, he notes the valuable advice given to the actor Rupert Everett by his manager: "It's okay, just don't let them *see* you *crash*."

The point is that the audience will believe that almost anything done by the person on stage is intended. So, when Rupert Everett dried, "confidently and in his character, he called the script girl and make-up to attend to him as if this stoppage was somehow all part of the show. The audience wasn't given the chance to believe the unthinkable was happening." Michael Pennington says that as a last resort an actor will stop, go and get the script, bring it back on stage and carry on, giving the audience the impression that in some strange way this is all part of the play. Think how much easier life is for us as speakers, with no restrictions on having the script with us in the first place.

I have seen advice that goes as far as suggesting that speakers should make a mistake on purpose, inserting a planned mess-up early in their speech. They then make a wonderfully smooth recovery, showing their ability to think on their feet and putting the audience at their ease. This seems a rather extreme manoeuvre to me, but if it works for you then feel free to go with it. The general message of avoiding too much slickness in delivery is a good one. In the words of *Beeton's Art of Public Speaking*:

> "The style of language which the speaker should adopt...
> should not be too artful or laboured in construction. A little
> appearance of negligence, indeed, is often of service, in order
> to avoid the appearance of great preparation. This fact was
> fully recognised by the most eloquent orators among the
> ancients."

Go easy on yourself

A significant aspect of handling your mistakes is to be gentle with yourself after the event. Most people perform less well on the big day than they did in final rehearsals. That's because there is a lot less pressure in rehearsals. This point seems obvious, but few of the books on public speaking pay it much attention.

It is important, because it means we should be sympathetic and generous to ourselves if the actual performance does not meet our hopes and expectations. Normally, it quite simply doesn't meet those expectations. Our extreme motivation to succeed causes us to stumble. And, of course, however much we practise, we can never entirely predict what will happen at the event itself. So be forgiving if your performance is not quite what you hoped for.

Dan Ariely, a psychologist and behavioural economist, gives a good example in his book *The Upside of Irrationality*. He was severely injured as a young man in an accident that caused third-degree burns over 70% of his body. He tells how, at a conference in Florida, he and three colleagues were going to present their recent work on adaptation, the process by which people become accustomed to new circumstances. Instead of talking about his research findings, he planned to give a presentation about his personal experience of adapting to physical injuries and discuss some of the lessons he had learned. In fact, when he started to talk about his hospital ordeal, he welled up with tears and found that he could not speak. Though he quickly recovered by switching to an impersonal discussion of his research, he concludes: "It left me with a very strong impression about my own inability to predict the effects of my own emotions, when combined with stress, on my ability to perform."

This is a classic example of the things that can go wrong in public speaking that we cannot prepare for and should not beat ourselves up about afterwards.

Dan Ariely had practised his talk in full, he knew what he was going to say, and indeed, apart from the personal element, it was very similar to other talks he had given over the years. He could not have predicted his reaction before the live audience, and his approach of talking about his personal experience in preference to generalities was one that any public speaking coach should have encouraged. He deserves great credit for his attempt.

However well you prepare for your speech, you can never exclude the possibility of unexpected troubles on the day. When they happen, be gentle with yourself.

Beware of apologies

Here is an authoritative comment on the role of apologising, or rather not doing so, in public speaking. It comes from AC Benson in his piece on *The art of lecturing*:

> "One thing is of high importance. A lecturer must never yield to a temptation, which comes in the guise of modesty, to deprecate his efforts, to apologise for speaking at all, to plead that he does not do it willingly. After all, he would not be asked to do it if he was not wanted."

One of the great modern experts on apologising is Donald Trump. He says: "I think apologising is a great thing, but you have to be wrong… I will absolutely apologise, sometime in the hopefully distant future, if I'm ever wrong."

Given that most of your listeners won't notice your mistakes in the first place, you should always think twice before you offer your apologies to the audience. The great scientist Michael Faraday, who was also famed as a lecturer, commented: "I would wish apologies to be made as seldom as possible." He noted that: "I have several times seen the attention of by far the greater part of an audience called to an error by the apology which followed it."

In general, just get on with your talk, and leave the audience to make their own judgements. They will not thank you for being told at the outset that you did not have enough time to prepare so what follows isn't going to be very good. Don't take their hopes away, and don't prejudice them against you in advance. Similarly, don't apologise at the end; you never know, some people might have enjoyed what you had to say. Don't cause them to re-evaluate their experience.

This principle can be widened to say that you should normally avoid all commentary on your talk as you go along. Don't announce that you're about to tell a really funny joke or a really bad one. Just get on with it. The comedian Frank Carson performed his own critical review as he spoke; his catchphrases were "It's a cracker!" and "It's the way I tell 'em!"

But most of us, sadly, don't fall into his class, and so we won't get away with it in the way he did.

None of this is to suggest that one should ignore the basic politenesses of life. If I arrive late, or need to go off to the loo in the middle of my speech, or belch loudly, I should apologise appropriately to my audience. It is far better, of course, to avoid such problems in the first place if at all possible.

Conclusion

Some days it simply won't work.

You will be appearing at the wrong time, or in the wrong place, or both. You may be off form, or you may simply have a terrible audience. It happens to everyone.

If you're giving a factual talk, at least take comfort in the thought that your listeners may have learned something. A failed performance tends to be much worse for a comic speaker, because they have little in the way of incidental benefits to compensate for not making people laugh.

Bob Monkhouse recognised this, writing in *Over the Limit: My Secret Diaries 1993-98*: "Every comedian I know can recall with absolute clarity the times and places where their act died. I've died eleven times, and I remember every painful detail."

The compensation for the skilled funny speaker is that there will be far more successes than failures and that, as the performer and writer Catherine Tate puts it, "To get out on stage and make people laugh is intoxicatingly wonderful."

When you do mess up, remember that it is not a reflection on you as a human being. This is not an easy message to absorb, but we should all try to master it. If your personal sense of self-worth were to depend on the marks the audience gave you for a talk, the pressures would be intolerable.

Of course, it's important to learn the lessons when things do go wrong. Here is Donald Trump again:

> "You have to learn from your successes and your failures. And if you don't learn from mistakes, then you're a fool. Now, ideally you want to watch other people and learn from their mistakes, because that's less costly and less traumatic."

Points to take from this chapter

- You will make mistakes in every talk, and usually a lot of them.
- The audience does not even notice the huge majority of mistakes.
- The secret is simply to keep going without making a fuss.
- If you do feel you need to react, a great tactic is to make a joke of things.
- Consider drinking water or reading from record cards to give yourself thinking time.
- If the big day doesn't go as well as rehearsals, that's only natural: rehearsals are much less stressful.
- Beware of apologies: they draw attention to your mistakes.
- If it all falls flat, remember it's only a talk. Your life will still go on.

We've now completed our review of the major principles that underlie the long-term success of any speaker. Next, for the second section of this book, we'll move on to the key elements of preparation – the things to do in advance of giving your speech to ensure that all goes well on the day.

We'll start, in the next chapter, with the crucial importance of finding out about your audience to ensure your talk is relevant and appropriate for them.

Notes

The quotation from Richard Gerver comes from his helpful book *Simple Thinking: How to Remove Complexity from Life and Work*, Capstone, 2016. Sarah Palin did indeed say the exact words quoted here, and you can see her do it at https://www.youtube.com/watch?v=NNU5vmmXZVU. The extract from Mark Twain comes from *Mark Twain: The Complete Interviews*, edited by Gary Scharnhorst, University of Alabama Press, 2006. Donald Trump's comments are from *Trump on Trump* by George Beahm, Cassell, 2016. The extract from Michael Faraday is contained in *Advice to Lecturers: An Anthology Taken from the Writings of Michael Faraday and Lawrence Bragg*, The Royal Institution, 1974.

THE KEY PREPARATION

CHAPTER 14

Get to know your audience

Introduction

Up to now, we have been dealing with the Key Principles, the underlying approaches that will help us flourish as public speakers. We now move on to the second section of this book, the Key Preparation. By this I mean the thirteen detailed steps we need to take before our presentation to ensure victory on the day. As before, we will see that there is no magic in any of this. We will be discussing the straightforward, clear-cut ways of laying the groundwork that anyone can adopt on the way to a first-class performance.

I've heard it said that a talk is all about the audience, not the speaker. That is nonsense: of course the speaker's personality is vital. But it is certainly true that, to stand any chance of being successful, a talk must also fully take into account the character and mood of the audience. For that reason, we are going to start this section by looking at effective methods by which a speaker can get to know his or her audience. Only by doing this can we ensure a presentation that will be both appropriate and attractive to the people who will sit in the auditorium on the day of the speech.

The importance of understanding the audience

You must prepare and deliver your material according to your listeners.

Sometimes this can be easy. Shakespeare gives an example in *Romeo and Juliet* when Juliet says: "Every tongue that speaks but Romeo's name speaks heavenly eloquence."

You would immediately know what to talk about if you were in Juliet's company. By contrast, in Chapter 37 we will examine the cautionary tale of Tony Blair and the ladies of the National Federation of Women's Institutes to see how badly things can go wrong when a speaker misreads the audience.

Information to obtain

The initial challenge is to establish what the audience wants from the speech. Nothing works as well as simply asking them, usually through a representative, sufficiently in advance to give you time to prepare your whole script from scratch if need be. This conversation will, at the very least, help determine two key elements of what you will say:

- What the audience *would* like you to talk about.
- What the audience *doesn't* want you to talk about.

Once you are aware of the topics or themes you should focus on, and the ones you should avoid at all costs, the planning and preparation of your talk become relatively straightforward.

Though this point seems blindingly obvious on the page, history shows that an extraordinary number of otherwise skilled speakers (Tony Blair included) have failed to do this straightforward, basic research. As a result, they failed horribly when they came to give their talks.

The lists that follow set out other questions to ask. Needless to say, not all of them will be relevant in all circumstances. Although the issues overlap, and may in some cases appear to duplicate others, experience suggests that a thorough approach like this gives a speaker the best chance of preparing a talk that will be well received and avoid giving inadvertent offence:

Audience make-up

- What is the probable size of the audience?
- What will the make-up be regarding age/gender/ ethnicity/level of education/technical or professional qualifications/political allegiance/religious beliefs?
- What, if anything, do they have in common with each other?
- What will they be wearing?
- Who are the influential characters in the audience?
- Are there individuals who might be up for some good-natured banter as an initial icebreaker? (Always check with the person in question before you rely on anyone else's word for this.)

Audience mood

- What do they understand is in it for them to make their attendance worthwhile (such as new perspectives, great storytelling, motivational uplift, humour and conviviality)?
- What are their possible motivations, biases and beliefs?
- Will they be there willingly or under compulsion?
- Are they likely to be welcoming/receptive/hostile?
- How serious are they likely to be?

- Where will they be in the range between passive and demonstrative?
- What points of etiquette are important to them that might affect how you should dress, speak or behave?

Audience expectations

- Why will the audience be there?
- What issues are most important to them?
- What are they looking to get out of your speech?
- What style of presentation are they expecting (for example, professional, practical, motivational, humorous) and what format (formal lecture, group discussion, brainstorming forum, question and answer session, or some combination of these)?
- What, if any, expectations or preconceptions do they have about the use of technology, visual aids and handouts?

Audience knowledge

- How much do they already know on the subject?
- Are they technically minded, practically minded, or both (or indeed neither)?
- Do they use special terminology that you need to know about?
- Will there be individuals present who have more expertise on the topic than you do?
- What problems do they have that you might be able to help with?
- What do they, or will they, know about you, the speaker?

Audience logistics

- Where will the session take place, and at what time of day?
- How long will you have to speak for (including any question and answer session)?
- Is this an audience that likes to ask questions of its speakers?
- Will anyone else be speaking before or after you? If so, who, and on what topic? Can you be there to listen to previous speakers?
- When will you be able to get into the room to set up for your talk?
- Will you have a prior opportunity to carry out a dress rehearsal at the location of the talk?
- What distractions will there be for you to cope with?
- Confirm the specific logistics: the exact address and postcode of the venue, and the availability of parking, toilets and any refreshments.

Once you have the answers to your questions, you can start on some useful planning to make your talk genuinely relevant to your audience. Just one or two pointers from the information you gather can easily produce a significant improvement to your presentation. Bob Monkhouse will confirm this for us in a minute.

How to do your audience research

The primary approach to identifying an audience's issues is to go straight to them or their representative for a full discussion. Nothing beats a face-to-face meeting, and I will always try for that, even if in the end I have to make do with a lengthy telephone conversation.

Some speakers go so far as to ask each attendee to fill out a questionnaire beforehand to establish what they want from the session, but this can be counter-productive, particularly if audience members feel their comments are then ignored in the construction of the talk. You also need to avoid creating forms that are annoyingly long and unwieldy to complete, or come over as a blatant marketing ploy. I would suggest that, if you do decide to use individual questionnaires, you do it with delicacy and brevity.

Beyond direct contact with your audience, secondary methods of research can also be powerful:

- Talk to your contacts (or contacts of your contacts) who may know the business or audience in question.
- Go searching on the Internet.
- Look at technical journals.
- Read company accounts, annual reports, newsletters and any available minutes of relevant meetings.
- Look at any marketing materials issued by the event organisers.
- If the event (or one similar to it) has taken place before, research any course documentation or relevant videos that you can get your hands on.
- Search out relevant blogs. They can be invaluable for getting an unofficial opinion that is open and direct.

Two of my favourite sources of information are the letters page and the gossip or trivia section of a trade journal. They can give you a magnificently uncensored view of your potential audience.

The magazine of the English chartered accountants, *Economia*, is a good example. In a previous format, under the slightly less imaginative title of *Accountancy*, it reported the results of a poll of chartered accountants to test the Monty

Python image of the dullness and boredom of the profession. The respondents were asked whether they were, in fact, pretty boring people: 4% of those polled strongly agreed with this statement; 15% tended to agree; and, rather wonderfully, 17% were unable to offer an opinion either way. These statistics have added colour to my talks on accountancy for the past twenty-five years and continue to serve me well today.

Beware of potential pitfalls in your research

Be sure to do your research with a questioning mind, and don't necessarily take everything you find out at face value. I talked about dealing with the audience through a representative. In practice, their representative may well be the organiser of the event, perhaps a figure of authority in the business. Such spokespeople may well attach their personal feelings and concerns to the bodies they represent. Think carefully about whether you are being given legitimate information, and review your findings in a critical spirit.

Sometimes there will be things that you are not told about, perhaps because the organiser of the event thinks they are too obvious to be worth mentioning, or because they might give offence to you or the audience.

For example, I delivered an hour's talk to long-term prisoners in the Lifer Unit at Dovegate Prison near Uttoxeter in Staffordshire. The subject was the work of the Criminal Cases Review Commission, and how it might help the prisoners in their appeals against conviction. The prison staff were very helpful in giving me information and arranging accommodation for the talk. They explained how much the prisoners appreciated outside speakers coming in to make presentations, provided of course that they were not patronising or offhand. The prisoners were indeed very welcoming. But something I failed to think about or research in preparing for the talk, and that the prison staff did not mention to me, was that prisoners have generally had very limited schooling and education.

I now know that nearly a third of adult offenders have an intelligence quotient under eighty, and 20% to 30% of them have learning disabilities or difficulties that interfere with their ability to cope within the criminal justice system. It is the combination of undiagnosed learning challenges and a socially deprived background that leads many young people to frustration and truancy, then crime and prison. I omitted to take account of all this and started off at a pace and complexity that was completely unsuitable for the audience.

At least, by noticing the puzzled faces around me, I was able to recover the situation after the first few minutes. I slowed down, used lots of repetition and encouraged questions as I went along to ensure the prisoners understood me. The result was that I took an hour to cover my first twenty minutes' worth of material, before running out of time. I never made the same mistake again.

A further pitfall to avoid is the effect of your own egotistic characteristics. Your first tendency is to think that the audience will want for themselves exactly what you want for them. This can be fatal to the success of a talk. The good news is that being aware of this inherent bias gives us the best chance of achieving objectivity by checking on our prejudices and adjusting for them accordingly.

Moving on from your audience research

How can you bring a more in-depth focus to your preparatory work?

The communications coach Joey Asher has a helpful recommendation. He suggests asking yourself: "What are the three questions my audience would most likely ask me about this subject?" It then makes sense to use those questions as a primary element in the planning for your talk. They will direct you to areas where you should concentrate your subsequent research, and you will save time in the process.

A few general points about audiences

Audiences vary vastly from place to place and time to time. Ian Pattison, the Glasgow-based Scottish writer who created the memorable comic character of Rab C Nesbitt, noted that: "Here in Glasgow they can say 'Hello' like it's a declaration of war." The Glasgow Empire had the ultimate reputation of being the 'comedians' graveyard': if the audience there liked you, they still didn't applaud, but they let you live.

Each speaker will have his or her individual experiences of joy and disaster. I loved speaking in the United States because the audiences there were so warm and enthusiastic. Back in the UK, I tend to die – in speaking terms, that is – in Liverpool, and I don't go down very well in Luton either. However, the people of Portsmouth and Plymouth give me a great welcome. I clearly struggle with the Ls but should carry on taking the Ps.

These huge variations mean that it is highly dangerous to make generalisations about the characteristics of specific audiences. But my experience is that, on the whole, younger attendees are more politically correct, so you have to be more careful in your terminology and choice of humour.

Many speakers find their style appeals more to a particular gender. Women, on the whole, react more positively to me than men. When I am speaking I try to identify a lady in the audience, typically about three or four rows back, who smiles a lot, so that I can rely on at least one friendly face if things start to go wrong. Obviously, you wouldn't want to take this approach as far as to embarrass any individuals or make them feel you were inviting them out afterwards.

Often senior people in an organisation want just an overview of your topic, with an emphasis on the key points, while junior staff like to hear a bit more of the detail. Of course, it all depends on the circumstances. A low-key review of corporate strategy for business managers requires very different pacing and content from a stirring 'reach for the stars' motivational talk to the same people at the end of a conference.

The time of day when you speak can make a big difference. Early in the morning, it usually makes sense to keep things uncomplicated and businesslike, and to err on the side of brevity. Later in the day, particularly after dinner, an audience should be more relaxed and mellow. If you are talking to a business audience after work on a technical subject, they may well be tired after a long day, so take a bit longer to drive your points home and use some humour to maintain their goodwill.

The Bob Monkhouse masterclass

One of the finest, and most underrated, books on public speaking for a British audience is *Bob Monkhouse's Complete Speaker's Handbook*. It was first published with a different title, *Just Say a Few Words*, in 1988, and that complication may not have helped its popularity. Long before the days of Internet-enabled research, Bob Monkhouse showed how it was possible to understand your audience by taking the time to think intelligently and creatively about them.

In the book, Monkhouse describes an instance where he was engaged to give a speech to people running corner shops in the retail grocery business. He thought logically through the features of the trade – the role of cash and carry, the effect of television advertising, limitations on alcohol sales – until he hit upon an area rich in potential humour: "Dated food – ahah! Surely customers won't buy food that has passed its sell-by date and yet it seems unlikely that the small grocer could afford to dump it." It dawned on him that he had a great start for his speech. His opening words were: "You do look well. It's reassuring to look around me and see how healthy 600 people can be despite living off a diet made up exclusively from food that's passed its sell-by date."

This line got a great laugh, and deservedly so: Bob Monkhouse had taken the time to work through the life of a corner shop grocer in his mind. And note the skill with which he expressed that opening line, making it a compliment ("You do look well") rather than focusing on the food reaching the point of going off, before completing the joke and making his audience feel like a select club of exceptional individuals.

Conclusion

One of the greatest sins a speaker can commit is failing to research the audience in plenty of time before a talk. If you do not identify their underlying issues and concerns, the content of your speech may be utterly inappropriate, and you are likely to offend almost everyone.

Never try to cut corners on the effort you put into audience research. It will save you time in the actual writing of your talk and will repay you handsomely in the response you get from your listeners.

Points to take from this chapter

- Establish both what they do and what they don't want you to talk about.
- It helps to divide your research into audience make-up, mood, expectations, knowledge and logistics.

- If possible, do your research in a face-to-face meeting.
- Blogs, letters pages and gossip columns can be surprisingly helpful.
- Review your findings critically and with an independent mind.
- Beware of thinking the audience will want the same thing as you.
- Identify, and focus on, the three questions they are most likely to ask you.

In the next chapter, we will move on to look at the surprising importance of the title you give to your talk and the descriptive material you use to support it. We'll see how a good title can draw people to your presentation, while one that is poorly thought out can doom your entire session to failure.

Notes

Juliet's words are from Act 3, Scene 2 of *Romeo and Juliet*. Quotations in this book from Joey Asher derive from his wonderfully incisive work, *15 Minutes Including Q&A*, memorably subtitled *A Plan to Save the World from Lousy Presentations*, Persuasive Speaker Press, 2010. The quotation from Ian Pattison comes from *Now That's Funny* by David Bradbury and Joe McGrath, Methuen Publishing Ltd, 1998.

CHAPTER 15

Devise a striking title and a strong blurb

Introduction

Seemingly small details can make an amazing difference to the success of a talk.

Two prime examples of this rule are the title you give to your presentation and the promotional statement ('blurb') you use as an additional enticement for people to turn up on the day. In this chapter, we will review the key criteria that enable a title or blurb to work its magic, and we'll look at practical examples of both. We'll also encounter some cautionary instances of what can go wrong.

Crucial rules for titles

The title of your talk is there to catch people's attention and imagination quickly, so it is important to spend the time you need to get it right.

A good title should meet these tests:

- Is it accurate enough to explain what your presentation is really about?
- Does it indicate that your talk can help the audience solve a problem they have, provide a skill they need, or supply them with some other benefit?
- Will it grab their attention?

Titles that are snappy, or provocative, or humorous, or topical, or challenging, or distinctive, or ideally some combination of these, work well.

Never make your title so gimmicky that it becomes unclear what the presentation is actually going to be about. If the audience needs to know the precise particulars of what you're going to be speaking on, then a punchy title with a more detailed subtitle can be useful.

Practical examples

Here's an example of a great title. One of my favourite books on education (I am a school governor) is *Getting the Buggers to Behave* by Sue Cowley. It's an example of a strong, memorable title that still manages to make the underlying topic very clear. I'm sure it was the title that drew my interest in the first place. I would much more happily go to a talk called *Getting the Buggers to Behave* than one on *Developments in Student Management Methodology.*

I have already mentioned the international success of the TED talks. Here are the titles of the five most popular TED talks at the time of writing:

- Do schools kill creativity?
- Your body language may shape who you are.
- How great leaders inspire action.

- The power of vulnerability.
- Ten things you didn't know about orgasm.

You will see that there's nothing fancy here, but all the titles have a healthy mix of the qualities I am looking for. They are catchy, to the point (no more than eight words in each case) and largely self-explanatory. They all pass the initial test of making you eager to hear a talk on that subject.

Scott Berkun on titles

Scott Berkun says some sensible things about titles in *Confessions of a Public Speaker*. He deplores how often speakers reject the opportunity to use interesting, lively titles for their talks. He proposes some generic titles for presentations that are a vast improvement on the standard conference fare.

My favourites among his suggestions are:

- The top five problems you have with <insert thing here> and how to solve them.
- The truth about <insert thing here> and how it can help you.
- The good, the bad, and what we're doing about it.

These titles engage the interest of the potential audience member, who thereby becomes more likely to turn up on the day. They are expressed in terms of problem-solving and constructive action. They are sufficiently limited in scope and coverage that the title realistically reflects what the audience can expect to hear. Few talks in real life achieve the lofty aim of doing exactly what it says on the packaging, so that is no mean achievement.

Avoid wide-ranging titles

Here is a crucial point in Scott Berkun's advice: please don't make your title too sweeping.

In the brief span of a talk, there is no chance that you're going to tell the audience everything they ever wanted to know about, say, cricket, or cheese, or orgasm, or any other subject. If you give yourself too general a title, and hence too full a remit, two major things immediately go wrong.

First, you are dooming the audience to dissatisfaction and yourself to poor reviews, because you simply won't be able to cover the promised ground. Second, it means you have not properly thought through what you intend to say and, most importantly, what you are going to leave out. Your lack of focus invites failure from the outset.

In contrast, by thinking seriously about your title, you force yourself to think seriously about your content. That way, you have an ideal opportunity to plan a talk covering a limited amount of material that you genuinely want to speak about, and that the audience will genuinely want to hear.

Further pointers on titles

If the organisers of your event have the power of veto over your title, it's sensible to agree it with them well in advance. Remember that, even when you have a topic assigned to you, you can still try to increase the size of your audience by suggesting a stronger title.

Later in this chapter, I will be talking about the blurb, or prospectus, for one of the talks I have delivered on public speaking itself. The title the organisers had given me was *Presentation Skills* – not terribly exciting, to be honest. I persuaded the event manager to change it to *Perfect Presentations*. The *Perfect Presentations* wording was designed to be provocative and so attract a bigger audience: "Who is this insufferable wise guy who thinks he knows everything about presenting skills?" The talk drew twice the average audience for that series of presentations, so I may have been on to something when I suggested my title.

Beware the dangers of an ambiguous title.

There is a story that Lord David Cecil, a British historian and academic, once gave a lecture on *The Pleasures of Reading* and was surprised to find the poet John Betjeman in his audience. Betjeman had come expecting a talk on the architectural delights of the well-known town in Berkshire rather than a celebration of the joy of books. I do so hope that's a true story. I went to Reading once myself, but it was closed.

For this book, I worked through a whole range of possible titles, seventeen in total, before making a final decision. I'm glad I did: it's well worth investing the time to come up with the most appropriate title you can think of.

Polish your blurb

A 'blurb' is a short description of your talk to make people want to come and hear you. Typically, it will be sent out by conference organisers in their prospectus for the event. You could compare it with the description on the back cover of a book. Just as a good blurb for a book can make the difference between it being purchased or remaining on the shelves, so a good blurb for your talk can markedly bolster the size of your audience.

A good blurb should meet these tests:

- Does it fit your personality?
- Is it snappy and to the point?
- Does it make clear who the target audience is?
- Will it excite the interest of potential audience members by showing what's in it for them?

- In particular, does it suggest that people will enjoy your talk?
- Does it contain a brief description of what you are offering, sufficiently accurate so that at the end of the session no one will feel you misled them about the content?
- If there is something unique to your talk that other speakers don't offer, does the blurb make this clear?
- Does it include enough biographical details to confirm that you will be a competent and credible speaker?

Speakers often underestimate the value of inserting biographical material. It is important not to hide your expertise from your potential audience, and you can't demonstrate your skills to them much earlier than when you write your blurb.

A good blurb helps to structure what I call the 'terms of engagement' for the presentation in your favour. It is a means of imposing your will and your control over the event and what you're going to say, so that what takes place in your talk does, in fact, match what you intended to happen.

The blurb sets out what you are going to speak about, and also strongly implies the style in which you intend to do it. That way, your audience can turn up with clear expectations, and you can be in a much better position to fulfil them. All this is a vast improvement on leaving the organisers to second-guess you.

Let's look at a couple of examples.

Example of a blurb – one of my own

Ian Nichol on Perfect Presentations
Using examples from his work as a speaker and speaking coach, Ian will show you how to give an excellent

presentation with impact and style. This highly practical and interactive session will cover these key topics:

- Why good speakers are made, not born, and why it matters.
- Setting the terms of engagement.
- Knowing your audience (and possibly your subject).
- Preparation, preparation, preparation – writing your script.
- Dealing with nerves: the 4% rule and the use of drink and drugs.
- Notes, handouts and visual aids.
- Casing the joint.
- Answering and avoiding questions.
- Managing the audience from hell.

The seminar will be fun for all and will be of particular interest to anyone who has to speak in front of a business audience.

Your speaker: Ian Nichol

Ian Nichol is a chartered accountant (sorry!) who has been a successful public speaker and presenter since 1968. He has been a commissioner of the Criminal Cases Review Commission, the independent body based in Birmingham that investigates suspected miscarriages of justice. He is also a humorous after-dinner speaker for charitable causes. He previously ran his own training and speaking business, and before that was a tax and training partner at PricewaterhouseCoopers. Ian's variety and depth of speaking experience mean that he can offer valuable advice for speaking and presenting to any audience: the board of your company, the panel at your job interview, a drunken rabble after dinner, or (less commonly perhaps) a room full of murderous criminals.

The thinking behind my blurb

What I was trying to achieve with this blurb was to differentiate my talk from others organised by the same events manager by making it sound intriguing and potentially enjoyable – not a typical feature of that particular brand. For example, in the section on nerves you'll see that I am going to talk about the 4% rule and the use of drink and drugs. The '4% rule' was there to appeal to accountants, who were the larger part of the potential audience, and their unending love of figures and percentages. It was also there to be novel and enticing because, since I had invented it on the spot, no one would have heard of it before. The point I was going to make at the presentation was that it's crucial to perform well at the very start – for, say, the first 4% of the talk. (It corresponds to my emphasis in this book on the first few minutes.) The drink and drugs reference was similarly introduced to whet people's appetites; the theme will crop up here in Chapter 25 under the guise of managing your medication.

Example of a blurb – the Henry Wilcox approach

Here is one of my favourite blurbs. In a piece taken from his book *The Trials of a Stump-speaker*, Henry S Wilcox, an American jurist, is advertising his forthcoming speech (on the winning side) in the 1888 United States presidential election. The speech will be part of a concerted effort on his part to make his name as one of the world's best-known orators. (Spoiler alert: sadly, it didn't work, notwithstanding the success of this particular performance.)

> BEHOLD!!!!
> HENRY S WILCOX, THE GREATEST WIT, ORATOR,
> NOVELIST, IN THE KNOWN WORLD, WILL
> POSITIVELY SPEAK IN THE BEHALF OF THE
> REPUBLICAN PARTY AND ANNIHILATE THE
> OPPOSITION, AT THE OPERA HOUSE TO-NIGHT.
> LADIES AS WELL AS GENTLEMEN WILL BE
> PERMITTED TO ENJOY THIS GREAT TREAT.

I apologise for the sexist undertones here: the world has moved on somewhat since 1888. Subject to that, I love the sheer nerve of Henry's blurb – no messing around with timid expression for him. The speech that resulted was a triumph:

> "Almost every sentence was followed by lusty cheers. The applause at times was protracted and deafening… It took nearly two hours to deliver my address, so frequently was I compelled to stop on account of the enthusiasm of the audience. When I had finished, they gathered around me in great numbers. Many said it was the greatest speech that they had ever heard in all their lives."

And who are we to doubt the man's word for it?

Conclusion

Having a great title and blurb matters. It gives you your best chance to influence the type of people who turn up to your presentation and to maximise the number of them. (If you are not seeking the largest possible attendance, why are you planning to talk in the first place?)

And there is a substantial side benefit. If you get your title and blurb right, people will come with high expectations of your talk. And that in itself will positively shape their, and your, experience of the day. The feeling of having the audience with you as you begin is highly potent in helping you to deliver a successful speech.

Points to take from this chapter

- Your title should convey the essence of the talk, show that it can help the audience, and grab attention.
- Titles expressed in terms of problem-solving or constructive action work particularly well.
- Limit the scope of your title to avoid giving unrealistic expectations.
- Beware the dangers of an ambiguous title.
- The essence of your blurb is to make people want to attend.
- Always include sufficient biographical details to confirm your credibility as a speaker.
- An effective title and blurb will actively improve the audience's experience of the talk.

We have now reached the point where we can begin to work on the detailed contents of what we might say when we take the stage. In the next chapter, we're going to examine some cunning ways to cut down on the time we need to spend researching that material.

CHAPTER 16

Save time on research

Introduction

I am not alone in finding that researching a topic is one of the most enjoyable parts of the whole speaking process. However, speakers are busy individuals and need to control the amount of time they spend on preliminaries, particularly if people like me are going to insist they put in the hard hours working on the text of their talks. In this chapter, therefore, I'm going to discuss ways in which you can save time on research for your presentations.

Avoid perfectionism

For most talks, the essential desire of the audience is to gain a greater awareness of the topic and go away satisfied, preferably having enjoyed themselves in the process. None of that requires the speaker to become a world expert on the subject. However much it may go against the grain, you should not be aiming for perfection.

Graham Allcott, a productivity specialist, sets out the argument for doing 'just enough' expressively in his practical book *How to be a Knowledge Ninja*. He recommends that you treat your reading list as a restaurant menu:

"You might focus on a few key dishes, or you might try a sample menu where you try small portions of lots of things on offer, but trying to get through everything on the menu would just leave you feeling sick."

One element of avoiding perfectionism is not to reinvent the wheel.

If you are struggling to find the right words on a subject, remember that you are just a search away from discovering all kinds of penetrating quotations and comments from established experts. If you cannot improve on what they have said, why not reproduce it in your talk while acknowledging the source of the material? It is a principle I have tried to adhere to in this book.

Evaluating the research you need to do

The key elements in deciding what sort of research is required, and how much of it, are:

- The nature of the audience you will be speaking to.
- The objectives you have set for the session.
- How long you have to speak.

Once you have addressed these questions, you will be in a much better position to determine your research targets, to work out what kinds of research will be 'just enough' for this particular talk. By determining early on which areas of study are not crucial, you will have more capacity to address the areas that genuinely matter.

Don't set out on a fool's errands.

However tempting it might be to reveal hidden nuggets of obscure information about your topic, it won't help your talk if the audience find them irrelevant or unintelligible, or if they leave you insufficient time to cover the mainstream areas of the subject.

Make use of modern research aids

In a fascinating book called *Talent Is Overrated*, the journalist Geoff Colvin suggests a helpful approach for speakers. "In the age of YouTube," he writes, "it may be easy to find video of others giving similar types of presentations that one can then analyse and learn from, noting specifically how other speakers tried, well or badly, to convey the same key ideas that you want to put across."

Geoff Colvin suggests making notes of the various points in a presentation that you consider to be particularly well crafted, then, once you have forgotten most of it, using your notes to create a presentation making the same points. After that, you record yourself giving the speech and compare your recording with the original.

I took up the challenge and set myself the task of preparing talks on two topics I knew hardly anything about: buying garden tools and Mozart. I started by researching what material there was on YouTube about these subjects, searching for 'buying garden tools' and 'talks on Mozart' respectively. Astonishingly, I found about a dozen videos on buying garden tools alone. After that, I followed the method outlined by Geoff Colvin, and also consulted a couple of reference works. The result, though I say it myself, was two very decent talks, each prepared within a few hours.

Don't forget to sit and reflect

It can often be a better use of time to sit and think about a subject rather than rush off immediately to the reference material. Hold an interesting idea in your mind, and you may be surprised where it takes you.

Harold Ford, writing in a book called *The Art of Extempore Speaking*, put it this way:

> "Reflect upon your subject. Revolve it again and again in the mind. This will give birth to ideas. Ideas fertilise the mind and make it productive of original thought. Ideas will beget ideas. Thought will yield thought with astonishing fertility when we concentrate all the powers of our mind upon a subject."

Use your experience

Always make the most of your own previous exposure to the subject.

You may be speaking about a well-known topic, but no one else will have exactly your experience of it or your approach to it, your participation in both success and failure. Your own story of dealing with an issue will resonate with an audience more than researched accounts of what others have done. Your talks will gain polish and immediacy, and you will save time in the process.

One of the best commentaries on the power of using personal experience comes from Frank Cummins Lockwood and Clarence DeWitt Thorpe in their classic 1922 textbook *Public Speaking Today: A High School Manual*:

"Perhaps, in the long run, no subject matter will prove so useful as that which is drawn from experience. Here is a source of knowledge that is both fresh and true... What you have tried and tested for yourself you can rely upon. It is practical, that is, you have practised it yourself by going through it. Such facts as are gotten in this way almost always have weight and force. And when you refer to things in a speech that you have yourself seen, heard, tested, or had a hand in, you feel so certain of what you say that it convinces those who hear because of its solid reality...

Talk about things that interest you. If they truly interest you, they will interest other people. Anything that is sincere and human is good enough to talk about. You know about things that others do not know about. They seem very commonplace to you because they are so humble and familiar. But to others they may seem new and strange. At least these simple things well told, plus the warmth and flavour and colour of your personality, will interest and instruct others."

The experiences you talk about do not need to be momentous. The idea is to make the most of, to milk for all they are worth, events that have involved you. I gave a reasonably successful series of talks on tax investigations in the 1980s, and again in the 1990s, based on personal experience of just one major inquiry in each decade. I supplemented my knowledge by thorough reading, but it was my involvement in those two investigations that I concentrated on in my talks.

Seek out the experts

If you are relatively new to the subject you will be speaking about, consider talking early on to experienced people who are familiar with the topic.

In his involving hands-on book *The First 20 Hours: How to Learn Anything … Fast*, the business author Josh Kaufman writes: "Talking to people who have acquired the skill before you will help dispel myths and misconceptions before you invest your time and energy." For further rapid initial progress, Josh Kaufman suggests skimming through five books on the subject rather than examining one in depth – the fundamental idea being that by noticing the ideas, processes and techniques that come up in a variety of sources, you will have a much better notion of where to focus your attention.

Research critically

Always carry out your research in a critical, analytical spirit. Don't take anything that you read (including, of course, this book) at face value without asking some penetrating questions first. For example:

- Can you identify explicit or implied biases in the writer of the material?
- What was their motivation for writing in the first place, what's in it for them, and do they have a particular mission in mind?
- Are the arguments backed up by detailed evidence or academic studies?
- Do the supporting data come from credible sources?
- Is there anything in the material that is inconsistent or clearly illogical?

- Are there comments or pieces of information that appear misguided or just incorrect?

None of this is to suggest we should reject potential sources out of hand. Seneca the Younger, a Roman Stoic philosopher (and tutor to the emperor Nero), said we should never be ashamed of quoting from a bad author if a particular line or saying is good. Let's seek out strong material wherever it comes from.

Wikipedia

Wikipedia is a brilliant tool for obtaining an overview of a subject and for discovering links to original materials. It has been an invaluable help in the writing of this book. Its astonishingly broad coverage makes it endlessly useful. Because anyone can edit Wikipedia, it cannot be inherently reliable: but that's okay because it functions best as an outstandingly worthwhile first point of reference on the road to specialist sources.

Other tips

Malcolm Kushner and Rob Yeung offer a particularly cunning and helpful suggestion in their book *Public Speaking and Presentations For Dummies*. When doing library research, they suggest you go first to the children's section. A good children's book will cover the main points of your subject and do so in the most comprehensible way.

When it comes to the Internet, remember that you are not obliged to read all the information in front of you. If you press the Ctrl and F keys on your keyboard simultaneously while reviewing a website, you will bring up a search bar that allows you to look for specific words or terms. It can save you from wading through masses of irrelevant material, and it also works for Microsoft Office and many similar applications.

Research on the latest topical developments and news items on the subject you will be talking about is always worthwhile. Material of this kind appeals to almost any audience, so a Google news search can pay rich dividends.

Googling

Please do enjoy Googling. Other search engines are available, but for me Google is, quite simply, the most powerful research tool you can find. It's well worth spending the time to become skilled at carrying out Google searches.

At the most basic level, for example, if I search on Google for Ian Nichol, I get 419,000 search results, which is rather a lot to review. If, however, I use inverted commas and search for "Ian Nichol", it tells Google that I only want those precise words in that order, and I get a measly 5,980 results – much easier to work with.

I recommend doing a search on Google for 'how to use google search'. You will quickly learn about the latest techniques, including those that the Google support team recommend. The best guide I know in book format is *The Definitive Guide: Google Hidden Tools*, published in the MagBook series. Using these reference sources, I was impressed by how quickly my searching skills improved.

Conclusion

We saw in Chapter 11 that a successful speech can pass over only a very restricted amount of material – little more than a few core points. There comes a time when the more we research, the more we are likely to encounter diminishing, or indeed negative, returns as we no longer see the wood for the trees. I hope this chapter has given you some ideas for streamlining your research to save you time and also to ensure that you remain focused on the essential elements of your presentation.

Points to take from this chapter

- There's no need to seek perfection in your research: focus on the issues that matter.
- Use quotations and comments from authorities in the field.
- Look for videos of similar presentations.
- Give yourself thinking time to reflect on the subject.
- Make the most of your own previous experiences.
- If you can, talk to the experts.
- Do your research in a critical spirit.
- Take the time to develop your online searching skills.

Once you have done your research, you are in a position to start thinking about the construction and wording of your presentation. In the next chapter, I'm going to talk about the importance of the planning process which that involves.

CHAPTER 17

Plan what you are going to say

Introduction

Anyone who wants to give a successful talk should plan the structure and content of what they are going to say well in advance – and, within that overall aim, make sure they adapt the language they use appropriately for a listening audience. Because if they don't, horrors can follow.

In this chapter, we'll see some cringe-inducing demonstrations of the failure to plan one's words. Charles Dickens will then show us how to do it properly, and I'll give a detailed example by way of the preparation process I use myself. We will also learn how to adjust our speeches for audiences that, by their nature, cannot refer backwards or forwards in what we say.

The dangers of chancing it

Here is an excruciatingly embarrassing example of what can happen when you fail to plan what you are going to say. Kate Winslet is speaking off-the-cuff (or, as she puts it, on the cuff) at the start of her acceptance speech for winning Best Actress at the Golden Globe Awards in January 2009. She has beaten Anne Hathaway, Meryl Streep, Kristin Scott Thomas and Angelina Jolie to the prize:

> "Oh, oh, I'm so sorry (gasp) Anne (gasp), Meryl (gasp), Kristin, oh God, who's the other one? (Gasp) Angelina! I'm so… This is (gasp)… Okay. Now, forgive me. Gather. Is this really happening? Okay, um, I'm gonna try and do this on the cuff.
> Okay. Thank you so much. Oh, thank you so much. Oh, God. [To a member of the audience trying to help her out:] Oh, please wrap up? You have no idea how much I'm not wrapping up.
> Okay. Gather. Thank you to the Hollywood foreign press. This is absolutely extraordinary. I've had an amazing couple of years. I got to play these two remarkable women. And I want to thank my beautiful agents, Hilda and Dallas. I've known them since I was fifteen, and they really brought the script to me and helped me to hang on to it. My gosh. Oh. Okay, who comes next? (Gasp)…"

I'll spare you the rest: it didn't get any better, and I imagine you've got the point by now. But don't think that professional speakers like politicians, whom you might expect to have the gift of the gab, will necessarily be an improvement on this.

Bob Dole, the US Republican presidential candidate in 1996, had a loose style of speaking which, coupled with some unfortunate memory lapses, made his impromptu performances a walk on the wild side. We come upon him as he discusses the problems politicians face in keeping their public and private lives separate, referring to Benjamin Disraeli in the nineteenth century: "You read what Disraeli had to say," Mr

Dole commented. Then he paused for some time before saying: "I don't remember what he said. He said something." And then: "He's no longer with us."

I can offer no finer advertisement for having some speaking notes with you than the examples of Ms Winslet and Mr Dole.

The moral for would-be orators is clear: never, ever try to wing it when you could have prepared beforehand.

The Dickens masterclass

Charles Dickens is a shining example of someone who went to extraordinary lengths to prepare for his public performances. He limited his readings to comparatively few of his novels and tales, and from that source material he abridged or excluded large swathes of text. He happily rewrote his original work when he thought it would suit his dramatic purposes.

Here, in *Charles Dickens as a Reader*, his friend Charles Kent tells us how hard Dickens worked to prepare his material for the stage:

> "It was not by any means that, having written a story years previously, he had, in his new capacity as a reciter, merely to select two or three chapters from it, and read them off with an air of animation. Virtually, the fragmentary portions thus taken from his larger works were rewritten by him, with countless elisions and eliminations after having been selected. Reprinted in their new shape, each as *A Reading*, they were then touched and retouched by their author, pen in hand, until, at the end of a long succession of revisions, the pages came to be cobwebbed over with a wonderfully intricate network of blots and lines in the way of correction or of obliteration."

The readings that this method produced were less subtle than the books – rightly so, because a public platform is not the place for subtlety – but gained immediate and intense emotional impact. The result was a triumph for Dickens.

How I do my planning

Here is how I prepare my own text.

I draft a loose outline of the talk, with subject headings and bullet points for the key topics, that takes up no more than a couple of pages of A4 paper. This process also helps me with the blurb, the prospectus, for the talk. I do this work in chunks of about half an hour at a time because I seem to have better ideas if I operate in short sessions. This gives me the framework for the talk, the skeleton plan on which everything else will hang.

Then I start on the actual script. There is, of course, a huge choice in how you go about the preparation of the script, which we will discuss more thoroughly in Chapter 18. For example, you could write out a full text or a partial text, or you might employ PowerPoint slides, using the notes facility PowerPoint offers. When I am preparing the script, again I do it in chunks, this time working for up to sixty minutes at a time but no more, to avoid getting stale. In this process, I always need to remember that on the actual day of the performance I must be ready to go off-script and improvise where it feels right to do so.

I am not proposing this approach as a model for anyone else: indeed, the point is that each speaker should be prepared to spend the time it takes to develop his or her individual style.

Modify your approach for a listening audience

However you go about planning what you are going to say, please do remember that your script is going to be heard, not seen: you are preparing not for readers but for a listening audience.

In *On Giving a Talk,* a memorable radio performance of 1937, part of which I have abridged here, John Hilton talks about some of the consequences of this. He is discussing the process of giving a radio talk, but the essential principles apply to public speaking in general:

> "My notion is that to read as if you were talking you must first write as if you were talking. What you have on the paper in front of you must be talk-stuff, not book-stuff.
>
> It's queer how the mere sight of paper and the feel of a pencil set you thinking prose instead of talk. I don't know anything about others, but my way is to speak my sentences aloud as I write them. In fact, here's my rule, all pat: 'To write as you would talk you must talk while you write.'
>
> If you were outside my room when I'm writing a talk you'd hear muttering and mumbling and outright declamation from beginning to end. You'd say: 'There's somebody in there with a slate loose; he never stops talking to himself.' No, I wouldn't be talking to *myself*, but to you.
>
> With a book or a paper your eye can look ahead to see what's coming. It can look back to clear something up. In my belief it's doing that all the time without our knowing it. Over the air you can't listen ahead and you can't listen back. You can try to recall, of course, while still listening, what was said an instant before, but you can't *refresh* your memory. So many a good prose sentence just won't do as a radio sentence.
>
> Take this one. It's the first few lines of a letter in *The Listener*. It's by an eminent author and critic:

'SIR, Your note on the increasing emoluments which modern developments bring to the author is merely quantitative and might lead to unfounded complacency if not qualified by a consideration of other aspects of the question.'

Now, in print that may be all right. I think myself it's not very good even as prose; but it'll *do*. Your eye can travel backward and forward over it and make sense of it. Over the air it's completely unintelligible. To say over the air what he's saying in print you'd have to pull your thought to pieces and put it together again in a totally different way, and probably in quite other words. You'd have to build it up in stages. Like this, perhaps: 'About authors and what they earn. You, sir, had a note. It said they did quite well nowadays. That's only true for some…' And so on.

Of this I'm quite sure; that if in writing a talk you try to make your text at the same time good for talk and good for print, you'll fail in both. Since the talk comes first, I think one should write the talk, the talk only, and let the question of after-printing go hang."

Conclusion

It is easy to spend hours and hours on the research for a talk, and then take almost no time in planning what you are actually going to say in your presentation – the presentation which will be the only tangible expression of that research. Please don't fall into this trap, because it can make a mockery of all your hard work.

Points to take from this chapter

- Plan the structure and content of your talk well in advance.

- Take time to develop your own preparation style.
- You must write your material as though you were talking to people.
- The audience can't listen ahead or listen back while you are speaking.
- Be prepared to restructure your words drastically for a listening audience.

In the next chapter, we are going to continue our review of the preparation process by looking at the best ways of using speaking aids such as notes, slides or a script. It's a vital area because these are the supports that, if used correctly, will give us the confidence and the competence to deliver a great speech.

Notes

If you feel you must, you can see Kate Winslet's acceptance speech at https://www.youtube.com/watch?v=aS4OjocfPE4.

CHAPTER 18

Use the right speaking aids

Introduction

Our next area to review is a crucial one, not least because many of the textbooks on public speaking take an unhelpfully prescriptive approach to it. The route I recommend – do what works for you – may seem self-evident, but you'll find it discussed in surprisingly few writings on the subject.

I'm going to be reviewing the use of speaking aids – notes, slides and so on – to support our presentations. A reliable speaking aid will help us to a smooth and confident delivery of the right words in the right order.

I'll be recommending a process of experimentation to discover the approach that suits you best. I will then explain the value of having quite comprehensive notes at the start of your speaking career. I'll look at two detailed examples – my own and that of the academic AC Benson – of how an individual speaker can make a sensible choice of speaking aids, and I'll also reveal the secrets of the obscure but valuable art of reading out a speech successfully.

A cornucopia of speaking aids

By 'speaking aids' in this chapter, I am talking in the limited sense of whatever you use to remind your brain what you should say when you stand up to speak.

Your speaking aids could, therefore, be any of the following (the list is far from exhaustive):

- Brief mental planning for an impromptu delivery.
- Written notes, in varying degrees of detail.
- Slides to accompany your talk.
- Any of the various sorts of autocue.
- A detailed script.
- Memorisation.

A whole variety of technology – laptops, tablets, headsets, apps and so on – is available to help you in the process. You might be thinking, for example, about joining the increasing number of speakers who present their talk from an iPad or other handheld device.

The approach I recommend

For me, the key elements of success in a talk are the quality of the material and the confidence the speaker feels in delivering the speech. Everything else pales in comparison. It follows that you should use whichever speaking aid you feel most comfortable with, the one that will give you the most self-assurance when you perform in public.

You need to judge what you think might suit your personality and then go out and try it. Many people find that it takes a degree of experimentation to establish what works most advantageously for them.

I certainly needed a lengthy process of trial and error to discover the approach that suited me best. It is unhelpful to suggest that any particular style – be it memorisation, notes, speaking to an autocue, or anything else – is better in principle than some other style. It all depends on the individual and the occasion. In the words attributed to Henry Ford, "Whether you believe you can do a thing or not, you are right." The form of speaking aid that gives you the most self-belief is the one that will work for you.

You might prepare a script for your presentation, or detailed notes, or less detailed notes, or simply, though not without difficulty, work it all out in advance in your mind alone. Remember that, whichever approach you use, you must continuously engage with the audience and maintain eye contact with them, and not get lost in your notes or other speaking aids. In all circumstances, you will need to be familiar with your material before you ever get up to speak. We will look at methods of familiarisation later in this chapter.

Whatever form of speaking aid you use, do remember that the finished product will be a spoken talk, not an essay on paper.

John Hilton gives some helpful advice on this in *On Giving a Talk*:

> "In speech we say, 'It's', not 'It is'. So I write 'It apostrophe s', and not 'It is' on the paper. I know if I wrote 'It is' I should say 'It is'. The lips utter what the eye sees. So, through every text, apostrophes in the writing wherever there's elision in actual speech; underlinings if you want them; dots or spaces where pauses should be. Make what the eye sees look like what the lips are to utter."

The value of fuller notes

I'm going to be focusing on situations where speakers use more detailed notes or a script, because they get less attention in most modern reference works. I would certainly recommend that, while you are going through the process of establishing what works best for you, you err on the side of having reasonably thorough notes. That way, you will have far better reserves for those moments when your mind goes blank.

There is a thoughtful comment on this point by Spencer Leigh Hughes in *The Art of Public Speaking*:

> "It often happens that a man will speak successfully because he has notes, though he may never look at them... The consciousness that they are there gives him confidence. He knows he has something that will keep him afloat in case of need. And he is never more likely to need them than if he is very successful at the outset... Applause is sweet – it may be intoxicating – but the wise speaker utilises the opportunity by taking a glance at his notes, and making quite sure of his next point."

I saw the comedian Jimmy Carr give an interesting example of this approach at a tribute show for the comic writer and performer Peter Cook in 2002. It was at a point in Carr's career when he was breaking through to national celebrity. He had his material with him on a clipboard, which undoubtedly gave him extra confidence, and he read from it at times rather like a university don. It suited his stage persona as a smooth-talking, Oxbridge-educated smart alec. As I understand it, he subsequently continued using the clipboard on occasions when he was trying out new material. This 'safety first' approach goes back at least as far as Charles Dickens, who always had with him on his lectern marked copies of the books from which he took his public readings, long after he knew the words by heart.

How I do it myself

I have spoken impromptu, I have spoken from brief notes, I have spoken from very full notes, and I have spoken from a complete script, with or without additional ad-libs that come to me on the spur of the moment.

What has become apparent through feedback over many years is that audiences like me best when I speak from a fully prepared script – in other words, I read out my speech – but go off the beaten track and ad-lib when the time feels right. The full, detailed script works best for me because it gives me the confidence to go off on a tangent and improvise successfully when it's appropriate to do so. The memorisation route simply doesn't work for me, because I have a truly terrible memory.

The circumstances in which one speaks are, of course, a major influence. These days my speaking is mostly done after dinner, where you haven't got much time and every word counts, so that working from a precise script seems very fitting. A suggestion from Mitch Murray suits me just fine:

> "Instead of sitting up night after night, attempting to learn fourteen hundred crucial words, use just a fraction of that time and effort to develop the knack of presenting your speech in a natural and relaxed manner."

I save time trying to memorise my script by not bothering to do it in the first place.

After nearly fifty years of experimentation, I now use six-inch by four-inch (fifteen- by ten-centimetre, for younger readers) plain white record cards when I'm speaking. Because they are stiff and compact, they are not liable to wave around in the breeze while I am in action. They are also small enough for me to be able to make all the hand gestures I desire while still holding them. Beware of using larger, flimsy pieces of paper for your notes; if your hands are shaking even slightly on account of nerves, the movements of the sheets may make your anxiety obvious to the audience. In any event, the size of the paper and its wobbliness serve as distractions from your talk.

I number each card, so that if I do have an accident and drop them – which, touch wood, has not yet happened to me – I can at least get them back in order quickly. I don't recommend going further and securing your note pages together by way of staples or paperclips; it may be a good idea in theory, but in practice the effect is just too awkward and clumsy.

I put the text on one side of the card only: using both sides is a recipe for getting confused and losing one's place. Since I cannot read my writing, it is an easy decision to type out my script for the cards. The font that I seem most comfortable with is Arial in size 14: I find it difficult to refer readily to material in a smaller font size. Many experts recommend having a speech typed double-spaced between lines, but I don't seem to need that. What I find works well is to use line breaks to denote pauses: in other words, I will break off the text and start again on the next line to mark a point where I should pause for effect, even if it is in the middle of a sentence. (You can see an exaggerated example of this in the way I have set out Queen Elizabeth I's speech later in this chapter.) It all helps the performance to sound truly conversational.

I put key passages **in bold** or <u>with underlining</u> for emphasis, so that the most significant words will immediately catch my eye. Alternatively, or in addition, you could use, say, a yellow highlighter; it is entirely a matter of choice. If it suits you, you may want to go even further in your preparation. For example, some speakers use subheadings in their notes. They won't read them out as part of their talk, but the subheadings help them to structure their delivery in their minds. Some use ellipses (such as *use... ellipses* or even *ellip... ses*) to note pauses or words that should be broken up for effect. Others put instructions or stage directions for themselves like *wait for applause* or *speed up here* in the margins. Charles Dickens used this particular technique, so you will be in distinguished company if you adopt it.

What I have described here, simply as an illustration, is the approach that gets results for me. Your challenge is not to copy my style, or that of any other speaker, but to discover what works best for you by a process of gentle experimentation over time.

Becoming familiar with your material

Regardless of whether or not you memorise your script, it's vital to become as comfortable and familiar with your material as you can before the big day.

I have set out below a list of tips which actors employ when they are learning their lines. They are as helpful for becoming familiar with your text as they are for memorising it. Of course, not everyone learns in the same way, so try things out to see what works for you.

- We know that talking aloud helps you become acquainted with the material more successfully than a simple perusal of the text. Read the words out loud, clearly and quite slowly, to become more familiar with them. This way you are forcing your brain to recognise and digest the words by both speaking and hearing them. Be prepared for the strange looks you will get if you do this on public transport: a muted muttering under your breath may then be more advisable.

- When you are learning information, it is more efficient to try to retrieve it from your brain than just to go over it again. Test yourself on whether you know it rather than simply rereading it. It can be beneficial to do this with a friend or loved one helping you, but do it in moderation, in case they cease to be your friend or loved one.
- The basic procedure of writing the material down again can often help fix it in the mind.
- Many people find the use of colour for emphasis is an aid to retention, so see whether those coloured pens and highlighters work for you.
- Others find it helps to move around as they practise giving voice to their material. The idea is that the body, as well as the mind, becomes familiar with the text.
- During sleep, your brain, at a subconscious level, processes what has gone on during your waking hours. Not surprisingly, the last part of the day gets particular attention. Reviewing your script by reading the text out loud in the final fifteen to thirty minutes before you go to bed can be very effective. Studying it again early the following morning then helps to consolidate the process.
- If you do decide to memorise your material, do it with extraordinary thoroughness. Kelly Stoetzel, the director of content at TED, has said that she tells speakers who plan to memorise their talks: "You have to go so far that you can walk backwards while delivering it at double speed, or on one foot with the TV blaring. Because then, when you give it, you can feel really present, and do it at your own speed."

To state the obvious, the more you practise, the easier it all becomes.

In defence of reading from a script

Imagine that someone who is going in for public speaking for the first time is told not only to prepare a great talk but also to memorise it. The pressure imposed upon them is enormous. To perform well in such circumstances is well-nigh impossible. It is the public speaking equivalent of being asked to climb Everest solo without oxygen after a week's mountaineering lessons. It is no wonder that so many novice speakers are put off for life because of the stress levels under which they have been encouraged to function.

There is a modern fixation with memorising a speech, perhaps influenced by the success of the TED talks where speakers often do go down the memorisation route. The TED talks are excellent, but to my mind that's because of the careful choice of speakers and the degree of preparation they go through, not because the speakers learn their words. (And, even then, remember that the TED videos you see online have been edited to leave out the embarrassing parts: if the speaker fluffs their lines or indeed loses the plot entirely, don't expect to see that bit.)

Away from TED, sensible people ignore the trend unless they have first-class memories. Bill Clinton, for example, is a master of using the autocue. Abraham Lincoln read out his oratorical masterpiece, the Gettysburg Address, from a piece of paper, even though it was under 300 words long. The tradition of reading from a script is well established.

Yet the prevailing feeling today is almost as though there's something nasty and immoral about speaking from notes or a text, as though it is cheating. Nonsense: it's simply a useful element of the tools of the trade (and if people want to regard them as tricks rather than tools, it won't worry me).

The fundamental point is that it works in practice.

In a brilliant book about succeeding in stressful situations called *Choke: The Secret to Performing under Pressure,* the psychologist Sian Beilock notes the benefit of what she calls outsourcing your cognitive load, in this case by writing at least some things down rather than trying to keep everything in your mind. "As a result," she says, "you may be less likely to mix up information or forget important details of what you are doing."

The best validation of all for reading from a script must surely be Barack Obama, who I think is unparalleled in modern times as an orator. In the formative years of his speaking career, the period that took him from fledgling political player to US president, Obama relied very heavily on his use of the autocue, the device that displayed the visual text of his speeches. He used it to build his confidence in the knowledge that, if he faltered in his speech, the autocue would immediately come to his aid. It was his crutch and salvation. His autocue rapidly developed a media personality of its own until it came to be known as TOTUS, or Teleprompter of the United States: you don't often find an autocue device developing a cult following. It gave Obama the confidence to produce some of the finest speeches of the early twenty-first century.

The important point here is that it is irrelevant whether on an objective analysis Obama needed the autocue. My guess is that he knew his material so well that he could have dispensed with it altogether. But that doesn't matter. The autocue gave him confidence, and in public speaking confidence, when allied with preparation, is the absolute key to success.

How to read out a speech

I can't deny that there are real issues to be addressed before a speech can be read out successfully. There is a great danger that the reader will proceed much too fast, or give insufficient thought to what he or she is saying.

A good example was Jeremy Corbyn's speech as new leader to the Labour Party Conference in 2015, where he appeared to read out a stage direction from his speech writer, telling the puzzled audience: "Strong delivery here." Speakers can overcome these objections by gaining full familiarity with the script and by effective eye contact to ensure that the audience is keeping up with them. A century ago James A Winans, professor of public speaking at Cornell University, set out what the orator needed to do. "He should speak very slowly," he wrote, "and especially should pause deliberately while getting each new statement in mind, and then deliver it as directly as possible to his hearers."

That's all very well, but how can it actually be achieved?

Quite easily, as it happens. There is a highly effective technique for looking as though you are speaking naturally, when you are in fact reading from a text. Few people seem to know about it, and even fewer use it: so, it gives a unique opportunity for you to shine out among the speaking community. Quite simply, when you move your head down to refer to your notes or script, stop talking. Only start talking again when your head comes back up. The same principle applies if you turn your head towards a screen you are using for your presentation.

This technique was promoted by the work of James C Humes, a US author and former presidential speechwriter (and, incidentally, the man credited with joint authorship of the text on the Apollo 11 plaque on the surface of the moon). He calls it the 'See–Stop–Say' technique – "Look down and *see* the words. Bring your head up and *stop* for a second. Then *say* the line in your own words." It is a technique that generations of great orators have used: not least Winston Churchill, Franklin D Roosevelt and Ronald Reagan. The key principle is: "Never, never, never let words come out of your mouth when your eyes are looking down." Otherwise, you lose contact with your audience.

The pause after bringing your head back up, once you have read the words, is to ensure you don't start speaking again while your head is still moving up. It is vital to be looking at the audience whenever you are talking to them, and the pause is an essential element of that. The technique takes a while to perfect, mainly because we have an irrational mental block about periods of silence in our speech. To begin with, the length of the pause seems excruciating to the speaker. In fact, it is hardly noticed at a conscious level, if at all, by the listeners. It gives the speech a highly appropriate communicative style, allowing the audience to take in fully what the speaker has just said and to get ready for what is coming next.

The technique I adopt when I read from a script could not, therefore, be more elementary:

- Look down.
- Scan the material.
- Look up at the audience and pause.
- Speak one thought.
- Repeat the whole process as often as it takes.

It's all very straightforward, with the practical side effect that the pauses divide the speech into chunks or segments to capture an authoritative conversational tone. This echoes John Hilton's approach, again set out in *On Giving a Talk*. "My belief," he says, "is that listeners hear speech, not in a sequence of words – one after the other – but in chunks; and what I try to do, though I may seldom succeed in my good intentions, is… to throw out my words in bunches… like that… and then pause long enough for the listener to take that bunch in." That, incidentally, is the reason why you may see this style of speaking also referred to as 'chunking'. An astonishingly good example of the technique was given by Malala Yousafzai, the young Pakistani humanitarian and activist for female education, speaking at the United Nations on her sixteenth birthday in 2013.

A good way of practising is to try out the approach for yourself on this extract from the famous speech of Queen Elizabeth I in 1588 to the troops at Tilbury, who had gathered to defend their country against an invasion by Spain:

> "I know I have the body [pause]
> but of a weak and feeble woman; [pause]
> but I have the heart and stomach of a king, [pause]
> and of a king of England too, [pause]
> and think foul scorn that Parma or Spain, [pause]
> or any prince of Europe, [pause]
> should dare to invade the borders of my realm."

For me, the massive value of reading out a speech in this way has been highlighted by the number of times audience members have said to me after a completely scripted talk, "How do you manage to improvise so much all the time?"

If you still don't believe me, I highly recommend videoing yourself before using the method, and later comparing that video with what you look like after a couple of weeks of practice. You should be impressed by the improvement.

I can recommend a further sleight of hand. Mitch Murray gives a great additional tip for leaving people unaware that you are reading your speech verbatim. Start with a couple of announcements, he suggests – something that would seem quite natural to the audience to be read from a script – and then go straight into your speech. They won't notice that you are still reading word for word. He gives an example: "'Ladies and gentlemen, before I start, I've been asked to make the following announcements... [Announcements follow, then you move straight into the speech proper.]'" Remember that it remains crucial for you to look up frequently and scan the audience as you continue your address.

A case study: AC Benson

Here are some detailed excerpts from *The art of lecturing* by AC Benson. To me, they represent a valuable example of the thought processes we should each work through in establishing the speaking aids that suit us best:

> "I remember in my undergraduate days that there was a young don in my college who was an excellent preacher, and has since become a famous one. He held a strong view that clergymen ought, at all events in the earlier stages of their ministry, to write their sermons. He held that it was easy to become fluent, but that the temptation, if fluency was once attained, of trusting to the inspiration of the moment became so strong that men practically gave up working out their sermons at all. He said to me that he always took a manuscript into the pulpit, but that he often did not keep to it, if a more effective method of treatment came into his head.
>
> ... Ruskin, whom I heard lecture thrice, used a mixed method. He used to begin by reading an elaborately written paragraph or two, and then, as he gained confidence, he would desert his manuscript altogether, talk in the most frankly conversational way, and even, as happened in his

lectures on birds, imitate the gait and flight of crows and swallows, as far as a wingless biped could. On the other hand, I have heard Mr Gladstone deliver a long lecture on a Homeric subject, full of curious learning, without a single note, and employing all the time a sustained felicity of phrase and a magnificent accompaniment of oratorical gesture. But in my own very humble sphere the only chance for me to deliver a lecture worth hearing, with any order or structure, any ornament of humour or rhetoric, is to write the whole discourse, and then 'golly' it out with what emphasis and vehemence I can muster. It depends to a great extent upon the pace at which the mind works. I have personally had a good deal of practice in writing and very little in public speaking; and though I can write grammatical English, and even turn a phrase or two on paper with rapidity, I cannot do it with any certainty on the public platform. My mind keeps pace with the written word, but lags behind the spoken word. … If one is conscious, as I am, that I cannot carry the structure clearly in the head, or be sure of the details; if one cannot expatiate easily and lightly, if one cannot be sure of saying exactly what one means, then the only resource is to fall back on a written manuscript. I have heard lecturers say that the sight of the old and battered bundle of papers becomes a kind of horror. I do not personally feel that; the more often I deliver a lecture, the more effective it becomes: one has made obscure passages clearer by interlineations; one has erased unemphatic paragraphs; one brings out the points better, and the whole becomes a much more living thing with each delivery.

The one point I have learned by practice is the absolute necessity of clear enunciation. I am always careful to observe at the beginning of the lecture whether the most distant persons in the audience are exhibiting signs of impatience or inattention. It is very easy to see in the faces and gestures of the audience whether they can hear or not; if they cannot, I go slower, and am careful not to drop my voice at the ends of sentences, a frequent cause of inaudibility.

… [A] well-known preacher said once in my presence that he always took a manuscript into the pulpit, though he seldom if ever used it, because thirty years ago, preaching without notes, he forgot not only the thread of his discourse, but his text and subject, and indeed was not sure for a moment who or where he was – an incident which, it may be added, passed wholly unnoticed by his audience.

The main point, then, is that a lecturer should form a perfectly definite theory and method of his art, and discover by preference and practice how he does his work best."

Conclusion

The efficient use of speaking aids is crucial to every speaker. Very often it will mean the difference between a highly successful talk and a lamentable failure.

The choice of aids has to be a personal one: take your time to get it right, to ensure you do what works for you. I believe that each speaker will benefit tremendously from going through a detailed examination, as AC Benson did and as I have done, to determine the right approach for them as an individual.

Points to take from this chapter

- To maximise your self-confidence, use the speaking aid that makes you feel most comfortable.
- Experiment to find out what works best for you.

- No class of speaking aid is inherently preferable to any other.
- Whatever approach you take, you need to maintain eye contact with the audience at all times.
- When you begin as a speaker, err on the side of having fuller notes.
- It's vital to become familiar with your material before you speak.
- There's nothing wrong with reading from a script if you use the right technique.
- The Humes 'See–Stop–Say' approach ensures you are looking at the audience whenever you speak to them.

In this chapter, we have been reviewing the use of speaking aids in general. Next, we will move on to look at perhaps the most controversial issue in modern public speaking: the use of one specific aid – slides, and in particular PowerPoint slides. We will acknowledge the criticisms of PowerPoint, but we'll also see that simple, pictorial PowerPoint slides can be a great addition to a talk.

Notes

Mitch Murray's suggestions come from *Mitch Murray's One-liners for Business: And How to Use Them in Your Speech.* The quotation from Kelly Stoetzel is from an excellent article, *18 minutes to change the world,* by the novelist and travel writer Samantha Weinberg in the January/February 2016 edition of *Intelligent Life* magazine. James A Winans was writing in his magisterial tome of 1915, *Public Speaking – Principles and Practice.* James C Humes describes fully his technique for reading from a text in his great book *Speak Like Churchill, Stand Like Lincoln.* Malala Yousafzai's speech at the United Nations can be seen at https://www.youtube.com/watch?v=3rNhZu3ttIU.

CHAPTER 19

Avoid death by PowerPoint

Introduction

We move on to a topical and, as I indicated at the end of Chapter 18, contentious subject.

As I was writing this chapter, there were no fewer than five books on public speaking listed for sale on Amazon with the phrase *Death by PowerPoint* not merely discussed in the text, but even included in the title.

In the book *The Stupidity Paradox: The Power and Pitfalls of Functional Stupidity at Work* by Mats Alvesson and André Spicer, the use of PowerPoint slides is effectively treated as a synonym for stupidity in the workplace.

In this chapter, then, I want to examine why the world's most popular slide presentation program attracts such negative publicity.

The answer goes to the very root of what we are trying to achieve when we talk publicly. We will see that slides can normally only be subsidiary to our role as speaker. Their incidental value can, indeed, be highly potent – as Bill Gates will show us – in adding vibrant pictorial effect to what we have to say. Even so, we will end on a cautionary note when the Columbia space shuttle disaster gives us a grim warning of what can happen when slides are inadvertently used to dumb down a complicated argument.

The limitations of a slide presentation

With a possible exception for teachers and lecturers, speaking in public should mean passing over to the audience a small number of key points to take away and use, while we influence and perhaps entertain them in the process. We can most naturally achieve those aims by way of the words we use to address the audience.

It is, therefore, a logical starting position to say that, for much public speaking, slides are likely to be secondary, if not superfluous, to our primary purpose.

I find it helps to ask a tough question whenever I am thinking of using a PowerPoint template: do I want my audience to listen to me or to read my written slides? As we saw in Chapter 11 when we talked about keeping things simple and forceful, they cannot do both effectively at the same time. Consequently, if the answer is 'to read the slides', then I should think again whether public speaking is the right medium to get my message across.

The Gettysburg lesson

The most withering (and the funniest) exposition of the limitations of PowerPoint comes from Edward R Tufte, a noted writer on information design and professor emeritus of political science, statistics and computer science at Yale University. His work incorporates a miraculous transformation, created by the computer scientist Peter Norvig, of Abraham Lincoln's Gettysburg Address into a PowerPoint presentation.

The slide show brilliantly converts Lincoln's poetic wording of 'four score and seven years ago' into a graph showing '−87 years'. If you are like me, you may find that the comic horror of the experience will deter you from using PowerPoint slides again for some weeks afterwards. In six delicious slides, we learn the key lesson of PowerPoint. When used sensibly in the right context, it can be an active support for a talk. But if the context is not right, or the use is not sensible, disaster can follow. Literally so, as we shall see.

Use pictures for your slides

The most important principle of slide design is that people tend to remember images – photographs, paintings, drawings, cartoons and the like – better than they remember words alone. This is the picture superiority effect, the concept that we learn better by viewing images than by seeing their equivalents or counterparts in word form. Indeed, the research shows that, in human memory recall, pictures dramatically outperform text.

It follows that in presentations we do not want to encounter slides full of words. By definition, they cannot offer the picture superiority effect. Beyond that, research has made it clear that, if I am talking and at the same time using slides that are full of words, the audience is likely to lose the plot in trying to shift between the two information sources. Consequently, there is a great reduction in the effectiveness of the talk. When the audience is torn between you and your slides, they end up missing out on both.

The obvious consequence for public speaking is that, if you are using slides to accompany your presentation, your message will be better understood if:

- The slides incorporate relevant pictures as well as words or, even better, in place of words.
- You limit the words you do use on the slides to crucial material and nothing else.

The best slide displays take advantage of the fact that human brains excel at handling visual information, while the verbal side of things can be dealt with perfectly adequately by the speaker just, well, speaking.

Someone who recognises this point brilliantly, and who understands that this approach can work as well for complex technical issues as for lighter topics, is Bill Gates, the philanthropist and former chairman of Microsoft. Two of his finest presentations are his 2009 TED talk on *Mosquitoes, malaria and education* (TED spells it mosquitos, but we know better), which we will be discussing in Chapter 30, and his 2010 TED talk on global warming, *Innovating to zero.*

Bill Gates keeps his slides simple and pictorial. He avoids the mistake of putting too much information on each slide, and he uses photographs rather than graphs or charts wherever he can. He realises, for example, that a close-up image of a man's arm covered with mosquitoes will tell the audience more than any number of words on a slide. In my own career, I worked with the tax expert John Whiting who, despite the extreme technical content of his subject, used short, simple, funny slides in picture format to great effect.

When you are preparing pictorial slides, please don't clutter them with detail: big, clear and straightforward images, with consistency in slide design, usually work best. Use bright colours and sharp contrasts. Your computer and projector systems, if they are anything like mine, will conspire to drain your colours and eliminate your contrasts, so make sure you use slides that are bright and sharp in the first place.

Tips for word-based slides

When you feel you must use words on slides, these guidelines can be helpful:

- Audiences would like to be able to read the slides, and even better to do so without straining. The 7 x 7 rule is useful: the maximum number of lines of text on a slide should be seven, and so should the number of words on a line. More stringent commentators would limit you to 6 x 6, but personally I won't complain provided you stick to less than fifty words of text in total. Even then, remember that the words on the slide have to add something fresh to your presentation.
- For your slides to be legible, you need a large font size. If, say, you are using Arial, I suggest an absolute minimum of 24pt for text and 32pt for headings.
- The need for freshness applies to a slide overall just as it does to the individual words. A slide is worthless if it does not add anything to your talk. In that situation, you get what is known as a PowerPointless presentation. If a slide just duplicates what you are saying to the audience, it lacks meaning and there is no point in using it.
- Use a font that is straightforward, clear and elegant. Arial and Helvetica are both safe choices. I mostly start with Arial, think about using more exciting stuff, and then use Arial after all. Fonts like Comic Sans MS that are full of personality are, I find, best used for things like Christmas newsletters. I do indeed use Comic Sans MS for my Christmas newsletters and, to be honest, no one seems to like

it, but that probably says more about my newsletters than my choice of font.

- Avoid any excess detail, leave lots of white space, and keep things simple.

- Use clear titles for your slides, so the audience doesn't have to search for their meaning. 'Growth in profit 2015–18' tells you what is coming up; 'Slide No 1' doesn't.

- Once you have decided that a slide has sufficient intrinsic value to be worth showing to the audience, for heaven's sake show it to them long enough for them to comprehend it properly. I will walk out of your presentation if you show me slides where I am never given the time to digest the material below the second line.

- Switch off the screen lighting when no slide is showing. I will not thank you for dazzling me with white light on a blank screen.

- Use a very limited number of good slides. I would hope never to see more than twenty slides in a presentation lasting an hour or less. I distinctly remember attending a talk where the first slide had the helpful numbering '1 of 94'. I was out of the room well before slide '2 of 94' appeared. Showing how to do it properly, in 2010, Bill Gates carried out a speaking tour of US colleges to encourage more people to tackle 'the world's biggest challenges'. His PowerPoint presentation consisted of just one brilliant slide, which showed the decline in death rates for children aged under five in the previous fifty years.

- Restrict your slides to the information your audience needs to understand the essential substance of the topic, not the information you would love them to have. That way you will make your slides much less wordy.

- Know that, if I am in the audience and you say, "I don't think you can read this slide, but what it says is…", your audience is about to become smaller.
- Don't let the presence of PowerPoint stop you telling stories: storytelling is a fundamental component of successful presentations. Stories do not transfer well to wordy PowerPoint slides. You should still tell the story, but don't accompany it with word-based slides.
- Don't read your slides out. The audience can do that for themselves if they want to. Talk around them or analyse what's on them, but don't reproduce them word for word in your speech.
- Focus on the audience, not the slides.

Be cautious of using slides to plan your presentation

For the initial planning of your talk, I recommend an old-fashioned brainstorming session with pen and paper. Slides come as a later add-on. If you create a presentation by way of PowerPoint slides from the outset, you may well struggle to identify your key theme or your key points. You may also sacrifice logical flow and produce slides that are far too detailed. Slides can be a useful supplement, but they should not be the basis for the talk.

Don't allow PowerPoint to dumb down your argument

In this chapter, I have recommended using simple slides. However, that should not lead you to oversimplify complex topics in your talk.

I once specialised in advising firms of management consultants on their finances. Management consultants are the people who borrow your watch and then charge you to tell you what the time is. I got to know one particular company's style of working rather too well. The centrepiece of their services to businesses was a slide-based final presentation, using less than half an hour to sum up the findings of many weeks' research. This was in the 1980s, before the advent of PowerPoint – yes, there was an age before PowerPoint – but they prepared their slides in a way with which today's PowerPoint audience would feel very much at home.

This approach created a severe difficulty that we did not properly appreciate at the time. Quite simply, it reduced a multiplicity of complicated and interrelated issues to single points on a slide, lacking any nuance or depth. It was easy to obtain general agreement to that simple slide because, though it was shallow and naïve, there was nothing actively incorrect on it. The result was that inadequate or wrongly focused action points were agreed, based on the limited picture given by the slides. If the business went wrong as a consequence, you could be sure that the management consultants weren't going to be the ones to suffer. They would be invited back a couple of years later to have another go at sorting things out.

It is scary to think that slide shows have the power to make intelligent brains turn to mush when making business decisions. I had hoped things were improving, but *The Stupidity Paradox* is a cautionary and convincing warning that they are not.

This facile approach can occasionally have tragic consequences, as Edward Tufte notes. In February 2003, the Space Shuttle Columbia disintegrated as it re-entered Earth's atmosphere, killing all seven crew members. While the craft was still orbiting the Earth, NASA engineers had used a PowerPoint presentation to summarise their investigation into whether a piece of foam that struck the shuttle's wing during launch had caused serious damage.

Edward Tufte carries out a brilliant analysis of the key slide in the presentation. Most notably, the foam was hundreds of times larger than anything the scientists had tested before (or, as the slide rather inscrutably put it, 'Volume of ramp is 1920 cu in vs 3 cu in for test'), but this was demoted to the last point on the slide and effectively reduced to insignificance.

The independent board that investigated the Columbia disaster wrote that "it is easy to understand how a senior manager might read this PowerPoint slide and not realise that it addresses a life-threatening situation." The board also said that: "During its investigation, the board was surprised to receive similar presentation slides from NASA officials in place of technical reports. The Board views the endemic use of PowerPoint briefing slides instead of technical papers as an illustration of the problematic methods of technical communication at NASA."

The lesson is still to be learned.

In the US campaigns in Iraq and Afghanistan, the overuse and misuse of PowerPoint became a standing, if grim, joke with military leaders. One general commented: "It's dangerous because it can create the illusion of understanding and the illusion of control. Some problems in the world are not bullet-isable." One amazing slide in particular turned military strategy in Afghanistan into something more like a bowl of spaghetti, and led General Stanley McChrystal, the leader of American and NATO forces in Afghanistan, to comment: "When we understand that slide, we'll have won the war."

In my view, none of this is the fault of the PowerPoint program: it is the fault of people using PowerPoint sloppily, in the wrong place at the wrong time for the wrong reasons.

Quite simply, the complexity of the Columbia situation was such that a detailed technical paper was called for, not a simplified slide. If you are fighting a war, go for formal written orders in preference to a PowerPoint display. If you are dealing with complex or difficult underlying topics that you need the audience to understand, give them a written paper or a detailed handout to support your arguments.

The workplace psychologist Tony Buon would have us avoid corporate-style PowerPoint templates in general, and in particular would ban PowerPoint from any meeting or presentation involving statistical, technical or complex ideas. I wouldn't go that far, but his basic point is exactly right; before using PowerPoint, we should do a proper analysis to ensure that its value will outweigh its disadvantages.

Conclusion

I am not the first person to notice that you rarely see people on the edge of their seats at a PowerPoint presentation. What is vital is that the speaker's personality shine through to the audience, and that is hard to achieve if you allow yourself to become the oral expression of your slides. They can be a useful support for your performance, but don't let them become your crutch or Zimmer frame. You must dominate the slides and not vice versa: the audience's attention must focus on you, the speaker, and not on your PowerPoint display.

Points to take from this chapter

- Slides can only be secondary to your main purpose as a speaker.
- Use pictures for your slides, because people learn better by seeing images rather than words on a screen.
- Beware of dividing audience attention between you and your slides: they end up losing out on both.

- Limit the words you use on your slides to essential matters only.
- Don't allow simple slides to oversimplify complex topics.

That is quite enough for the moment on slides, a subsidiary aspect of speechmaking. In the next chapter, we are going to progress to something that is absolutely fundamental – the words we utter. We will review how the use of plain, clear, straightforward language can contribute massively to a compelling talk.

Notes

Edward R Tufte exposes the limitations of PowerPoint in a booklet called *The Cognitive Style of PowerPoint: Pitching Out Corrupts Within*, Graphics Press, 2006. You can see the conversion of the Gettysburg Address into a PowerPoint presentation at http://www.norvig.com/Gettysburg/. The recommended Bill Gates TED talks can be found at https://www.ted.com/talks/bill_gates_unplugged and https://www.ted.com/talks/bill_gates. The astonishing PowerPoint slide on the American strategy in Afghanistan, with an accompanying discussion, can be seen at http://www.dailymail.co.uk/news/article-1269463/Afghanistan-PowerPoint-slide-Generals-left-baffled-PowerPoint-slide.html. Tony Buon's views are set out in his thought-provoking book *Communication Genius: 40 Insights From the Science of Communicating*.

A book highly recommended for people who want to make better use of PowerPoint is *PowerPoint Surgery: How to create presentation slides that make your message stick* by Lee Jackson, Engaging Books, 2013.

CHAPTER 20

Watch your language

Introduction

The average human attention span fell from twelve seconds in 2000, about the time that the smartphone revolution started, to eight seconds in 2015. (Treat goldfish with respect; they are thought to have an attention span of nine seconds.) Moreover, in 2030 the typical attention span will be… Well, let's move on.

The point is that we haven't got long to make our listeners take notice. The language of our talks must be designed to grab and keep their attention. This chapter examines methods of doing that.

We'll look at the value of using direct, straightforward speech and then review a variety of ways to keep things simple. I'll warn you against the dangers of flowery expressions and, even worse, the use of unnecessary jargon. We'll discuss the importance of signposts and transitions in a presentation for a listening audience, and – from bitter experience – I'll tackle the perils of using rude or risqué vocabulary.

As a result of all this, we'll produce talks that can both seize and retain the attention of our audiences.

Keep it plain and simple

If the person receiving my message does not understand it, then communication is empty and pointless and I might as well not have bothered.

We should choose our vocabulary for talks with this in mind, using sentences that are generally brief and to the point, direct language and straightforward words. If you keep your speech uncomplicated, your listeners will be much better able to comprehend it. Winston Churchill put it this way: "Broadly speaking, short words are best, and the old words, when short, are best of all."

The key motto of the 1954 classic *The Complete Plain Words* by Sir Ernest Gowers, still regarded by many as the Bible of plain English, is: "Be short, be simple, be human". It is a maxim that also applies in full to speechmaking. There are many downsides of long sentences in speeches, not least the danger of running out of breath as you work your way through all those subordinate clauses.

The emphasis on simplicity is not new.

Quintilian, the leading Latin writer on rhetoric, demanded that the speaker should ensure not simply that he could be understood, but that it should be absolutely impossible to misunderstand him. Julius Caesar said, or was said to have said, that we should "avoid a strange and unfamiliar word (*insolens verbum*) as a sailor would avoid a rocky cliff".

Flowery language just doesn't work

In putting the words together for a talk, we should not hunt around for ornate and grand language. Otherwise, we will come over to the audience as stilted and pompous, or just unintelligible.

Not everyone takes this point. Gordon Brown, prime minister to be, certainly didn't at a seminar in 1994. "Our new economic approach," he said, "is rooted in ideas which stress the importance of macroeconomics, post neo-classical endogenous growth theory and the symbiotic relationships between growth and investment, and people and infrastructure." Newspaper articles that followed had headlines like *The gift of tired tongues* and *You've never had it so incoherent.* The message is clear: don't try to impress audiences with overcomplicated terminology, because it doesn't work. (Some people remember a younger Gordon Brown as a fine speaker who could dazzle an audience with his wit and brilliance. I have no idea what went wrong.)

In fact, there is substantial research evidence that it just does not work to put big words into a speech to sound clever. If you use complex language which the audience struggles to understand, they regard your message as less convincing and you personally as less intelligent. In a series of studies, a psychologist, Daniel Oppenheimer, asked people to read various passages including job applications and academic essays and assess the intelligence of the people who wrote them. Simpler language led to materially higher ratings of intelligence, confirming that the unnecessary use of complex language makes a bad impression.

Mr Oppenheimer set out his findings in a paper appropriately called *Consequences of Erudite Vernacular Utilized Irrespective of Necessity: Problems with using long words needlessly.* Equally appropriately, his paper won him the literature prize at the parody 2006 Ig Nobel Prizes. In summary, if you use straightforward language you will almost certainly be more convincing than those who speak in elaborate sentence formations.

Of course, Julius Caesar's rule of avoiding the 'strange and unfamiliar word' can pose practical problems. It is not always easy to decide when a word is unfamiliar, and even when there is no doubt that it is, it may still be the only one to express the desired meaning.

As Spencer Leigh Hughes puts it:

> "There can be no harm in using a word however unusual when it is the only word to express your meaning – and surely it is better to do this than to employ a word that is not unusual when it has a meaning quite different from that which you would convey. It is possible to indulge in affected simplicity of style on the platform, and I think that the man who would address a grown-up audience in the style of *Mary had a little lamb* ought to be chased round the town."

It's not only in using new and unfamiliar terms that we need to be careful. Common words can also prove hard going if you employ them in a technical sense that is new to the audience. If you are in any doubt, test your material out on some listeners before you give your presentation.

I doubt whether the US Secretary of Defence Donald Rumsfeld did that before an infamous news briefing in 2002. In answering a question about the lack of evidence linking the Iraqi government to the supply of weapons of mass destruction, he said:

> "Reports that say that something hasn't happened are always interesting to me, because as we know, there are known knowns; there are things we know we know. We also know there are known unknowns; that is to say, we know there are some things we do not know. But there are also unknown unknowns – the ones we don't know we don't know. And if one looks throughout the history of our country and other free countries, it is the latter category that tend to be the difficult ones."

Even the kinder commentators noted the tortured language used by Mr Rumsfeld. His remarks led him to victory in the Plain English Campaign's annual Foot in Mouth award for 2003. The terms 'known unknowns' and 'unknown unknowns' came from project management theory, but he used them without enough adaptation or explanation to make them intelligible in a new context. People tell me that you can genuinely make sense of his comments. I found it takes at least five minutes to do so, and your audience members cannot indulge themselves that way if they are to follow the remainder of your talk.

How to keep it simple

How in practice does one achieve the right level of simplicity? Here's what I try to do when I am preparing a talk:

- Make the main subject I will be talking about very clear, very early on.
- Always consider what the audience will know of the subject at the outset, and what might prevent them from understanding and accepting what they hear.
- Constantly think about the drafting: what's the purpose of that passage, what's that particular word doing, is it needed in the first place?
- Remember the value of brevity and keeping things simple, not least by ordering my sentences in a logical sequence.
- Try never to overestimate people's ability to see where I am going. This involves helping them out by providing signposts of where I am heading ("I'm going to talk about this…") and recaps of where I have been ("So we have demonstrated that…").
- Aim for specific, concrete speech – not 'a period of

unfavourable weather set in' but 'it rained every day for a week'. The more concise, concentrated and focused the words, the clearer the picture I will create in the mind of the listener.

- As my teacher Miss McManus taught me long ago, in general use active language ('eight out of ten cats prefer Whiskas', not 'Whiskas cat food is preferred by eight out of ten cats') because it is more direct and vigorous and is easier to understand than the passive voice.

- Avoid jargon wherever possible and, if I have to use difficult words, explain them.

- Limit the use of abbreviations. And, when I use one, I always say the unabbreviated phrase in full the first time it arises.

- When editing a speech, look out for complex or clumsy sentences where the meaning is unclear, and rewrite them.

- Use software programs to check for document readability. (For example, I use the readability tests that come freely available with Microsoft Word.)

- At an early rehearsal, encourage listeners to stop me if I seem to be making things complicated and get them to ask me, "What do you mean by that?" When I tell them what I mean, I will almost certainly express myself more simply than I did before.

- During rehearsals, look out for the stodgy bits. I find it's often helpful, after the first rehearsal, to ask myself which 300 words (about two minutes of the speech) I would cut out first, and then cut them. Repeating the process can work remarkably well after the second and third rehearsals too. (I learned this technique from book editors. Gary Smailes, a leading developmental editor who has worked with me on this book, describes his approach this way: "I always train editors to come at a book with the question 'what should we keep?' I urge them to start with the idea that the whole book should be scrapped and rewritten. This is not often literal, but it shifts the view of the book to a place where each sentence must justify its existence. If a sentence is not essential to the book's topic, it can go." I think this is a great maxim for speakers to keep in mind as well.)

- Never underestimate how long it will take to achieve all this. Plain, clear sentences take longer to prepare than vague, unspecific, generalised waffle because I have to think much more carefully about what I am doing.

It follows from this that a red pencil is helpful in reviewing the text of a talk. Cut the filler words if possible, and use shorter conjunctions and intermissions between one sentence and the next. Here are some potential 'befores' and 'afters' with this approach:

Before (excess verbiage)	After (simpler stuff)
and therefore	so
for the duration of	during
for the purpose of	to
I must point out that	JUST LEAVE IT OUT!
in order to	to
in spite of the fact that	despite
in the event of	if
in the vicinity of	near
in view of the fact that	because
meet with/meet up with	meet

prior to	before
subsequent to	after
until such time as	until
with reference to	about
with regard to	about

We can take this approach further and say it's usually a good idea to use a little, traditional, Old English word in preference to a longer and less powerful word that may have come into the language from Latin.

Just to take a few of the 'A's:

Apprehend *becomes* catch
Approximately *becomes* about
Ascertain *becomes* learn
Assistance *becomes* help
Attempt *becomes* try

Always remember your speech is not aimed at readers

You are preparing something which you are going to speak out loud. In his diaries, Jock Colville, who was Assistant Private Secretary to Winston Churchill in the Second World War, tells us he would alter the official text of a speech Churchill had delivered to improve the style and grammar. This was because "the PM's speeches are essentially oratorical masterpieces and in speaking he inserts much that sounds well and reads badly."

Your task is to go in the opposite direction from Jock Colville and prepare something that sounds well.

I like the example given by John Hilton in his radio talk *On Giving a Talk*:

> "It's queer how as soon as we start putting words on paper we go sticking in the word 'that' all over the place. You find yourself writing: 'He said that he thought that the book was his.' No living mortal ever uttered such a sentence. What we say in normal speech is: 'He said he thought the book was his.' Then why, in writing, do we stick in the two 'thats'? I don't know. But I'm always on the job with my own scripts, cutting out unnecessary 'thats'. A needless 'that' in a printed sentence is like… like a stone in a currant bun. Three needless 'thats' in a talk is like… like sand in spinach. So… out with all the useless 'thats'."

At the most basic level, remember to adapt the words you use from what might appear in a written piece – not, for example, 'the matters discussed above' but 'what I said earlier'.

Use standard pronunciation

There are some straightforward points to make about pronunciation in a talk. First, it is a good thing to finish one word before starting on the next, instead of slurring one into the other. This might be obvious, but it can be easy to forget in the tension of the moment, and it is more important in public speaking than in private conversation.

At the same time, pronunciation that tries to be ultra-precise can be annoying. Spencer Leigh Hughes gives an example:

> "Let me take the word 'often'. I know quite well that it contains the letter 't', but I also know that the ordinary way of pronouncing it is 'off'n', and that I maintain is far better than the style affected by some miserable little precisians

> who insist on saying 'off-TEN', with a huge emphasis on the 'ten'... Though there may be no absolutely fixed rule for the pronunciation of all words there is generally an ordinary way, and it is the way for ordinary people."

So far, so good, but I don't think that that implies one should follow the way for ordinary people if the ordinary person is just being sloppy. If someone starts out to say 'deteriorate', loses patience with the number of syllables they have let themselves in for, and settles for 'deteriate' instead, I for one will be groaning in the audience. Say it properly, or even better use a nice short Old English form like 'get worse' instead. Indeed, shorter words have the bonus that they're easier to pronounce and less likely to be stumbled over by a nervous speaker.

Don't forget to research pronunciations that might be difficult or that you're unfamiliar with. For example, Tannadice Park is a football stadium in Dundee, the home of Dundee United. It being in Scotland, Tannadice is pronounced 'Tanna-DICE', as in the things you throw in a gambling game. But newsreaders have been known to pronounce it as though it were some kind of Italian pasta, 'Tanna-dee-chay'. Much embarrassment can follow. And there's an unpleasant trap to fall into with 'misled', the past tense of 'mislead': for those who have seen the word in print but not previously spoken it, it's easy to say 'myzled' rather than the correct 'miss-led'.

There's nothing wrong with repetition

Don't worry about repeating yourself in a talk: it can be very powerful, as we saw in Chapter 11. This reminds us of the differences in style between speaking and writing. Speakers will often need to repeat themselves, conveying the message several times, and often in several different ways, to ensure the audience fully takes it in. Their listeners do not have the advantage, as in reading a book, of being able to turn back to an earlier page or to take time out to think at length about what they have not fully understood so far.

In his highly pragmatic book, *Persuade: Using the Seven Drivers of Motivation to Master Influence and Persuasion,* Philip Hesketh, an expert on the subject, tells us that in one of his first speeches as prime minister David Cameron used the term 'values' twelve times in five minutes. It was clearly (at least at the time) a theme dear to his heart. Philip Hesketh writes:

> "If we hear something repeatedly it becomes familiar. And we like the familiar. And because familiar things require less effort to process, we assume them to be true. If your argument is strong don't be afraid to repeat it often and with gusto."

Avoid clichés, jargon and meaningless rubbish

Limit your use of words or phrases that are short on meaning, much overused, or designed just to show how bright you are. Here is a list of my own top twenty-five. I believe their absence enormously strengthens a speech:

Ballpark figures
Benchmark
Changing the goalposts
Connectivity
Core competencies
Deep dive
Elephant in the room
Empowerment
Future-proof

Helicopter view
Holistic
Incentivise
Interface
Knowledge base
Leverage
Paradigm
Pushing the envelope
Re-engineering
Strategic fit
Thinking outside the box
Thought leadership
Touch base (or even 'touch base offline')
Transformational change (why not just 'change'?)
Transparency
Twenty-four-seven.

In your researches for a talk, you will commonly encounter the jargon, the technical argot, of a particular subject. After a while, you will become familiar with it, take it for granted and start using it yourself. Remember that it is likely to remain unintelligible jargon to your audience. You must always translate into their terms, their language, if your talk is to succeed. Nothing turns an audience off quicker than mysterious technical expressions. Once they stop understanding you, their minds wander and they soon lose the thread irretrievably.

Use signposts

A speaker needs to use clear signposts and transitions. To stress the point again, if you are reading a book or magazine, it is easy to go back and reread items to clarify your understanding and to check cross-references. The person listening to a talk does not have these opportunities and needs additional help. Here are some examples of linking phrases to help maintain the logic as the discussion moves on:

After all
As it happens
By that I mean
By the way
For example
Funnily enough
In addition
In any case
Incidentally
Mind you
Nevertheless
Now, let's review
Okay
The next point to look at is
To be fair
What can we learn from this?

Phrases and link words like these can help to make the logical sequence clearer to the audience, tie separate subjects more tightly together and close the gaps between different themes.

Be aware of the speaker's power to offend

Occasionally, a point made by a speaker can depend on the use of a rude word to gain maximum impact. Think carefully before you venture into this dangerous territory. It involves having to make a guess in advance about the tolerance and maturity levels of your audience, and sometimes the differences between particular gatherings can be utterly baffling.

Once, at an annual meeting of the accountants PricewaterhouseCoopers, I heard Simon, one of the partners, tell an anecdote to add colour to the topic of dealing with colleagues in a global multilingual organisation.

A tax partner from Moscow called him and got straight to the point in effective, if not idiomatic, English.

"Simon," said the man from Moscow, "Simon, you nasty man, you think we Russians know fuck nothing about international tax… But, let me tell you, we know fuck all."

This brought the house down.

I naturally decided to steal the joke for my own use, and a couple of months later I told the same story as a guest speaker at the annual dinner of the Beds, Bucks & Herts Society of Chartered Accountants. About a third of the audience laughed, but everyone else was completely shocked. You could see them mouthing, "What did he just say?" Rude words in this context were clearly unacceptable, and I had lost them for the rest of the speech.

The moral has to be: if you don't know your audience well, err on the side of caution. I've never used that joke again in public – well, not more than a dozen or so times.

More generally, a speaker has a responsibility to treat any audience with respect. Don't put any material into a presentation simply for shock value: that would be a wretched approach.

A brief checklist for watching your language

Joseph Berg Esenwein, a distinguished American editor and lecturer, included a digest of eighty-six rhetorical rules in his 1902 work, *How to Attract and Hold an Audience*.

Here are my top ten picks from his listing:

- Do not use a word in more than one sense in the same paragraph.

- When in doubt, consult the dictionary.
- Simple words are most effective.
- Use care lest long sentences confuse the meaning.
- Use just one main thought to dominate each sentence.
- Do not crowd together conflicting ideas, nor thoughts not naturally related.
- Repetition, both of words and of sentence forms, adds emphasis.
- Use climax.
- Plain, specific, short and strong words give vigour to sentences.
- Avoid the use of unnecessary words.

Conclusion

The best thing I know about the style of language to use in front of an audience comes from the unnamed author of *Beeton's Art of Public Speaking*. Here is what he or she had to say about the key features of a successful speech:

> "The first are simplicity and force. The most familiar words and illustrations should be chosen. No matter what the thoughts of the speaker may be, let them find expression in such language as all can understand."

If, making use of the suggestions in this chapter, you can deliver your presentations in "such language as all can understand", you will have passed one of the greatest tests for a public speaker.

Points to take from this chapter

- Our use of language must be designed to grab and

maintain the audience's attention.
- Use sentences that are brief and to the point, direct expressions and straightforward words.
- If you use complex language, you devalue yourself and your message in the audience's mind.
- Provide recaps, transitions and signposts to ensure they stay with you.
- Adapt your speeches for listeners, not readers.
- If you've got a good argument, don't be afraid to repeat it often.
- Avoid clichés and jargon, and express your thoughts in the language of the audience.
- Be aware of the speaker's power to offend.

In the next chapter, we are going to move on from looking at our use of language in general to reviewing the critical importance of the start of our talk. We'll learn how to make an initial impression that should keep the audience hanging on our words for the remainder of our time on stage.

Notes

The information on attention spans is taken from *The Telegraph* for 15 May 2015. Winston Churchill's words come from a speech on receiving *The Times* Literary Award in 1949. Julius Caesar's maxim of the *insolens verbum* was discussed in Samuel Taylor Coleridge's *Essays on the Principles of Method*. John ('Jock') Colville's comments are from *The Fringes of Power: Downing Street Diaries, 1939–55*, Hodder & Stoughton, 1985, in the entry for 8 October 1940.

CHAPTER 21

Concentrate on the first few minutes

Introduction

Here is Alexander Burton, someone who knew a thing or two about oratory, writing in 1920 about the introduction to a speech:

> "The beginning, or introduction, is a matter of taste. With the speech, just as with a short story, the manner of opening is subject to no law. An orator may choose to startle his hearers with an opening sentence of dramatic fervour. Or he may begin with a quiet compliment to the intelligence of his audience. Or he may say anything else under heaven."

Doesn't that make life easy for us?

To be honest, things are not quite that simple. The Burton approach may give us lots of flexibility, but the start of a talk still poses a real challenge. Whichever writer first compared the opening of a presentation to the first minutes of a blind date had it exactly right. Both sides are wary. *This could be awful,* thinks your new acquaintance in the audience; *I've got to spend an hour with this strange person I've never met before.* As the speaker, you need to deal with this quickly. Whatever you say, the implied message has to be: 'Don't worry, it's going to be all right', so that you and the audience can begin to relax into each other.

The good news is that if the first few minutes of your talk go down well, it sets you up for all that follows. Focus on the opening. Alexander Burton was right: there's no best way of starting, no key thing you have to say. But you must still make sure you have convincing material as your banker for those tense opening minutes, to build your confidence for the rest of the session.

In this chapter, we'll look at what science says about the importance of the opening. After a quick reminder about the value of a speaker being introduced, I'll examine a variety of methods for you to get off to a strong start. In particular, I'll focus on easy ways to break the ice so that the audience feels comfortable with you, and you with the audience, for the remainder of your speech.

The importance of the opening

Scientific research supports the emphasis on the start of your presentation. Audiences tend to be more sensitive to the first things they hear in a talk (this is called the primacy effect) together with the last things (the recency effect). They remember beginnings and endings rather than what happens in between, which is why politicians among others plonk their weakest stuff in the middle. Many experiments on the human memory confirm the potency of the primacy effect.

Apart from anything else, of course, you never get a second chance to make a first impression.

That first impression you give to the audience will colour

their views and influence the way they regard the rest of your talk. This effect is almost wholly illogical (why should your reaction to a joke I will make in half an hour's time be determined by something I say now?), but you are stuck with it. You might well think that it is utterly unfair for your listeners to judge you based on the point in your talk at which you are at your most exposed and nervous, but there is nothing to be done about it. Each of us has to make the best of the situation by ensuring that we get going in the most effective way.

Let's stress again the most obvious point: that we should use some of our strongest material for the first five minutes or so of the presentation. Moreover, we need to be able to deliver it smoothly, so let's have no long sentences, complex clauses, or tongue-twisting pronouncements. And we should know it thoroughly, or at least have full notes, to ensure that we speak fluently at this crucial time in our performance.

Be introduced

We talked about the useful practice of being introduced in Chapter 10, when we looked at getting the audience onside. Here, I just want to remind you to brief your introducer properly. Otherwise, you might suffer the fate of Henry S Wilcox, as told in his book *The Trials of a Stump-speaker*:

> "In presenting me to the audience [my introducer] said he had the pleasure of introducing a political giant, whose fame was so great that his name had become a household word in every cottage in the State! And then he had to stop and ask me what my name was."

Even at a lower level of embarrassment than poor Henry suffered, introducers struggle surprisingly often to get names right. My surname is Nichol without an S at the end, but I have been introduced to audiences throughout the land as Nichols. If you are the speaker and something similar happens, the best practice is simply to get on with your talk: correcting your host serves only to pile awkwardness on awkwardness.

If you think I am paranoid about the need for competent introductions, listen to Spencer Leigh Hughes, picking up the baton from Henry Wilcox in his 1918 book *Press, Platform and Parliament:*

"It is a little embarrassing when a chairman introduces you as one whose name is very well known to everybody (a very familiar form of introduction), and then has to stop and to peer carefully through his glasses at the programme to find what your name is. And a sensitive beginner may have been caused to wince when the chairman puts it this way: 'Mr Hughes will now give us his address on life in Parliament – but may I say, before he begins, that next week we shall have a really splendid lecture from…'"

So, please be introduced, and try to make sure it is done well by following the basic rules we discussed in Chapter 10.

Getting their attention

You have been listening to what your introducer has been saying, all the while thinking pleasant thoughts and reminding yourself how much you are going to enjoy making your presentation. Now your host has finished talking, and it's over to you.

Some of the textbooks assume that the speaker will have a quiet and attentive audience from the outset. You are therefore free, in a hushed room, to make a dazzling opening remark that will ensure a rapt reception for the rest of your speech. That may work if you are Barack Obama, or if you have had a helpful introduction, but it will not always be the case.

There are two main approaches to an ill-disciplined audience who are still talking among themselves and seem not to have noticed that you are waiting to speak.

The first strategy is to remind your listeners of your presence by making some fluffy opening remarks that aren't significant to your message, so that it doesn't matter if they get drowned in the general hubbub. Take a final deep breath, look up and out at the audience to let them know you are ready, and say something like, "Ladies and gentlemen, thank you, it's a great pleasure to be here." Speak clearly and forcefully, saying the words slowly and smiling as you do so. I find it oddly comforting to tell a challenging audience what a delight it is to be present, at a point when I am feeling anything but delighted and would rather like to go straight home.

The second strategy with an inattentive audience is the preferred approach for an experienced speaker. Quite simply, wait for the house to settle before you start: say nothing until they have all shut up. You will find that peer pressure from those members of the public who do want to hear you will shush their more recalcitrant colleagues remarkably quickly. This is certainly the textbook solution, but if you're a nervous new speaker unwilling to outstare a noisy audience into silence, the first alternative may well be preferable for you in practice.

Getting off to a strong start

Once you have their attention, you can get going. Here are some fundamental principles for those crucial first few minutes:

- Look around the audience, scanning the whole room so that everyone feels involved. We examined the vital importance of making excellent eye contact, and tips on how to achieve it, in Chapter 10.

- As you scan the room, look out for any particularly friendly faces that are likely to build your confidence in the opening minutes.
- Try not to duplicate what the person who introduced you said. If they told the audience your name and the subject you were going to talk about and, heaven be praised, got it right, you are wasting precious seconds by repeating that information when you could be saying something new, something they don't already know, and making an impression.
- Be prepared to show undisguised enthusiasm for your topic. It helps demonstrate your warmth as a human being and so makes the audience more likely to engage with you. If *you* are not enthusiastic about your subject, why should the audience be?

A helpful ABCD mnemonic sets out four key areas well worth considering for the opening minutes:

- A is for *Attention* – getting the audience focused on what you have to say and building a rapport with them. By breaking the ice quickly and starting powerfully, you gain people's attention from the outset. Telling a story is an excellent way of achieving this, and we shall look shortly at how Monica Lewinsky did it in a TED talk.
- B is for *Benefits* – making it very apparent what they will get from listening to you. They are much more likely to pay detailed attention if they have obtained a clear view of 'what's in it for me' at the start of the talk. For example, explain the importance of the

subject you are talking about, and in particular why it should matter to *them*, to that particular audience. If it is realistic to do so, I recommend promising them goodies. Say, "This talk will save you money," and then, if you can, tell them exactly how much money.

- C is for *Credentials* – demonstrating why they should listen to *you* in particular, rather than anyone else. What entitles you to make public statements on this topic?
- D is for *Direction* – telling them what your objective is, what you are trying to achieve, and so indicating where your presentation will take them.

We will be looking at two of these areas – breaking the ice and building rapport to gain *Attention,* and demonstrating your *Credentials* – later in this chapter.

For the moment, I would just encourage you to make the most of whatever opportunities come your way in those vital opening minutes of your talk, by noting a classic example of a speaker doing just that.

Speaking in Milwaukee in October 1912, Theodore Roosevelt, running for a third term as US president, was able to grab the crowd's attention from the outset with the words: "Ladies and gentlemen, I don't know whether you fully understand that I have just been shot." That is a true humdinger of an opening. He had indeed been shot in the chest on his way to the auditorium. He went on to deliver an eighty-four-minute speech, despite blood seeping into his shirt, and only afterwards did he get medical attention. You could say that this was a rare example of public speaking saving a person's life: it was the long, folded-up speech in his breast pocket together with his glasses case that slowed the bullet and stopped it reaching his lung.

Do the housekeeping and set the ground rules

If things work well, the person who introduces you should deal with the practicalities of the session before you ever start talking. That way you avoid getting bogged down by the tedious detail of administrative issues in the vital early minutes of your speech. But if your introducer fails to do their job properly, you may need to take over.

These are some points you might want to cover:

- How long your presentation will last. If your listeners remain puzzled as to when the next break is coming, they are less likely to be concentrating on what you have to say.
- Whether you will welcome questions and comments from the floor and, if so, at what times – throughout the talk, for example, or just at the end. Remember that interactive sessions often work better than monologues from the stage and that the more effort your listeners put in, the less you'll have to do. Sorry, that's to say: the greater the contribution from the audience, the more they'll get out of the experience.
- What to do if a fire breaks out or there is some other emergency.
- Turning off mobile phones, and appropriate frighteners to ensure that audience members do so. I was once moved to say: "In the unfortunate event that a phone rings, one of my larger applicants from the Criminal Cases Review Commission will be in touch with you to discuss how such a sad event can be avoided in future." It seemed to work rather well. These days I find that threatening non-compliers

with a surprise appearance on the *Jeremy Kyle Show* often does the trick.

- In a session with audience participation, you may want to remind people of the spirit you are looking to work in: showing respect for others, keeping confidences, letting other people speak, starting back from breaks on time. If anything said during the proceedings is to remain confidential, it is vital to emphasise this at the outset.

Breaking the ice

Monica Lewinsky is the former White House intern who was in her early twenties when President Bill Clinton notoriously had what he termed an 'inappropriate relationship' with her in the mid-1990s. Much later, she came back into the public view as a social activist, speaking out against shaming and online bullying.

In 2015, Monica Lewinsky gave a TED talk: *The price of shame.* By her own account, she was a nervous wreck in the hours leading up to the talk, but she had planned a brilliant tactic: very early on, she told a story which she was confident would work well with the audience. Here is an extract:

> "At the age of forty-one, I was hit on by a twenty-seven-year-old guy. You know what his unsuccessful pick-up line was? He could make me feel twenty-two again.
> I realised later that night I'm probably the only person over forty who does not want to be twenty-two again."

After a great audience reaction, she was able to sigh in relief. She knew it was going to be all right.

Her example shows the power of breaking the ice quickly.

It dissipates the early tension and allows you and the audience to loosen up. A warm feeling spreads over the gathering as your listeners recognise that they are in the company of an engaging and fully human speaker. Once they have done that, you, and they, can concentrate on the serious points you want to make.

There are lots of things you can do to break the ice with an audience.

Tell them something intriguing about yourself, for example, as Monica Lewinsky did. It's not difficult, because people are intrinsically interesting.

In his book *Press, Platform and Parliament*, Spencer Leigh Hughes tells the story of the man who started his maiden speech in Parliament with the sentence, "Mr Speaker, Sir, I am a manure merchant in the north of Ireland," which, he notes, "had an arresting effect".

Perhaps you could describe some exciting event that has happened to you, or some challenging aspect of your personality, and link it to your presentation. When I am breaking the ice myself, I try to do it in the self-effacing style that seems to suit me. If I am talking to would-be speakers, I often start with my experience of pronouncing difficult names, particularly the challenge of Mihaly Csikszentmihalyi that we discussed in Chapter 5, as an example of the issues they might face.

Alternatively, I might talk early on about how my accountancy experiences caused me to change my name. I tell the story of how I was a partner in an accountancy firm called Coopers & Lybrand when it merged in 1998 with another company called Price Waterhouse. External consultants were hired at, allegedly, the cost of several million dollars to come up with a name for the merged enterprise. After a lengthy discussion, they produced the not entirely earth-shattering name of PricewaterhouseCoopers for the new body; arguably the finest single name in accountancy, and at twenty-two letters certainly one of the longest. The new business was very precious about that new name: people got very cross if you didn't spell it as just a single word, with that hugely significant capital C in the middle.

Always a good company man, I pondered at length on what I could do to mark the historic importance of the merger and the new name. Then it came to me. I was informally reborn for the years that followed as a man with a single name, IanniChol – just the one word like PricewaterhouseCoopers, and with a capital C in the middle. I thought about changing my name formally by deed poll to IanniChol but never quite got around to it. Those close to me were allowed to call me Ianni for short.

Twenty years after the merger, this story still succeeds at breaking the ice in the early minutes of a talk and gets a good laugh; and my wife calls me Ianni to this day.

Another example of breaking the ice

I was speaking one evening about presentation skills. The audience were tired, they knew nothing about me, and I got the distinct impression that many of them did not want to be there. I thought that a relaxed, less demanding style would go down well in the circumstances, and that turned out to be the case. The event took place in Birmingham, which accounts for the number of references to the Midlands. I started the talk by introducing myself to the audience:

"Hello, my name is Ian, and I am... an alcoholic.
Oops, sorry, wrong audience. That's for tomorrow night.
The chair told me that you have been waiting several years for a knowledgeable, professional speaker on presentation skills, so... I'm here to help out while the search goes on.

I want first to tell you a bit about my background, to show you what gives me the nerve to stand up and talk on this subject.

Well, I grew up in the West Midlands.

I went to Solihull School – it's a fine school, but unfortunately, speaking personally, I got bullied and beaten up a lot.

So I decided to give up teaching [long pause] and look for another job."

[This is the point when I know how tough it's going to be tonight. If they don't laugh at this point, I'm in real trouble.]

"I had to make my mind up what to do next.

Aptitude tests showed that I had a devious and cunning mind, unrestrained by moral scruples or any sense of decency.

Accordingly, I decided to become a tax accountant.

I ended up as a partner at PricewaterhouseCoopers.

I did do quite well at tax – I had my own loophole named after me.

It was then that my interest in public speaking got started..."

By this point the ice had melted, and I could move on to deal with my points of substance.

Building rapport

Try to establish an early bond with your audience. We talked about ways of getting to know them in Chapter 14, and, if you have done that, giving some concrete demonstration of your knowledge will impress them at the very start of your presentation.

Tony Blair gave a classic example of how *not* to achieve this in his encounter with the ladies of the Women's Institute, which we will be talking about further in Chapter 37. He started by telling the audience how scared he was of them. People would be happier if a speaker told them how friendly or welcoming or attractive they were. To say they are terrifying fails to display any specific knowledge of them and attributes a quality to them that they would rather not claim for themselves.

By contrast, just saying something that shows you appreciate who the audience are and where they come from can be extremely valuable. Bob Monkhouse's story in Chapter 14, about the grocers' food that had passed its sell-by date, is a classic example of this approach. The most basic comments that provide a link between you and the audience – even ones like "Isn't it cold in here?" or "Isn't this a huge hall?" – can get the goodwill flowing in your direction.

Demonstrating your credentials

What gives you the right to be there?

Ensure the audience knows what it is that makes it legitimate for you to speak in public, that you have the credentials to justify your nerve in taking up their time. By making them aware of why you're entitled to be their speaker as early as you can, you start off with their respect. And, by demonstrating that they can trust you as a credible authority on your topic, you will also be reminding yourself of that fact: nothing is better designed to damage your self-confidence than going on stage feeling like you're an impostor.

Get in early. As we discussed in Chapter 15, the best way of getting in early was to set out your hard-earned skills and experience in the blurb for your talk. If that didn't quite work out, or if some of the audience may not have seen the blurb, the person who introduced you should have done the job instead in their opening words. If that, in turn, was not a success, the task falls to you in the first few minutes of your performance. Early references to "the last time I gave this talk", "the audience at the Barbican last week", and "the reaction I've had from young people to this" will show you as an old hand at this kind of thing. (You don't need to tell them that the only previous time you've given this talk was at the Barbican Primary School last Thursday.) However, try not to be too blatant when demonstrating your right to be there: the speaker who referred to "my highly acclaimed best-seller on the subject" went a bit far for my liking. Subtlety and gentle implication of ability work better than explicit boasting and extravagant self-plugging.

Other points on the opening

If you are trying out new or unfamiliar material, hold it back until later on in your talk, when you are more confident and less can go wrong than at the start.

Resist the temptation to rush your speech at the outset. Remember that your audience will be slower to react to you at the beginning than at the end. They are finding their way with you, as you are with them. Take your time and force yourself to speak in a measured way. We will be talking about the value of slowing down in Chapter 34, and it applies even more crucially to the opening minutes of your session.

Conclusion

Your anxiety level will be at its highest when you start your talk. It is vital, therefore, that you use strong material in the opening minutes, and that you have rehearsed it thoroughly. This approach will get you through the hardest part of the whole experience. It will allow you to capture the audience's attention and set the tone for all that follows.

Once your nerves start to abate after the first couple of minutes, you will find the rest of your performance much smoother sailing.

Points to take from this chapter

- The start of a presentation has much in common with the start of a blind date: the audience needs assurance that it's going to be all right.
- You need your best stuff at the beginning, to build your confidence for all that follows.
- To ensure you deliver your opening words well, use simple language to guarantee a smooth delivery, and make sure you are thoroughly familiar with your material.
- Be introduced, and make sure it is done competently.
- Use the ABCD mnemonic (Attention, Benefits, Credentials, Direction) to help you prepare compelling content for the opening.
- Breaking the ice early on removes the tension and allows the audience to focus on the serious matters to come.
- Don't forget to demonstrate your credentials as the speaker.
- Avoid rushing your speech: just take your time.

In the next chapter, we are going to look at another topic that is central both to developing your self-belief as a speaker and to giving an outstanding talk – rehearsals, and how to use them to make the presentation itself a much less intimidating experience.

Notes

Alexander Burton was writing in his book *Public speaking made easy.* You can see Monica Lewinsky's TED talk at https://www.ted.com/talks/monica_lewinsky_the_price_of_shame.

CHAPTER 22

Rehearse, rehearse, rehearse

Introduction

In 1553, Thomas Wilson, who was later to be a prominent diplomat under the first Queen Elizabeth, wrote one of the early works in English on public speaking, *The Arte of Rhetorique*. One of his crucial passages is still relevant today:

> "What maketh the lawyer to have such utterance? Practice. What maketh the preacher to speak so soundly? Practice. Yea!... Therefore, in all faculties diligent practice and earnest exercise are the only things that make men prove excellent."

More recently, the violinist Fritz Kreisler turns up in several tales on the same theme. A tourist on 57th Street, Manhattan stops a man carrying a violin case to ask, "How do I get to Carnegie Hall?"

Kreisler, for it is he, replies: "Practise, practise, practise."

In another story, a music student goes up to Kreisler and exclaims, "I'd give my entire life to play as beautifully as you just did."

Kreisler replies: "I did."

These stories may be apocryphal, but they identify a crucial principle which applies to speaking as much as to music. The way to get better at public speaking (and almost any activity involving any level of skill) is to take it seriously, work hard at it, do as much of it as you can, and practise.

The tennis player Ivan Lendl put it neatly: "If I don't practise the way I should, then I won't play the way that I know I can."

For public speaking, the fundamental form of practice is rehearsal.

In this chapter, we will examine the contribution that rehearsal can offer to the success of any speaker, and then look at the practical rules for making it the hugely powerful process it can be at its best. I'll also explain the benefits of testing your material out on mentors – in the form of family, friends and colleagues – and show how they can work with you to maximise the quality of your talk. First, however, we have a lesson to learn from a man who was once Mr Universe, the world's greatest bodybuilder.

You have to do the reps

"I am a great believer in luck. The harder I work, the more of it I seem to have."

The aphorist Coleman Cox came up with that maxim in 1922, and public speakers do well to take note of it. Rehearsing is all about giving yourself the best chance of having good luck on the day. The more you rehearse, the more familiar and confident you will be with your material, and the less you will suffer from excess stage fright in the actual performance.

You have to do the repetitions. In his autobiography *Total Recall*, Arnold Schwarzenegger, the actor and politician (and former professional bodybuilder), gives as an example the opening page of an address he gave to the United Nations in 2007 on fighting global warming. Each time he rehearsed the speech he put a mark at the top of the page: he made fifty-five marks in total. It is the detailed rehearsal that develops bodily confidence and allows you to sound spontaneous on the day.

Talks at TED conferences have been one of the great public speaking successes of the twenty-first century. Much of that is down to sheer hard work in preparation and practice. The process for helping presenters to deliver their talks commonly starts six to nine months in advance and involves an exceptional level of focus on scriptwriting and revision, coupled with an extensive rehearsal programme. It is not a process for the fainthearted, but the vast amount of hard graft pays dividends in the final performance.

Of course, not everyone is able to dedicate as much practice time as Arnold Schwarzenegger did for his United Nations address or as the TED speakers do. Indeed, the TED approach involves the ultimate in dedication. Often, we need to be pragmatic and look for the middle ground.

The communications coach Carmine Gallo has suggested a high achieving but more manageable approach for achieving a polished presentation, involving ten hours of rehearsal to boost confidence and performance. Ten hours should be within most people's capability, yet it is a rehearsal period far greater than most business presentations receive. And if you are worried about going stale through too much practice, remember that the dangers of under-rehearsal are far worse.

For my part, I advise people I coach to rehearse any talk at least three to four times as a minimum, and to do it in full on each occasion without cutting any corners. Each time you rehearse, make sure that you incorporate all the changes that have come out of feedback from earlier practice sessions. We will be talking about feedback later in this chapter.

A comprehensive rehearsal programme becomes even more important if you have composed your talk on paper in the first instance. Reading it aloud will reveal sentences that might look good in a book, but are not suited to a listening audience. Your listeners will not have the advantage of the paragraphing or punctuation or cross-referencing that a book offers. Rehearsal is critical for identifying places in the talk where you need more signposts and directions for the audience. It will also reveal sentences that would be more successful if they were shorter or broken in two. Modern political speeches, for example, tend to work best with a big helping of very short sentences, as Nick Clegg showed us in Chapter 11.

Some practical tips

Start the rehearsal process as early as you can, ideally at least a week (or preferably two) before the presentation itself. You need to do this to give yourself the time to revise and rewrite without panicking along the way. Don't be surprised when things don't go well at the outset: they never do.

Indeed, that's the point: it is far better to get things wrong now so you do them right in front of the final audience. At first, you will slip and stumble. You will forget what you meant to say next, and it may take you a minute and a half to express a thought that will later take ten seconds. The key thing is to keep going and complete the talk as well as you can each time you rehearse. Most people are surprised by how quickly they improve, and this, in turn, builds their confidence.

To know how well you are progressing, it's not enough to work through the presentation silently in your head: when you rehearse, speak out loud. This is an example of a critical aspect of effective rehearsal – making the practice runs as much like the real thing as possible. It's tough to start with, but it gets easier as your talk becomes smoother and more polished.

Similarly, if you are going to be standing up for your talk – as I recommend, to put you in better physical control of the auditorium – you should be standing up in rehearsal. Turn your mobile off. Have water with you for the rehearsal, as you will for the actual performance. Use any slides or other props that you will be using on the day. Always aim to have a final dress rehearsal in the suit or outfit you will be wearing at the presentation, and if possible do it at the actual venue where you will be speaking. It is a major boost to your confidence at the event itself to know that you have already been there and done it.

At the start of rehearsals, I perform in front of a mirror, not least to ensure I make eye contact. I cannot deny that making eye contact with yourself is not the same as with an audience, but it gets you working in the right direction and makes you more aware of your mannerisms. Winston Churchill, one of the greatest speakers of the twentieth century, practised in front of a mirror, and if it was good enough for him, then it will do for me. As I mentioned in Chapter 8, I have a tendency to put my hand in front of my mouth when I'm talking, which, apart from anything else, isn't helpful for audibility. Seeing myself in the mirror reminds me not to do it in a public performance. The habit never quite goes away, and so neither does the need for me to check myself for it on a regular basis.

I time my rehearsal so that I have a good idea of the length of material I need to cut out (or, much less often, add on) for the actual performance.

I must make sure that I have left enough time for any question and answer session. Even without the timing issue posed by Q&A, I need to remember that the presentation on the day may take anything up to 25% longer than the rehearsal. There will be distractions and interruptions, and there will be the time needed for getting to and from the podium or other place where I will be speaking. If things are going well, I am likely to do lots of ad-libbing; and, on a good day, it can be surprising how much time is taken up by the audience laughing or clapping. As an example, if I am asked to do a twenty-five minute after-dinner speech, I know that I will get into time trouble if I go over twenty minutes in rehearsal.

Whenever possible, I record my rehearsal: an audio recording is helpful, but a video is even better.

Once you have made your video recording, then you are in a position both to listen to your talk and to watch it. And you simply must do this. It is much, much more easily said than done, particularly the first time, because many people find it excruciating to observe themselves in action. A surprising number of actors, for example, can hardly bear to see themselves on television or film. But a budding speaker simply can't do a decent job in identifying problems or developing their personal style until they have found the courage to hear and watch themselves on video. You have to get over the anguish and just do it.

I recommend a very stiff gin and tonic to get you started the first time: I needed three. And have a friend with you to share the experience, to give you support, make constructive comments and, in particular, stop you obsessing about personal quirks that the audience would not even notice.

Watching yourself on video gets a lot easier after that first experience, which is not to say that it ever becomes a particularly relaxing process. However, you learn so much that the discomfort is absolutely worthwhile. I like to remind myself that this process is something that most of my speaking rivals have opted out of because of the pain it involves, and it is for that reason that I gain my competitive edge.

When you summon up the courage to review your recording, you may find above all else that you hate the way you sound. I certainly did the first time I heard myself, and I still do, to be honest. Again, though, you get used to it pretty quickly.

Beyond the way your voice sounds, you may find that your whole personality comes across very differently from what you expected; again, this is normal.

People often discover that their performance on video is more subdued and sedate than they would have wished, and this acts as an encouragement to add a greater variety of gesture and vocal expression. Public speaking commonly succeeds best when it is overstated: exaggeration, embellishment and amplification of tone and feeling can produce optimal results. It's not surprising that many speakers learn from their videos that some extra colour and drama would work wonders for them.

If there is to be a question and answer session, don't forget to think up some likely questions and rehearse the answers to them, just as you would rehearse the main body of your speech.

After each rehearsal, I also recommend reviewing your speech to make sure that:

- You know which bits you would cut out if time runs short.
- You have an escape route in terms of a conclusion you can move to swiftly from any point in the presentation, just in case anything should happen out of your control that makes an early finish necessary.

Get yourself an early audience

By all means, start off by rehearsing on your own. However, as soon as you get moderately familiar with your material, do test it out on an audience. It is invaluable to have other people watch and listen to your rehearsal. Try your speech out on work colleagues, friends and family members – anyone who is likely to give you an honest but constructive appraisal. It can be more frightening to have a partner or friend who knows you well hear you rehearse than to encounter a whole audience of strangers on the day itself. That is exactly the point, because it is far better to work your way through the nerves and anguish while you prepare in private for the talk than to encounter them on speech day for the first time.

Get accustomed to the pressures of performance, simulating the conditions under which you will give the speech at a time when it will be no great disaster if you do mess up. It will make your future public speaking a lot less daunting. Scientific research confirms the value of this approach: practising under pressure significantly reduces our chances of succumbing to stress on the actual day of the performance.

Make it clear to your listeners, your mentors for this purpose, that you want truthful, specific feedback and suggestions for improvement. They are there to support you (which is not the same thing as humouring you or making you feel good in the short term), and their input can help turn a substandard speech into a great one.

Susan Cain, the author of *Quiet: The Power of Introverts in a World That Can't Stop Talking* (and an introvert herself), has demonstrated that this process can succeed for introverts working at their public speaking, just as well as for extroverts. Indeed, she has gone on to substantial success as a professional public speaker in her own right.

As an intermediate step to rehearsing in front of people, some speakers perform in front of their dogs. (Cats are thought to be less sympathetic.) The American University in Washington DC, for example, supports students working on their public speaking skills with the use of 'audience dogs'. Dogs are mostly enthusiastic and non-judgemental, so I can see how this can help speakers develop their confidence early on in preparing their presentation – though the dogs' detailed feedback perhaps lacks the more precise approach of a human's.

For myself, when I was younger I rehearsed in front of my mother's dog, Toby, but with hindsight I suspect he was in the early stages of doggy dementia, and so he was not a particularly supportive listener. In fact, I found my pet rabbit Richard the Lionhead much more enthusiastic. To be fair, a number of other speakers have had a positive experience with a canine audience, while my bunny success seems not to have been duplicated elsewhere.

Some questions to ask

Here are some helpful questions to ask yourself when you review your recording:

- Do I stand up straight and smile?
- Do I look energetic and enthusiastic, confident and authoritative?
- Where do I sound particularly interesting, convincing or passionate?
- Which parts of the presentation need more work?
- Which parts feel like dead ends that would be better left out?
- Am I speaking slowly enough?
- Does the argument flow logically?
- Do I achieve my objective – whether it be to entertain, inform, persuade or call to action?
- Are there places where I trip over the words – where what looked good on paper doesn't work well as spoken language?
- Is the timing right, or have I overrun?

And here are some questions to ask your audience of mentors:

- Could you hear me easily?
- Which bits did you like?
- Which bits didn't you like?
- Which bits would you cut out or shorten?
- Was anything missing?
- What did you think of the start? Of the ending?
- What key points (no more than two or three) did you take away from the talk? (Check the extent to which they coincide with the points you wanted them to take away.)
- Were you left wanting more or wanting less?
- Were there any mannerisms that annoyed you?

When you and your mentors do this kind of review, always be constructive and try not to be overly critical. I know this is particularly hard when you are judging your own work, but take the long-term view. Getting better at public speaking involves a steep learning curve; the practice you are doing will have immense benefits, and it is unfair and unhelpful to be harsh on yourself as you set out on the road to success.

Further tips for mentors

Over the years, I have picked up some useful tips for mentors to help them make the most of their role:

- The first act of the mentor should always be to comment on something positive in what they have seen. There are always positives to be identified, not least the personal bravery of the speaker in going through this exceptionally challenging process.

Scott Adams, the creator of the *Dilbert* comic strip, tells a wonderful story of the transformative effect of four simple words from an instructor, "Wow. That was brave," on the performance of a struggling student in his class.

- A good way of making progress is often to encourage the speaker to discuss their thought processes: "Kendra, what made you approach the speech this way? How did you go about selecting your examples?"

- It can help to make suggestions without being judgemental: "Keanu, what would happen if you were to leave out the section on earthworm mating rituals?" Or, "Kailey, have you considered changing the order of parts two and three?"

- Mentor comments are unlikely to go wrong if they fall into any of the categories of the REF mnemonic, that is to say:

  Recognition – particularly of what the speaker is trying to achieve.

  Encouragement – which speaks for itself.

  Feedback – of a constructive nature, of course.

Conclusion

You must rehearse a lot, and do it out loud and standing up – as near to the conditions on the actual day as you can manage. I don't care how bad you are, or think you are, to start with: the rehearsal process will make you vastly better.

I have coached novice speakers who went from walking disasters at the beginning to stars by the time they gave their talks. And that outcome had hardly anything to do with me: it was their commitment to the rehearsal process that made all the difference. The influential author Malcolm Gladwell sums it up nicely: "Practice isn't the thing you do once you're good. It's the thing you do that makes you good."

Incidentally, if you think I've been tough on you in my demands for rehearsal in this chapter, I should mention that some people go even further than I have suggested here. Gary Smailes, my editor, told me of speakers he knows who intentionally rehearse in more extreme conditions than they will encounter on the day of the performance. One man, in particular, does it when drunk, or in the garden in shorts on a winter morning, or after staying up all night without sleep.

Perhaps I'm making things too easy for you in this book…

Points to take from this chapter

- The keys to better public speaking are hard work, doing as much of it as you can, and focused rehearsal.
- Rehearsals will make you familiar with, and confident in, your material.
- Don't worry when initial rehearsals go badly: you are identifying the challenging issues early on, which is the key to success on the big day.
- Make your rehearsals as much like the real thing as possible.
- Practise in front of a mirror.
- Be sure to time yourself.
- Record yourself, then review the recording: short-term pain will lead to outstanding long-term gain.
- Get yourself an early audience of mentors and ask for specific, constructive feedback.

In the next chapter, we are going to look at the surprising havoc that can be wrought by the misuse of handouts to accompany a talk. We'll end up with some sensible guidelines for the practical use of a basic addition to the speaker's armoury.

Notes

Carmine Gallo's suggestion can be seen at https://www.forbes.com/sites/carminegallo/2014/06/28/the-shortcut-to-the-10000-hour-rule/#6d92f06278d5. For the value of training in stressful situations before the actual performance, see (for example) Sian Beilock's book *Choke*. You can see the story of the American University 'audience dogs' at http://www.cbsnews.com/news/audience-dogs-help-students-reduce-public-speaking-anxiety-american-university/. The Scott Adams story comes in his book *How to Fail at Almost Everything and Still Win Big: Kind of the Story of My Life*. The Malcolm Gladwell quotation is from *Outliers: The Story of Success*.

CHAPTER 23

Beware of handouts

Introduction

Speakers' handouts are more fraught with danger than you might imagine.

I'll start this chapter with an example that shows just how hazardous they can be, incidentally demonstrating that handouts should never be more than a secondary aspect of your talk. We will go on to discuss the best time to distribute a handout and what items to put in it. Despite my initial scepticism, we'll end up with a document that will form a useful supplement to our presentations.

The Cambridge Union experience

In 1995, I attended a speech in the Debating Chamber of the Cambridge Union Society. It was a talk on customs duties or reclaiming value added tax in the European Union or something equally horrible. It soon became apparent that the speaker was reading out the text of her presentation word for word. *This isn't very exciting,* you thought as she got going. It was then that you saw that the full copy of the speech was in your conference folder, and you realised that she was about a third of the way down page 1 of 19. What followed was as close as I have come to a near-death experience. Not only was it dismally dull when the presenter started, but you had warning that it was going to be dismally dull in the middle and at the end. Given that page 1 of 19 took the lecturer four minutes to read out, you quickly established that you had over seventy minutes of dismal dullness still to come. The experience was so agonising that I didn't even manage to doze off.

Be very careful, therefore, how much you distribute by way of a handout at the start of a presentation. Otherwise, there is a substantial likelihood that people will focus on *it* rather than *you* during your talk. You will lose eye contact with them, as well as all sense of audience expectation. A logical attendee would walk out with the literature at the start of the presentation: in practice, politeness means they will stay, and your talk will suffer a lingering death.

General considerations

The Cambridge Union presentation broke the prime directive of handouts: that any handout should always be subsidiary to your talk. It should be an aid but not a substitute.

What sort of aid should we be aiming to provide?

The position is complicated by the discrepancy between the enthusiasm audiences express for having a handout and what they do with it afterwards. In real life, my suspicion is that, other than in areas like commercial proposals where your documentation will no doubt be reviewed in detail after your presentation, barely a soul goes on to read the materials you have distributed.

So by all means provide a handout, and it may well gain you extra brownie points in those horrible questionnaires that delegates are asked to fill in at the end of a presentation, which we will come back to in a minute. But don't spend too long on it. The important thing is to get the talk itself right. And remember that the fuller the handout, the less chance there is that anyone will read it afterwards. I try never to go over half a dozen pages, even for a very technical subject.

To stress the point again, never forget that the potential benefits of offering a handout may be more than cancelled out if it distracts the audience during the talk.

Having said all that, I'd still have to admit that a well-designed handout can be a genuine help to a presentation. If you can prepare one that will be useful for your audience without going to an inordinate expense of time, then please do so.

When, then, if you are providing a handout, should you give it out, bearing in mind the horrors of the Cambridge Union debacle?

My firm preference is for the end of your session, so that the audience is not distracted while you are speaking. However, if you take this approach, remember to tell the audience at the outset that they will indeed be getting a handout afterwards covering the key points of the presentation, so they are not obliged to take notes. And then, of course, do remember to distribute the handout at the end.

What to include in the handout

The thing to put into the handout above all else is some thought on your part. Beyond that, you might consider including:

- The key facts underlying your talk.
- Relevant definitions and quotations.
- Copies of any examples and numerical calculations you use.

- A mixture of text, graphs, diagrams and pictures in preference to a wordy text alone.
- Your name and your contact details in big letters on the front page.

Go for quality rather than quantity. In general, consider providing a simple key information sheet or sheets rather than a bulky document. Use good quality paper, give it an attractive design, include some colour, and consider having it laminated so that the attendee has a focused, long-lasting record of your talk.

An alternative approach, suggested by the psychologist and business consultant William Lareau, is to give the delegates at the start of your talk a word-for-word copy of the overheads or slides that you will be using. This allows people to add their own notes in the margins, thereby increasing the chances that they will connect with what you're saying, while ensuring they pay attention to the talk rather than lose themselves in the text of the handout.

By contrast, some speakers get into the habit (often because it is encouraged by conference organisers) of distributing copies of their slides, and nothing else, *after their talk*. This strikes me as an odd idea. If your slides make sense on their own without the further explanation offered by what you have to say, why bother giving the talk in the first place? Or, to look at it another way, how much better might your slides have been if you were not lumbered with using them as a handout afterwards?

There are, of course, many individual exceptions to the general pointers we have discussed here. A handout will not normally, for example, accompany an after-dinner speech, though you will no doubt wish to carry a plentiful supply of business cards to distribute to your eager listeners.

The special problem of professional conferences

I referred above to the questionnaire (known in the trade as 'happy sheets'), often given out for completion at the end of a presentation at a professional conference, on which the audience is asked to assess the speaker. Often it will require a judgement on the handout. This is remarkably silly, because if people were focusing on the speaker as they should have been, they wouldn't have had nearly enough time to digest and evaluate the handout in time to give a sensible mark.

In these circumstances, experience suggests that sheer length and quantity of detail, as opposed to quality of content, will get the best marks. So, this time, the greater the number of dead forests, the higher will be your credit. I don't want to encourage you to join in the silliness, but it helps to know that it exists. Look out for the SPQR (Society for the Promotion of Questionnaire Reform), which I may well establish once I have finished this pesky book.

In a more sensible world, instead of worrying about a lengthy handout, conference organisers and their speakers would be encouraging attendees to take notes of the session by such obvious means as providing them with paper and pens. I am constantly surprised at how rarely this happens. I have always derived the greatest learning from other people's presentations by taking my own notes, and I know I am far from alone in this. Moreover, as a technological Luddite, I'm pleased to say there is now evidence that taking longhand notes is more effective than using a laptop to make your record of the event.

Conclusion

I can't finish this chapter without mentioning one of my own favourite strategies – to provide no handout at all at the actual presentation, but to announce that the notes or script of the talk will be available to attendees if they contact you at your given email address. That way, fewer forests will die as a result of your speech, and only people who genuinely want the notes or would like to take matters further will get the handout. They then have the chance to come back to you with questions, while you will have the opportunity to contact them again in the future using your email database. It is a useful way to build up a relationship, assuming that everyone acts with integrity.

Overall, I urge you to remember the prime directive. Handouts can be nice add-ons, but in the end it is the talk that counts. The chances of attendees reading the printed materials after the event are not high. Take the detailed work on handouts seriously, but not *all that* seriously.

Points to take from this chapter

- Handouts should always be subsidiary to your talks.
- Keep them brief and go for quality, not quantity.
- Don't let them distract the audience from what you have to say.
- When in doubt, give them out at the end of your session, not earlier.
- Provide paper and pens to encourage people to take notes.
- Longhand notes tend to work best for attendees.

In the next chapter, we will get down to the real nuts and bolts (sometimes literally, in the case of the backing gear and equipment) of the speaker's trade, discussing the inspection we should carry out of the auditorium where we will be performing. We might initially view this as an annoying triviality, but we'll soon see that it can frequently make the difference between triumph and disaster.

Notes

For a fuller picture of the Cambridge Union, Stephen Parkinson's excellent book *Arena of Ambition: A History of the Cambridge Union*, Icon Books Ltd, 2009, is recommended. William Lareau's suggestion comes from his highly practical handbook *Conduct Expected: The Unwritten Rules for a Successful Business Career*, New Win Publishing Inc., 1997. The evidence that taking longhand notes is more effective than using a laptop is set out in a 2014 paper in the journal *Psychological Science* by Pam A Mueller and Daniel M Oppenheimer (yes, it's that man Oppenheimer again) with the wonderfully self-explanatory title *The Pen Is Mightier Than the Keyboard: Advantages of Longhand Over Laptop Note Taking.*

CHAPTER 24

Case the joint

Introduction

People quite often look at me as though I am off with the fairies when I tell them how vital it is to carry out a thorough inspection of the venue where they will be speaking, and to do so well in advance of the talk itself.

In this chapter, I'm going to justify (I hope) the strength of my conviction, showing that I'm following in distinguished footsteps in my approach. I'll go on to explain the underlying rationale: to ensure the best possible lines of communication between you and your audience. We'll then examine the specific areas to look out for when you do your tour of the auditorium. As a result of all this, you will find that you have a much sturdier level of confidence when it really matters: that moment when you take the stage.

Why it is so important to acclimatise yourself to the venue

Here, Charles Kent writes about his friend Charles Dickens, a model example of my suggested method:

"Announced to read, for instance, for the first time in some town he had never before visited for that purpose, or in some building in which his voice had never before been raised, he would go down to the empty hall long before the hour appointed for the reading, to take the bearings, as he would say, or, in other words, to familiarise himself with the place beforehand."

Dickens knew why this familiarisation process was so important. For a reading, or indeed any other form of presentation, to succeed you need:

- A receptive audience.
- Sitting comfortably.
- Not too hot or cold.
- Able to hear you without having to work too hard at it.
- Able to see you – and vice versa, so that you can make eye contact and judge their reactions.

Your best chance of achieving all this is to get to know the auditorium beforehand and be prepared to adjust your style to fit the conditions. As an example, in larger venues, or where your listeners are spread out, it will take longer for your words to sink in. (Similarly, laughs and other reactions will come back more slowly to you from the audience.) Accordingly, you will need to pause for longer than usual for your words to hit home before you start talking again.

The general approach

Get to know in advance the place where you will be talking –

if possible, on an earlier day, or failing that by looking around at least an hour or two before you are due to speak. The more professional you are in 'casing the joint', the more likely you are to avoid unexpected disasters.

If, for example, you are one of a number of presenters during a conference, try to attend from the outset of the session to listen to the speakers before you. You will almost certainly learn something:

- You will spot things that could easily go wrong at that particular venue.
- You will get a better idea of the sort of questions that are likely to come up in your presentation.
- You will identify areas where other speakers have duplicated what you were going to talk about. You can then quietly drop that material from your talk, or earn brownie points by saying, "I thoroughly agree with Sansa's comments earlier that…" or "Arya said…, and I would just like to give my own interpretation on that point." You gain extra credit by demonstrating that, like the audience, you have been there from the outset and have been paying attention.

Even more important is that by turning up early you get a feel for the audience, and that will make you more comfortable and relaxed during your talk. You discover whether they are quiet or demonstrative, uninterested or keen, and whether their questions tend to be penetrating or superficial. Moreover, you get a sense of the pace of the day, whether the talks show light and shade, whether they are too technical and heavy or too light and frothy. You can then amend the style and depth of your own presentation accordingly – though I recommend limited rewrites rather than wholesale changes, which can take you too far into unknown territory.

Specific tips

Here are the things I focus on when I do my reconnaissance of the venue.

The room

Walk around the stage and the auditorium so that you feel increasingly at home. How does the room strike you? Is it spacious or cramped? Space is not always a good thing since ultra-large rooms tend to lack atmosphere and have a dead aura.

Check the layout at the front. Is anything likely to block the sightlines between you and the audience, or the audience and any screen you use? Ensure there is adequate space between you and the audience, so that you will have room to move about and impose your presence on them. Plan whatever you need to do to eliminate obstructions, whether it be stray tables or chairs, or even the person who introduces you if they outstay their welcome at the front.

Is a lectern going to be available for your talk? If so, are you going to make use of it?

There is no right answer to questions like these, but you need to think about them. David Cameron gave a lectern-free speech at the Conservative Conference in October 2005, which was widely considered the turning point in his bid to lead the party. His rivals seemed to hide behind the lectern, whereas his openness and ease in full view of the audience won him a three-minute ovation.

Sit in the seats the audience will be using, to get a feel for what their experience will be like. The more uncomfortable the seating, the quicker the audience will start fidgeting and the earlier you will need to allow a stretch break. Seats that are close together may well help the audience to feel involved, but they should not be so close that people feel their personal space is being invaded. Also, if you want them to take notes, they need space to do so.

Never hesitate to ask for the layout to be changed to suit you. Angela Merkel, the Chancellor of Germany, has been known to rearrange the chairs to improve communications at a conference, and we should all be happy to follow her example.

Check that the room is clean and tidy: you should not be expected to perform in a dump. As you look around, be on the alert for those little things – as with David Cameron and the lectern, or rather David Cameron without it – that can help put you in charge as the owner of the event rather than a passive participant.

Lighting

Will the lighting be powerful enough for you to see the audience and vice versa? Again, there is no right answer here. You may be someone who finds it reassuring *not* to be able to see them. The point is simply that it helps to know in advance.

Will the lighting be sufficiently strong for you to read your notes? If not, you might need to ask for a lectern with a light attachment.

Remember that, in those occasional instances where there *is* good lighting, it could heat up the venue, so you will need to check that it doesn't get too hot for the audience.

Temperature

Check the heating and ventilation. It is important for you to be comfortable, just as much as for the audience.

In the American presidential elections of 1960, it was Richard Nixon's profuse sweating in the televised debate that helped bring him defeat against John F Kennedy: those who listened to them on the radio felt that Nixon came out the better of the two.

You are looking to avoid any extremes of temperature: a hot room may send your audience to sleep, but equally a speaker will need to work harder than usual to gain their interest if it is chilly. If their primary short-term concern is how to get warm, they won't be paying you the attention you deserve.

Sound system

Carry out your sound checks and rehearsals well before your presentation is due to start. Make certain you are happy with the acoustics and that the venue doesn't reverberate with echoes.

Will you need a microphone? If in doubt, err on the side of caution and use one. There is no excuse for the audience being unable to hear you.

Having checked on the sound system well before your talk, check it again if you can in the minutes before you are due to start.

Other equipment and supplies

Check well in advance that the right sockets and leads for your laptop are available. And check all the other supporting equipment, however insignificant it might seem. For example, nearly every venue I have spoken at provided flipchart pens that were either dying or long dead, so I always take my own with me.

If you want audience members to take notes, make sure pens and paper are provided.

Check when and where, if at all, tea and coffee will be provided for the attendees, and try to arrange for this to be done in such a way as to minimise disruption to your talk.

Make sure you have water and a glass. This is to keep you hydrated, to prevent or combat a coughing fit, and to give you a helpful prop that you can use to play for time if your mind goes blank and you need to regain the thread of your talk. Nichol's ninth law states that the chances of a coughing fit or losing the thread are raised exponentially if you don't have water with you from the start.

Noise and other disturbances

What unusual noises are likely to come from nearby rooms? This is a particular challenge in hotels, which have an interesting habit of rearranging rooms, or setting up lunch or dinner, at crucial points in your talk. The sound of crockery being crocked is the loudest and most distracting and annoying sound in the entire world. You heard it here first.

I recommend talking informally to people in the know at the venue about its good and bad points, especially the bad ones because they can have unique destructive power. 'People in the know' usually means hotel or kitchen staff on the ground, rather than the top brass. I always ask about the occasional noise that may come in from adjacent parts of the building, kitchens being the worst offenders, so that I can time critical points of my presentation to avoid major clashes.

In extreme cases, be prepared to ask for a change of room.

Toilets

Never underestimate the importance of the loo facilities. Where are the toilets, for your comfort no less than that of the audience? Are they ample regarding urinals and cubicles? The adequacy of the toilets is a key factor in determining how long people will take to get back from breaks.

Remember that one of the great crimes of modern civilisation is that, in general, ladies receive inadequate toilet facilities by comparison with men. I did once get a bit carried away in my lavatory checks and found myself obliged to justify my presence in the ladies' loos. I said I had lost my mum, an excuse that fortunately worked well with anyone who knew my mother.

Car parking

Beware the absence of promised car parking, or the car park being full. You may need to delay your talk while people desperately seek somewhere legal to abandon their vehicles before joining you.

Smokers

In these days of political conformity, the nearest place to smoke legally may well be several miles from the auditorium, or indeed in the next town. Allow for this in your calculation of how long breaks will last.

Safety precautions

You need to know what the evacuation procedures are for the venue in the event of a fire or other emergency. Have an eye to the worst case. Who would there be to take charge, apart from you as the speaker, if the fire alarm went off? If the person to take charge is you, check you would know what to do.

Organise your helpers

If there is someone responsible for technical facilities at the place where you will be speaking, talk to them as soon as you can before your performance. They can add enormously to the quality of your presentation, and you want to make sure they are on your side.

James Schofield, the author of Collins' incisive *Presentation Skills in 7 simple steps*, is helpful on this. "The moment you agree to give a presentation," he writes, "you should be trying to make a new BFF (Best Friend Forever) – the person responsible for technical support and equipment at the venue."

As James Schofield says, we should explain what we want to the technical specialist; be persistent in trying to get it, while showing respect for their suggestions; and be sure to thank them appropriately when the presentation is over. This is crucial because nothing can go wrong in public speaking with such disastrous consequences as the technology. We will return to this subject in Chapter 29.

Beyond the technical guru, arrange if you possibly can to have at least one assistant at the venue to act as a troubleshooter for you. The presence of a skilled helper is invaluable: it allows you to focus on your proper job of delivering your talk well.

The role of a top-class assistant should include:

- Checking the lighting and the room temperature.
- Helping out if equipment malfunctions.
- Monitoring the internal noise level – alerting you, for example, if your voice falls away so they can no longer hear you at the back.
- Monitoring the external noise level, particularly annoying sounds from adjacent rooms, and taking swift action if problems arise.
- Dealing with audience administration; for example, name badges, handouts, and procedures for late arrivals, not to mention getting audience members back from breaks on time.

While I am on the subject of name badges, can I quickly make a plea for them to be in large letters? Then people will be able to read them without having to squint or move embarrassingly close to your body.

Some personal experience

When I was doing half or full day seminars on tax, I would always turn up at least ninety minutes before the start to case the joint. That way, I would have the time to identify potential problems and put them right.

I saved myself from some horrors:

- The many days the sound system did not work or was amazingly distorted.
- The day they'd double-booked speakers so that I got the job just by arriving first and gaining the right of possession. (I was also larger than my rival, which may have helped.)
- The day the handouts had not turned up.
- The day the handouts turned up but were the wrong ones.

In both the handout disasters I had time to organise helpers to drive in from fifty miles away, not necessarily at entirely legal speeds, to rescue the situation with replacements. The audiences never noticed that anything was wrong.

The tough gig – the small audience in a big hall

One of the hardest audiences to work with is a limited number of people in a large auditorium; say, thirty in a place meant for three hundred. When an unexpectedly small audience turns up, you need to take decisive action early on.

Here, Walter Dill Scott, writing in *The Psychology of Public Speaking*, suggests a solution:

"One of the most helpful methods [of dealing with this issue] is to get the audience to sit close together. It is easy to speak to a packed house, but it would take a Demosthenes to make an impression when separated from his audience by a yawning abyss of empty seats. 500 people scattered over an auditorium which seats 3,000 can scarcely be welded into a

> homogeneous audience… This fact forces itself on all public speakers and leads them to attempt to have only certain groups of seats occupied and preferably the front ones in order that the vacant ones may not form a barrier between the speaker and the hearers."

Here, in an interview, Mark Twain gives a good example of how to deal positively with a small audience and make Walter Dill Scott's approach work in practice:

> "Personally some of my most enthusiastic audiences have been small ones. I remember on one occasion many years ago, I delivered a lecture in St Louis. The hall was a very large one, with a seating capacity of about 1,600 persons I believe, no galleries, but every seat occupying the same level. The night was terribly stormy and there were perhaps thirty people in the hall and with that exception a vast acreage of chair backs confronted me. The feeling of a lecturer at such junctures should not be despondent. Every man's presence should be regarded as an individual compliment… I requested everybody present to come forward and sit in a solid phalanx. It was like lecturing to the disciples on the edge of the Sahara but I started off, and instead of lecturing for an hour and a half only, I kept it up for more than two hours."

Conclusion

It is hard to overstate the importance of casing the joint thoroughly before your talk. Once you feel familiar with the room where you will be performing, it is so much easier to own that room by way of your commanding presence, so the audience feels, and more importantly you feel, that you have every right to be there, in control. Once you can begin your talk with the quiet assurance and self-confidence that proclaims, "This is my space, and what I have to say to you is valuable," the battle for success is already half won.

Points to take from this chapter

- Remember the aim – a receptive audience, sitting comfortably, not too hot or cold, able to hear and see you.
- Get to know the venue thoroughly before you speak.
- Be ready to adjust your style to suit the conditions.
- Arrive early to get a feel for the audience.
- Get to know the person in charge of technical facilities.
- Take an assistant to act as your troubleshooter.
- Get a small audience in a large venue to sit together.
- Familiarity with the venue breeds confidence in your performance.

In the next chapter, we're going to take a walk on the wild side, looking at the thorny issue of whether drink or drugs (or possibly both together) could ever have a positive effect on our performances as speakers. I hope you'll join me with a mind open to some surprising discoveries.

Notes

The extract from Mark Twain again comes from *Mark Twain: The Complete Interviews*, edited by Gary Scharnhorst, University of Alabama Press, 2006.

CHAPTER 25

Manage your medication

Introduction

In this chapter, we are going to examine some artificial means of stimulation for a public speaker. I'm referring to the use of drink and drugs in an attempt to improve your performance, or perhaps simply to persuade you to take the stage in the first place. I will review the questionable role of alcohol in a speaker's toolkit, and then move on to talk about medicines in general.

This is, of course, a controversial subject. It is such a hot topic that most textbooks on public speaking ignore it entirely, often on the basis that serious professionals should have no truck with synthetic ways of enhancing their presentations. In reality, so many people do seek chemical help before appearing in front of an audience that it would be wrong to turn a blind eye to it here.

I have to declare an interest.

When taking my first driving test, I was such a bundle of nerves that I accelerated on what should have been my emergency stop. I doubt whether the examiner ever worked again. For my second test, a low dose of Valium calmed me down and got me through. I find it hard to accept the wholesale condemnation of using artificial aids to help a stressful performance succeed.

It is, at any rate, important for there to be an open discussion on this topic.

Writing in *The Guardian*, Scott Stossel tells the story of a phone call one night, in 1965, to a professor at Pennsylvania State University, asking if one of his students was due to give a speech the next day. The student had just been rescued before she jumped from one of the highest buildings on the campus. She said she could not face giving another speech. The worried professor subsequently found that, of fourteen recorded student suicides at the university in recent years, thirteen had been enrolled in mandatory public speaking classes.

It is a grim reminder that, in particularly vulnerable individuals, the effects of uncontrolled stage fright can be devastating.

Alcohol

Let's start by having a look at what usually does *not* work – the use of drink-inspired courage to get us through a speech.

"The best audience is one that is intelligent, well-educated and a little drunk." That is a comment credited to an American lawyer and politician, Alben W Barkley. I prefer my listeners that way myself: a modicum of alcohol, but not too much, can do wonders for an audience's good nature. But it doesn't follow that the best speakers should follow the same path.

The textbooks on public speaking that are prepared to talk about drinking in advance of a performance tend to condemn it out of hand. I have to agree with them, for most speakers in most circumstances. The key text on alcohol before a speech is *Right Ho, Jeeves* by PG Wodehouse, where the wonderfully named Gussie Fink-Nottle gives a classic demonstration of what can go wrong.

Having addressed his stage fright by way of an alarming

mixture of gin and whisky, Gussie presents the prizes at Market Snodsbury Grammar School. With self-confidence oozing from his every pore, he soon corrects the headmaster when he gets Gussie's name wrong in his introduction. (As we have seen, the standard advice must be to grin and bear such annoyances.) Gussie proceeds to call the headmaster a silly ass (though admittedly he does it in a friendly way) and laughs explosively at his own joke.

When he starts on his speech proper, he again insults the headmaster, insults the Irish and insults a key member of the audience ("the fellow with a face rather like a walnut"). He makes offensive comments about his friend Bertie Wooster, who is in the hall. He is magnificently rude to a prizewinner: "So you've won the Scripture-knowledge prize, have you?... You look just the sort of little tick who would." He goes on to accuse the boy of cheating, suggests that he is well known to the police, and hints at a guilty liaison between the boy's mother and the headmaster. Only the singing of the national anthem intervenes to bring proceedings to a close. To be fair, nearly all of Gussie's antics go down remarkably well with the boys. Even so, while countless books urge us to speak like Churchill or Obama or Jobs and the like, there is no sign of a *Speak like Fink-Nottle* bestseller on the booklists just yet.

My own experience of alcohol before talks has not been a happy one. I went on a first date with a lady in London. We were both terrified, and within half an hour we had drunk a bottle and a half of the house white on empty stomachs. The problem was that I was due to give an after-dinner speech later that evening. When the moment of destiny came, I was awful: my timing went completely awry and I sped up when I should have slowed down. Jokes came thick and fast, but with the punchlines in the wrong places. Unsurprisingly, they never invited me back. On the other hand, I married the lady in question two years later, so the evening did present certain compensations.

Though you might have thought the point was self-evident to begin with, the latest scientific research confirms that, for most people most of the time, alcohol makes you worse at public speaking. It does indeed calm your nerves, but, as with my after-dinner speech, the audience will rate you less well than a sober speaker.

Even if you have no initial intention of imbibing, beware the well-meaning host who attempts to ply you with a succession of drinks before the event. And, if you do find you've exceeded a prudent level of alcohol intake in advance of your speech, switch to water and drink a lot of it as soon as you possibly can to sort out your internal systems. Then carry on sipping water during the speech itself so that you stay hydrated and your mouth does not dry up.

On occasions like that, there is nothing for it but to drink a large amount of water, but at other times never forget the incidental consequences of fluid consumption. The former Scottish Labour Party leader Jim Murphy has told how too much liquid at lunchtime ruined his maiden Parliamentary speech in 1997. By the time the Speaker, Betty Boothroyd, called on him to speak, his distress was such that he just stood there, wriggling and writhing. "Are you willing, Mr Murphy?" the Speaker asked. "Willing, but not able," he spluttered, hastening from the Chamber – not the most glorious of speaking debuts.

Once your event is over, you can, of course, relax properly. This is how Mitch Murray puts it in his splendid *Handbook for the Terrified Speaker*: "Don't forget, once your speech is over, go straight back to alcohol… Just think: if water can rot the soles of your shoes, imagine what it can do to your stomach!"

Pills

In 1975, Basil Boothroyd published his humorous classic,

Accustomed As I Am, subtitled *The Loneliness of the Long-Distance Speaker Or, All You'd Never Guess About Public Speaking*. In it, he writes: "I'm not often on the pill. But there are times." He talks about the two types of medication: the 'bracer-upper' and the 'calmer-downer'. Of the two sorts, he says, the calmer-downer is not necessarily going to be the safer option. This applies in particular if you should "find yourself reflecting, as the toastmaster screams your name, that you don't give a damn whether you talk to these people or not, whoever the hell they are." He also notes the difficulty of timing your medicinal intake to achieve the right level of sprightliness or relaxation, given the unpredictable length of any meal or other speeches preceding your talk.

There is still a good deal of logic behind the calmer-downer.

Public speaking anxiety can show itself in a variety of unpleasant physical ways: a speeding or irregular heartbeat, nausea, sweating, breathlessness, feelings of faintness or dizziness, or even a full-blown panic attack before the event.

Some people do find they need medication to get them through, regardless of all the helpful tips we'll meet in Chapter 27 on dealing with the stress. This happens in real life considerably more often than the idealistic literature on public speaking and other high-pressure public performances might suggest.

In her fascinating book *The Society of Timid Souls: Or, How to be Brave*, Polly Morland, a writer and documentary maker, tells of the plight of orchestral musicians. The issue of trembling hands means they can suffer even more problems from stress than public speakers. Studies suggest that somewhere between 16% and 24% of orchestral musicians have experienced the most severe forms of performance anxiety.

"Forget about rock stars in rehab," Polly Morland writes, "take a look in the orchestra pit."

Beta blockers

The pills of choice for orchestral musicians to manage their nerves have been beta blockers, which are drugs used to treat conditions such as angina, heart failure and high blood pressure. I know beta blockers only too well because my doctor prescribes them to control my blood pressure. They work by blocking the action of hormones like adrenaline, so decreasing the activity of the heart. Stopping the heart from racing makes us feel calmer and less shaky.

Fortunately, beta blockers are usually free of major side effects, and they are not physically addictive. Their key attraction, unlike alcohol or tranquillisers, is that they can take away the nasty symptoms of fear without affecting your mental control or your performance. They remove the physical side effects rather than the actual feelings of anxiety.

At their best, they are not going to enhance your performance, as steroids would do for an athlete, but rather allow you to perform to your potential. The most popular pill for both orchestral musicians and public speakers at the time of writing seems to be propanolol (marketed as Inderal), which was the first successful beta blocker to be developed.

A wide range of sports have banned beta blockers on account of the advantages they offer in situations of stress. Because your hands will shake less, it's not surprising that archery, shooting and snooker prohibit their use. Snooker fans may remember the magnificent Big Bill Werbeniuk, whose career came to an untimely end when propanolol was banned in competition. He also had a prodigious alcohol intake before and during matches that makes Gussie Fink-Nottle look a rank novice in the drinking stakes.

Public speaking is not a competitive sport, so the comparison with such events is of limited relevance to us here, except to the extent that the ban on beta blockers in athletic activities seems to confirm their potential effectiveness.

In her book *Choke*, Sian Beilock writes: "Rather than improving overall performance per se, [beta blockers] may allow those who get most anxious in competitive situations to show what they can do." She notes that, in a study with musicians using the beta blocker oxprenolol, the results varied in a significant way. Overall, those who took the drug trembled less and performed better. Significantly, however, it was the players most prone to stage fright who improved with the help of the drug. Those players who did not normally get stage fright did not benefit from the oxprenolol at all. This appears to support the common-sense approach that you should only ever consider the use of drugs if stage fright is a debilitating issue for you.

The Scott Stossel case study

Someone who certainly falls into that category is Scott Stossel, a man who suffers from extreme anxiety. In his deeply impressive book *My Age of Anxiety*, he describes his regime for speaking at a public event. He needs to get going on the pills early, or else no amount of medication will save the day.

About four hours ago, he got started by taking some Xanax, a tranquilliser used to treat anxiety and panic disorders. Then, an hour ago, he took more Xanax together with some propanolol. He probably swallowed a shot of scotch or vodka at the same time. Between fifteen and thirty minutes ago he most likely took a second shot, perhaps a double or triple measure.

As he now stands up to speak, he has Xanax and a miniature vodka or two readily available in reserve. If he has got his dosage wrong and taken too much, he may already be slurring his words. If he has consumed too little, well, he may be off the stage by now. However, he says: "If I've managed to hit the sweet spot... then I'm probably doing okay up here: nervous but not miserable; a little fuzzy but still able to convey clarity."

He is under no illusion about his approach: he is aware that it is dangerous, but he also knows it works.

The Ronnie Corbett experience

The comedian Ronnie Corbett tells the story of his solo debut. He is nowhere near the Scott Stossel league in terms of anxiety, but he still uses one of his friend Harry Secombe's 'nadger' pills to combat his nerves. The outcome is problematic:

> "He gave me one of his pills and I went on to do my five minutes. Unfortunately, thanks to the nadger, I don't remember anything about that night. This important milestone in my career, my first solo spot, passed in a blur."

Conclusion

What can we conclude from the accounts of Scott Stossel and Ronnie Corbett?

Above all, if you are thinking of taking a pill or any other kind of medication for your performance anxiety, please, please talk to your doctor first. This is vital to ensure that any particular drug is safe for you, taking into account any medical conditions you have and the possible interaction with other pills you take. Beta blockers are prescription-only medicines, which means they can only be prescribed by a general practitioner or a similarly qualified professional.

Beware of the downsides.

For example, you don't want to eliminate so much of your nervous energy that your performance becomes dull and flat.

It is always advisable to have a couple of test runs using your proposed medication before the day of your presentation, to make sure there are no unpleasant side effects. Even then, take into account the likelihood that you will be much more agitated on the day of the performance, so the trial run may not be an entirely reliable guide. Moreover, while beta blockers are not addictive in physical terms, as alcohol and tranquillisers are, they can be addictive in psychological terms, so that we come to feel we cannot do anything that challenges us without popping a pill. Trust me on this: I've been there.

It will always be a delicate balance. Using medications may calm your nerves very successfully, but you have to set that against the potential loss of the concentration, focus and sheer enthusiasm that are so important to a speaker. And, whatever you do, never ignore the dangers of resorting to chemical assistance to deal with the stresses of life.

Points to take from this chapter

- For some vulnerable people, stage fright can be devastating.
- Alcohol almost never works as a solution.
- Beta blockers may relieve the physical symptoms of fear without damaging your performance.
- Consider using drugs only if your stage fright is debilitating, and only after consulting a doctor.
- Always carry out test runs of your medication before the actual speech.

In the next chapter, we are going to examine a much more down-to-earth topic – the use of the humble checklist to ensure that you are fully prepared for your presentation, avoiding any mishaps along the way.

Notes

Scott Stossel's piece in *The Guardian* appeared on 6 July 2015. The story about Jim Murphy appeared in *The Times* Diary column (TMS) on 16 June 2015. The Ronnie Corbett quotation again comes from his delightful autobiography *High Hopes*.

CHAPTER 26

Use a checklist

Introduction

For many years it was regarded as a blunt and unhelpful tool of officialdom, but the reputation of the simple checklist was emphatically restored by the American surgeon and writer Atul Gawande in his 2009 book *The Checklist Manifesto: How to Get Things Right*. He demonstrated the importance of organisation and planning by way of checklists in medicine and the wider world.

In this chapter, I want to set out the straightforward rules for making the most of public speaking checklists. I'll then show you three examples of useful checklists:

- A brief list covering the content of a presentation.
- My schedule of items to consider when I decide whether I should be speaking at all.
- My personal checklist of preparatory points to review before any talk.

I hope that these examples will convince you that, far from being a bureaucratic waste of time, a concise, well-planned checklist can be immensely valuable in the preparation of a great talk.

How to make the most of your checklists

For a checklist to work well, it must be short and limited to essential steps. Otherwise, it becomes a meaningless chore to be rushed through unthinkingly, rather than a critical project for an engaged brain. Also, it must be fully adapted to suit your individual personality and circumstances.

For example, I suffer from borderline obsessive-compulsive disorder, which makes me liable to anxiety characterised by repetitive, ritualised behaviours. (Do you know how hard it is to make sure you have turned the tap off?) My personal checklist is geared to confirming just once or twice that the microphone is working, not half a dozen times.

An abundance of material is available from the Internet, not to mention the book you are reading, to help you put together a list that suits you personally. An excellent source, with a significant focus on the logistical aspects of a presentation, is the *Public Speaker's Checklist*, available as a free PDF file download from John Zimmer's *Manner of Speaking* website at http://mannerofspeaking.org.

A helpful tip, suggested by Simon Raybould in his book *Presentation Genius*, is to spend five minutes at the end of any presentation to go over the experience in your mind, asking yourself what you should add to your checklist. Ask also, I would suggest, what you should leave out for the future to avoid the list becoming too lengthy.

The content checklist

For the actual content of your presentation, I have found nothing to beat an excellent, brief list set out more than a hundred years ago in a 1912 work, *Extemporaneous Speaking* by Paul M Pearson and Philip M Hicks. It asks some searching questions about each of the introduction, the middle ('discussion') and the conclusion of your speech:

Introduction.
- Is it needed to win the goodwill of the audience?
- Does it set forth the speaker's theme clearly?
- Will it arouse interest in what is to follow?

Discussion.
- Does it have:
  * Unity?
  * Logical order?
  * Clearness?
  * Force?
  * Elegance?
  * Appeal?
- Is it convincing?

Conclusion.
- Is it the natural climax of the speech; or
- Is its purpose merely that of leave-taking?
- Is it brief?
- Is it strong?
- Is it appropriate?

I particularly like the implicit reminders here that:

- If parts of your introduction serve no purpose in winning over the audience, they would be better left out so you can get on with your primary business.
- It's good to work up to a climax.
- The conclusion, though it should be brief, needs

to have more substance than a simple message of 'thank you and goodbye' to the audience.

The checklist for deciding whether you should speak in the first place

It helps at times to go back to first principles. My next checklist is an aide-memoire for anyone thinking of giving a talk – a useful list of questions to ask yourself at that key early time when you're deciding whether to commit to speaking in public:

- What am I trying to achieve?
- Is this the right format?
- Should it be someone else?
- What's in it for me?
- What's in it for them?
- How much effort will it take on my part, and am I prepared to make it?

Let's look at these questions in more detail. If you can give favourable answers to each of them, and can do so realistically, then all systems are go, and you have a potentially successful talk on your hands.

What am I trying to achieve?

We looked at this subject in Chapter 4. Approach the question with a broad mind. The presentation might be part of your career development plan, to help you get a promotion. You might be seeking to enthuse and energise the audience, to move them to action by what you say. When you are speaking to workmates or other colleagues, you may be trying to make them feel good about their work or the organisation. You might be going for applause and laughter, the immense joy and boost to self-esteem that a speaker can derive from an audience that is enjoying itself. Alternatively, if you are being paid for a speech, you might simply be doing it for the money.

There can be a thousand different targets. But it will help your focus in preparing for the talk (or, indeed, deciding not to do it) if you concentrate keenly right from the outset on what you are aiming to accomplish. Remember that the achievement you are looking for will usually have to be significant to justify the time commitment.

Is this the right format?

Public speaking is very time-consuming.

It's not just your preparation time and your time on the actual day of the performance. There's the time of the audience too, including travelling to and from the venue.

Would another format be more efficient? If you are passing over detailed information, would an email or a widely circulated letter be better? It is almost always better to convey extreme detail in written form: the reader can go back, reread the material, cross-reference it, and go at a pace of their choosing with tea breaks to suit them. We talked in Chapter 11 about the small number of points you can reasonably hope to convey in a speech.

Where public speaking comes into its own is the situation where you want to make an emotional link with the audience, to motivate them, to bind them together, to make them laugh or cry. A prolonged talk on the detailed aspects of a technical subject, or a presentation on a topic that plainly does not inspire popular interest, may not do any of these things.

The novelist and playwright JB Priestley wrote a piece on one of the pleasures of later life called *Not Going*, commenting that "One of the delights known to age and beyond the grasp of youth is that of *Not Going*." Two of the less successful TED talks were entitled *My journey to yo-yo mastery* and *How to tie your shoes*. (I'm not making this up, honestly.) Mr Priestley may have had talks like that in mind.

Should it be someone else?

Are you the right person to give the talk? Do you have sufficient expertise in the subject? If someone who knows your work has asked you to do the speech, that is a pretty big hint. But beware of being dragged into speaking for negative reasons – in particular, the fact that no one else wants to do it. They may have first rate grounds which you too would be unwise to ignore. Remember also that being in a position of authority or power in an organisation is not of itself a convincing reason for you to give the talk. Is a more junior person more knowledgeable or otherwise better equipped to talk on the subject? Quite simply, would they be a more effective speaker than you?

I regret the times I should have given way to a junior colleague who would have given a stronger performance, not to mention the other times when I would have improved on the boss's effort. In general, use the speaker who will have the best combination of intellectual and emotional impact.

I worked as a commissioner at a UK public body where the chair failed to learn this lesson. As a consequence, they lost their job, and the institution itself closed down shortly afterwards. It can be painful to make way for someone else when a speaking opportunity comes up, but to do so can sometimes be essential for the organisation's future welfare, not to mention that of the individual. If the status of the speaker is a real issue for the institution or the audience, then have the business leader on the platform but consider limiting them to the introduction and the close, leaving the main body of the talk to the best speaker available.

On the other hand, if the boss is keen, competent and enthusiastic about speaking and they know the subject, let nothing stop them doing the talk. If it is you who is the obvious choice, don't let any qualms you may have about public speaking put you off: read this book, then get on with the presentation.

What's in it for me?

To speak well in public is a high-preparation, energy-draining occupation. In my experience, you won't do it with the necessary commitment unless you stand to gain a lot in the process. As we have seen, the potential rewards can take various forms – winning people over, carrying a motion, getting applauded, creating laughter, gaining understanding, being paid, experiencing sheer excitement at taking part – but make sure you have realistic expectations of getting those rewards. Otherwise, as my biology teacher would say, "the whole experience could end up a damp squid for you."

What's in it for them?

It helps to be clear in your mind what you're expecting the audience to get out of the experience of listening to you. It focuses you in deciding whether to speak in public and, if so, what sort of things to say.

Will your talk be so enjoyable that people will want to be there just for the pure pleasure of the moment?

Will you be giving them a message that they can take away and implement, a message that will make a positive difference, however small, to their lives or the lives of others?

Will you be imparting information that is either intrinsically valuable or of practical application?

Here's an example.

I was asked to take over at the last minute from a speaker who was going to be talking to an audience somewhere in Hampshire about the indirect tax (that's to say, value added tax and customs duties) implications of international trade. When I arrived, it immediately became apparent that no one in the audience had, or was likely ever to have, the slightest involvement in international trade. Like so many audiences – this is something the books don't tell you – they were there for the sandwiches. To my mind, this was an assignment that the original speaker, using the thought processes we've discussed here, should not have accepted. The prawn mayonnaise sandwiches turned out to be tastier than usual, but that's not sufficient justification for all the hours needed to prepare the talk.

However, we were where we were, in the function room fifteen minutes before I was due to speak, and there was no question of cancelling. What I tried to do was to make the most of the experience for the audience (beyond the sandwiches), by radically simplifying the content of the talk and making it as entertaining as possible. My French onion joke went down particularly nicely that evening.

How much effort will it take on my part, and am I prepared to make it?

To an extent, public speaking is a collaborative work. Always look for every opportunity to make use of the skills of talented people to support you in creating and performing your speech. They may come up with all sorts of ideas for helping you choose a topic or improve the content of your talk. They may coach you, or perhaps give constructive feedback when you rehearse. They may help with sound systems or other technology on the day, or relieve you of much of your administrative work.

But in essence – and it's a big but – public speaking remains a lonely occupation where the individual speaker must always bear most of the burden. I firmly believe that speaking success is straightforward to accomplish. There's no secret about what you need to do, and all the fundamental principles are set out in this book. Although the rules are simple, however, that doesn't mean they're painless to implement. The question that each of us must ask is: are we prepared to commit the time and effort to achieve the success we deserve?

Checklist for preparation immediately before the event

Here is a list I use to address some preparatory points for my talks that might not be immediately obvious:

- Tee shirt.
- Handkerchief.
- Bladder.
- Bart Simpson socks.

Tee shirt
A light-coloured, absorbent tee shirt worn as an under layer of clothing usually works well to combat the perspiration that accompanies your adrenaline flow. Anything that combats the soggy armpit effect, as demonstrated for example by Tony Blair when under pressure, has to be a good thing.

Handkerchief
Taking at least one handkerchief with you to a talk is a must. It will combat an unexpectedly runny nose, not to mention issues of excess perspiration. A suitably bold handkerchief may also

stand as a style statement for those who are concerned about such things.

Bladder

Enoch Powell, the classics professor turned politician, was a man of original, if often questionable, views, and an undeniably impressive orator. He liked to speak with a full bladder, presumably to sharpen his faculties before a speech. My advice is the exact opposite: a loo visit in the twenty minutes before a talk calms me down, focuses my thoughts and makes sure I eliminate at least one potential hazard for when I am speaking. The poet Philip Larkin once forgot this crucial wisdom before a presentation, with deeply embarrassing consequences. His intake of alcohol to steady his nerves before the talk probably didn't help much either.

Bart Simpson socks

Many people are superstitious about public speaking and it's not surprising, given the significance of the event. The story goes that a man visiting the famous scientist Niels Bohr was surprised to see a horseshoe hanging over his door. Incredulous, he asked Bohr whether he believed in that superstition. "Of course not," replied Niels Bohr, "but I've been told it's supposed to be lucky whether you believe in it or not."

For a major speech twenty years ago that went down unexpectedly well, I was by pure accident wearing a pair of Bart Simpson socks (still available on Amazon for £2.99 upwards). To this day I still wear my Bart socks when I speak in public.

Conclusion

I was a late convert to the power of checklists, but now I would not do without them. For me, the key is to make my lists short and punchy, so that they never subside into a bureaucratic burden.

Though I say it myself, I was particularly pleased with the 'checklist for deciding whether you should speak in the first place'. If I can't produce positive responses to the questions it raises, I will do myself and my prospective audience a service by not speaking. I'll save a great deal of time, and they will escape what would have been a decidedly second-rate talk.

Points to take from this chapter

- A well-planned checklist can be exceptionally useful to a speaker.
- Effective checklists are short and limited to essential steps.
- Adapt your checklists fully to your personality and circumstances.
- Review what items you might add to or subtract from your list on a regular basis.
- The checklist for deciding whether you should speak in the first place can be particularly useful.

This chapter concludes the second section of the book. We have now reviewed the thirteen key areas of preparation that effective speakers will engage with thoroughly before they take to the stage.

We will now move on to the third section, the key techniques – the strategies we can employ to bring high levels of polish and professionalism to our talks.

We'll start in Chapter 27 with a particularly crucial technique, or rather set of techniques – the uncomplicated ways by which we can avoid an excess of nerves when we stand up to speak in public.

Notes

The specific link for John Zimmer's checklist is https://mannerofspeaking.org/2011/07/06/a-public-speakers-checklist-free-pdf-file/. JB Priestley's piece on *Not Going* can be found in his essay collection *Delight*, William Heinemann Ltd, 1949.

THE KEY TECHNIQUES

CHAPTER 27

Use these simple methods to control your nerves

Introduction

Early on in this book, I told you that you should welcome the fear that accompanies public speaking because it makes you a much better performer. That rule applies to nearly all speakers nearly all of the time, and to me it is a sacrosanct principle of our trade. We did, however, see that, under the impressively named Yerkes-Dodson law, it is possible to be that little bit *too* aroused (which, in this instance, means too nervous) during the course of a speech. The result is that our performance can lose a degree of impact.

In this chapter, therefore, I want to look at a variety of easy ways to manage our nerves so that our talks maintain top quality.

I'll begin with a reminder that the effect of nerves differs from speaker to speaker, meaning that there can be no one solution for excess nerves. I'll emphasise that far and away the most problematic issue with our fears is that they could stop us preparing properly in the first place, and I'll explain the straightforward way to eliminate this problem. A psychologist called Alison Wood Brooks will then reveal to us the best – and scientifically proven – method for dealing with those superfluous butterflies, before I go on to describe a host of other ways to calm the anxious soul. There truly should be something for every speaker here.

None of this detailed advice will remove all your nervous anxiety. Nor, as you know by now, do I want it to. What it will do is help you to speak at the initial level of tension that will bring you the very best results on stage.

Nerves affect us all differently

It may be that some people are born without a fear gland. I'm not sure that would be helpful if, for example, you were evaluating the benefits of single-handedly circumnavigating the world in a dinghy, but it would assist in getting you up to speak in public, if not in ensuring that what you said was worthwhile material.

To those who laugh in the face of fear, this chapter will be pleasingly irrelevant. Assuming, of course, that such people exist.

Mark Twain made a classic comment on glossophobia, the fear of talking in public, to cheer us all up: "There are two types of speakers: those that are nervous and those that are liars." So please do remember that it is not just you feeling the nerves. My researches confirm that at least eight out of ten people admit to feeling anxious when they speak in public and, as Mark Twain suggested, the other two are probably telling porkies.

One of the hoariest bits of public speaking lore is that many people are more scared of giving a speech than they are of dying. It led to the great Jerry Seinfeld joke that, for the average person going to a funeral, they'd be better off in the casket than doing the eulogy. For my own part, I once gave a talk in Leeds where the lack of audience reaction led me to believe that speaking there was, in any event, much the same thing as dying.

In practice, people are affected very differently by nerves.

Unlike many speakers, I have always been more relaxed in front of a big audience where I can barely see individual faces in the crowd. I like the sense of anonymity that a large group gives me, while I find an intimate talk to ten or twenty people much scarier. Some speakers enjoy having the support of friends and family when they are performing, while others say they would be reduced to tongue-tied idiocy if their mothers ever turned up to hear them.

In the sporting arena, the boxer Joe Calzaghe balanced the adrenaline flow which he needed to perform at his best in the ring with relaxing with friends before the fight, listening to his iPod and using breath control techniques. By contrast, Lennox Lewis tried to sleep before a match; this would not have been possible or desirable for Calzaghe, who could not have kept still during the build-up.

Such differences in individual styles and preferences mean that no one rule for combating anxiety will suit everyone. Each individual has his or her optimal method of dealing with nerves, and each individual faces the challenge of working out for themselves what that method is.

The recommended approach

Though we each have to find the way that suits us best, we can note some helpful general pointers:

- Often the best way of dealing with your concerns

is the most direct one. Recognise the fear, get to know it, and be prepared to live with it. Then just get on with your talk. The maxim made famous by the psychologist Susan Jeffers, 'feel the fear and do it anyway', applies in spades to public speaking: you have to do the speaking before the fear can go away. The message is to acknowledge your nerves and then just carry on. It is the carrying on that counts.

- As we saw in Chapter 3, you need to be nervous before you start. I know that if I am not on edge when I begin speaking, my talk will fall flat. Remembering the confirmation from the Yerkes-Dodson law that nervousness is mostly good for your speech helps you deal with your fears that much better. The edginess gives you the best chance of hitting top form because the adrenaline must flow if you are to perform successfully.

- Each time you finish a speech and no one has laughed at you or ridiculed you, your internal confidence level rises just a little. That will make next time's performance more comfortable, and you will have set out on a virtuous circle of improvement. The anxiety starts to lessen and, you never know, eventually it might peter out. At that stage, you will face the opposite challenge of raising your nervous energy to ensure an adequate flow of adrenaline.

The physicist Sir Lawrence Bragg took this approach to the limit. "A good lecture," he said, "is a *tour de force*; a good lecturer should be keyed up to a high pitch of nervous tension before it and limp and exhausted after it. In my experience, the occasions when I have felt confident before a lecture have been disasters." You might regard this as unduly melodramatic, but I think the underlying principle is sound. Accept some discomfort as an essential element of giving a talk, and then just go for it.

The aim is to control your nerves rather than lose them.

The worst thing that fear can do

What we mustn't let the fear do is interfere with our build-up to the talk. That is the real issue: the danger that our worries will destroy our momentum in getting going in the first place.

As speakers, we can get fixated about our possible fears on the actual day of the speech. Instead of that, what we need to watch out for and guard against is the fear in the weeks beforehand that leads us to procrastinate and shy away from laying the groundwork for the big day.

Preparation and rehearsal are critical to our success, and we must not let our qualms get in the way. The simple solution is to get up a good body of steam, to start preparing for the talk as early as we can and keep speeding ahead. That way, the only time that fear will raise its head is the right time: the moments just before the presentation.

The key principle – embrace your nerves and tell yourself you are excited

Here is the constructive way to deal with nerves. Stop thinking of them as a Bad Thing. Regard them as what they are: the release of hormones into your body to put you into an alert state of readiness. Seen in this light, the results of the latest investigations into performance anxiety make a lot of sense.

The research now tells us that the best advice in the face of your nerves is *not* to try to calm down. Instead, the trick is to use that nervous energy to work actively for you. Nervousness is much the same feeling as excitement, so channel the energy positively into excitement. People perform better when they tell themselves they are excited, rather than when they say, "I am anxious" or try to pretend the feelings are not there.

In other words, the key to greater success is to reframe any public performance as a game to inspire and enthuse you, rather than an examination to pass or fail. Actively focus your mind on your speech as an opportunity, not a threat. Move on from your doomed attempts to dump your nerves: they are an entirely proper and appropriate accompaniment to the start of your talk. Over time, repeated public speaking performances will reduce those nerves, but not, if you are like me and the vast majority of speakers I talk to, by a huge amount. That's as it should be: you need them to get you into an alert and ready state.

There is substantial scientific support for this approach.

Alison Wood Brooks of Harvard Business School carried out a series of experiments to test what happens when we reappraise performance anxiety as excitement, the results of which were published online in December 2013. Participants were given instructions, before a variety of public speaking, singing and mathematics challenges, to tell themselves they were excited, or anxious, or calm, or nothing at all. Their performances on the challenges were objectively rated, and across all tasks participants who told themselves they were excited performed better. As speakers, they were more fluent, flowing and in control.

Saying "I am excited" out loud genuinely does lead you to feel more excited. Your mindset moves from feeling threatened to seeing opportunity. You are exploiting the fact that it is much easier to translate a powerful emotion like fear into a different emotion than to attempt to conquer it. In this case, the replacement emotion, the equally strong feeling of excitement and enthusiasm, drives you on to deliver a successful talk.

To be honest, it's a bit embarrassing to find out that human beings are so easily suggestible that this kind of self-talk can transform their behaviour, but it works, so let's make the most of it.

Alison Wood Brooks sums it up: "Compared with those who attempt to calm down, individuals who reappraise their anxious arousal as excitement feel more excited and perform better." If you can regard a situation and your physical response to it in a positive way, you are significantly more likely to succeed. Let's all accentuate the positive.

Manage the difficult half-hour before you start

Many people find that the worst time of all comes just before their speech is due to start. Here is Spencer Leigh Hughes, writing in his book *Press, Platform and Parliament* about his maiden speech in Parliament: "I was restless until called on, and it is the waiting to be called, not the speaking itself, that is the real ordeal."

How, then, should we approach the waiting period?

I admire the style of a bomb disposal expert who was asked how he overcame his fear. Quite simply, he said he did this by staying extremely busy and concentrating on the task, and so not having time to be scared. This approach allowed him to be fully focused.

At a much more mundane level, this tactic has worked for me in dealing with my speaking nerves. I remind myself that my role is to contribute all I can to the whole event from the outset, rather than just the segment where I will be doing my speaking.

This approach drives me to absorb myself in the workings of the day, for example:

- Doing my best to get to know the venue.

- Checking heat and light and ventilation.
- Monitoring food and drink supplies.
- Testing the sound system.
- Greeting and getting to know members of the audience.

By mingling with the crowd before I speak, being there as they sign the attendance list and introducing myself to as many people as possible, I remind myself that I am dealing with normal pleasant individuals, not evil extra-terrestrials from the planet Mongo. Moreover, I simply don't have the time to develop an excess of nerves beyond what I need to get my adrenaline flowing appropriately for my talk. This approach also has the incidental benefit of increasing the number of friendly faces in the audience as I start my presentation.

This style won't work for everyone. From your self-knowledge, and from experience, you have to work out what is best for you.

Take the example of whether or not to meet the audience beforehand. Sir Lawrence Bragg wrote:

> "If a sensitive lecturer is to give of his best, he must be left in peace for a period before the lecture starts. It is the refinement of cruelty to expect him to be social, to introduce him to a number of people whom he has not met before and to whom he must be polite."

I know how he felt: I have often been with him in spirit, hiding away in the toilets while trying to get my nerves under control. In time, I worked out that committing myself fully to the event as a whole worked better for me and was a lot more fun. But it was different for Sir Lawrence, and it may well be different for you.

In any event, here are some specific actions, offering practical benefits in their own right, that you can do, all alone if you wish, to keep you occupied in the awkward minutes before you are called on to speak:

To avoid embarrassment, always check how you look in a mirror. Review the state of your hair and clothes to ensure that nothing is amiss. Watch the hair gel incident in the film *There's Something About Mary* to see the extreme importance of this point. For a male speaker, the mnemonic XYZ (eXamine Your Zip) can be especially useful before embarking on a presentation.

When you look in the mirror, smile at yourself as happily as you can. Fake a happy look if you can't achieve it by any other means. The ABC maxim – '**A**lways **B**e **C**heerful' – applies to the whole of a presentation, but it is particularly important at the start. If you look happy before you take the stage, you have a better chance of staying that way.

Warm up your voice.

Make sure you have no loose change or keys in your pockets. They rattle.

Turn off your mobile phone: in my experience, more presenters' phones ring during presentations than any belonging to audience members. To be on the safe side, keep your phone a long distance away from you throughout your talk, preferably in a neighbouring village, lest the speech gremlins mysteriously turn it back on again. It's best to avoid the need for grovelling apologies of the 'I could have sworn I turned it off' kind.

Scout the stage and surrounding areas for malicious props. Be cautious of stray furniture, objets d'art and the like. Items as varied as pot plants, pianos and filing cabinets have in their time caused havoc by attacking unprepared presenters. I shall never forget the palm fronds that encased me while I spoke at an Ernst & Young accountants' dinner. With fronds like these, I thought, who needs anemones?

Make sure you have a good supply of water to get you through your speech.

Commit to keeping going

If you have prepared well beforehand, the secret to success on the day of the performance is simply to commit yourself to the speech. Just do it; just get on with it.

Spencer Leigh Hughes captures the essence of this principle in *The Art of Public Speaking*, writing of:

> "the feeling of bewilderment and panic, and the sudden mental blankness, that overtakes some men directly they are on their legs. There is only one way of overcoming such a feeling, and that is by a man forcing himself to go on, to say something, however rambling and incoherent it may be. It is the same in regard to learning to skate, or to ride a horse, or to swim – a man must be prepared to blunder and flounder about at first, or he will never do anything."

In his later book, *Press, Platform and Parliament*, SLH shows how this principle worked out in his maiden speech in Parliament:

> "Though I was not in the least nervous when I began, I distinctly remember not recognising the sound of my own voice for the first few minutes. Indeed I experienced a sense of unreality at the outset, as if I was not quite sure as to where I was or what I was doing. But I pegged away..."

It's the pegging away that counts. Otherwise, the outcome can be harrowing, as when – as we touched on in Chapter 3 – the *Transformers* director Michael Bay made an unscheduled early exit from a Samsung press conference after an apparent autocue failure. (His disaster is one of the reasons why I put so much store in this book on having appropriate backup for all the technological aspects of a talk.) The better option for a speaker is almost always to keep going.

A variety of tips

You don't want to get *far* too nervous. Here is a potpourri of tips for controlling the fear. Try them out and see what works for you:

You want to get off to a good start, so work hard on the opening of your talk. As we saw in Chapter 21, you should aim to become thoroughly familiar with your script for the first few minutes. If you can begin well, it will relax you and make your audience comfortable, with good omens for the rest of your presentation. For me, using humour early on usually achieves that, and it also gives me a good gauge as to the mood of the audience.

Exercise a few hours before your presentation. There is growing evidence to suggest that physical exercise is helpful in preparing the brain to deal with stress in other forms. For me, a five-kilometre jog at the gym seems ideal. You need to find out what suits you personally. Remember not to knock yourself out in the process; you need to have enough energy left to mount the lectern, let alone give your talk.

Get to the venue in plenty of time to avoid rushing.

Establish a warm-up routine which you will employ each time before you speak and in the same order. Do this both in rehearsal and for the real thing. There's no such thing as a right or wrong routine; it's the one that works for you that counts. A standard procedure offers the comfort of familiarity, prepares you for the talk and calms you down at the same time. Never underestimate the power of developing your personal rituals.

Be ready to acknowledge your fear to yourself before the event. You could say to yourself: "You are feeling anxious, which is entirely appropriate since you're about to do something which matters a good deal to you and to the people who are going to be listening to you." The idea is that, by legitimising your fear in this way, you are treating it in an adult fashion and are therefore more likely to take it in your stride.

Let's develop the previous point a little. Scientific research has now been carried out, believe it or not, on the best ways of talking to yourself. In one study, undergraduates were given five minutes to put together a speech on why they were qualified for their dream jobs. They were asked to write down how they were preparing themselves psychologically for the exercise. Some were told to use the first-person pronoun (I), while others were to use either the second person (you) or their name. The undergraduates in the former category, the ones who referred to themselves as 'I', were more anxious about the forthcoming speech, and recorded comments like: "I was only given five minutes to prepare my speech and was thus almost set up to not do well." The students in the latter category had more confidence ("You can do this!") and, according to the independent reviewers, performed better in the actual speech.

What seems to be happening here is that, when people address themselves as 'you' or use their first names, they see their situation as challenging rather than threatening. Using your name, speaking to yourself as a third person ("Come on, Ian, you're good at this"), distances you from issues of self-doubt and takes the damaging self-examination out of the equation. It therefore allows you to give yourself helpful and supportive feedback.

Try using visualisation techniques to prepare you mentally for the outcome you desire. This process can help to keep tension under control because it makes the whole speaking experience more familiar and commonplace. I picture in my mind how I want the event to unfold and how I will deal positively with things that might go wrong – the technology failing, say, or a member of the audience asking annoying questions. When I rehearse, I think about successful past performances, reconstruct how the best bits felt, and project these feelings and attitudes forward to the approaching presentation.

At its simplest, visualisation involves closing your eyes and imagining things going well.

Picture the scene. What would you be doing? What would the audience be doing? How would you be feeling? How would your face look? What would your body posture be like? Paint in your mind your picture of a successful outcome – success, that is, according to your personal definition.

In my visualisations, I often use the theme that 'I am going to enjoy this talk', which is entirely positive but does not put me under excessive pressure to perform. I know that, if at the most basic level I have an agreeable time during the presentation, my pleasure will radiate around the audience.

Someone who shows us the way on visualisation is Muhammad Ali, one of the world's greatest sportsmen. He rehearsed his fights in his mind, again and again, before he ever stepped into the ring. He called this visualisation process 'future history'. I read that, out of nineteen fights where he predicted the result, Ali got it right on seventeen occasions. Before his fight with Archie Moore, for example, Ali (then Cassius Clay) said: "Don't block the aisle and don't block the door. You will all go home after round four." And that's exactly what happened.

Recent research has shown that meditation training, even in very limited amounts, may be helpful. Meditation skills increase our ability to attach ourselves to an experience or to detach from it. We are therefore more able to focus our attention on the practical things that will make our talk succeed, while identifying and then discarding the distracting thoughts produced by the fear of failure.

It helps to remember that the audience almost always wants you to succeed. People are fundamentally decent, and anyway it is no fun listening to a failing speaker.

We discussed exercising before a presentation. Some people take this approach further and jump up and down outside the venue immediately before their talk. This works well as a last-minute way of loosening yourself up physically, but please try not to do it so vigorously as to scare off potential audience members.

Some people find it helps to give themselves instructions on dealing with the nerves in the notes they take with them to the presentation. Simple written directions like 'BREATHE!' remind you what to do and can make a positive difference to your performance. The joke went that George W Bush, who as US president had an uneasy relationship with public speaking, went even further than this and wrote notes on the backs of his hands to remind him of the basics. It said 'Breathe in' on his left hand and 'Breathe out' on his right.

Yes, please do breathe, and make sure you do it throughout your presentation. Take some slow, deep breaths from your belly before you get up to speak. It helps your stress control, not to mention your voice. An opportune time to do this is when the chair is introducing you to the audience. You will find lots of useful breathing exercises on the Internet. I find the suggestions on the NHS Choices website particularly helpful – search for their 'Breathing exercise for stress'. And you will find some helpful videos on YouTube if you search for 'breathing exercises for public speakers'. I like the *5 Minute Vocal Warm Up for Actors & Public Speakers* by the vocal coach Page Clements.

Stand up in a power pose, big and full of vigour, before you start to speak, as we discussed in Chapter 12.

I mentioned the ways in which I keep busy immediately before a presentation. For other people, different sorts of distraction techniques can be highly effective. I heard of an actor who had memorised *Jabberwocky*, the nonsense poem by Lewis Carroll, and repeated it continuously in his mind before a performance, particularly on first nights. It's a great example of finding something to occupy you as a method of coping with the fear.

Over the years, speakers have used a variety of other tricks to calm themselves down. They might imagine audience members in the nude, or in high chairs like young children, or mentally put them on the loo, or use some combination of such things. It's not easy to be frightened of a roomful of naked people sitting on the toilet. Modern writers are scornful of such devices, but if it works for you, then go ahead. I once had a rather fearsome boss called Richard who would attend my talks with a countenance that suggested he was undecided whether to walk out or just hit me. Somehow, mentally dressing him in a rather daring string bikini seemed to reduce my stress levels enormously.

In fact, the use of tricks to lull oneself into a sense of confidence goes back through time. One stratagem known to the Victorians to ease their speaking fears was to imagine that they could see before them only a vast number of heads of cabbages. Louis Bourdaloue, a fiery French Jesuit preacher of the seventeenth century, seems to have addressed his demons by speaking with his eyes closed. I cannot honestly recommend this approach for general use, but his oratory undeniably held his audiences in rapture.

I suggested earlier that you will often be able to find at least one person in the house who will respond warmly to you and make great eye contact. Even in a tough audience, there's usually a friendly face to be found, the shining beacon you can look to in your moment of pressing need. Try to identify that special person who is willing to smile back as early as you can in your performance. In my experience, it tends to be a woman more often than a man, regardless of the gender of the speaker. Of course, if you are lucky enough to end up making good eye contact with that person, don't forget to continue scanning faces all around the room as well, so that the whole audience feels involved.

You might go so far as to arrange beforehand to plant a supporter in the crowd: it can make a real difference. I love having my wife, Val, in the gallery. She is supremely encouraging and has the unique talent of laughing at my jokes when those around her look as though they have recently experienced multiple family bereavements. Scientific research has, in fact, now confirmed the effect on speakers of other halves being present. If you are a man, it can indeed be helpful for your spouse to be present, provided the two of you have a good relationship. Women, on the other hand, generally do better if male partners are absent, regardless of the state of their union. I have the feeling this says more about the helpfulness of men, or lack of it, than anything else.

One approach I have found useful is to combat my fears by doing something even scarier. Once I had done some after-dinner speaking, day-to-day tax lecturing seemed very straightforward by comparison. Someone who had a similar idea was the journalist Hugo Rifkind. He conquered his fear of giving a speech by taking part in something a lot more challenging: doing stand-up comedy. It was an open mike night at a comedy club in Glasgow, a city which, as we have already noted, can be a challenging venue. Hence Ken Dodd's comment: "Freud's theory was that when a joke opens a window, and all those bats and bogeymen fly out, you get a marvellous feeling of relief and elation. But the problem with Freud is that he never had to play the Glasgow Empire second house on a Friday night."

Hugo Rifkind was scared – he walked down the gloomy corridor towards the stage feeling fear unlike anything he had ever known – and he tells us that he bombed on stage. However, the world carried on turning, and any other form of public speaking would be a comparative doddle for him in the future. I like the idea of addressing your concerns about public speaking by doing something in advance that scares you far more. For me, it would be skydiving or, even worse, attending one of those horrific networking events where you do nothing other than talk inanely to a whole succession of people you have never met before.

One of the best ways to deal with excessive nerves – and remember, it's not the nerves you want to eliminate, but the excess – is a slightly gentler version of the Hugo Rifkind approach. Just speak in public as often as you can so that it becomes routine. Take all the chances you get to do so. In particular, try to work up from a handful of listeners at the start – so that your early mistakes don't come on major occasions – to bigger events.

Are you afraid of success?

Are you afraid of success rather than failure?

This issue has arisen surprisingly often with people I've

coached. At some level, might you be fearful of what could happen if your talk goes well? Perhaps you feel you couldn't cope with all the attention that might follow, or that it's easier to blend in than to stand out, which might take you into unknown territory in your life.

Signs that fear of success might be a problem include:

- Feeling that you do not deserve to succeed, or that you wouldn't be able to maintain any success you did achieve.
- Delaying your writing and preparation for the talk.
- Being unwilling to move beyond the planning phase to create a memorable presentation.
- Avoiding the practice and rehearsal stage.

This issue can affect anyone, however talented. Star Trek fans, for example, may remember Dr Julian Bashir, the doctor from *Star Trek: Deep Space Nine*, who deliberately confused a preganglionic fibre with a postganglionic nerve to avoid coming top of his medical class.

One of the best ways to address the fear of success is simply to recognise the problem in the first place. Here is an excellent practical tip on the *Lifehack* website from the business coach Kushla Chadwick: "One of my favourite things to do is use the words 'even though'... For example: 'Even though I have to give this talk in front of the class and I'm embarrassed, I'm open to giving a brilliant talk and feeling good about it.'"

Conclusion

Some useful general principles bring together what I have said throughout this book to put the fear of public speaking in proper perspective:

You need to get yourself up to a significant level of nerves and adrenaline if you're going to perform well.

We are all different: stress affects us in a variety of ways, and we need to work out the coping mechanisms that suit us as individuals. I hope that this chapter has given you a plethora of them to choose from.

There is no point in waiting for the fear to go away: it won't. But we can dramatically alter our relationship with our nerves by becoming more confident in our performance and gaining the sense of accomplishment that comes from pushing through the fear.

Confidence is indeed crucial. Whatever you do to address your anxieties, if you *believe* it works for you, it is likely that it truly *will* work for you.

If you have dealt with the situation before, and been successful, you are less likely to be afraid the next time. Hence preparation, practice and volunteering to speak again will all give added self-assurance for future presentations.

It's the previous lack of groundwork and practice, not the nerves on speech day, which can destroy a performance. Get stuck in early to the detailed work of thoroughly preparing a talk. Familiarity with your material breeds a positive approach.

Points to take from this chapter

- As Mark Twain said, "there are two types of speakers: those that are nervous and those that are liars."
- The direct route is the simplest: get to know your fear, live with it, and just get on with your speech.
- Accept some discomfort as an essential element of giving a talk.

- You will perform better if you tell yourself you are excited.
- See your talk as an opportunity, not a threat.
- Stay busy beforehand, so you don't have the time to be scared.
- Work through the variety of tips in this chapter to see what works for you.
- Make sure you don't have a problem with the fear of success.

Much of the book thus far has discussed the preparation of a relevant, incisive talk wholly appropriate to the audience you will be addressing. That's all very well, but none of it will be of the slightest use if your listeners can't actually hear or decipher what you are saying. The next chapter, therefore, will explain how to use and control your voice so that your delivery is distinct and audible. That way, you will join the alarmingly small group of speakers whose words can be fully understood and appreciated by the audience.

Notes

Alison Wood Brooks' study, *Get Excited: Reappraising Pre-Performance Anxiety as Excitement*, was published in the US *Journal of Experimental Psychology* in 2014. The hair gel scene from *There's Something About Mary* can be seen at https://www. youtube.com/watch?v=9NesjZbF1Ls. The research project on talking to yourself was led by Ethan Kross, a psychologist at the University of Michigan, and was published in 2014 in the *Journal of Personality and Social Psychology* as *Self-Talk as a Regulatory Mechanism: How You Do It Matters*. You can find the article at http://selfcontrol.psych.lsa.umich.edu/wp-content/uploads/2014/01/KrossJ_Pers_Soc_Psychol2014Self-talk_

as_a_regulatory_mechanism_How_you_do_it_matters.pdf.
Hugo Rifkind's article was originally published in the February
2014 issue of British *GQ*. Kushla Chadwick's piece can be seen
at http://www.lifehack.org/articles/communication/what-you-
have-fear-success.html.

CHAPTER 28

Manage your voice

Introduction

Making the most of one's voice must be a fundamental concern for any speaker. The audience needs to hear you without straining, and, beyond that, you'd like your manner of delivery to be sufficiently varied and compelling to keep their attention as your talk continues. This chapter will ensure that you meet those objectives.

We'll review what past experts on the subject have had to say. Then I'll introduce and explain the helpful CAVE mnemonic, which gives you a simple and quick checklist to ensure that all is well with your speaking voice. We'll look at a couple of genuinely easy exercises to improve your vocal tone, and finish with a variety of general tips coupled with a blatant plug for a particular brand of throat lozenge. If you haven't improved your oral prowess after all that, quite frankly I shall be left speechless.

Past writers on vocal management

Hugh Blair, the Scotsman who wrote one of the first great

treatises in English on practical oratory, had some sensible things to say on this subject. His influential work, *Lectures on Rhetoric and Belles Lettres*, is a compilation of talks given to his students at the University of Edinburgh where he was Chair of Rhetoric and Belles Lettres until his retirement in 1783.

These abridged extracts come from that work:

"It is [a] useful rule, in order to be well heard, to fix our eye on some of the most distant persons in the assembly, and to consider ourselves as speaking to them. We naturally and mechanically utter our words with such a degree of strength, as to make ourselves be heard by one to whom we address ourselves, provided he be within the reach of our voice.

In the next place, to being well heard and clearly understood, distinctness of articulation contributes more, perhaps, than mere loudness of sound. The quantity of sound necessary to fill even a large space is smaller than is commonly imagined; and with distinct articulation, a man of a weak voice will make it reach farther than the strongest voice can reach without it.

To pronounce with a proper degree of slowness, and with a full and clear articulation, is the first thing to be studied by all who begin to speak in public; and cannot be too much recommended to them. It is a great assistance to the voice, by the pauses and rests which it allows it more easily to make."

I think that's excellent general advice. It's when the recommendations of the experts get more specific that one needs to apply extreme caution. Each generation seems to have its fads, and here the author of *Beeton's Art of Public Speaking* tells us what was all the rage in 1882:

"There are several general rules... The first is connected with the time for practising, which should be between ten and twelve in the morning and from five to eight in the evening. 'To commence too early in the morning,' says Mr Hunt in his *Philosophy of Voice and Speech*... 'is injudicious, the secretion of mucus being more abundant about that time, the voice is thereby affected.' It is neither advisable to speak on an overloaded or an empty stomach. Four hours after a moderate meal may be considered as the proper time... Colds should be carefully guarded against, and this is to be done not so much by going muffled up in great coats and cravats as by bathing daily in cold water and taking daily exercise in all weathers... Certain things are known to be injurious to the voice, and are therefore to be avoided. Amongst these are figs, apples, pears, and nuts. Alcoholic liquors and smoking are said to do more damage to tenor than to bass voices."

Gosh! It confirms my belief that you should regard everything you read in books about public speaking with extreme scepticism.

What do you sound like?

Let's quickly move on to a topic that is important and, thankfully, has a reasonably solid base of knowledge. Do you know what your voice sounds like to others?

It is a question that is more challenging than might initially appear. The first time we hear ourselves on a recording can be a surprisingly tough experience. It's not what we expected to hear, and we tend not to like the outcome.

In normal life, we hear ourselves by way of the vibrations

from our vocal cords passing up through the neck to the bones in our ears. The way other people hear us is by our voice vibrating through the sinuses around our nose and then moving out to them through the air.

To put the difference more starkly, we could say in rough terms that we hear ourselves from behind while other people hear us from in front. The moral is that, however unpleasant the initial experience may be, we do need to record ourselves and listen to the results if we want a reasonably accurate view of how we sound to others as a speaker. Only then can we properly start to judge our vocal effectiveness in any talk we give.

Some basic guidelines

How, when we listen to our recording, can we reach a view on how effective our voice is?

Two centuries ago a work called *The Universal Preceptor*, a preceptor being a teacher or instructor, gave an excellent basic set of guidelines. My copy is the Improved Twentieth Edition of 1827, so we can safely say that this was a popular book of its day.

Its author, the Rev David Blair – the history of British oratory is full of Blairs – had this to say:

> "A distinct and audible *delivery* is essential to a good orator.
> The *first* rule is, to open the mouth sufficiently, and not to mumble or mutter the words.
> The *second* is, to pronounce distinctly every letter and syllable without hurry.
> The *third* is, to fill the room with the voice, so that the most distant part of the auditory may hear.
> And the *fourth*, so to modulate the voice, as to be able to become energetic whenever energy is specially required."

These requirements don't seem too unreasonable to me, so it is surprising how many speakers fail to meet them, particularly in today's world when the availability of microphones means there is no excuse if the most distant part of the auditory cannot hear what is going on.

Incidentally, the very reasonable requirement for distinct, unrushed pronunciation is not a justification for pedantry. We want words pronounced clearly according to orthodox principles, but without any additional fussy or finicky touches. (We saw an example of this in Chapter 20.) At the same time, we don't want words to be run together or mangled so as to become unintelligible to the audience.

Always make the most of your CAVE

I use the mnemonic CAVE, standing for Clarity, Audibility, Variety and Enthusiasm, as a present-day reminder of the basic principles set out by the Rev David Blair. Here is what I think you should aim for in the voice department:

- **Clarity.** Your voice should be clear and articulate, not muffled. The great thing about clarity is that it is more important than volume. If your voice is clear enough, it should also normally be loud enough: if it isn't, use a microphone. If you are working in an auditorium with poor acoustics, pay particular attention to speaking slowly and distinctly, with lots of pauses, to make it as easy as possible for the audience to follow you. Don't mumble or swallow your words, and be aware of verbal twitches like 'um', 'okay', 'like' and 'you know'.
- **Audibility.** Make sure your voice carries to the back of the room and no one strains to hear you.

The simple act of looking towards the back of the auditorium helps project your voice, so remember to perform to the very last row at the rear.

- **Variety.** Vary the pace and tone of your delivery. For example, go faster to emphasise excitement, slower for gravity and deeper meaning. Use pauses to break up your speech and give the audience time to gather themselves. Highlight individual words or phrases for effect. Don't get carried away in this: as Spencer Leigh Hughes puts it, "The speech in which there is no emphasis is a dreary business, but not worse than one in which the man puts a resounding emphasis on every other word."
- **Enthusiasm** and energy. Always sound like you want to be there and have something important to say. Never forget that faking enthusiasm when you are nervous goes a long way towards making you much more enthusiastic and much less nervous.

When you listen to recordings of your speech, check through to see how well you have done on each of the CAVE criteria, and plan how to address any issues you identify.

A couple of easy, enjoyable exercises

Experience confirms that very few people are prepared to follow through a programme of voice exercises, so I will just recommend two that are both helpful and fun to do.

The smile. 'Smiling and dialling' is a technique used by cold callers to improve their chances of selling their dodgy products. They force themselves to smile as they talk on the phone, and this helps give them a cheerful tone of voice. It works: research confirms that people can accurately perceive a smile coming from the person at the other end of a telephone call. Imagine, then, the effect of a smile when your listeners can actually see you.

I suggest that you record yourself saying a sentence like this: *Smiling and dialling is a technique used by cold callers to improve their chances of selling their dodgy products.* First, record the sentence with a deadpan, impassive expression. Then do it again with a smile on your face, not necessarily a big one, since just a hint of amusement will do. If you're like me, you will be surprised by the difference in tone when you compare your recordings. Once you've learned the power of smiling, I think you'll be impressed by the effect it will have on audiences for your talks.

Dr Seuss. I saw this excellent tip in an article by Ed Sykes, an American motivational speaker. To improve your vocal variety, read books by Dr Seuss out loud. I find it impossible to do this without a smile on my face, so, unless you are clinically dead, this second exercise automatically incorporates the first one. Ed Sykes particularly recommends *The Cat in the Hat* and *Green Eggs and Ham.* To these I would add my personal favourite, *Oh, the Places You'll Go!* – the last book published in the author's lifetime, dealing with the journey of life and its challenges.

The rhythms and rhymes of Dr Seuss provide great practice for articulating one's words clearly and with appropriate emphasis while conveying detailed nuances of meaning. Every speaker can benefit from reading Dr Seuss out loud – well, nearly everyone, or as he puts it in *Oh, the Places You'll Go!*:

> "And will you succeed?
> Yes! You will, indeed!
> (98 and 3/4 percent guaranteed.)"

Do the reading enthusiastically: it's difficult not to, given the wonderful material the author provides.

Don't be afraid to move your mouth more for better articulation, or to exaggerate as much as you like. It will do marvels for your vocal range. Record yourself, and listen to the results. Ed Sykes particularly recommends performing to children, who will give you great feedback on whether you are doing it properly. I have followed his advice, and the results are gratifying.

There are many other examples of writers who have produced works that are brilliantly enjoyable in their own right and also provide great practice for speakers. In particular, there is a considerable variety of compilations in print of poems that are ideally suited for reading aloud. My personal favourite is Tom Atkinson's 1983 selection, *Poems to be Read Aloud: A Victorian Drawing Room Entertainment*. It contains many of the classics: *Gunga Din*, *Ozymandias*, *Vitai Lampada*, *Kubla Khan* and *The Shooting of Dan McGrew*, not to mention *Eskimo Nell*. I cannot, sadly, recommend the last of these for younger readers.

Speaking with a speech disorder

There should normally be no reason why a speech disorder should prevent someone from becoming a successful speaker. We met the great Patrick Campbell back in Chapter 2. Demosthenes, the great Greek orator who set the standard for all who followed, had a speech impediment which may well have been rhotacism – difficulty in pronouncing the letter R. The many distinguished speakers who appear in Wikipedia's list of stutterers include Demosthenes himself, Winston Churchill, the former US vice president Joe Biden, and of course King George VI, the man whose speech training was the subject of the 2010 film *The King's Speech*. The list extends to actors such as Rowan Atkinson, Samuel L Jackson and Marilyn Monroe, among many others. Indeed, people with a speech disorder figure disproportionately highly in the lists of powerful speakers, thanks to the discipline and determination they bring to the challenge.

Having said all that, I know it can be a frightening experience for a person with a speech disorder to come to the lectern for the first time. The following tips, which I have gathered from people who themselves have speech disorders, may help smooth their path:

- When you have a speech disorder, it is even more important than usual to take your time. Slow and careful speaking pays dividends.

- When preparing your presentation, try to avoid difficult words. For example, people with a lisp can struggle with the letters S and Z, while stutterers will tend to avoid words starting with M or W. Pre-planning at the writing stage can be a real help. If you are going to have to pronounce a difficult word you cannot avoid, take it slowly when it arrives and be prepared to make a joke of it. You could take a similar approach to the one I used with Mihaly Csikszentmihalyi in Chapter 5. The audience will be on your side.

- The point about being ready to make a joke is significant. The audience will be relaxed with you if they can see that you are relaxed about your speech disorder, so gentle, humorous self-deprecation works well. The writer and public speaker Ben Allen, who has had a lisp all his life, says this: "In my presentations, I tell about how I was once asked what country I was from and told I have a unique accent. This stimulates a laugh, and it demonstrates to the audience that I am comfortable with my lisp and they should be too."

- If you do make a mistake, just move on. Don't hang around to have another go at a word you have mispronounced: it creates too much unnecessary pressure. Don't apologise. All speakers make mistakes all the time, and the audience still very easily comprehends the gist of what is being said. You are not participating in an elocution competition.
- Many people with a speech disorder find that the longer they speak, the more noticeable it becomes. To counter this, try to give yourself frequent breaks, whether that be taking a drink of water, punctuating your talk with a relevant video or audio passage, or organising a coffee or toilet break for the audience.
- Ben Allen suggests that, contrary to the general advice in this book, someone who has a speech disorder should beware of recording themselves, because of the effect it may have on their self-confidence. Instead, he suggests practising in front of others, or recording yourself but then sending the recording to a friend for feedback rather than listening to it yourself.

The crucial point is that, if you are enthusiastic about your topic and have prepared well, the fact that you have a speech disorder should in no way affect the success of your talk. As Ben Allen says, "Be passionate about what you have to say, and if you have laid the proper groundwork, you will deliver a remarkable presentation."

A medley of general tips

Here are some, mostly obvious, points about managing your voice that I find helpful:

- Warm your voice up before you speak. At the start of your speech, stand tall to produce your best voice; stand up straight and take a deep breath. Then, while you are talking, stay hydrated by sipping water. Cool to tepid water is thought to be a better bet than the ice-cold stuff.

- If you speak in a large auditorium, your voice takes much longer to get to the people at the back, while reactions from the audience come to you slowly and in waves. In general, this means you need to slow down your speech because the interactions between speaker and listeners take so much longer to percolate through.

- Don't let your voice fall away at the end of a sentence. If the audience can't hear your final words, they are very likely to lose the meaning of what you are saying.

- If you are performing for a long time, say, half a day or more, then, to protect your voice, try to avoid speaking during the breaks. Ask people to save any extra questions for the very end of your talk.

- My next point is unashamedly dedicated to Theresa May, prime minister at the time of writing, who has a problem with coughing fits. "*Vocalzone throat pastilles are ideal for public speakers and voice professionals to help relieve an irritated throat.*" Yes, I know that's a blatant puff, and I did get it from the Vocalzone website, but their pastilles have worked for me for the past twenty years, so it would seem a bit churlish not to mention them here. During a full day's speaking engagement, I take one every couple of hours, and they keep me going very nicely. "I Want The Word To Get Out That Vocalzone Are

The Best Throat Pastilles In The World," says Sir Tom Jones with an abundance of capital letters, again on the website. Well, I'm doing my best to help you out here, Tom. Again, I must stress that I have not been paid by Vocalzone to write this, though that shouldn't stop them sponsoring future editions of this book if they feel like it.

- When you listen to your recording or have someone else listen to it for you, watch out for excessive vocal mannerisms. The filler words like 'you know', 'um', 'er', 'oh', 'okay' and 'like' become annoying if overdone. We experienced a masterclass in the use of filler words from the actress Kate Winslet in Chapter 17. Filler has actual value in telling the audience that you are going to carry on talking once you have got your thoughts together, but if overused it can sound desperately unprofessional. The best way of reducing one's use of filler is simply to be aware in advance of the extent of the potential problem: that way, it is much less likely to strike in practice.

- If you speak with a regional accent, by all means be aware of it in terms of the overall impression you make and the responses you get from others. Beyond that, my advice is to glory in it and not try to change it. Your accent adds to the richness of our language. In practice, it takes an enormous amount of time and effort to lose an accent, and success is far from guaranteed. Yes, I know that the singer Cheryl (or Cheryl Cole, as she was then; her name will probably have changed again by the time you read this) was released from the American version of *The X Factor* because it was feared the audience would not understand her Geordie accent. But then, life has a lot worse to offer than a non-appearance on *The X Factor*. And right-minded people agree with the newspaper survey which held that the Geordie accent is the most attractive in England.

- Above all, if you are in doubt about whether your voice will carry, always err on the side of using a microphone if one is available. There is nothing wimpish about the proper use of technology. If your attempt at being macho by not using the equipment means I can't hear you in the back row, I will come to the front and ritually disembowel you. Don't say I didn't warn you.

Conclusion

In 1828, a correspondent of *Jameson's Journal* from Dunfermline in Scotland said that he had "overheard part of a sermon then delivering at a tent at Cairney Hill by Dr Black". He did not miss a word, "though the distance must be something about two miles; the preacher has, perhaps, seldom been surpassed for distinct speaking and a clear voice; and the wind, which was steady and moderate, came in the direction of the sound."

Far be it from me to say whether that account strains credulity. What I do know is that, even if the barnstorming speakers of the past are no longer with us, the use of a clear, well-directed voice is as important as ever. If we carry out the easy exercises recommended in this chapter and then check on a regular basis how we are managing our voices according to the CAVE mnemonic, we should find ourselves comfortably within the top 20% of speakers for vocal ability.

Points to take from this chapter

- Record yourself to get a better awareness of how you sound to others.
- Focus on the four elements of the CAVE mnemonic: Clarity, Audibility, Variety and Enthusiasm.
- Learn the power of smiling.
- Practise by reading out loud, and do it energetically.
- Warm your voice up before you speak.
- Don't let your voice fall away at the end of a sentence.
- Watch out for too many filler words.
- Use a microphone if you have any doubt about whether your voice will carry.

The human voice is far and away the most important piece of technical equipment available to the speaker. In the next chapter, I'll move on to the more recently developed technology that can support us in our presentations. We have a whole range of modern aids at our disposal. They can do a brilliant job, so long as we manage them correctly; we will be looking at how to achieve that.

Notes

Ed Sykes' advice can be found at http://www.thesykesgrp.com/CatinHat.htm. Ben Allen's comments come from an article of his on Andrew Dlugan's public speaking and presentation skills blog, *Six Minutes*. You can find it at http://sixminutes.dlugan.com/speech-disorder/.

CHAPTER 29

Control the technology

Introduction

I'd like to start this chapter by telling you what I'm *not* going to do in it. I'm not going to attempt a review of the latest technology for the all-singing, all-dancing multimedia display that's going to turn your talk into a masterpiece, or enter into an in-depth analysis of the most recent public speaking apps for your smartphone. These things are peripheral at best to how well you will do in your talk, and they certainly won't turn failure into success.

In any event, the technology and the specific applications are so fast developing that, if you are technically minded, you will want to do an Internet search on what is available and highly rated at the time you read this. What I *am* going to do in this chapter is discuss a few critical issues about technology and pass on some tips I have found helpful.

After an initial caveat about the potential for the technical equipment to misbehave, I'll look at the use and abuse of two particular tools that, if appropriately managed, can make an excellent contribution to a successful talk – microphones and autocues. I will then emphasise the importance of dealing effectively with the technical support specialists you will encounter during your speaking career. Finally, I'll set out my list of suggestions for making the most of the technology available to you.

You won't be a technical guru by the end of the chapter, but you'll have a practical basis for avoiding the horrors that can befall us when the equipment gets up to mischief.

The double-edged sword of technology

As you will have noticed by now, I am ambivalent about the use of technology in public speaking.

In theory, I recognise the tremendous benefits it can bring. In practice, I am conscious of having seen about five times as many presentations ruined by technology going wrong as materially improved by using it. The more intricate the equipment, the quicker it breaks down; and speakers ignore that rule at their peril. Moreover, you may well have wondrous animated slides to show me, but if your talk is ten minutes late starting because it takes that long to get them working, I shall not be impressed. I would rather you just spoke to me instead. That is, after all, a somewhat more important aspect of public speaking.

If you think my moaning is over the top, there is research to back me up. Barco, a global technology company, published a press release in 2016 which said:

> "9 in 10 office workers experience seriously elevated stress levels when dealing with troublesome technology during meetings, Barco research shows. People's heart rates reached 179bpm when struggling with technology during a meeting, compared to resting heart rates of around 60-100 bpm

> – a clear indicator of stress… In trying to deal with tech problems, staff are wasting significant amounts of their valuable time: 66 percent try to fix problems themselves, 50 percent call IT/tech support, 29 percent end up giving up with the tech and going to their plan B. 15 percent even postpone meetings until technology problems can be fixed."

I rest my case.

Microphones

As I understand it, microphones (from the ancient Greek *micros*, meaning small or inadequate, and the modern *phoney*, meaning unreliable and treacherous) were sent to earth by Emperor Ming the Merciless as a side order with the death rays that were to destroy humanity.

In their most venomous strain, microphones take the form of lapel mikes, so inconspicuous that you forget to remove them or turn them off on leaving the stage.

The thing to avoid at all costs is going for a comfort break wearing a lapel mike still in its fully functioning state. A sage once noted that urination and ruination differ only in the positions of the U and the R. The audience may be interested in many aspects of your life, but that does not include your peeing habits or your comment to a friend in the next cubicle echoing back to the main hall about it being the worst house since Virginia Ironside played Helmsley.

My own most embarrassing moment was a rather loud "I wonder if this thing's still on" as I entered the gents at Rugby Theatre, but fortunately reception back in the auditorium was a bit crackly, and I got away with it.

Gordon Brown as Labour prime minister had a much more

distressing experience. In the 2010 general election campaign, he forgot to switch off his microphone during a campaign visit to Rochdale in Greater Manchester. He was then picked up as describing a lady he had just been talking to, Gillian Duffy, a widow and Labour voter, as a "bigoted woman". After the pair of them had clashed on immigration, Mr Brown was heard telling an aide: "That was a disaster. You should never have put me in front of that woman." A matter of days later, Mr Brown became the ex-prime minister. You have been warned: turn your microphone off promptly once you no longer need it.

Here are some more pointers about microphones:

- Unfortunately, even though most microphones are pernicious offshoots of the devil, it's still better to be safe and use one if you've got any doubts at all about the projection of your voice. It truly is preferable if they can hear you at the back.
- Check your microphone thoroughly before you speak for snap, crackle and pop. Ask a friend or two to sit in turn in various parts of the auditorium to confirm that you are easily audible but not too loud, and to check that you and the microphone are well positioned relative to each other. You can, of course, always ask the audience at the start of your talk: "Can you hear me at the back?" (This can be turned into a joke if you follow up with: "The last time I asked that question, a lady said yes, she could, but she'd happily change places with someone who couldn't.") The speaking authorities do not consider the "Can you hear me at the back?" question a cool way with which to start your blockbuster speech, but there really is nothing worse than sitting at the back and

being unable to hear, except for sitting at the front and being unable to hear.

- When you practise, allow enough time to get truly acclimatised to the sound of your voice coming at you through the speakers. If you have not spoken with a microphone before, you are likely to find the noise your voice makes quite strange at first. And watch out for speaker feedback (a dreadful, high-pitched whistling – you will know it when you hear it).

- Remember that the conditions when you rehearsed before your speech may be different from the ones during your actual performance. During your talk proper, aim to have an ally sitting towards the back of the audience who can indicate to you by way of previously agreed sign language if anything goes wrong.

Autocues

An autocue, or teleprompter in the American wording, is, in Wikipedia's elegant definition, 'a display device that prompts the person speaking with an electronic visual text of a speech or script'.

We first encountered autocues in Chapter 18, when we discussed Barack Obama's use of them. They have suffered from a dodgy reputation in recent years, to some extent because of the alleged over-reliance on them by Obama. In July 2009, one of Obama's ever-present autocues crashed to the floor in the middle of his speech. "Oh, goodness. Sorry about that, guys," he said. He was left with only the defunct autocue's abandoned partner to help him through the remainder of his remarks, but he survived.

Anyway, I like autocues. They can help you deliver speeches to large audiences, or presentations to a camera, more effectively. As with all other forms of technology, the key is to use them as a tool, not a life support system.

At their best, they let you focus on making emotional connections with the audience to get your message over, rather than desperately trying to remember what you were supposed to say next. Here are some recommendations for working with an autocue:

- Finish writing your speech well before the event, so that your text is ready in plenty of time for you to do at least two or three rehearsals using the autocue.
- Find out what is available to you in terms of the autocue software, for example, formatting features such as bold type and underlining, to help you speak effortlessly.
- Rehearse as often as you need in the actual location where you will be speaking.

As with any other aspect of public speaking, using an autocue gets easier the more you do it and the more you practise.

Put it in writing

When you are requesting equipment for a talk, it often helps to put it in writing so that you have an exact record of your requirements. This helps avoid misunderstandings, and usefully gives you someone to blame if things go wrong.

Here is an example of one of my email requests for technological assistance. Sarah, Azhar and Emma were members of the excellent Information Technology Administration team at the Criminal Cases Review Commission:

From: Ian
To: Sarah
Subject: Speaking in Public Seminar 10am 20th October – equipment request

Hello Sarah

I've got a PowerPoint™®© presentation for the seminar next week which I have created on my home computer. My cunning plan is to bring a USB flashy drive, if that is the right term, into the office containing said presentation.

Is it possible therefore please that you could organise for me to have, at about 9.30am on 20th October:

- a functioning laptop – into which the USB can be plugged – in the Boardroom (hopefully with a screen to project the presentation onto).
- a zapper-type thingy (if possible) so that I can operate the slide show as I move around the room.
- an Azhar-or-Emma-type person to show me how to turn things on, etc.

Many thanks for your help with this.
Best wishes, Ian.

As you will have seen, I always recommend laying on the pleasantries when you are trying to get someone to do something for you in connection with a presentation.

I received a pleasant email in reply. It confirmed that all the equipment would be supplied and, as an unexpected bonus, said: "Incidentally, to save you embarrassing yourself in the future, the correct term for a USB flashy drive is, I believe, a 'USB thing-a-ma-jig.'"

Never forget...

Here are a few more pointers about coping with public speaking technology:

Technology is by definition evil and capricious, as anyone from Gordon Brown to Doctor Who will confirm. By carrying out a dry run of the presentation in the actual location where you're going to speak with the actual equipment you're going to use, you will significantly reduce the chance that it will not work at all. Rehearse using all the equipment, allowing yourself plenty of time to correct anything that goes wrong. Even so, always have a backup plan which will allow you to give the talk even if your equipment dies on you.

In 1988, I gave a seminar in Harrogate which included a video presentation. The video went into spontaneous rewind halfway through. The absolute horror and fear that shot through me live with me still. But I just about managed to remember that courage is feeling the fear and carrying on in the face of it. If you can soldier on nobly and talk your way through a situation like that, you will find the audience enormously supportive. I got one of my best receptions that day.

Ensure that embarrassing personal material does not intrude on your presentation. Computers have their individual concerns and interests that do not necessarily align happily with those of the presenter. An executive was doing a PowerPoint presentation to his management committee. Microsoft Outlook was still open. In the middle of the talk, a window came up informing him of a new message. The heading for all to read was: 'RE: job application for the post of Marketing Manager'. Sadly, it was not for an internal appointment within the company. Try to avoid that sort of thing.

However good your files and equipment may be, never forget to check that you and the organisers possess between you all the necessary programs, wires and connections to link them up and make them work at the actual venue.

Following on from the last point, please do treat equipment that serves to connect other bits of equipment with total love and affection. Loose fittings tend to go wrong before anything else.

Remember to have with you spares for any equipment that could possibly give up the ghost on you during your presentation, and change your batteries well before there is any chance of them running out of juice.

The importance of being kind to the technical people is worth emphasising again, as in my example with Sarah, Azhar and Emma. They work in difficult conditions and under a lot of pressure. Thank them as you go along and at the end.

Conclusion

The use of technology to give glossy presentations can contribute a lot to your talk, but never forget the risks. Work on the basis that, if something can go wrong, it will. My cardinal rule is to use only technology with which I, or trusted helpers who will be present throughout, feel completely comfortable. This approach has served me well over the years.

Points to take from this chapter

- The technology is peripheral to your talk.
- Beware of over-complicated equipment.
- Check your microphone thoroughly beforehand; turn it off immediately you no longer need it.
- Autocues can be a genuine help if you rehearse appropriately with them.
- Always have a backup plan for dead equipment.
- Be nice to the technical people.

Now that we have mastered the technology, or at least are keeping it on a tight rein, we'll move on to look at a number of areas where we can enhance our presentations by infusing them with added verve and variety. In the next chapter, we are going to start by reviewing the power of visual aids to make our talks more stimulating.

Notes

The Barco press release can be found at https://www.barco.com/en/News/Press-releases/9-in-10-office-workers-experience-technology-related-stress-in-meetings-survey-shows.aspx.

CHAPTER 30

Make the most of visual aids

Introduction

At its essence, public speaking involves one person saying something to an audience, then saying some more and, after that, saying something else. Evidently, there is the potential here for monotony and boredom, and a bored audience is not a happy audience. You can avoid all that, and add great substance and richness to what you say, by bringing variety into your talk. In the next few chapters, we will look at some specific ideas for achieving this.

I'm going to begin with a review of visual aids. We looked closely at one specific aspect of this subject in Chapter 19 when we discussed PowerPoint presentations. Here, I want to talk about visual aids in more general terms.

I will remind you that such supports go far beyond the use of slides alone, and we'll discuss the range of props available to us as speakers. Bill Gates will then deliver a masterclass on the topic, and finally we'll meet a man called Rob Peck who represents perhaps the last word in visual ingenuity for a public speaker.

The effective use of visual aids

There is much more to visual aids than slides alone.

A whole range of props can add significance and point to our presentations. In my talks on finance, I have used thousands of pounds in Monopoly money, countless apples and oranges to remind people not to make misleading comparisons, and on one memorable occasion a blow-up sex toy (don't ask). Putting on a dunce's cap if you make a mistake in a technical presentation can relieve the tension wonderfully, and shows your ability to laugh at yourself. After dinner, I have given my speeches accompanied by a succession of rubber chickens together with outsized glasses of beer or wine and a great deal of cough mixture.

Props do not have to be complicated, and indeed the simplest ones are usually the most readily intelligible and striking. At a wedding speech, the father of the bride described his daughter's numerous suitors. Holding up a fifty pence piece, he said: "And this is the coin with which she chose between them."

One of the classic examples of the power of visual aids is Bill Gates' 2009 TED talk, mentioned in Chapter 19, on *Mosquitoes, malaria and education*. He quite simply released a jar full of mosquitoes to make a point about the deadly effects of malaria. He did admittedly tell the audience that the mosquitoes were not infected, after a brief delay that must have seemed much longer if you were there at the time. The jar probably held no more than a dozen or so mosquitoes, but enough to make the point. The joke afterwards was that the headline for the talk should have been, 'Gates releases more bugs into the world'.

In any event, it was a striking demonstration, showing how a simple use of variety can dramatically enhance a presentation. Bill Gates has become an engaging speaker, and the mosquito episode employed good humour and comic timing as well as the exciting visual effect. One of the fascinating aspects of his performance was the impact it made on the audience despite the small number of mosquitoes used and the even smaller number that anyone could realistically have seen.

The use of slides as visual aids

The key point about visual aids is that they should be visual.

For me, that generally means pictures. If you extract some words or numbers from your talk and put them up on a slide, that does not make them visual aids. They remain words or numbers – a mostly pointless duplication of what you say to the audience. So, for the slides in an accountancy talk, I would always want to transform detailed figures into graphs and diagrams for discussion, not tables of numbers.

As we discussed in Chapter 19, what we don't want are slides full of words, because they compete with what the speaker is trying to say. By contrast, simple slides in picture format can be remarkably powerful.

For inspiration, I recommend frequent viewings of TED talks, where the slides used by speakers maintain an outstanding level of relevance and visual interest. There is, of course, an enormous amount of other material on the Internet to support your use of visual aids. One crucial caveat: clip art (pre-prepared images used for illustration) is freely or very cheaply available, but do be aware that some of the materials that were developed in the clip art boom of the 1990s and early 2000s look rather tired and dated now.

Visual aids should also be properly visible, and that means visible to everyone in your audience. If you are speaking in a large auditorium, you will need to make doubly sure that people at the back can see clearly what is on your slides. Remember that the slides are there to support you, not vice versa.

The ultimate visual aid – the juggling public speaker

Of course, there are limits to how far you may wish to go in your search for visual variety. In an entertaining book about the world of American motivational speakers, *Yes You Can! Behind the Hype and Hustle of the Motivation Biz,* Jonathan Black writes of one particular speaker, Rob Peck, who gives his entire presentation while juggling. "The audience jumps to its feet with delight when he's done," says Jonathan Black.

I have the feeling that that might be slightly over the top for British audiences, but you never know…

Conclusion

Visual aids are a tremendous way of adding flavour to your talk. They can give context to what you are saying and help your subject stick in the minds of your listeners.

Images and pictures last longer in people's brains than concepts or technical terms. Whether or not a picture can tell a thousand words, a suitably chosen image can convey a great deal of information to your audience in a highly persuasive manner.

Points to take from this chapter

- Simple props can provide striking images to support your talk.
- Visual aids should be visual, so make the maximum use of pictures.
- Turn detailed figures into graphs and diagrams.
- Simple pictorial slides can work brilliantly.
- The slides from the TED talks can be a helpful source of inspiration.
- Visual aids must be visible to everyone in the audience.

In the next chapter, we are going to look at the most fundamental of all the ways in which a speaker can add variety to his or her performance – the vital craft of storytelling. We'll see that it's a much easier skill to acquire than you might first think. It is one of the most uncomplicated ways imaginable to win over an audience.

Notes

Two excellent books for people who are seriously interested in improving the quality of their slides are *Slide:ology: The Art and Science of Creating Great Presentations* by Nancy Duarte, O'Reilly Media, 2008, and *Presentation Zen: Simple Ideas on Presentation Design and Delivery* by Garr Reynolds, New Riders, 2011.

CHAPTER 31

Tell stories

Introduction

In this chapter, we will discuss the crucial topic of achieving variety in our talks by way of storytelling. The telling of tales is one of humanity's oldest art forms, and its positive psychological effects can be unparalleled.

We'll look at the inherent ability of a story to enhance our understanding, and Michelle Obama will use the example of her father to show its heart-rending emotional power. I'll demonstrate that, to be effective, stories need not be concerned with big events, or of great length, or of literal truth. Finally, Barack Obama will give us his own virtuoso demonstration of the storyteller's craft.

The inherent value of stories

The logic behind telling stories is easy to understand. In *Public Speaking – Principles and Practice*, James A Winans wrote:

> "The average person finds difficulty in holding his mind upon an abstraction. Ability to do so comes as the result of training. A concrete idea is more vivid... We are relieved by an occasional illustration. When a speaker indulges in much abstract discussion we either cease to listen, or do our best, hoping we understand and waiting for the welcome 'Now to illustrate.'"

To illustrate is, of course, to illuminate, to let in the light.

Stories and emotion

Nothing illustrates like a story.

I like the definition of a story as 'a fact, wrapped in emotion, that can have the power to transform the way people think or act'. That gives an idea of the potential value storytelling can have in public speaking, and indeed whole books have been written on this single topic. It is estimated that about two-thirds of all human conversations are about who is doing what and with whom – that is to say, telling stories.

Earlier, when we discussed the role of emotion in public speaking in Chapter 7, we looked at Kevin Murray's devastating true story about the fatal consequences for one child of safety procedures being disregarded. The singer Annie Lennox, talking in the context of her role as a UNAIDS ambassador, expressed the principle starkly when she said: "Human stories touch people when you show them one child – not a statistic, a child."

In a similar vein, here we have an extract from the text of Michelle Obama's Democratic Convention speech in August 2008. She is talking about her father. Note, in particular, the use of telling details to bring passion and force to an overall theme:

"My dad was our rock. Although he was diagnosed with multiple sclerosis in his early thirties, he was our provider, our champion, our hero. As he got sicker, it got harder for him to walk, it took him longer to get dressed in the morning. But if he was in pain, he never let on. He never stopped smiling and laughing — even while struggling to button his shirt, even while using two canes to get himself across the room to give my mom a kiss. He just woke up a little earlier and worked a little harder."

It is the specific, individual consequences of his illness – the fight to button his shirt, the use of the two canes – that help to make this passage so affecting. Michelle Obama returned to the same theme at her Democratic Convention speech in September 2012. With four more years of oratorical experience behind her, she gave a performance that was even more poignant:

"Even as a kid, I knew there were plenty of days when he was in pain… I knew there were plenty of mornings when it was a struggle for him to simply get out of bed.
But every morning, I watched my father wake up with a smile, grab his walker, prop himself up against the bathroom sink, and slowly shave and button his uniform.
And when he returned home after a long day's work, my brother and I would stand at the top of the stairs to our little apartment, patiently waiting to greet him… watching as he reached down to lift one leg, and then the other, to slowly climb his way into our arms.
But despite these challenges, my dad hardly ever missed a day of work… He and my mom were determined to give me and my brother the kind of education they could only dream of."

The rules for storytelling

Make your talk interesting by including anecdotes and stories. They make you appear more approachable and human, particularly if they come from your own experience. If you want people to remember an important point, tell them a story.

Of course, there are caveats.

Ensure that any story you use is relevant to your theme; it must have a clear bearing on the issue at hand, or else it will distract the audience's attention from what matters. And avoid anything that could be deemed off-colour or embarrassing to the audience.

Stories don't have to be about big news

Subject to those qualifications, any shape or size of story can work well. An example does not have to be particularly exciting to have a special effect. In his helpful *Storytelling Pocketbook*, Roger E Jones tells the sweet tale of an executive at the Chase Manhattan Bank, who would always clear up any litter he came upon in the office building. He writes: "The consequence of his action, and his simple story being retold, was that his floor of the office building was the tidiest I have ever seen."

One of the most shocking stories I know of concerns a cup of tea.

The journalist Robert Crampton described in *The Times* how he tells audiences of his encounter with Andie MacDowell. "When I got to how the rather haughty American actress had failed to offer me a cup of tea from the pot brought for her during our interview," he writes, "there was a gasp of pure Middle English outrage. 'Now that,' someone said emphatically to his neighbour, 'that is just Bloody. Bad. Manners.'" A story like this works brilliantly with a British audience.

On the same theme of small-scale but fascinating stories, I like the technique used by Ivanka Trump as she spoke on behalf of her father, Donald, at the 2016 Republican National Convention in Cleveland, Ohio. Her stories are not dramatic, but they make great use of potent pictorial detail. She remembers her childhood, "playing on the floor by [her] father's desk, constructing miniature buildings with Lego and Erector sets, while he did the same with concrete, steel and glass." She describes him writing in "[his] signature black felt tip pen", and emphasises the scale of his vision: "When I was a child, my father always told me, Ivanka, if you're going to be thinking anyway, you might as well think big."

Stories in business

Business speakers can easily ignore the potential for storytelling.

Suppose the number of customer complaints coming into your service department has gone up by 3% in the last quarter, and you want your store managers to take it seriously. By all means, produce graphs and statistics showing a worrying trend and potential loss of profitability. But if you can bring focus and power to your presentation by concentrating on the story of a single irate customer, it can make all the difference between polite nods of recognition from the audience and managers genuinely changing their behaviours to combat the problem.

Examples of keeping your stories short

Speakers often worry that stories will take up too much of their talk, to the exclusion of their main business. This involves the mistaken assumption that stories are not part of the important stuff, and it wrongly suggests that stories need to be long to be effective. Monica Lewinsky's powerful introductory story in Chapter 21 needed less than fifty words.

Here are some sources which have inspired me in writing very short stories for speeches:

- The science fiction writer Brian Aldiss invented the genre of the 'mini-saga', a whole story told in just fifty words. The *Daily Telegraph* has run several mini-saga competitions, with the best entries collected in book form: several of those books are still easily obtainable. (Search for 'Mini Sagas – Daily Telegraph' on Amazon.) Here is a great example from the Wikipedia article on mini-sagas, with the writer Daniel H Pink showing that brevity is, indeed, the soul of wit:

  "When I was shot, fear seized me at first. No surprise that. But once I realised I wasn't going to die – despite the thermonuclear pain and widening puddle of weirdly warm blood – my mind recalibrated. And one thought, comforting yet disturbing, leapt into my head: I need to Tweet this."

- The *Reader's Digest* has an annual competition for stories of one hundred words and publishes the best examples in the magazine. As with the *Telegraph* contests, the standard is extremely high.

- More traditional sources include the parables of Jesus, and before that the fables of Aesop. These are ideal places to go if you are looking for inspiration in the area of moral or motivational concepts. Here, for example, is a piece based on one of Aesop's fables:

> "Among the ancient Greeks, there was a legend that went like this. At the start of time, Jupiter gave each man two wallets – one to contain his neighbour's faults, and one for his own. The practice developed of hanging the wallets over the shoulder, the bag for the man's own failings on his back and the bag for the neighbour right in front of his nose. That is why men are quick to see the faults of others, but often blind to their own."

Making stuff up

If stories do not come readily to your mind from your past experiences, why not use your imagination?

I am not talking here about material for technical, informational lectures, where matters are, for the most part, necessarily clear-cut, but rather issues of belief or emotion where, in words attributed to the architect Frank Lloyd Wright, "the truth is more important than the facts."

It's a debate that goes back at least as far as Aristotle, but in my view a greater truth can often be attained by presenting a picture that is not factually accurate. It's what I call, rather grandly, the 'speaker's licence'. It has also been described as 'being comfortable with ambiguity' or, by those of a contrary view, as 'talking bullshit'.

We saw in Chapter 8 that complete honesty can often be counter-productive. To develop that theme, I can tell you that all of my public speaking encounters described in this book did happen to me in one form or another, but a certain amount of embellishment has gone into making them more dramatic and pertinent.

Mark Twain put it this way: "Get your facts first, and then you can distort them as much as you please." You are allowed to do the same. If an experience does not quite fit the point you want to make, don't hesitate to rearrange the details of it for your presentation. You have the speaker's licence. You are giving a performance, and that is often not the place for literal truth. With a little dressing-up, a story can move an audience from restrained signals of approval to overwhelming enthusiasm.

At times, simply leaving things out can be effective. In the acknowledgements at the start of this book, I thanked John Dascombe for judging me the winner of my school's public speaking competition at the tender age of thirteen. I may have implied that it was a competition open to the whole school, but I never quite said that. I actually won the prize in the under twelves category (don't ask), and from memory there was only one other entrant, and he had the flu.

Here's a marvellous denial of the importance of literal truth. It is the wistful farewell from our friend Henry S Wilcox at the end of his book *The Trials of a Stump-speaker:*

> "What I have written now shall stand. To me, it seems a jolly tale, full of mistakes and mirth-provoking scenes, such as may cheer an idle hour and still give some instruction. As such I finish it and send it forth to sink or float, as pleases those who read. The gay may laugh and credit me with wit, the solemn frown and hold me much to blame; the critic pierce each fancy with his pen and write me down a fool. All this I can endure. The grass will grow as green upon my grave. But heaven forfend that these, my wavering lines, shall ever meet that dense, unmitigated ass, that stupid, mournful, addle-pated imbecile, who shall, with solemn visage, sadly ask if all my tales be true."

Barack Obama weaves his magic

We have looked at Michelle Obama's storytelling masterclass; now for her husband. In a riveting victory speech in Chicago following the US presidential election of 2008, Barack Obama tells the story of a lady called Ann Nixon Cooper:

"This election had many firsts and many stories that will be told for generations. But one that's on my mind tonight's about a woman who cast her ballot in Atlanta. She's a lot like the millions of others who stood in line to make their voice heard in this election except for one thing: Ann Nixon Cooper is 106 years old.

She was born just a generation past slavery; a time when there were no cars on the road or planes in the sky; when someone like her couldn't vote for two reasons – because she was a woman and because of the colour of her skin.

And tonight, I think about all that she's seen throughout her century in America – the heartache and the hope; the struggle and the progress; the times we were told that we can't, and the people who pressed on with that American creed: yes, we can.

At a time when women's voices were silenced and their hopes dismissed, she lived to see them stand up and speak out and reach for the ballot. Yes, we can.

When there was despair in the dust bowl and depression across the land, she saw a nation conquer fear itself with a New Deal, new jobs, a new sense of common purpose. Yes, we can.

When the bombs fell on our harbour and tyranny threatened the world, she was there to witness a generation rise to greatness and a democracy was saved. Yes, we can.

She was there for the buses in Montgomery, the hoses in Birmingham, a bridge in Selma, and a preacher from Atlanta who told a people that "We Shall Overcome". Yes, we can.
A man touched down on the moon, a wall came down in Berlin, a world was connected by our own science and imagination.
And this year, in this election, she touched her finger to a screen, and cast her vote, because after 106 years in America, through the best of times and the darkest of hours, she knows how America can change.
Yes, we can.
America, we have come so far. We have seen so much. But there is so much more to do. So tonight, let us ask ourselves – if our children should live to see the next century; if my daughters should be so lucky to live as long as Ann Nixon Cooper, what change will they see? What progress will we have made?
This is our chance to answer that call. This is our moment."

In this way, Obama presents the story of a hundred years of American history in the most vivid terms, and sets it in the context of the life of one elderly black woman. He truly is a class act as a speaker.

Conclusion

Telling stories is one of the things that make us human. So speakers need to tell stories, first to show that they themselves are human, and secondly to win an inordinate amount of audience goodwill in the process. Their tales may be entirely prosaic and humdrum: it doesn't matter in the slightest, as long as they convey a human message.

Points to take from this chapter

- Stories can transform the way people think and act.
- Small details can be immensely powerful.
- Make sure you use examples relevant to your theme.
- Tales of your personal experiences work particularly well.
- Stories about seemingly trivial matters can still be highly effective.
- Storytelling has surprising power in business settings.
- Be prepared to let your imagination run free.

In the next chapter, we'll look at a further dynamic way to bring variety to our talks that too many people are unnecessarily wary about – the use of humour.

Notes

The Annie Lennox comment comes from an interview in the October 2010 issue of the *Harvard Business Review*. The scripts for Michelle Obama's convention speeches can be found at https://www. npr.org/templates/story/story.php?storyId=93963863 and https:// www.npr.org/2012/09/04/160578836/transcript-michelle-obamas-convention-speech. Robert Crampton's story of his encounter with Andie MacDowell was from an article, *My year of public speaking*, in the *Times Magazine* of 26 December 2009. Ivanka Trump speaks at https://www.youtube.com/watch?v=QXGmQfRNA08. You can see Barack Obama's victory speech in Chicago at https://www. youtube.com/watch?v=Jll5baCAaQU.

CHAPTER 32

Don't be afraid of using humour

Introduction

Laughter, like telling stories, is one of the distinguishing characteristics of being a human being. It reduces stress and helps us cope better with illness. It connects people and builds relationships. A speaker with a sense of humour has a sense of proportion, and audiences like that. There are major misconceptions about humour: that it cannot coexist with powerful emotion in speeches, and that it can't say anything important. That is nonsense. As an example, some of the most potent and heartfelt funeral tributes are laced with a life-affirming humour that shows a real feeling for the departed person.

For myself, I have always found that, if you can persuade people to laugh in the first instance, you can get them to listen more attentively to your serious points later on. And an audience that responds to humour is one of the greatest experiences available to a speaker. The actor Richard Briers put it this way: "I may sound over the top but to hear an audience roar with laughter at something you've timed well is, to me, the most lovely thing on God's Earth."

In this chapter, I will talk about the particular importance of humour to a British audience. I'll sing the praises of a self-deprecating approach, and give some examples to show that you don't need to know any complicated jokes, or indeed any jokes at all, to be amusing. I'll also set out a checklist of points on how to make the most of working with humour in practice.

By the end of the chapter, I hope to have shown you that the use of humour can be a highly rewarding experience for speaker and audience alike, and that it's not nearly as tricky a skill to pull off as some writers on the subject might have you believe. The secret, as always, is to identify the approach that suits you best as a speaker.

Humour and the British

A British audience loves humour.

As long ago as 1882 the author of *Beeton's Art of Public Speaking* wrote that "To be a good platform speaker one should have a considerable fund of humour, especially in this country, for an English crowd has a large sense of the humorous." Just before the First World War, Spencer Leigh Hughes commented in *The Art of Public Speaking* that "Jokes are always welcomed after dinner, and it is really pathetic to observe how eagerly a very humble effort at jocularity is welcomed on such occasions, and how amply it is rewarded."

Great British humour can arise even in the most unpromising places. The story is told of a sermon delivered by Ian Paisley, Northern Ireland's fire-and-brimstone Protestant preacher and politician. Dr Paisley was preaching on death and damnation, favourite topics of his. "There will be weeping," he bellowed, "and wailing and gnashing of teeth." An old lady in the congregation raised her hand and pointed out that she did not have any teeth. Dr Paisley looked upon her with a mortifying gaze: "Madam," he slowly replied, "teeth will be provided."

The value of self-effacing humour

Perhaps the safest way of using humour in public speaking is at the speaker's own expense. Here is a tremendous example of poking fun at yourself.

Chris Mullin, the Labour MP for Sunderland South, is seconding the Queen's speech in Parliament in May 1997, following Labour's landslide win in that month's general election. He recognises that some self-deprecating humour is the key to getting the House's attention. He has been sitting trembling in the Chamber awaiting his turn to speak – another reminder that nerves are essential to speaking success.

He begins his speech: "Things are looking up. On Monday, I was allocated an office with a window, thereby fulfilling one of my few remaining political ambitions."

He goes on:

> "As hon Members know, we count the votes very fast in Sunderland. For twenty minutes on the evening of 1 May, I was the only Member of Parliament in the country. It occurred to me that there was a slim window of opportunity, should I care to seize it, to form my own government. I would have had to be Chancellor of the Exchequer, Foreign Secretary and Prime Minister, but that has not done the Sultan of Oman any harm…
>
> My route to respectability has been an odd one. When I was first elected in 1987, *The Sun* published photographs across a full page of what it called 'Kinnock's Top Ten Loony Tunes':

I was number eight. If my memory serves me right, at least one of those who was higher than I in that top ten has been appointed to the government – I shall mention no names. I now keep my *Sun* headlines framed on the wall of my study at home. There is 'Mr Odious'. Yes, I once briefly displaced my hon Friend the Member for Brent East (Mr Livingstone) as the most odious man in Britain – the highest honour that *The Sun* can confer. There is 'Loony MP backs bomb gang', which was given a full front page, and 'Twenty things you didn't know about crackpot Chris.'"

By this stage, Chris Mullin has easily won over his audience and has fully prepared them for the serious themes he proceeds to discuss. He writes in his diaries, published as *A Walk-On Part: Diaries 1994–1999*, of "a wonderful and rare feeling to be (however briefly) in total command of a packed House... All evening people were coming up saying how good it was." It was his finest hour in Parliament.

In my experience

Here is how I state the case in my lecture on the use of humour in training:

"Laughter helps boost our learning abilities.
We now know that the body reacts biochemically to laughing.
Laughter produces changes in the chemical balance of the blood, leading to an increase in the body's production of the neurotransmitters needed for alertness and memory.
Researchers examined several courses in the teaching of Latin at the University of Illinois, where the lecturers

> made a conscious effort to inject humour into their material.
>
> They found that the knowledge retained by participants following these training sessions improved by 23.5% over a period of six seamstresses – sorry, that should read semesters – in 1997 and 1998. However, the one problem with this, and a point never to forget in my presentations, is that 44.7% of statistics are invented on the spot, as I just invented that one."

For me, the value of a humorous approach was intensified because for twenty years I specialised in tax training, which is seen by most people as a rather dry subject. (Hence the expression: "An empty taxi drew up, and a tax specialist got out.") The use of humour in training sessions had real value in relieving the pressure on the trainees and lessening their tension.

For example, in examining the taxation of sportspeople I would tell the story of the late, great footballer Bobby Moore.

The Inland Revenue took him to court. As England's captain in our 1966 World Cup winning team, he had received awards from the Football Association and Radox Bath Salts for being part of the team and for being England's best player and presumably the nicest smelling.

The judge held that the payments were not taxable in Bobby Moore's hands, as England winning the World Cup was an exceptional event; and history has, of course, proved him triumphantly right.

The Ken Robinson masterclass

Don't just take my word about the power of humour.

The stand-out feature of the most watched TED talk as at the time of writing, *Do schools kill creativity?* by Sir Ken Robinson, is its use of exceptional good humour. If you watch the talk, you will see how he gets the audience laughing in the first ninety seconds; then they are hooked. There are no complicated jokes involved: you don't need them. Ken Robinson simply makes great use of situational humour, getting laughs out of our everyday encounters.

Working with humour in practice

If you can make people laugh early on in your talk, they'll stay with you and pay attention in the expectation of laughing again. This applies everywhere – in church, at school speech days, in prison – and it applies to all speakers. John F Kennedy employed humour in the openings of his speeches to establish a rapport with his audience, and Bill Clinton uses much the same approach. Sir Ken Robinson was following in a distinguished tradition in his TED talk.

You never know in advance if humour that appeals to you will go down well with other people. The only way to find out if something is funny is for the audience to tell you. It therefore makes sense to test your comic material out on smaller groups of friends and acquaintances first, rather than go straight into a large public auditorium with it. Things will look promising if the smaller group likes it, provided that the style of humour is suited to the actual audience you will encounter on the day.

Don't attempt humour that you don't find funny or amusing yourself. It was always deeply disconcerting to watch Margaret Thatcher read out jokes prepared by her speechwriters that she did not quite understand. It never worked. Seek her out on YouTube performing the *Dead Parrot* sketch from Monty Python (yes, really) and you will see what I mean.

Similarly, don't try any form of humour that you are not comfortable with, or does not fit in with your character and personality. For example, I mentioned earlier my problem with long jokes. I found that the lead-up to the funny bit put me under too much pressure, and I simply wilted under that pressure. By the time I got to the punchline, I was so tense that there was no chance I was going to get it right. Instead, I discovered that simple, genuine comments that have a touch of humour to them, one-line jokes and the like, could work well for me and be reliably successful. One-liners are less risky and allow the presentation to move on with greater pace. If you do feel that longer jokes are your style, telling them frequently to other people is the best way of mastering them.

When you find an existing piece of humour you think will be suitable for you, always make sure you adapt it so that it is entirely relevant to your theme. Try to bring in topical and local details, so that it becomes your own joke. A good story can have many lives, and you can edit it to suit many different audiences.

Don't force your humour. Listeners do not care for the speaker who rambles on earnestly for an hour, but every fifteen minutes or so puts in a long, elaborate joke that doesn't arise from the subject matter. Spencer Leigh Hughes is masterful on the subject of forced humour:

"While a joke, and especially a good tale, will be received with gratitude, there ought to be some connection between the joke or tale and the subject about which the man is supposed to be speaking. You will often hear a man break off in the middle of a speech to say, 'Talking of so-and-so reminds me of a tale I heard the other day,'

> and then it is soon made evident that the tale has no connection whatever with his topic. When this trick of dragging in a tale by its ears has been played half a dozen times the hearers perceive that the gentleman has nothing to say."

Give people time to take in your humour. With less obvious jokes, you have to allow a couple more seconds for the audience to work them out and get the point before they actually laugh: the thinking process leads to a slower reaction. The same issue arises if you are speaking in a large auditorium or to an audience that is spread out. Your challenge is to hold your nerve until the audience starts laughing. If they never start laughing, simply use one of the recovery techniques we discussed in Chapter 13. (I find "That's the last time I get my jokes from *The Beano*" works well.) Beyond that, never worry too much about your precise comic timing. In the words of the great radio comedian Ted Ray, "The secret of timing is not to talk when the audience is laughing." It's no more complicated than that.

The primary origin of a speaker's funny material should be their individual personality. Beyond that, everyone will have their preferred individual sources. *The Week* magazine is my personal favourite: sections such as *Spirit of the age, It must be true... I read it in the tabloids, Pick of the week's Gossip*, and a *Wit & Wisdom* compilation of quotations provide a treasure trove of entertaining, topical stories. *Reader's Digest* is a traditional favourite for many people, and helpfully its humour has lost much of its earlier blandness. I like to have a good book of humorous quotations to hand, such as Gyles Brandreth's *Oxford Dictionary of Humorous Quotations*. Any book with a title starting something like *The Wit of...* is usually a safe bet. In carrying out your research, remember that the humour with the most to offer is often found in places where you don't expect it: Winston Churchill, for example, could be incredibly funny, but his reputation for formal oratory tends to overshadow that aspect of the man.

There are some very sensible caveats about the use of humour. Sometimes the use of expletives gives extra force to your humour, but always be sure to judge very carefully whether they are appropriate for the circumstances of your talk and the audience in question. Never pick on particular people among your listeners, other than by prior agreement. Never tell jokes about a minority group. In all circumstances, remember the value of good manners. As an example, people ask where we would be without a sense of humour. The answer, as the great satirist and comedian Willie Rushton told us, is, of course, Germany. But, from personal experience, I would recommend against telling that joke at an event where the German ambassador is present.

Some of the important don'ts of humour were set out in William G Hoffman's *Public Speaker's Scrapbook* of 1935, and they remain entirely relevant today:

"Don't say, 'That reminds me of a story.' Don't tell a dialect story, if you are not pretty good with the dialect. Don't tell a long or complicated story. Don't tell a story at all if you don't feel at ease with it. Don't tell irrelevant stories. Don't start with 'There were two Irishmen.'"

If you decide that the use of humour is not for you, never underestimate the power of simply smiling at your audience. Victor Borge, the Danish entertainer and pianist, wrote in his autobiography that "the smile is the shortest distance between two persons." At the very least, by smiling at the audience you will relax your facial muscles. More than that, a surprising number of people will smile back at you and thereby give you confidence. In fact, a 1991 research paper on reactions to smiling suggested that, while not all the audience will smile back at you, roughly half of them might.

More from Spencer Leigh Hughes

Spencer Leigh Hughes was one of the greatest humorous speakers of the early twentieth century, and he left us a helpful essay on *Humour in Public Speaking*. Here are some extracts:

> "Few men can with success make a long speech that is entirely humorous, and few audiences can endure any such attempt. Humour should be a condiment, and not a main ingredient of the dish. But when judiciously applied it is of enormous value in getting the hearer to swallow the other parts. Nothing clinches an argument and makes it 'go home' better than a really good joke that is obviously appropriate to the occasion... Audiences are surprisingly quick to see when a joke really illustrates an argument or enforces a statement.
>
> ... There is nothing disgraceful in not being able to make a humorous speech. Some of the greatest masters of the platform, and some of those who have dominated Parliament, have had no gift in this direction. And as a rule, though not always, they have been conscious of not being able to excel in this direction, and have been satisfied with their other triumphs. It has not always been so, however, and I think there is no more painful experience than to see and hear a really great and gifted speaker laboriously trying to be amusing when he cannot.
>
> At the same time I believe there are men who could amuse and fascinate their hearers by bright and cheery speeches, but who repress their natural impulse, thinking that it

would be undignified to make an audience laugh. This is a great mistake. True humour is a valuable gift, and it will enable a man to get a hearing often, so that he can put in his more serious matter, when without it perhaps he would have appealed in vain for a hearing. I know some practised speakers who, when they are confronted by an audience known to be 'ticklish' – that is to say, not too friendly – always begin with a joke or two, to put everyone in a good humour, and then come gradually and warily to the more contentious part of the business. Directly the audience begins to be a little restive such a speaker soothes it again by something amusing, and so the end is gained. But the man who does this must feel he has it in him, and must do it with art and skill.

… And let me repeat that the humour that provokes the most general laughter is good humour, just as the wit that succeeds in this way should be like the sheet lightning that illuminates without hurting, not like the forked lightning that scorches and withers."

Conclusion

Lots of books on public speaking warn you off trying to be humorous unless you are an accomplished master of the subject. My experience, both personally and with people I have coached, is that audiences warm to a speaker who makes any genuine attempt at humour.

I remember reading in an article in *The Sunday Times* that the average man laughed for eighteen minutes a day during the 1950s, compared with six minutes today. Let's redress the balance. The most joyous feeling I know is that of people laughing. Humour entertains your listeners, lets them feel good, and makes them more responsive to what you have to say. Used with care, it clarifies your points and makes them more memorable. The audience then pays attention and stays involved.

What's not to like?

Points to take from this chapter

- There is no better experience for a speaker than an audience laughing with them.
- The safest form of humour is self-effacing humour.
- Complicated jokes are not required.
- Never employ humour that you are not comfortable with yourself.
- Adapt any humour you use so that it is relevant to your theme.
- Try to bring in topical and local details.
- Don't underestimate the power of simply smiling at your audience.

We have looked in recent chapters at three great ways of adding variety to your talks – the use of visual aids, storytelling and humour. There are, of course, vast numbers of other ideas for adding zing and zest to your talks, and we'll examine a range of these in the next chapter.

Notes

Chris Mullin's speech can be found at http://hansard. millbanksystems.com/commons/1997/may/14/first-day#S6CV0294P0_19970514_HOC_100. You can see Ken Robinson's record-breaking TED talk at https://www.ted. com/talks/ken_robinson_says_schools_kill_creativity. The

1991 research paper on the reactions to smiling was by the psychologists Verlin Hinsz and Judith Tomhave, and was entitled *Smile and (half) the world smiles with you, frown and you frown alone.* Spencer Leigh Hughes' essay on *Humour in Public Speaking* comes from Volume II of *The Book of Public Speaking.*

CHAPTER 33

Use other ways to bring variety into your talk

Introduction

In this chapter, we will look at an array of other ideas for bringing flavour to your presentations.

We'll review a number of rhetorical devices that have come down to us through the ages, adding flair and dynamism to our words. Victoria Wood will give us a virtuoso demonstration of the use of rich, vivid language to brighten our talks, and we'll end with a wealth of further suggestions.

Use the rule of three

I'm not writing a handbook on rhetoric, but it is worth mentioning that it's hard to go wrong using some of the traditional rhetorical devices. I'll mention just a few of these.

The rule of three – an important and easy-to-use technique – is based, quite simply, on the principle that things that come in threes are more successful than other numerical combinations. From ancient times, gathering phrases in groups of three has been recognised as having particular power. Wikipedia explains the underlying reasoning as being that 'having three entities combines both brevity and rhythm with having the smallest amount of information to create a pattern. It makes the author or speaker appear knowledgeable while being both simple and catchy.'

Julius Caesar showed the way: *Veni, vidi, vici* ("I came; I saw; I conquered"). William Shakespeare borrowed the device in his play *Julius Caesar* when he wrote: "Friends, Romans, countrymen, lend me your ears." The Gettysburg Address by Abraham Lincoln celebrated government "of the people, by the people, for the people". Charles de Gaulle called in turn to men of the army, navy and air forces: "de terre, de mer et de l'air", with the rhyme and rhythm reinforcing his message. Tony Blair famously set out his priorities for government as "Education, Education, Education". Superman still fights for "Truth, Justice, and the American Way".

The rule of three can be used to provide humorous effect as well, as in Rory Bremner's "I've been to the top of the mountain, I've parked my car, I've paid and displayed." An example that works well in the motivational field goes: "You've heard about our past; you've contributed to our present; and we hope you'll be part of our future".

It is always worth thinking about sprinkling your talk with some juicy threesomes.

Use other rhetorical devices

Our next technique to review is anaphora. Anaphora (from the Greek meaning 'carrying back') is the repetition for effect of a word or phrase at the beginning of a clause or sentence.

Its use goes back at least as far as the Psalms:

"**The voice of the Lord** is over the waters;
the God of glory thunders,
the Lord, over many waters.
The voice of the Lord is powerful;
the voice of the Lord is full of majesty.
The voice of the Lord breaks the cedars;
the Lord breaks the cedars of Lebanon…" (Psalm 29)

The technique was used to brilliant effect by Abraham Lincoln ("**With** malice toward none; **with** charity for all; **with** firmness in the right…") and by Martin Luther King Jr ("I have a dream"). In Britain, Winston Churchill could not resist anaphora:

"**We shall** not flag or fail. **We shall** go on to the end. **We shall** fight in France, **we shall** fight on the seas and oceans, **we shall** fight with growing confidence and growing strength in the air, **we shall** defend our island, whatever the cost may be, **we shall** fight on the beaches, **we shall** fight on the landing grounds, **we shall** fight in the fields and in the streets, **we shall** fight in the hills. **We shall** never surrender."

By contrast, epistrophe (from the Greek for 'return'), also known as epiphora, is the repetition of words at the end of sentences or clauses.

The apostle Paul, in the King James translation of the Bible, uses the technique: "When I was **a child**, I spoke **as a child**, I understood **as a child**, I thought **as a child**." Here's Donald Trump getting in on the act, closing his acceptance speech at the 2016 Republican National Convention:

"To all Americans tonight in all of our cities and in all of our towns, I make this promise: we will make America strong

> **again**. We will make America proud **again**. We will make America safe **again**. And we will make America great **again!**"

The geeks among us might wish to know that the Donald Trump piece displays the technique of symploce (from the Greek for 'interweaving'). Symploce represents a combination of anaphora and epistrophe, so that you get the same words at the start of the sentence and the same words at the end.

Use contrasts

In his inaugural address as US president in January 1961, John F Kennedy famously said: "And so, my fellow Americans: ask not what **your country** can do for **you**, ask what **you** can do for **your country**." In rhetorical terms, this type of word arrangement where clauses are reversed in structure is called chiasmus, from the Greek word for 'crossing'.

Contrasts of all kinds can be hugely useful in public speaking. Margaret Thatcher gave us: "You **turn** [U-turn] if you want to. The lady's **not for turning**." (This was the speechwriter's pun on the title of Christopher Fry's verse play *The Lady's Not for Burning*, though it is doubtful whether Mrs Thatcher herself took much note of that.)

Max Atkinson was quoted on the value of contrasts in a BBC News Magazine article in 2009: "Using contrasts is a real winner," he said. "Research shows 33% of the applause a good speech gets is when a contrast is used... It makes your point bigger and better." He notes the forceful impact of the move from a negative point to a positive ('**ask not**' to '**ask**' in the Kennedy example). The Thatcher excerpt shows that the effect can be equally potent when the order is reversed ('**turn**'... '**not for turning**').

Abraham Lincoln is the ultimate master of the use of contrast. We looked at the text of the Gettysburg Address in Chapter 4.

Despite its brevity, it is full of contrasts, in both language and ideas, that are striking and memorable:

Four score and seven years ago	now
Our fathers	we
We have come to dedicate	those who here gave their lives
We can not consecrate	the brave men… have consecrated
The world will little note	but it can never forget
What we say here	what they did here
We have come to dedicate a	It is for us…
portion of that field	to be dedicated

Ask rhetorical questions

We will look at the issue of question and answer sessions separately in Chapter 36, but for the moment I want to recommend the value of asking the audience questions, particularly rhetorical questions, to gain rapport. A rhetorical question is broadly one that you ask without expecting an answer, or perhaps where the answer is evident but you ask the question to win a point in your argument.

A great example came at the end of the second US presidential debate of 1980 between Jimmy Carter and Ronald Reagan. Reagan asked the audience some simple but powerful questions, making effective use of epistrophe in the process:

> "Next Tuesday all of you will go to the polls, will stand there in the polling place and make a decision. I think when you make that decision, it might be well if you would ask yourself, are you better off than you were four years ago? Is it easier for you to go and buy things in the stores than

it was four years ago? Is there more or less unemployment in the country than there was four years ago? Is America as respected throughout the world as it was? Do you feel that our security is as safe, that we're as strong as we were four years ago? And if you answer all of those questions yes, why then, I think your choice is very obvious as to whom you will vote for. If you don't agree, if you don't think that this course that we've been on for the last four years is what you would like to see us follow for the next four, then I could suggest another choice that you have."

I love the flow of this passage, from the clear, strong opening question, "Are you better off than you were four years ago?" to the understated ending, "then I could suggest another choice that you have." Unsurprisingly, Reagan went on to win the election.

Variety in lecturing

It is a well-established principle that a lecture is a process by which the notes of the lecturer pass into the notebook of the student without passing through the brains of either.

Professor RV (Reginald Victor) Jones was a man who saw things differently. He was a British physicist and scientific military intelligence expert who played a significant role in Britain's defence during the Second World War. After the war, he was appointed Chair of Natural Philosophy (physics) at the University of Aberdeen, where he gained a reputation as a brilliant lecturer. He believed that you should have something significant to say, say it in clear English that was free of jargon, and make sure everyone in the audience could see and hear you.

In a letter to *The Times* in September 2016, Alexander Grant, who had been a first-year student with Professor Jones, described his teaching technique, which came from a day with somewhat less rigorous health and safety requirements:

"His lectures were indeed brilliant, backed up by visible, very audible practical demonstrations. How did he measure the speed of a bullet? He fired it from a handgun across the lecture bench into a six-inch cube of solid wood suspended by string from a clamp stand... There were no protective screens in front of the one hundred or so attentive students. Memorable lectures indeed and I think I still remember the physics. For his final lecture to the first year he provided beer for the students, whose numbers were much enhanced by others with a thirst (for knowledge)."

Use vivid language

I would encourage any would-be speaker to watch DVDs of the great writer and comedian Victoria Wood.

It was said of her that she would never just mention a biscuit when she could talk about a Rich Tea. This was a classic example of the wealth of the language she used, of the pleasure she took in doing so, and of her commitment to using specific terms rather than generalities. The specific example raises deeper and more meaningful associations in the mind of the listener. Many of her finest and funniest lines have this same quality: for example, "My first words were Cadbury's Dairy Milk," "Beat me on the bottom with a *Woman's Weekly*," and – my favourite – "Life's not fair, is it? Some of us drink champagne in the fast lane, and some of us eat our sandwiches by the loose chippings on the A597."

She knew well that concrete terms create vivid impressions

– a maxim that goes back at least as far as George Campbell, a Scottish minister who, with Hugh Blair, was one of the finest early British writers on rhetoric. "The more general the terms are," he wrote, "the picture is the fainter; the more special they are, 'tis the brighter."

Victoria Wood took this point brilliantly. Her love of words and language, and her precision in using them, are compelling.

Some other ideas

Here is an assortment of further ideas you might consider to add variety to your presentations:

- Bringing in some of the history of your topic, and showing how it has developed over the years, can often make a rather dry subject more interesting. For example, in talks for non-specialist audiences about accountancy, I have often spoken about the Italian Luca Pacioli, or, to give him his full name, Fra Luca Bartolomeo de Pacioli. He was a Franciscan friar and a mathematician, and he worked with Leonardo da Vinci. But above all, he was the man who is commonly regarded as the father of accounting, being the first person to publish a work on double-entry bookkeeping. He has helped me make finance talks that little bit more interesting – not much, perhaps, but it all helps.
- Keep your eyes open for developments in current affairs that could be relevant to your subject. Topical allusions or popular cultural references resonate with your audience, and can bond them to you more effectively than any technical argument. If you try hard enough, you will be amazed how apposite you

can make the prime minister's recent bout of flu or Chelsea's latest victory appear to a discussion of your current archaeological dig. It's certainly no harder than fitting Cadbury's Dairy Milk into a book on public speaking.

- The use of relevant quotations can be powerful, particularly if they are funny or inspirational. Here is William Emeny, writing in his stimulating book *100 Things Awesome Teachers Do*, on the power of a quotation attributed to Mahatma Gandhi: "One of my teachers at school had Gandhi's famous quote 'Be the change you want to see in the world' displayed prominently in their classroom. It is still informing my decisions over a decade on."

- I have already mentioned the value of rhetorical questions. More generally, questions posed to the audience can give emphasis to your arguments or help ideas become fixed in their memory. If you are speaking for your organisation, a simple question like "So, what are we going to do about this?" can be forceful in demonstrating your willingness to address problems proactively, provided you can follow the question up with a reasonably appropriate solution. Asking challenging questions makes people think more deeply and engages their curiosity.

- Depending on the circumstances of your talk and the size of your audience, light-hearted quizzes can be a great way of increasing audience participation, having fun and relieving yourself of some of the pressure, while helping your points to sink in. I always used to give small prizes in the form of chocolates – nowadays you might want to include some healthy alternatives – and the enthusiasm and competitive spirit this generated were out of all proportion to the small cost involved.

- Consider including in your talk a surprising or little-known fact about your subject: a few minutes' searching on the Internet can produce some fascinating results. Did you know that Australia exports camels to the Middle East? That the banana is a type of berry? That William Shakespeare is an anagram of 'I am a weakish speller?' That no word in English rhymes with orange? That no baby boy was named Ian in the United Kingdom in 2016, so that I am one of a dying breed? Strange but true items can instantly grab or recapture the audience's attention. But they should have some connection, however tenuous, with your topic. And bear in mind that much of the trivia you find on the Internet can be misleading or even outright nonsense. So, to correct myself, there is no *common* word that rhymes with orange, but it does rhyme with sporange, an enclosure in which spores are formed in ferns or similar plants. So there.

- By contrast, stating the obvious, or what would be obvious if people thought about it in any depth, can be intensely powerful. I am lost in admiration for an example given by the neurosurgeon Henry Marsh in his extraordinary book *Do No Harm: Stories of Life, Death and Brain Surgery*. He writes: "The idea that my [operating tool] is moving through thought itself, through emotion and reason, that memories, dreams and reflections should consist of jelly, is simply too strange to understand."

- It can help to vary the tone of your words. Winston Churchill was particularly good at mixing elevated, statesmanlike language with phrasing that was more colloquial and popular. In a speech in Canada in 1941, he developed the story of how, in the summer of 1940, the French generals had dismissed the prospects for Britain in the war. He quoted them as saying, "In three weeks England will have her neck wrung like a chicken." His simple, one-line conclusion was: "Some chicken: some neck," and it went down a storm with his audience.

- Consider varying the emotions you use in a talk. As an example, honesty can be compelling, particularly when it is not a quality often associated with you. In his farewell speech at the 2006 Labour Party conference, Tony Blair made a comment about his wife: "At least I don't have to worry about [Cherie] running off with the bloke next door." It combined humour with an honest recognition of his differences with the bloke next door, Gordon Brown, and so contributed to one of his most successful political speeches.

- The occasional use of verse in your speech can have a refreshing effect. The worse the verse, the greater tends to be the audience enjoyment. We will look at an example of this in Chapter 35 when we discuss making the most of the last five minutes of a talk.

Conclusion

Variety is indeed the spice of life, and we should employ it liberally in our talks. It makes a real difference by helping us pace our performances effectively, mixing elements of light and shade into the texture of what we have to say.

Chapters 30 to 33 have, I hope, given you an assortment

of new ideas for bringing extra colour to your talks. As ever, I recommend that you try out the ones that appeal to you, to see what works for you personally.

Points to take from this chapter

- Gathering phrases in groups of three adds force to your argument.
- Repeat words at the start or end of a sentence for extra effect.
- Make use of contrasts.
- Ask rhetorical questions to gain rapport.
- Use vivid language – specific terms rather than generalities.
- Don't be afraid to use the wide range of further techniques set out in this chapter.

We talked earlier (in Chapter 28) about the most effective ways of managing your voice in public speaking. A related topic, worth considering in its own right, is the general pace of speech that works best for a talk or presentation. In the next chapter, I am going to suggest that it's slower than you might think.

Notes

The Max Atkinson quotation can be found at http://news.bbc. co.uk/1/hi/magazine/8128271.stm. The extract from George Campbell comes from Book III, Chapter 1 of his *Philosophy of Rhetoric*. The story that no baby boy was named Ian in the UK in 2016 can be found at http://www.express.co.uk/life-style/life/857037/2017-baby-names-popular-unpopular-top-uk-2016. If the *Express* says it, then clearly the point is incontrovertible.

CHAPTER 34

Slow down!

Introduction

In recent chapters, we have been focusing, not surprisingly, on the kinds of things you might say in your talk. I want now to examine the speed at which you might say them. I'll be extolling the benefits of using a slower pace, and we'll also discover the wonders of an invaluable but underused tactic available to the public speaker – the unassuming pause.

The case for speaking slowly

David Niven PhD (that's the other David Niven, the one who hasn't to my knowledge been a film star) expresses a particularly forceful view on our pace of speech in his book *The 100 Simple Secrets of Successful People*. He writes: "Communication is not about the number of things we say, it's about the number of things that are understood. Good speakers master a practice that is simple but powerful: they speak more slowly than others." He cites research from 1995, showing that people rate speakers who speak more slowly as being 38% more knowledgeable than faster speakers, though the research seems to have been based on a small sample size.

One of the leading British experts on public speaking, Max Atkinson, agrees with David Niven. In his great book, *Lend Me Your Ears,* he argues that most people talk too fast when they are speaking in public. To maximise our speaking effectiveness and audience understanding, he suggests that we should bring our pace down from a normal conversational rate of about 170 to 180 words per minute to between 120 and 140 words per minute, doing this by a combination of speaking more slowly and pausing regularly. (One of the easiest ways to work out your speed is to time yourself dictating a document where you know the word count.)

Max Atkinson acknowledges that at the outset most of us will feel uncomfortable speaking this slowly, and so we will need to practise and work at it. He sets out a principle that has certainly been successful for people I have coached and for me personally:

> "There's a useful rule that works for the vast majority of speakers: if what you are saying sounds to you to be too slow, and if the pauses sound too long, then you have probably got the pace about right."

In the view of Amy Cuddy, the American social psychologist we met earlier, our approach to speaking in public ties in with our feelings of power and control. She says: "When we feel powerful, we expand. When we feel powerless, we shrink." In that perceived state of powerlessness, we feel that we don't have anything good to say and we do not want to take up people's time: so, of course, we speed up. When we have a sense of power, the body tells the mind that it is not under threat, and we slow down appropriately.

This all ties in with my experience of listening to the speeches of the great orators. Perhaps the most famous of all twentieth-century speeches, Martin Luther King Jr's 'I have a dream', starts very slowly. In the first minute, he says less than eighty words. He is going to do whatever it takes for his words to soak into the minds and hearts of his listeners. Barack Obama is another example of someone who speaks slowly and deliberately and is all the more impressive for it. And, going back to those TED talks, in Sir Ken Robinson's presentation, *Do schools kill creativity?* he says just 2,700 words in nineteen minutes, at a rate of little more than 140 words per minute.

The case for it not mattering very much

I don't know of any leading authorities who suggest we should speed up when we speak in public, but there are certainly those who feel that too much emphasis is placed on slowing down.

In his book *Presentation Genius,* Simon Raybould suggests that an increased speed of delivery may have the advantage that people are swept along by our flow, without being given a chance to think of counter-arguments. He also notes that slow speakers might be regarded as having to think too hard, suggesting they don't know their material.

I cannot agree with his point that talking slowly might reduce a speaker's credibility. Certainly, in many years of reviewing feedback for a large number of speakers, I have never seen the suggestion raised that a slow speaker was not the master of his or her material. Quite the reverse, in fact. The situation is very different, of course, when speakers perform in fits and starts because they haven't prepared properly and are making it up as they go along. They deserve all the criticism that comes to them, as do those who speak fast in an attempt to cover up the weaknesses of their arguments.

In general, thinking of my own speeches and those of the people I have coached, my belief is that a slower delivery has produced greater success for all of us. If you are dealing with important information, challenging views, complex arguments or sophisticated humour, you simply have to give the audience enough time to get to mental grips with your point before you move on. You have no choice in this: as we have said before, the audience does not have the opportunity to go back for another attempt at hearing and understanding you, and they can't cross-reference what you have said to a non-existent written text. If in doubt, slow down.

When I was much younger, I gave an after-dinner speech to a golfing society somewhere in the West Midlands. I spoke at a relatively rapid pace. The humour was, in my view, dry and sophisticated: in the view of the golfers, it was unintelligible, not to mention unfunny. I died on my feet. If, in my golfing speech, I had slowed down the delivery and paused sufficiently at the end of each joke for people to think it through and take it in, I might have given myself a decent chance of getting some laughs. Well, maybe not a decent chance, because the audience seemed to be largely composed of the living dead that evening, but some slight possibility anyway.

Learn the power of pauses

Let's say a bit more about pauses, because they are a speaker's best friend.

The great comedian Jack Benny built an entire career on his pauses and his assumed stinginess. His defining moment comes in the scene where he is held up at gunpoint by a mugger.

"Your money or your life," shouts the mugger. Jack stares at the mugger and pauses for an age. "Look, bud," screams the frustrated mugger, "I said, your money or your life!"

"I'm thinking it over!" says Jack.

It's well worth going on to YouTube for his masterclasses in the use of the pause. His friend, the comedian George Burns, summed him up: "This was some great act this guy had: Jack Benny carried a violin that he didn't play, a cigar he didn't smoke, and he was funniest when he said nothing." To see a man working his humorous pauses in more recent times, watch that great TED talk by Sir Ken Robinson again. He goes beyond the original rule of comic timing ('don't talk while they're laughing') and challenges the audience *not* to laugh at his jokes.

The role of pauses is by no means limited to comedy. I like the saying, 'Don't mind the silence, it's the sound of thinking': and that can be thinking being done by you or the audience, or both. Pause as much as you need to, to get your thoughts together.

Or to get your breath.

Or to give the audience time to think through your latest statement and admire your wisdom.

Or to drink some water.

Or to walk across the stage.

Or to prepare them for the next major point you are about to launch into.

By pausing, you avoid the suggestion that you are rushing, and you look as thoughtful as can be, even if your brain cells are a complete blank at the time. Beyond that, the use of the pause can be particularly helpful if you are reading from a text, as we saw in Chapter 18, using the example of Elizabeth I's speech to her troops.

Max Atkinson gives an excellent example of the power of the pause. In the final part of Winston Churchill's famous *This was their finest hour* address to the nation in June 1940 after the fall of France, he pauses on six separate occasions to drive home the force of his message. The passage "Let us therefore brace ourselves to our duties, and so bear ourselves, that if the British Empire and its Commonwealth last for a thousand years, men will still say, 'This was their finest hour'" consequently becomes:

> "Let us therefore brace ourselves to our duties, [PAUSE]
> And so bear ourselves, [PAUSE]
> That if the British Empire and its Commonwealth [PAUSE]
> Last for a thousand years, [PAUSE]
> Men will still say, [PAUSE]
> 'This [PAUSE]
> Was their finest hour.'"

Max Atkinson notes that pauses of half a second, a second or even a second and a half can work well in public speaking, while in ordinary conversation they might feel intolerably long. He suggests marking your planned pauses in the text of your speeches, writing a single slash (/) for a short pause and a double one (//) for a longer pause. I have stolen this tactic, and it works well for me.

Conclusion

In my view, the pace of normal speech is too fast for most public speaking, and that's even before you take into account the speeding-up effect produced by nerves and the urgent desire to be finished talking.

If you go too quickly, your message will be unclear, and the audience won't be able to follow the thread of your argument. Your lack of confidence will show – it is the rate of speech above all other factors that gives away the speaker's fear – and the audience may decide to give up on you.

So, just slow down. This is especially important at times when you feel you are not performing well; we will have more to say about that when we talk in Chapter 37 about the speaking engagement from hell.

One of the best ways of slowing down is to increase the number and length of the pauses in your speech. They have significant dramatic power, not to mention the side benefit that the more you pause, the less material you have to write for your talk.

I would give speakers rather more latitude than Max Atkinson, but I would not recommend going much above 150 words per minute if you want to be confident that the audience will stay with you. My own speeches these days work out at 140 to 150 words per minute on average.

While working within such an overall speed restriction, remember the need to vary the pace and tone of your delivery to keep the audience alert and interested. 'V' for variety is a fundamental element of the CAVE mnemonic (Clarity, Audibility, Variety and Enthusiasm) which we discussed in Chapter 28 on managing your voice.

Above all, remember Max Atkinson's golden rule: if you think you are speaking too slowly, and that your pauses are too long, you're probably going at just the right pace.

Points to take from this chapter

- What matters is how much the audience understands, not how much you say.
- Most people talk too fast when they speak in public.
- Speaking more slowly feels uncomfortable, so you have to work at it.
- Pauses are a speaker's best friend, particularly when your brain goes blank or if you are reading from a text.
- It is particularly important to slow down when you feel the talk is not going well.

We talked in Chapter 21 about the importance of making your mark in the first few minutes of your talk. Just as you want to make an early impression on your audience, so you will be keen to go out with a bang at the conclusion of your performance. That's what we will be discussing in the next chapter.

Notes

Amy Cuddy's words again come from her February 2016 lecture, *Have Presence, and be Self-Assured in Moments of Pressure.*

CHAPTER 35

Use the last five minutes to advantage

Introduction

The words 'In conclusion' have a wonderfully invigorating effect on an audience. You at once have their full attention, and you want to make the most of it. Indeed, throughout the history of oratory, the experts have encouraged us to pay particular attention to what the Romans called the *peroratio*, the peroration or conclusion of our talk. In Cicero's day, this was the part of the speech where the legal orator summed up his arguments, cast the other side in a negative light (oratory has never been an entirely blameless pursuit) and raised sympathy for himself and his client.

In this chapter, I'll set out my recommended method for dealing with the ending. We'll discuss topics particularly suitable for the last few minutes of your talk, not least the well-designed call to action that will send your audience away inspired. We'll review some strong final words you might use, and then Franklin D Roosevelt, the great American president, will give us a demonstration of how to conclude an oration with power and conviction.

The way to approach the ending

The last part of your speech needs careful construction, not least because it has to sound as though you have reached your natural finish. The conclusion must conclude: it should form a logical ending to the speech and be fully related to it, not something appended as an afterthought.

Whether or not you have used notes or memory for the earlier part of your speech, I recommend that, at least as an initial step, you write your conclusion out in full so that you can become utterly familiar with it. And remember that a brief ending is normally the best ending, so be prepared to edit out ruthlessly material for your last five minutes that isn't essential.

Another key rule is that the ending is not the place for understatement or delicacy. Make it blindingly clear that you are finishing. Don't be afraid to say "In conclusion" or to write it on any slides you are using. Make the words you use direct and telling. Winston Churchill's maxim from Chapter 11 about using a pile driver to make your point is doubly important for the ending of your speech.

Topics for the last five minutes

If you are giving a humorous speech, there's nothing particularly clever you need to do with the last five minutes apart from carrying on being humorous and aiming to finish with a strong joke or witticism. Things get more complicated if you have been giving a talk with a serious purpose. For that situation, my list of trusty servants for the end of a speech follows. Remember that, to avoid making the conclusion too long, you will only select a few of them at most for any particular talk:

- A reference back to the beginning. This might include revisiting your opening argument and developing it in the light of how you have expanded the audience's understanding.
- The conclusion of an example or story that you began earlier in the talk.
- A summary or reinforcement of your overall argument or explanation.
- Any reasonable deduction or lesson you can draw from the points you have made.
- A memorable message.
- A story or fable that encapsulates that message.
- A rhetorical question to get the audience thinking.
- An emotional appeal.
- A powerful quotation.
- A call to action, asking the audience to act or behave in a certain way, often coupled with an explanation of how they stand to benefit from doing so.
- A demonstration to the audience that you, like Franklin D Roosevelt later in this chapter, are the right person for the task ahead.

In making your selection from these topics, don't worry about repeating important information from earlier in your talk. It reinforces what you have said in people's memories, and gives them a much better chance of retaining the material. This is a good reason why the traditional approach to delivering a speech (tell them what you're going to tell them; tell them; tell them what you've told them) that we encountered in Chapter 11 can still work so well. In telling them what you've told them, for the sake of brevity please do focus on the critical issue or issues only.

The call to action

If your talk is to be any more than a pleasurable short-term diversion (not that there is anything wrong with that), you will want your audience to do something with what you have told them. This could be as simple as remembering the key points you've raised, or it could be as much as undertaking a whole course of action.

The advertising guru David Ogilvy, writing in his book *On Advertising*, summed up the importance of the call to action aptly, comparing two great Greek orators: "When Aeschines spoke, they said, 'How well he speaks.' But when Demosthenes spoke, they said, 'Let us march against Philip.'" Like David Ogilvy, I'm for Demosthenes.

In modern times, Winston Churchill's wartime eloquence was one of the foundations for his people's belief in their darkest days that Britain and her allies could still win the Second World War; and win it they did.

In America, the speeches of Martin Luther King Jr not only gained him iconic status but also secured genuine improvements in civil rights in the United States, not least through the passing of the Civil Rights Act of 1968. Barack Obama's civilised and eloquent speeches in the years leading up to the US presidential election of 2008 convinced the bulk of a still racially conflicted American population that they could elect a first black president without fearing for the consequences. These were heroic steps for America and the world.

The rest of us may not be able to change history on such a scale. However, I suggest that you too in your speeches should be seeking to influence, for the better, the people who are listening to you. As we have seen, a speech is not the best place for subtlety and gentle suggestion. If you want to have any lasting effect on your listeners, if you are to change their attitudes or lead them into some particular action, the best route is the straight route, asking them directly to do it, and making your instructions as specific as possible with no scope for misunderstanding.

In this process, it may help to reinforce your message by:

- Giving your listeners a handout to take away (despite all those provisos in Chapter 23), setting out plainly what you want them to do.
- Giving them a deadline.
- Encouraging them to feed back to you on progress.

Remember that any actions you call for should be reasonably achievable within the period you state.

The call to action may well be the most significant part of your whole presentation, but it doesn't have to be particularly grand. Here are some everyday examples:

- "Vote for me in the election on Thursday!"
- "Please give the go-ahead for this project *today*."
- "Starting now, use these safety procedures every time an employee has an accident at work."
- "I'm asking you to donate £10 before you leave this room, and sign the Gift Aid form I've provided."

Audience members will be much more likely to support your call to action if they can see a consequential benefit for themselves in doing so. So, always think about the possible value of giving them an appropriate 'benefit statement'. Here are two examples:

- "By agreeing to this pay restraint, you will protect your jobs by avoiding future redundancies."

- "If you approve these plans, we can get going straight away and ensure that you meet budget this year."

The benefits you promise must, of course, be realistic if you are to maintain credibility with the audience.

If you have missed something out...

It quite often happens that, as you come to the end of your talk, you realise that you have left out something that you really wanted to speak about. Think twice before you attempt to tack it on at the end.

Spencer Leigh Hughes has some sensible advice here:

> "This temptation should be resisted, for a point that might be telling in its proper place loses its force if dragged in by the ears. Let it go – nobody other than the fond author will know what is being lost, and very likely the point was not such a wonder after all. At any rate, it will keep, and can probably be made to do service in some slightly altered form on another occasion."

He is right.

The audience will almost always be oblivious when you have left something out. Listeners simply do not have the time or opportunity to notice gaps in your argument that the reader of a written text might spot. By bringing your point in at the very end, you are drawing attention to a mistake that would otherwise have gone unnoticed.

If, on reflection, you still think the point is vital and must be stated, then act as though you deliberately kept it until the very end. This approach might be appropriate if, for example, you had been giving a talk on world religions and had forgotten about

Christianity and Islam, or one on creationism without mentioning that there were alternative views. In situations like this, instead of panicking, say: "Before I end, I want to give you just one last thing to think about..." and then insert the missing link.

This approach gives you a good chance not only of recovering the position but also of leaving the audience grateful that you have given them additional information as a freebie. Indeed, if done with panache, the technique can be so effective that some unscrupulous speakers plan it deliberately from the outset. It is not, however, for the cautious of spirit.

And for your final words...

One of the biggest challenges late on in a talk is to come up with appropriate final sentences. Here are some suggestions.

If you want to be gushing towards the audience, this is certainly the best time to do it. An example is: "Thank you so much for your welcome. I wish you all the best."

At the end of a humorous talk, some lines attributed to the American poet Richard Armour go down well, perhaps followed by a simple "Thank you":

> "I love a finished speaker,
> I really, truly do –
> I don't mean one who's polished,
> I just mean one who's... through."

Other strong finishes – usually followed up with steady eye contact, then brief silence and a "Thank you" – that have worked well for people I have coached and for me include:

- "I have one final thought that I want to leave you with..."

- "If you remember just one thing I've said today, remember this…"
- (At the end of a pitch or proposal) "Whoever you choose to do this work, are they going to deliver the goods?"

Let's now look at a couple of examples of the conclusion of a talk.

An example of an ending – a talk on public speaking

These are the points I put to the audience in the final five minutes of a talk about public speaking:

- "You look like you've enjoyed yourselves;" *[I only say this if it genuinely looks that way, which thankfully is usually the case]*: "you see, it's not such a scary subject after all."
- "I want you to carry on feeling good about speaking – you can do it!"
- "Do take up any opportunity for public speaking that comes to you: you get a lot better simply by working at it."
- "I can support you in the process."
- "So, if I can help you in any way with a talk over the next twelve months, just let me know."

An example of an ending – FDR mobilises America

In March 1933, Franklin D Roosevelt gave his first inaugural speech as president of the United States. With the country gripped by the Great Depression, the speech had been much anticipated, and Roosevelt did not let his people down. The speech is best known for its early reference to 'fear itself' ("So, first of all, let me assert my firm belief that the only thing we have to fear is… fear itself") but the conclusion is also outstanding. There is a great sense of urgency, of swift and determined action to follow, and of Roosevelt offering himself as a strong leader for troubled times.

The speech was broadcast nationally on several radio networks, and so was heard by tens of millions of Americans, preparing the stage for Roosevelt's commanding response to the crisis. His confident and inspiring oratory was extremely well received. "Any man who can talk like that in times like these," said one listener, "is worthy of every ounce of support a true American has." Another politician, Gordon Brown, was later to write: "It was one of those rare speeches that in themselves change the course of events… On that inaugural platform, his eloquence ended once and for all the… profound depression of national spirit that had afflicted and paralysed America."

Here is the conclusion to the speech:

"In the field of world policy, I would dedicate this nation to the policy of the good neighbour: the neighbour who resolutely respects himself and, because he does so, respects the rights of others; the neighbour who respects his obligations and respects the sanctity of his agreements in and with a world of neighbours.
If I read the temper of our people correctly, we now realise, as we have never realised before, our interdependence on each other; that we cannot merely take, but we must give as well; that if we are to go forward, we must move as a trained and loyal army willing to sacrifice for the good of a common discipline, because without such discipline no progress can be made, no leadership becomes effective.
We are, I know, ready and willing to submit our lives and

our property to such discipline, because it makes possible a leadership which aims at the larger good. This, I propose to offer, pledging that the larger purposes will bind upon us, bind upon us all as a sacred obligation with a unity of duty hitherto evoked only in times of armed strife. With this pledge taken, I assume unhesitatingly the leadership of this great army of our people dedicated to a disciplined attack upon our common problems.

Action in this image, action to this end is feasible under the form of government which we have inherited from our ancestors. Our constitution is so simple, so practical that it is possible always to meet extraordinary needs by changes in emphasis and arrangement without loss of essential form. That is why our constitutional system has proved itself the most superbly enduring political mechanism the modern world has ever seen.

It has met every stress of vast expansion of territory, of foreign wars, of bitter internal strife, of world relations. And it is to be hoped that the normal balance of executive and legislative authority may be wholly equal, wholly adequate to meet the unprecedented task before us. But it may be that an unprecedented demand and need for undelayed action may call for temporary departure from that normal balance of public procedure.

I am prepared under my constitutional duty to recommend the measures that a stricken nation in the midst of a stricken world may require. These measures, or such other measures as the Congress may build out of its experience and wisdom, I shall seek, within my constitutional authority, to bring to speedy adoption.

But, in the event that the Congress shall fail to take one of these two courses, in the event that the national emergency is still critical, I shall not evade the clear course of duty that will then confront me. I shall ask the Congress for the one remaining instrument to meet the crisis – broad Executive power to wage a war against the emergency, as great as the power that would be given to me if we were in fact invaded by a foreign foe.

For the trust reposed in me, I will return the courage and the devotion that befit the time. I can do no less.

We face the arduous days that lie before us in the warm courage of national unity; with the clear consciousness of seeking old and precious moral values; with the clean satisfaction that comes from the stern performance of duty by old and young alike. We aim at the assurance of a rounded, a permanent national life.

We do not distrust the future of essential democracy. The people of the United States have not failed. In their need they have registered a mandate that they want direct, vigorous action. They have asked for discipline and direction under leadership. They have made me the present instrument of their wishes. In the spirit of the gift I take it.

In this dedication of a nation, we humbly ask the blessing of God.

May He protect each and every one of us.

May He guide me in the days to come."

There is nothing particularly novel about the construction of Roosevelt's speech. What he does is to take strong themes – neighbourliness, respect, interdependence, discipline and, in particular, leadership coupled with the need for action – and bind them thoroughly together so that the whole appears greater than the sum of the parts.

At the end of the speech comes the call to action, or rather the confirmation that here we have a man who will indeed act. The people want energy and activity and change; they have selected Roosevelt as their agent; and he has committed himself to that role.

We now have the hindsight of history to tell us that he succeeded magnificently in his task. But, at the time of his speech, no such guarantee of success was available to the American people, which is why the stirring confidence and determination expressed in his words made such an impact in March 1933. David Ogilvy would have approved.

Conclusion

In recent times, the behavioural psychologists have given us research evidence to underline the importance of the ending.

The Nobel Prize-winning psychologist Daniel Kahneman and his colleagues have demonstrated that what we remember about the quality of our past experiences is very largely determined by two things:

- How the experiences felt to us when they were at their peak (the most intense point, either the best or the worst).
- How they felt when they ended.

This is referred to as the peak-end rule. In his book *Thinking, Fast and Slow*, Daniel Kahneman writes:

"We want pain to be brief and pleasure to last. But our memory… has evolved to represent the most intense moment of an episode of pain or pleasure (the peak) and the feelings when the episode was at its end."

The combination of the peak and the ending represents the way in which we sum up the experience to ourselves, and how we subsequently go on to regard it. It is why rock bands focus on their greatest hits at the close of a concert, and why a great meal can be ruined by problems with the bill at the very end. It is why the conclusion of your speech matters so much. This is not to say that you can ignore the quality of what goes before, but it certainly gives you a great incentive to make the ending as rich and as powerful as you can.

Points to take from this chapter

- Make the most of the heightened audience attention during the final minutes of your talk.
- The conclusion should be a logical ending to what has gone before.
- Make sure that you are completely familiar with your material for the conclusion.
- Be prepared to reinforce what you have said earlier for added emphasis.
- Make your call to action, and do so clearly and directly.
- If you have missed something out earlier, normally just let it go.

In the next chapter, we'll move on to a topic that fills many speakers with unnecessary foreboding – the question and answer session. We will see that it can enhance your performance hugely. Equally encouragingly, we'll learn that you have nothing to fear from awkward or embarrassing questions, provided you follow a few simple rules which we will review in detail.

Notes

Gordon Brown's comments on Franklin D Roosevelt's inaugural speech come from *The Guardian*'s book of *Great Speeches of the 20th Century*, Preface Publishing, 2008.

CHAPTER 36

Have a painless and profitable Q&A session

Introduction

Don't be scared of a questions and answers (Q&A) session. In fact, it is a thoroughly good thing for lots of reasons we will examine in this chapter, not least that:

- Breaking up your monologue as a speaker adds freshness and variety to your talk.
- It involves less preparation time than the formal part of your presentation – which is not to say that it doesn't need preparing, as we shall see.
- It gives you as the speaker a much-needed break: while audience members are talking, you aren't.

In this chapter, I want to focus on the concerns people have about the Q&A session and, I hope, allay them. I will describe the specific planning steps for you to carry out in advance of the presentation, and discuss in sequence the actions to take on the day itself. We'll get into the nitty-gritty of the techniques for listening to questions and then (but only once the questioner has stopped talking) for answering them. The chapter will also include a discussion of the various painless options available to you when you don't know the answers. At the end, I'll recommend a variant strategy, whereby it's you as the speaker who asks questions of the audience.

Why fears of Q&As are largely misguided

If a Q&A session has all the advantages I mentioned above, why are so many speakers reluctant to engage in one?

Some people fear that the looser structure of a Q&A may lead them to lose control of the audience. In practice, I have never known that to happen in any question session that has been properly, or indeed half decently, planned. The reality is that the speaker most likely to lose their listeners is the one who talks away without any variety and sends the audience to sleep in the process.

Perhaps the greater concern for many speakers is that they may not know *all* the answers. If that worries you, then relax. It is not a requirement that you should answer all the questions correctly on the spot, or even that you should be the most knowledgeable person in the room on the subject. You are being judged on the overall value of your presentation rather than as a *Mastermind* contestant. As we will see in a minute, what is necessary is that, if you do not know the answer, you make sure that you subsequently provide the questioner with either the answer itself or the means to discover it. That is not a complicated process.

What to do in advance

The key to a successful Q&A is to prepare for it seriously, well in advance of the big day. Your aim will normally be to take advantage of the heightened audience attention in the Q&A session to amplify and develop the overall case you will be setting out in your talk. You must have a strategy for this part of your presentation: it cannot just be an afterthought.

It follows that, right at the outset of your preparation for a talk, you need to decide how much time you are going to devote to a Q&A and, if necessary, agree that figure with the organisers of the event. If you want to achieve a good level of audience participation, I would suggest that you allocate up to 50% of your session to a Q&A. You will, of course, need to adjust the length of the formal part of your presentation accordingly. So, if you have sixty minutes allocated to you, you may have only thirty minutes for your talk proper. This, speaking personally, is something I can happily live with.

Spend some time before your presentation thinking through the questions you *are likely* to be asked, and equally importantly the questions you *would like* to be asked.

Identifying the questions you would be delighted to receive from the audience should be a key factor in determining the content of your formal talk: you can gear what you say so as to invite the kinds of questions you want. At this stage of your planning, I find it helps to focus clearly on what you want to say, or have the audience ask you, during the presentation, rather than on what you want to avoid saying.

Henry Kissinger, the former US Secretary of State, is said to have opened a press conference by asking, "Does anyone have any questions for my answers?" Following his lead, I try to think of the top ten questions likeliest to come up and prepare my answers to them carefully.

In practice, my experience suggests that, by thinking in depth about your topic, you can anticipate about three-quarters of the questions you will get on the day of the presentation. That gives you a minimum of three strong answers out of four. It leaves you to make realistic judgements on how to deal with the remaining 25% of questions on the day, including the option of saying you'll come back to people rather than answer on the spot.

Simply being aware that this is the likely outcome on the day, that the Q&A session is very largely controllable, is a real help in giving me plenty of advance confidence that the presentation will be successful.

If the administration of the event makes it feasible, consider making a brief request to attendees in advance of the session for questions they would like answered. This gives the day an added layer of predictability, gets the audience thinking (and hopefully enthusing) about it well in advance, and creates a better opportunity for you to field some intelligent questions.

Another good tip at this stage is to come up with issues that you would want to raise if no one else does. For example, if there is likely to be an obvious truth or problem that you may not otherwise address, an issue which people may be too scared to ask about, have a question on it ready to raise yourself. It should lead to a fascinating discussion on the day.

Before the start of the session

The thing that goes most wrong in Q&A sessions is an embarrassing absence of questions. Typically, the speaker makes a half-hearted request for questions, and a painful silence follows. The average member of a British audience tends to be highly reticent until someone else has taken the plunge and got things started.

The greatest challenge, then, is to induce the first question.

I recommend that you address this issue before your talk even starts. As people mill around before the session, seek out a couple of smiling and enthusiastic audience members (they are there if you look for them) and plant questions on them. It is even better if you have got a personal friend or acquaintance in attendance and you can brief them to ask a question.

This is a powerful technique: you will find that, once even a single individual has asked a question and you have replied in a helpful and friendly way, it gives the green light to the rest of the audience.

At the start of the talk

The audience needs to know what to expect from your talk. And so it helps right at the start to make it clear to them at what stage you will take questions. Preferably this should be done by the person introducing you, rather than you as the speaker, so that you can get straight into your talk without worrying about administrative points. This is another strong argument for having someone introduce you.

If you are not willing to take questions, something not usually to be recommended, then this should similarly be made clear at the outset. In the talk by Amy Cuddy which I referred to in Chapter 12, it was announced at the very beginning that she would not be taking questions. It was a disappointing decision, but at least the audience knew about it early on, so they could then focus on the talk itself.

At the start of a session of my own, I, or the chair who introduces me, encourage the audience to raise points, ask questions and (though hopefully not too often) correct my mistakes. I usually welcome questions throughout, rather than in a block towards the end, but I don't think there is any one right style.

If your request for questions is to work, you have to say the words as though you mean them, with due emphasis. A gabbled "If there are any questions, please let me know," without any following pause for the audience to digest what you have said, does not meet this test.

At the start of the Q&A

When you do come to invite questions, I'm hoping that your plants in the audience will come up trumps for you. If they hesitate, you could try being shameless: "I was talking to a couple of people beforehand, and I believe they had some interesting points…" In case that still fails, always have a suitable first question (and, even better, a second and a third question) ready that you can pose out loud to the audience or to yourself. That way, at the very least, you won't be struggling to get going right at the start of the Q&A session.

The best questions get asked of speakers who look as though they want to receive them. Here is a great tip from Joey Asher:

> "Pause and ask, 'What questions do you have about this?' Then you need to pause. Really pause. Pause for five to ten seconds. It will seem like an eternity to you. But if you wait, people will get the idea that you really want them to ask questions."

Some experts recommend that you should set out ground rules at the start of the Q&A period. For example, to avoid having a few questioners take over the session, you might specify that everyone will be confined to a single question to start with. For myself, I would rather play it by ear and only impose rules if it becomes necessary. That is on the basis that I don't want to do anything that might deter people from asking questions from the outset.

The techniques for listening and answering

The crucial time comes when you are actually asked a question.
    At that point:

- Cease talking immediately, if you have not already done so, and pay attention.
- Do not interrupt while the questioner is still speaking, even if parts of what they say are incomprehensible, unless the question threatens to last longer than your talk.
- Nod in understanding (if there is some part of their words that you do in fact understand).
- Maintain eye contact with the questioner throughout.
- Look interested and, if possible, appear genuinely pleased that the question has been posed.
- If it is a good question, say so.

Once the question has been asked:

- Continue to make eye contact with the questioner, while also scanning the wider audience.
- Avoid the temptation to criticise the question, however silly it may be.
- Pause to sort yourself out and get your brain in gear before replying.
- Repeat or summarise the question from the stage. In that process, you can paraphrase or reframe it – while not altering its basic nature – if you think that that will be helpful to make the question either more coherent and intelligible for the audience, or more logically answerable by you. (Refocusing and reframing the question can also help when the words used by the questioner are emotionally charged, and you want to take that emotion out of the equation.)
- Repeating the essence of the question is often vital so that the rest of the audience knows exactly what point it is you are answering. It may sometimes

not be necessary if microphones are being passed around for questioners to use, but even then err on the side of caution as to whether people have fully heard the question. This repetition stage has the added advantage of giving you more time to think about your answer.

- It especially helps to summarise long questions: "So what you're asking is…?"
- Consider asking for clarification on any ambiguous point in the question. This course is almost always preferable to trying to bluff your way through. Be prepared to say something like: "Unfortunately, I didn't quite get that point. Could you rephrase it for me, please?"
- Be prepared to counter-question the questioner to draw out any issues that may underlie what they have asked. Explicitly address hidden agendas: "It sounds like you have some thoughts of your own…" And be ready to dispute any wrong assumptions or alleged facts inherent in the question.
- In *Public Speaking and Presentations For Dummies*, Malcolm Kushner and Rob Yeung offer an idea for dealing with loaded or obviously hostile questions that I have found particularly helpful in containing difficult situations. "Don't even bother giving an answer," they suggest. "Just say, 'May I ask, why did you ask that?'" These words may sound innocuous, but experience confirms that they will often shame the questioner into toning down their approach. They then ask you a revised question that you can answer a lot more constructively.
- It helps to be aware that a number of the questions you will receive may represent the questioners'

search for their flash of glory in the spotlight rather than genuine questions. Let them have their moment, provided it doesn't take too long or stop you making your point. On the other hand, if one questioner starts hogging the question time, invite them to continue their discussion with you after the formal session has ended, so others can take their proper turn.

When you come to speak in reply:

- Remember that you will almost always have more information to answer the question than the audience needs. They are not looking for a detailed display of academic learning from you.
- Always stop your reply when you have said enough. The general rule is that you have said enough thirty seconds before you think you have.
- It is tempting to embark on a speech when replying to an open-ended question. Don't.
- Use specific examples, particularly personal experiences of your own, to make your answers more memorable.
- In general, don't be satisfied with saying, "I agree with that." Wherever possible, try to add something – for example, supporting evidence such as a reason, a quotation, a statistic or a detailed instance of background information.
- Try to vary the length of your answers to avoid the session becoming predictable and samey. Mix punchy replies with responses in greater depth. I aim at a compact initial answer – a couple of sentences as a maximum – to get the key point over, and then

expand my reply whenever it feels right to do so.

- Remember that the energy you show during the Q&A session is a vital part of your message as a speaker, and of the overall success of the presentation.

Here are some pointers which I have found helpful for dealing with trickier questions:

- You are not obliged to answer every question (though, if you do decline to answer, you should say why). In particular, I would caution against entering into a debate in reply to a hypothetical question. Instead, just say something like: "I'm not expecting that to happen, so we'll deal with it if and when it occurs."
- Where a question remains largely incomprehensible despite your efforts to ask for clarification, a variety of techniques can be useful:
    - Restating or summarising the part of the question that you do understand ("The key issue you've raised is, I think…"), and responding to just that part.
    - Asking for responses from other members of the audience, especially those people you think might understand what is going on. Thank them if they do manage to help you out.
    - Passing the question back to the questioner: "What do *you* think about this?"
- At the end of an answer, if you find that the questioner is looking perplexed, there is a reasonable likelihood that others in the audience will be puzzled too. A good follow-up here is: "Was there part of your question that I didn't answer?" or simply, "Does that make sense?"

- If you then still sense puzzlement after your second attempt, say that you will see the questioner afterwards to discuss the issue further. Otherwise, your session may get hijacked by this single point. If the questioner is simply suffering from a lack of intelligence, an open forum is not the best place to address that problem.

Remember not to overrun the time that you have allotted for the Q&A session. If you are in danger of an overrun, act in plenty of time and be honest with the audience. Tell them that you will take just, say, one or two more questions now and that they can come and see you at the end with any other points.

What to do if you don't know the answer

Speakers can get very perturbed at the thought of the tough questions they may receive in a Q&A session. But don't worry: you don't need to know all the answers. Stay calm, pick one of the options that follow, and all will be well.

These are the tried and tested strategies for what to do when you don't know the answer:

- Say you don't know the answer: "That's an excellent question. I don't currently know the answer, but I'll find out. Let me have your email address or your telephone number at the end of the session, and I'll come back to you as soon as possible." Of course, if you take this approach, you have to follow through and get back to them with the answer within the next few days. If you do follow through fittingly, it's a great way of gaining credibility, not least because, in my experience, surprisingly few speakers deliver on their promises.

- Ask the audience. If it was good enough for *Who Wants to Be a Millionaire?* it's good enough for me. Involving the rest of the audience to find out what they think shows your openness and maturity. You will be pleased to discover how often someone among your listeners does know the answer, and how well it reflects on you that you are prepared to involve the wider gathering. Remember that you are there to give a helpful talk, and not necessarily to be the person who knows the most about every aspect of the subject.

- Use a holding approach where it seems appropriate. It can at least give you more time to think. You might say, for example: "I'm coming to that later [if you truly intend to deal with it subsequently]" or "I think that takes us down a separate path I wasn't going to talk about today [if that is indeed the case] – can you come and see me at the end, so we can discuss it separately?"

- Suggest how they could go about finding the answer. This can be a good approach for topics that are peripheral to your subject matter or were not really on the agenda for your session in the first place.

- Say that you cannot give an answer. That will be appropriate, for example, where you don't know the answer and have no means of finding out what it might be because it all depends on future developments. So, for example, the truthful and correct answer to the question "Will there be redundancies?" will often be "I'm afraid it's too early to say that," and that is the answer you should give.

Here is what you should *not* do when you don't know the answer:

- Make something up, or bluff, or guess. Trust me: you will be found out. I once saw a speaker make a wrong guess in an accountancy lecture. It was not pleasant. Someone in the audience immediately said, "That's wrong." The speaker said, "I was only talking in general terms." The audience member said, "It's wrong in general terms too." The talk never recovered after that. A professional speaker is likely to suffer an even worse fate when they are not found out on the spot, but rather suffer the legal and disciplinary consequences that can follow when someone in the audience acts disastrously on the basis of their comments.
- Huff and puff and try to move on to the next question. Again, you will be found out.
- Try to make the questioner look foolish or stupid, because then you will be the one to look silly. This seems a point so obvious as to be barely worth stating, but – trust me again on this one – you will encounter questioners so obnoxious or annoying that you will need a truly heroic temperament not to answer back.

Moving the discussion on to the question you want to answer

Most speakers have had the experience of preparing points that they want to bring out in the Q&A session, and then being asked questions that don't quite cover them. Long experience of upset questioners confirms that you should never answer an entirely different question from the one they have posed. Unless you are exceptionally cunning and the audience exceptionally dim, people will spot what you are trying to do, and you will lose their esteem. So always answer the actual question first, before moving on to what you truly want to say.

I know there is a big practical exception to this rule, in that politicians are endlessly seeking to answer the question they hoped they would get as opposed to the one that was asked. I don't think this is an example the rest of us should follow, and, of course, it is one of the reasons why politicians are not generally held in high esteem.

To be fair, there is research which suggests that people who evade questions adroitly are liked and trusted more than those who respond to questions truthfully but not as eloquently. I would, however, be very cautious about going down the road suggested by this research, even setting aside the moral issues. The study was centred on showing people different videos of a political debate, and I have the feeling that after a lifetime's bitter experience people expect less honesty to start with in a political context. They might have higher awareness and expectations in other circumstances. Also, dodging questions skilfully is such a hard business for most people, and done so badly by them, that being honest and addressing the question as actually asked seems a less stressful alternative.

I still think it best to answer the actual question, as asked, in the first place. Then, quite simply, move on to what you *do* wish to say: "More generally, I think the key issue here is…" This approach should leave both you and your questioner content.

After the Q&A session

While a Q&A session is highly valuable, I recommend that your presentation should always conclude with you giving some final words from the platform: perhaps a summary of your message, or a call to action. This will end the session on a high note, something compelling and memorable that will stay with the audience, as opposed to the anti-climax that can result from addressing questions that are not terribly relevant to your theme as the very last part of the event. As we saw in Chapter 35, we need to do all we can to maintain the significance of the last five minutes.

In praise of asking the audience questions

We pay considerable attention to inviting and answering questions *from* the audience, but it's worth remembering also that asking questions *of* them can bring variety to a talk and keep their attention, as well as giving the speaker a break. More than this, asking questions to which you'd genuinely like an answer shows the audience that you are interested in them, and it may help elicit valuable information. By asking "Who of you has experience with X?" followed by "How much?", you get an up-to-date picture of what the audience currently knows about X and, consequently, the length and depth at which you need to deal with it in the remainder of your session.

In a talk about changes in the taxation of pensions at Harrogate in 1988 – the presentation in which my video show went into spontaneous rewind – I asked these questions and found that I had the leading national expert on the subject in the audience. This was genuinely helpful to me, and by a process of rapid ingratiation I established a friendly face among the crowd able to answer the questions to which I didn't know the answers.

Conclusion

A Q&A session is ideal for interaction with the audience, getting them more engaged than a one-way flow of information could ever achieve. It raises the energy level of your presentation and it's the best way of checking that your listeners are getting to grips with what you are talking about. You can win over the sceptics in your audience in a way that a formal presentation alone could never achieve.

So why not have a go at doing a Q&A session? You never know – follow the hints here, and you might even end up looking forward to questions and answers.

Points to take from this chapter

- The secret is to prepare seriously, well in advance of the Q&A session.
- Rehearse your answers to potential questions.
- Make it clear, at the start of the session, when you will take questions.
- Always have a first question that you could raise yourself.
- Look as though you are genuinely keen to take questions.
- Repeat or summarise each question from the stage.
- Apply one of the recommended strategies when you don't know the answer.
- Never bluff or make things up.
- Answer the actual question before moving on to what you'd prefer to discuss.
- Always end with some final words from the platform.

In this third section of the book, we've been looking at a whole variety of wondrous techniques to ensure that nothing can go wrong on the day of our speech.

But, wait! Surely it isn't always like this? Won't we, like everyone else, on rare occasions have experiences as speakers that are the stuff of nightmares?

Yes, you're absolutely right. There is no escaping real life. What we can do, though, is to salvage all we can from our horrible experiences to make them that little bit less harrowing, and then recover quickly to face the world again. The strategies to achieve this will be the subject of our next chapter.

Notes

The research on people skilfully evading questions is discussed in an article called *People Often Trust Eloquence More Than Honesty* by Todd Rogers and Michael I Norton in the November 2010 issue of the *Harvard Business Review*.

CHAPTER 37

Survive the speaking engagement from hell

Introduction

However much you have planned for your talk and cased the joint beforehand and anticipated the audience's needs and motivations, there's not much you can do to make a speech successful when the audience is falling-over drunk, or when half of them learned an hour ago that they are facing redundancy. Not even the finest speakers can shine on days like that.

But that doesn't make the experience any less terrible, I know. You feel very alone in the world when it happens to you, and your whole ego seems to seep away from you. It is desperately scary. The challenge is to remember that you will have few days like this in your speaking career, that the good days hugely outnumber the bad ones, and then get back on stage again as soon as you can.

In this chapter, I'll mention a few genuinely horrendous experiences encountered by some distinguished speakers, if only to put our own trials and tribulations in context. I'll talk about my personal toughest appearances, and go into some detail about an awful day endured by Tony Blair during his time as prime minister – not primarily to enjoy his suffering (though there might be an element of that), but to show that we often have opportunities to alleviate the pain even in our most challenging performances.

After the Tony Blair story, I'll make some suggestions for dealing with problems like hecklers, illness in the audience and hostile crowds. Finally, I'll recommend a general approach in tough situations that has worked best for me over the years. None of these tips can entirely take the edge off our most excruciating sessions as speakers, but they can offer some reasonably strong pain relief.

The worst of bad times

In *Confessions of a Public Speaker*, Scott Berkun has a section called 'You can't do worse than this', in which some accomplished speakers describe their worst public speaking experiences.

How about these for starters?

- A US law professor had been invited to *attend* (which is not usually taken to mean *make a major speech at* without further elaboration) a conference. Immediately on arrival, he was asked to give a "one-hour talk comparing the German, French and American constitutions, with any special insight for Georgia". Yes, that was Georgia as in the country in the Caucasus region of Eurasia, not the US state.
- The guest speaker at a company dinner in Moscow was thirty seconds into his talk when hooded and heavily armed Russian troops entered the room and, guns drawn, marched one of the diners out with them.

The most harrowing description I've read of how a British public speaker can feel when things go wrong comes in the book *Don't You Know Who I Am?*, a tremendous diary of reminiscences by the journalist and television personality Piers Morgan. He gives a searingly honest account of a speech to a hostile audience on a media awards night. Things went wrong when he told a story that was usually a guaranteed winner for him. His punchline produced none of the usual laughter. "I panicked," he says, "looking out at 1,000 people staring at me... I could feel my cheeks go crimson, my breath shorten, my mouth parch. This was not supposed to happen." He ended up by asking the audience, "Do I take it that you've had enough of me, then?"

A gut-wrenching reply came back: "YES!"

At this point, unsurprisingly, "My shame was complete, and I abandoned the speech then and there – the first time I've ever had to do that."

By comparison, any unpleasantness I've experienced in my speaking career seems very trivial, and I have done a lot of speaking. You cannot prepare for experiences like that because they are utterly unforeseeable. You just have to be sure not to blame yourself when they happen. Piers Morgan quotes Geoff Miller, the former England cricketer and leading after-dinner speaker, who puts it this way: "[It happens] usually when you least expect it... It comes out of the blue, and it happens to everyone. You just have to dust yourself down and forget about it, because if you try and rationalise it, you'll go mad."

My own most challenging talks

I was giving a talk at a conference in Cambridge on the afternoon of 11 September 2001 (so it was morning in New York), when terrorists attacked the World Trade Center. The conference involved people working in global businesses who had many contacts and friends in the United States. News of the atrocity filtered through slowly, and for some time it was not clear what was happening.

There can be no formal rules for what to do when you are speaking in a situation like this. The speakers knew more about what was going on in New York than the audience, but not much more. The organisers decided that the alarm that bringing the conference to a premature close would create would not be justified. I think that was the right decision.

The speakers carried on speaking, which was itself a test of their professionalism. Giving a talk when your heart is not in it is not a great place to be. In the coffee break between speakers, we gave the audience a considered update on what was known so far. The last session of the conference was shortened to deal with immediate business only, and was effective in those terms. As I think back on that day, the lesson I learn, beyond the fact that no set of instructions could be created in advance to deal with such circumstances, is that speakers must take responsibility in stressful situations; be resolute in trusting their judgement about what actions to take; and then improvise accordingly.

Let's move on to a far more mundane example.

The later in the day a speaking engagement starts, the higher is the chance of that unwelcome challenge: the drunken audience. I was once asked to give a mixture of after-dinner speech and motivational talk to a group of professional accountants in the East Midlands. I didn't know that each member of the audience had been given a bottle of full-bodied Rioja on arrival in their rooms that afternoon by the conference organisers. That was before they descended to the bar, where they had a further happy hour or two before they encountered me. An added complicating factor was that no one had told them there was going to be a speaker.

I got up to talk to people who were already very, very

drunk and by this time had neither the interest nor the mental capacity to listen to any speaker, let alone one they had not been expecting. When the first coherent thing a speaker hears from his audience is "Why aren't you the disco?", with a few Anglo-Saxon expletives thrown in for luck, he knows this is not going to be his day.

To be fair to myself, I gave it a go. All subtlety went out of the window. I knew that, with a drunken audience, I had to make my points very plainly, hammering them home with Winston Churchill's pile driver from Chapter 11, or they wouldn't get them. I did try to do that, but after a minute or two of trying to out-shout the mass heckling I realised (arguably rather late in the day) that I was never going to get control of these people, gave up and sat down. "Good riddance," said the man in charge of the disco by way of showing solidarity with his fellow entertainer. Well, you win some, you lose some.

The positive lesson I derive from this experience is that, if you have done all you can to rescue a difficult public speaking situation and nothing is working, there is no shame at all in stopping short before the end of your allotted time. In this case, it came as a relief to all concerned. If your audience is out of control, consider giving up and going home, except when you think that that might provoke an even worse riot.

Tony Blair's bad day

Let's look at a case where a speaker did not prepare suitably and so brought disaster on himself, and see what he might have done to lessen the damage.

On 7 June 2000, at Wembley Arena, Tony Blair gave an infamously unsuccessful speech as prime minister to the National Federation of Women's Institutes. He was jeered, barracked and given the slow handclap. The WI chair had to intervene to appeal for members to listen politely. Mr Blair went on to be accused of hijacking the occasion by making a political speech to an organisation which prides itself on being non-sectarian and non-party political.

I don't believe his outlook was cynical or exploitative. It was a clear case of a speaker who had not thought properly beforehand whether his message was appropriate to his audience that day. This is how Tony Blair subsequently described it in his autobiography, *A Journey*:

> "I decided to make the philosophical case about the nature of our society, how it had changed, how we could retrieve the sense of values lost if we were prepared to think afresh. Unfortunately, I decided to visit this sociological essay upon the good matrons of the Women's Institute Triennial Gathering at Wembley."

It seems that Mr Blair managed to upset his hosts before he had even started on his speech, because Downing Street had already publicised to the newspapers what he was going to say. Always think twice before you send out advance copies of a talk, because it commits you to your text without any chance of adapting to changing circumstances on the day. You also lose all potential elements of novelty and surprise in the speech, and your listeners may well feel you are using them as pawns in your campaign for wider publicity.

It should go without saying that you have to engage the audience on something that matters to them. According to Mr Blair, he came to realise the potential danger, but did so late in the day: "I remember reading the speech through in a little anteroom and having a vague premonition that maybe it might have been a little more appropriate as a lecture to a bunch of professors."

Circumstances did not do much to help him. Wembley Arena was a vast and uninviting place in which to speak, with awful acoustics. He was performing first thing in the morning, and it was freezing. The sensible thing to do would have been to recognise this, to share the experience with the audience and get them onside. As we saw in Chapter 21, people can be won over by just a simple remark like, "Are you as cold as I am?" We then become fellow sufferers rather than combatants against the speaker.

However, Mr Blair pressed on. Gyles Brandreth was also to speak that day, and was there to watch the unfolding spectacle. He wrote afterwards that: "The ladies felt exploited and patronised: they sensed that the Downing Street machine had hijacked their conference for base political gain... If he had simply spoken on issues that concerned the WI, if he had spoken entirely to them and for them, they'd have stayed with him all the way."

What was so annoying about what Tony Blair said, to exacerbate the problems with the cold and the acoustics?

Here are a couple of excerpts from the speech:

"A meritocratic society is the only one that can exploit its economic chances to the full... Community cannot be built without opportunity. But if we provide the opportunity, then these values we hold dear, of responsibility, respect for others, must be rigorously reasserted. For every new opportunity we offer, we demand responsibility."

"Business, work and, with it, community and social life are all in the throes of change... We have to rebuild Britain as a great and powerful nation for the twenty-first century. Shaped by the values of opportunity for all and responsibility from all, Britain will become stronger."

There's certainly not a great deal of party politics in it, but it's all a bit vague and waffly and abstract for a speech. It might be all right in a book, and in fact subsequent research suggested that Tony Blair had heavily borrowed his themes and content from a 1996 book by Bill Clinton called *Between Hope and History*.

Mr Blair became aware that something was wrong. With masterly understatement, he writes: "I had an uncomfortable feeling. I am acutely audience-sensitive – you have got to be in my profession – and somehow I knew this wasn't quite ringing the bell."

He seems to have had no thought of fall-back arrangements, no plan B. When the heckling started, he made the classic speaker's error of falling into 'the runs'.

Getting the runs means that you become aware that you are, in speaking terms, dying a death on stage, and you consequently start to speed up. That is exactly the wrong thing to do, and it is all downhill from there. You gabble, and you lose your pacing and timing. You make no attempt to bring in the pauses and changes of emphasis that give colour and variety to a speech. Instead, you are just desperate to get to the end. Tony Blair changed his pace of speaking, but the wrong way. He sped up when what he should have been doing was to take lots of deep breaths and speak more slowly.

Things got worse. Mr Blair, his shirt awash with sweat, was flustered and losing control. His message to the nation, complete with soundbites for the television news, was of no value to the audience that sat before him in the cold light of morning.

Even at this late point, he could have made some recovery, if only in disaster limitation mode. When what you are doing is simply not working, abandon it and try something else. Most obviously, he could have set aside his pre-written text and shown his audience that he was there for them (and not vice versa) by inviting questions. That might have led to an engaging two-way discussion, pleasing the audience and allowing him to recover some of his bruised pride. It would have meant tearing up the script that had gone to the media, but it would have been worth it. Instead, in his words, "I resolved to cut my losses, make some trivial extempore remarks and get the hell out of there. Which I duly did."

Every speaker will have a bad day, though this was an extreme example of ignoring the needs of a particular audience. Even this story has a positive message in confirming that there will generally be opportunities to recover the situation if things go wrong. Mr Blair did not take his.

It is not clear whether he ever learned any useful lessons from his hellish experience. In *A Journey,* he writes: "Afterwards, and though I say it myself, the thing that was most annoying was it was actually a good speech – thoughtful, well argued, and even if neither of those things, worthy of comment or critique."

Well, it has received comment and critique here. The reality is that there is no such thing as a good speech in a theoretical sense, in absolute terms, in a vacuum. A good speech given to entirely the wrong audience is what I would call a bad speech.

Hecklers

The hecklers who annoyed Tony Blair are a rare exception to the polite, attentive audiences most speakers experience. However, we still need to be prepared for the occasional presence of such people.

The Wikipedia definition of a heckler is 'a person who harasses and tries to disconcert others with questions, challenges, or gibes'. That sounds nasty, but remember that some interruptions from the audience – "We can't hear you," "Can you open a window?" and the like – are entirely helpful in ensuring that your message gets over and that your listeners avoid passing out in the process.

But the heckler who is there to harass you is indeed a nuisance.

Never forget that your principal obligation is to the audience which has come to hear you speak, not the annoying interrupter at the back. The aim has to be to quieten the heckler as efficiently as possible.

One of the underrated ways of coping is just to let hecklers get on with it and blow themselves out. This involves pausing and waiting until they stop, which can make you deeply uncomfortable. Waiting is far from easy for anyone in such a situation, and that is exactly why it can be such a powerful technique. You will be telling the audience that you have an inner calm and strength (even if you are in fact paddling frantically within) which give you enormous credibility.

Other methods of dealing with hecklers are more direct. Spencer Leigh Hughes sets out a nice example (albeit with some dodgy cockney accents) in his 1912 book *The English Character*:

"I remember an orator in a London park being told that he was a liar, and he fixed his eye on the man who made the uncomplimentary remark, and said, 'Ho! I'm a liar, am I? Well, perhaps I am, but I'm not the only one, by no manner of means – there's others abaht, Samuel Jones, so I tells you strite – put that in your pipe and smoke it.' The crowd approved of this, and as a name had been given to the interrupter, they thought the speaker knew him, so the fellow was hustled away and had to sprint for it. As a matter of fact his name was not Samuel Jones, and the speaker had never seen him before. It was the pointed and personal retort that inspired confidence in the audience, and I learned afterwards that it was a trick which the orator had often tried with success."

At a business event or social get-together, any heckling is likely to be very restrained and done in a positive spirit. But if people do start going on a bit, here are some retorts that I have found helpful:

- "It's great to work with you again, but I do wish you'd turned up to rehearsals."
- "Listen, for what you're paying me, you don't expect originality, do you?"
- "Did I give you permission to heckle?"
- "Did I say you could ask questions?"
- "I like you. You remind me of me, when I was young and foolish."
- "Nigel, it's over. Can't you understand that?" (I stole that one from Jeremy Hardy)
- "Yeah, I remember when I had my first beer" (and that one from Steve Martin).

This kind of thing works even better if you manage to look good-humoured and well-meaning as you say it. Some modern comedians have discarded this style and gone for the simpler approach of beating the heckler up. But, to my mind, that should be saved for the last resort.

If you are dealing with a sober, serious and well-intentioned heckler, I recommend a more thoughtful approach. Try saying something like, "It's clear you feel very strongly about this. Why not see me afterwards, so that we can have an in-depth chat?" In my experience, this succeeds surprisingly often.

Illness in the audience

As a speaker, your role is to behave like a decent, caring, compassionate human being and take responsibility for the situations you encounter, regardless of your role in creating them.

As an example, if a member of the audience is suddenly taken ill, your prime responsibility is to ensure that they get help and treatment before you carry on talking. Often there will be others at the venue – the organiser or chair, for example – to take care of this. But you still need to be confident that they are doing that job properly before you continue speaking. I know a speaker who, in the middle of a benign and entertaining talk, saw someone in the second row of the audience collapse with a heart attack.

I recommend doing what she did:

- Tell the rest of the audience what has happened – they will not automatically know.
- Ask whether anyone present is qualified with medical or first aid skills.
- Call an ambulance.
- Help make the individual involved as comfortable as possible.
- For the moment, just sit down and wait.

Yes, in normal circumstances the show must go on, but there are also times when it needs to stop for a while.

A more unusual example of the unexpected interruption

At a hotel in deepest Hampshire, I was in full flow to a hundred tax enthusiasts (yes, there are such people) about the finances of small businesses. Suddenly, a very purple man of fifty or so burst into the room in extreme agitation, shouting that we had blocked his car in the car park.

An individual like this is much tougher to deal with than the drunken heckler who simply thinks the speaker is crap. Whereas you can usually quieten a tired and emotional heckler with a scorching put-down, my man would not be assuaged until his car was unblocked or until he expired from apoplexy brought on by the stress of the experience.

The latter solution might be too much of a distraction, so the normal recommendation is for a trusty assistant to take the individual to one side and help him out of his difficulty car-wise. If no assistance were to be available, you could always invite two or three of the larger and stronger attendees at the conference to help him out. An alternative route, where you treat the interloper as part of a surprise double act with the speaker, goes down well with the audience, but the eventual outcome is unpredictable. What happened on the day was that our new joiner was helped by our seminar staff with the aid of hotel reception. The car doing the blocking turned out to be entirely unconnected with our conference, so we sent the man an invoice for his attendance at the seminar.

Sleepers

At any time of the day, various members of the audience may be asleep. Do not be concerned. It usually has much to do with their health issues, mental fitness and alcohol consumption, and little to do with the quality of your talk. The absolute and inviolable rule is never to refer to any members of the audience who might be asleep, except when they are snoring very loudly, in which case it is permissible to motion to one of their neighbours to give them a gentle nudge. In general, sleepers are good for the feedback on your presentation. Their embarrassment will usually drive them to give you good marks rather than admit their drowsiness. I once got an 'outstanding' mark from a seminar delegate who I could swear was not awake for a single sentence of my presentation.

Speaking impromptu

For many people, speaking hell at its most atrocious arrives when they are asked to make an immediate speech without any warning. The law professor we met earlier in this chapter gives us about as frightening an example as could be imagined. The degree of difficulty for speaking impromptu is extreme. Anyone who has heard the programme *Just a Minute*, in which contestants are asked to speak 'without hesitation, deviation or repetition' on a given subject for a minute, will know how hard it is, even for a professional speaker.

For what I think is the best impromptu speech ever given, I recommend the 1935 film *The 39 Steps*, where the fugitive hero Richard Hannay (played by Robert Donat) is mistaken for a guest speaker at a political rally while trying to escape his pursuers. He comes up with one of the greatest of all openings. "Ladies and gentlemen," he begins, "I apologise for my hesitation in rising just now. But, to tell you the simple truth, I'd entirely failed, while listening to the chairman's flattering description of the next speaker, to realise he was talking about me." Very few impromptu speeches in real life come anywhere close to Mr Hannay's performance.

For ordinary mortals, the best way to deal with an impromptu speech is to avoid doing it in the first place. If you can't do that, just identify two or three relevant thoughts in your mind, put them in a logical order with (ideally) a logical conclusion, say them as forcefully as you can, and then sit down. In general, limit an impromptu speech to no more than a couple of minutes. That way, no moments of complete panic or utter mental blankness should occur.

Above all else, before you embark on an impromptu speech, I recommend taking into account some cautionary words uttered by Mark Twain during one of his own after-dinner speeches. He is talking about what he calls 'the genuine impromptu speaker':

> "I mean the man who 'didn't expect to be called upon and isn't prepared', and yet goes waddling and warbling along, just as if he thought it wasn't any harm to commit a crime so long as it wasn't premeditated. Now and then he says, 'but I must not detain you longer'; every little while he says, 'Just one word more and I am done' – but at these times he always happens to think of two or three more unnecessary things and so he stops to say them. Now that man has no way of finding out how long his windmill is going. He likes to hear it creak, and so he goes on creaking, and listening to it, and enjoying it, never thinking of the flight of time; and when he comes to sit down at last... he is the most surprised person in the house to see... how unconscionably long he has been... As a rule, he finds that he hasn't said anything – a discovery which the unprepared man ought always to make, and does usually make – and has the added grief of making it at second hand, too."

Captive and hostile audiences

Very occasionally you may find yourself talking to an audience that has not come by choice and resents being there, or one that is fundamentally opposed to your point of view. It is shameful to say it, but I myself did not go into one of those speed awareness courses they offer you in place of points on your driving licence with a particularly receptive mind.

As the speaker, you can do little to avoid the anger of difficult participants on such occasions. If you are asked to lead a session like this, always first look into whether you could achieve your objectives by other means. For example, see what alternative training is available on the Internet. That should at least allow participants to do the training at a time and location suitable to them, thus taking some of the negative emotions out of the process. And, frankly, if it all goes wrong I would prefer the trainees to vent their spleens by kickboxing their computers rather than hitting you.

If there is no avoiding a talk to a live hostile audience, here are some recommendations:

- Take time before the talk to identify the benefits that attendees can expect to obtain if they give you a fair chance on the day.
- At the talk itself, stay cool and try to disarm the audience at once – by way of:
  * Being open and acknowledging the difficult issues up-front.
  * Recognising their views and the differences between you.
  * Talking about the potential benefits you've identified for them.
  * Establishing as much common ground as you can.
  * Telling them they'll get the chance to reply, either during the talk or at the end, and then making sure they do get that chance.
- Avoid the use of emotionally charged language.
- Use humour whenever appropriate, and stay positive.
- Maintain the appearance of calm, however frazzled you are inside.

- Give people the opportunity to speak individually with you at the end.

An attempt at a tentative strategy

No book or coaching can prepare you for the full range of experiences you might encounter as a speaker. But I think we can summarise a general approach that works well in challenging situations.

When you feel under pressure during a presentation, when you're nervous or losing confidence, SLOW DOWN your delivery. I know it's hard to do the first time, but keep working at it. This is by far the best way to get yourself and the audience back under control. Give yourself the time you need just to stop and think. There is great power in silence, so pause for breath and plan what you're going to say before you venture forth on your next theme.

After that, if you've still got a tough crowd for an audience, and what you're doing isn't working, don't pretend that it is. Do something different. Be prepared to abandon your script.

When deciding what to do next, consider sharing the burden with the audience: "You know, I spent ten hours preparing this. It doesn't seem to be working, but I'm here, so what would you like me to talk about, what questions do you have for me?" That way, at least it becomes more of a joint enterprise, and the audience has a greater vested interest in your success.

In general, however hellish the experience, keep going if you can see some sign of light at the end of the tunnel. Be prepared to wait and see what happens and go along with it if it feels right. The comedian Barry Cryer noted that: "I once continued speaking while sitting on a woman's lap, where I had been placed by a very large man with whom it was inadvisable to argue." Wisdom was once defined as 'the ability to cope', and your task is to cope as best you can in the circumstances.

Be realistic if things don't turn out as you had wished, and never feel guilty if it wasn't your fault. If you *have* had a bad day, remember that the other people who were there will have forgotten about it long before you do. Remember, too, that we are not the best judges of our errors; we have a strong tendency to overestimate mistakes. When other people say they think our overall performance was in fact rather good, they may well be right.

You must go back into the fray again as soon as you're ready for it. If nothing else, what happened today will have been a remarkable learning experience.

Conclusion

It's good being a speaker. At least nine times out of ten the audience wishes you well and wants you to succeed. It's in their interest to do so. If your performance is a success, if you inform them or entertain them or make them think new things, they will feel good about giving up their time to hear you. They will go away satisfied, liking themselves and incidentally liking you. This chapter has dealt with the occasions when it doesn't quite work out that way.

The key thing to emphasise is that, if you prepare properly for a talk, the bad experiences will be rare indeed. Not only that, but, again assuming you do prepare properly, the bad experiences will almost always arise from factors outside your control, for which you can have no responsibility. Your job will be to grin and bear it, to improvise on the spot and do the best you can, and to avoid blaming yourself, because there is nothing for which you should be blamed.

I understand that the United States SEALs, a special

operations force of the US Navy, are taught in their training that 'calm is contagious'. That, I think, is the ideal approach when one finds oneself in the speaking engagement from hell. At my very best, I am a perfect example of the 'calm is contagious' model. I'm still working on the other 99% of situations.

Points to take from this chapter

- Many bad experiences are utterly unforeseeable and have nothing to do with you as the speaker.
- They happen to everyone, so dust yourself down and move on.
- If you have done all you can, and nothing is working, don't be afraid to cut your speech short.
- Remember that some audience interruptions can be actively helpful.
- Consider arranging to see people afterwards if they have interrupted in good faith.
- Beware of impromptu speeches.
- If you have to speak to hostile audiences, be open and acknowledge the difficulties at the outset.
- When you feel under pressure, SLOW DOWN.
- Go back into the fray as soon as you can.

After the dollop of misery to which I've subjected you here, the next chapter is going to be much, much jollier. I'll be encouraging you to have a bit of a party – not only when your performance goes well, but also when you emerge still breathing after the engagement from hell. In addition, I'll explain why, rather conveniently, the very act of celebration will be helpful to you in your subsequent speaking career.

Notes

Gyles Brandreth's comments again come from his piece for the *Sunday Telegraph* called *Tony Blair at the WI*, collected in *Brief Encounters: Meetings with Remarkable People*, Politico's Publishing, 2003. The Mark Twain speech is from *The Complete Essays of Mark Twain*, edited by Charles Neider, Da Capo Press, 2000. The Barry Cryer story can be found in his book *The Chronicles of Hernia*, Virgin Books, 2009.

CHAPTER 38

Celebrate success

Introduction

You've worked really hard to get to this point in the book. Now I want you to go out and enjoy yourself as a reward.

In this chapter, I will remind you how much you deserve that celebration, not that you should need reminding. I will also explain the serious underlying rationale for honouring our accomplishments – that the very process of remembrance helps us to subsequent success. Finally, I'll use the sublime words of a former US president, Theodore Roosevelt, to urge you on to those future achievements.

Always celebrate!

Always celebrate your achievements as a speaker.

Celebrate if the talk went well, and if it didn't – if it was a Chapter 37-type experience – then celebrate the sheer effort you put into your preparation for the event. The speech of my worst nightmares is always placed in proper context by the belt-loosening experience of the chicken tikka biryani and the tandoori king prawns at the Maharajah Restaurant in Rugby.

By contrast, be prepared for the days immediately after a major speech to be challenging. You have put heart and soul into your performance. Once you are out of the spotlight, it is natural to feel tired and drained and have a great desire to lie down for the next five days. It just reflects how much effort you have put into your work. Alternatively, you may be pumped up with adrenaline after the success of your talk, so that you could celebrate long into that day and night and indeed the following night: that too is entirely natural. Just remember that you remain human, so that if you proceed to drink four celebratory cans of Tennent's Super, you will still fall over in a heap like anyone else.

Use your success to boost your subsequent speeches

There is another, longer-term, aspect of celebrating success that involves using your accomplishments to improve future performance.

In their book *Play to Your Strengths,* Donald O Clifton and Paula Nelson ask us to relive our successes in our minds. "The more times you think of yourself doing your very best work," they say, "the more you are inviting success in the future." Picture what went well and work through it again in your mind, so that the habits of success become engrained in you.

Clifton and Nelson go further and suggest we talk to others about what it feels like during our proudest moments. Provided I am genuinely talking about things that went well, this process of positive affirmation certainly does strengthen me for future performances.

The final point to make about success is that, once you've celebrated it, you should make damned sure you go out and get it again. Success breeds success, but only if you go back into the arena.

Speaking of the arena, this seems as good a time as any to quote Theodore Roosevelt's majestic words in *Citizenship in a Republic*, a speech at the Sorbonne in 1910:

"It is not the critic who counts; not the man who points out how the strong man stumbles, or where the doer of deeds could have done them better. The credit belongs to the man who is actually in the arena, whose face is marred by dust and sweat and blood; who strives valiantly; who errs, who comes short again and again, because there is no effort without error and shortcoming; but who does actually strive to do the deeds; who knows great enthusiasms, the great devotions; who spends himself in a worthy cause; who at the best knows in the end the triumph of high achievement, and who at the worst, if he fails, at least fails while daring greatly, so that his place shall never be with those cold and timid souls who neither know victory nor defeat."

It may be fanciful, but those words seem to me to sum up the spirit of the committed speaker of either sex – not least Roosevelt himself, whom we previously met in Chapter 21 speaking for nearly an hour and a half with a would-be assassin's bullet in his chest.

Conclusion

It might at first seem odd that I have included celebrations as one of the key techniques of a successful speaker, but I think it's an essential aspect of our work. The festivities are great fun in their own right, but, just as importantly, they commemorate our effort and commitment. By so doing, they remind us of our success and increase our confidence for the next occasion when we mount the rostrum. They also help to instil in us the growth mindset, so helpful to our longer-term progress, that we discussed way back in Chapter 2.

The very act of celebration makes a small but significant contribution to a positive outcome when next we speak in public.

Points to take from this chapter

- Always celebrate your achievements as a speaker.
- Honour the effort you put in, even if the talk wasn't a success.
- Don't worry if you feel drained afterwards – it's only natural.
- Mentally reliving your success invites more success in the future.
- Go out, speak some more, and gain further triumphs!

I'm confident that, if you've diligently worked through the book to this point, evaluated its lessons and gone out regularly to put them into practice, you are now comfortably within the top 20% of speakers. In that sense, my job is done.

I'm hopeful, however, that you'd like to carry on developing your public speaking just that little bit further. In that case, the next chapter has been written especially for you.

CHAPTER 39

Carry on developing as a speaker

Introduction

I hope that, having discovered that public speaking is not the horror some people suggest, you might get a taste for it and want to do more. This chapter looks at ways of developing and improving your speaking skills over time.

I'll talk briefly about what is required to become a true expert, while recognising that the effort involved in doing so might represent a step too far for many people.

For the majority of us – those with lower ambition, but who would still like to carry on progressing as speakers – I'll explain the crucial importance of getting relevant feedback, both from ourselves and from our audiences, as a significant step on the road to future development. By way of example, I'll discuss the reviews I carry out of my own performances.

Moving on, I'll cover activities such as amateur dramatics, improvisation and membership of speaking clubs. They can help our speaking careers while also being fun in their own right. I'll recommend some further reading and suggest that you consider getting a coach. Above all, I'll remind you that the best way of improving as a public speaker is to go out and do some more public speaking.

Becoming an expert

Shortly, I'm going to talk about the things that have worked for me in developing as, I hope, a pretty decent speaker. But, for those with higher ambitions, it's only fair that I should make you aware of the hard graft you need to put in if you want to become a truly outstanding performer.

The best summary I know of how to achieve ultimate excellence comes in a fascinating article from 2007 called *The Making of an Expert*. The authors demonstrate that outstanding performance derives from years of deliberate study and coaching, and not from innate talent or skill. Key factors that help bring success include intensive practice, committed teachers and family support.

What is vital to note is that there is no shortcut for intensive practice. Experts really are made, not born. Practice should be 'deliberate', in the sense of focusing on tasks beyond our current level of comfort and competence. We have to be prepared to make specific and sustained efforts to do things that we are not currently good at. In a 2016 interview, Anders Ericsson, the leading expert in this field, stressed that, for practice to be worthwhile, it must continually probe our weaknesses and focus on areas we find difficult.

We also need a coach to guide us through this deliberate practice and to help us learn how to coach ourselves. The potential rewards to match those efforts are, of course, very high, but it is likely to take you a minimum of ten years (or 10,000 hours) of intense training to get there.

All that is for those people who are looking for speaking superstardom. The rest of this chapter is devoted to more ordinary people – those like me who aim to get steadily better at public speaking without making it their lifetime priority.

Getting feedback

For me, getting decent feedback has been the key to progressing as a speaker.

If you review other people's speaking performances critically but constructively, you soon find that you can explain in reasonably objective terms why their presentations succeeded or failed. In just the same way, you can come to describe the characteristics that go towards a good presentation of your own. Once you can do that, you have a much better chance of being able to reproduce those qualities on a regular basis to give consistently accomplished talks.

Being your own critic

Every time I speak in public, I ask myself what I can learn from the experience. I look at what's gone right and what's gone wrong, and so draw out the lessons for next time.

I can't deny that it takes discipline to go through this process. It is so natural for a speaker, drained by the presentation experience, to want simply to forget it and move on. But, since I started taking this self-examination seriously, my performances have improved significantly. So I recommend that as soon as you can after your talk – no later than the following day, because authentic memories fade fast – you should review your performance and make a written record of what went well and what didn't.

Apart from anything else, it is immensely helpful when you come to give a talk on a similar subject, particularly in identifying stories or examples to use again and those to drop.

To take a simple example, by writing it down immediately after the event I have a lifetime instruction never again to use the self-effacing personal development joke:

> "I wanted to do better with the opposite sex and got a book called *How to Hug* out of the library. It turned out to be Volume 10 of the *Encyclopaedia Britannica*."

It looks pretty good on paper – well, I used to think it did – but it died a slow and silent death on the one occasion I told it to an audience.

The analyses I have done of each of my speeches have also shown me the more general areas I needed to focus on at various stages of my speaking career, for example:

- Microphone problems.
- Inferior material.
- Poor heckler control.
- Over-imbibing at the drinks reception beforehand.

At the same time, those analyses have given me comfort in the areas where I have made advances – use of humour, catching the mood of the audience, and staying calm and robust under pressure.

Making best use of audience feedback

We'll come on to the 'happy sheets', which are the key modern approach to gaining audience feedback. But never forget the valuable – and probably more reliable – feedback you get during the speech itself:

- What can you see on the faces of the audience –

smiles, nods of agreement, excitement, confusion, boredom?
- Do audience members look as though they need to strain to hear you?
- Are people asleep? (Remember that this is not always a bad thing, and it may refer to an over-indulgent lunch or an overheated auditorium rather than the quality of your performance.)
- What do the questions from the audience tell you about the clarity and relevance of what you have been saying?

To maximise your chances of getting helpful feedback during the actual performance, consider making yourself available to audience members during coffee or comfort breaks so that you can receive immediate comments on important issues.

The most common way of obtaining information on your performance from the audience is, of course, the questionnaire asking for their feedback, the so-called 'happy sheets'. You will find hundreds of examples of these on the Internet, and I'm not going to inflict any of my own on you. In practice, the organisers of an event will often impose their own questionnaire on their speakers.

For myself, I always try to design a survey for each particular talk and audience. The fundamental principle I follow in getting decent feedback is that it is not enough to ask for marks out of ten. Specific, detailed comments are usually much more helpful.

I am particularly interested in asking the audience:

- What was the most useful part of the presentation, the most valuable thing learned?
- What was the least useful part?

- How could the session have been made better – what specific changes would you like to see made?
- Was the session too long/too short/about the right length?
- If any handouts and visual aids were used, do you have suggestions for improving them?

When you tell the audience that you encourage feedback, please do sound as though you mean it. It can make a vast difference to the amount of helpful information that comes back to you.

Remember that the most useful feedback is going to be telling you about things that would be better done differently. "I couldn't follow your logic on point C" is more helpful to you as a speaker for the future than "That was brilliant!" That doesn't stop such feedback being uncomfortable to receive, but do try to make yourself as open as possible to it, even if it leaves you disappointed in the short term. Criticism is never pleasant, but detailed, constructive feedback is by far the best way to improve.

When you do get comments like "I enjoyed your talk – great work!", please accept them with grace, but then try to explore more deeply. Ask them what they thought was the best bit, which part resounded most strongly with them.

There is one exception to the rule of taking into account all the feedback you receive.

I usually try to discount the most favourable 5% and the most critical 5% of comments. They are usually too extreme to offer any value to someone seeking to improve their performance. They often have much more to do with the personal issues of the individual commenting than with your speech.

When you comment on other people's talks, can I ask you please on behalf of speakers everywhere to observe these principles?

- Try to understand the speaker's intentions: don't be critical if the presentation did not achieve what it did not intend to achieve.
- Criticise constructively so they can do it better next time.
- If there is something you disapprove of, be certain it's the speaker's failure, not the constraints of your imagination.

In all this, remember the limitations of audience feedback. Any happy sheet completed immediately after the speaker has stopped talking will only give the initial thoughts of someone keen to get out of the building, and will not be a considered view on the practical relevance of the talk. In particular, it will tell you nothing at all about the positive or negative nature of the actions, if any, that the listener took as a result of the talk.

Amateur dramatics and other speaking pursuits

There are other speaking activities, worthwhile in their own right, that many people find improve their public speaking.

Here are some suggestions:

- If you are still at school or college, check whether there is a debating society you can join. If not, find some like-minded people and set one up. Apart from being ideal for your speaking skills, debating encourages you to delve deeply into a subject and get to know it thoroughly. The essence of a debate is to expose people to the two sides of any proposition, and so it can also make us more open-minded in a world that has become sadly bigoted in so many areas.

- For me, the hobby of amateur dramatics has been especially helpful. (I do a brilliant impression of Prince Charles talking to his vegetables, though I say it myself.) Performing in front of an audience when other people are sharing the stage with you is less scary than solo public speaking, but still quite challenging enough. Am-dram helps you to:
  * Familiarise yourself with a script.
  * Learn how to position yourself on a stage.
  * Project your voice.
  * Recover when things go wrong, which is the very essence of amateur dramatics.
- Some people find it helpful to take classes in improvisational theatre, often called improv or impro. This is a type of theatre where, in Wikipedia's definition, 'most or all of what is performed is created at the moment it is performed.' In other words, you make it up as you go along. Improv comedy is a particularly popular area.

  Improvisation incorporates these elements that are helpful to a public speaker:
  * Living in the moment.
  * Encouraging a playful state of mind.
  * Feeling in touch with one's body.
  * Connecting with other people.
  * Making mistakes.
  * Being comfortable with making those mistakes, and then moving on.

Practice at improvisation can be particularly useful in giving you the strength and flexibility to deal with things going wrong in a presentation, whether it be a lack of interest from the audience, hostile questions or technology on the blink. It develops a sense of good humour in a speaker and an 'I can deal with whatever happens' approach.

- Less demanding, but still helpful, speaking pursuits include reading poems and speeches aloud to yourself, family and friends. These recitals will increase your vocal range, make you more comfortable with the practice of speaking to an audience, and – if you record yourself and then listen back – help you become more familiar and at ease with the sound of your voice in a public forum.

- Consider joining a local speaking club, such as those of Toastmasters International or the Association of Speakers Clubs. (If you are a member of the Society for the Prevention of Cruelty to Apostrophes, I can only apologise to you for the missing one after *Speakers* in the Association's title.) There you will work with like-minded people to improve your presentation techniques. Make sure that the particular club you join is one where people give and receive constructive feedback rather than count up your 'ums' and 'ahs'.

- In broader terms, there is much to be gained by watching and listening critically to other speakers. What makes them effective or ineffective? What tricks or approaches do they use that you can adopt, or would be better to avoid? But don't go quite to the extent that I do. Often, I'm so busy marking presenters for rhetorical merit or artistic impression that I completely fail to notice the substance of what they are saying.

- The Internet is a terrific resource. A search for 'great speeches' on YouTube provides endlessly fascinating and helpful material. The TED talks (http://www.ted.com/) are of a consistently high standard: they broaden the mind and entertain simultaneously. They are also models of focused content and appropriate brevity, two of the most difficult challenges for speakers. Their importance to public speaking is massive. The people from TED set out a helpful playlist at http://www.ted.com/playlists/226/before_public_speaking of talks that you might want to look at in preparation for a presentation.

- The idea of doing something even scarier than giving a speech to raise your confidence and performance levels is something we touched on earlier when we talked about Hugo Rifkind and his stand-up comedy in Chapter 27. As Sian Beilock says in her book *Choke*: "When you know what the worst thing that can happen is, and you have experienced it already, you will be less likely to worry about it."

Keep on reviewing progress

Beyond analysing any particular talk we have given, it's a good discipline from time to time to review more generally the areas we could usefully work on. It's much harder to improve if we don't have a period of reflection to evaluate how we are getting on.

In my most recent three-month review, for example, I identified the current areas I need to spend more time on as:

- Speaking more slowly.
- Keeping my energy levels up during longer talks.
- Involving the audience more.

Bear in mind that no such self-assessment is complete without a review of what you have been doing genuinely well. Celebrate your successes.

Further reading

With the advent of the Internet, it's now cheap and easy to find the texts of some great orations of the past online. For speech compilations in book form, *The Penguin Book of Historic Speeches* and *The Penguin Book of Modern Speeches,* both edited by Brian MacArthur, are invaluable. And because I think he is currently the greatest speechmaker of all in the English language, I always recommend people to obtain the most up-to-date collection of speeches by Barack Obama they can find. As I write, the title that wins that prize is *We are the Change We Seek: The Speeches of Barack Obama,* published in January 2017.

For those who are looking for something not quite so political in nature, there are some great speeches and talks in the non-fiction collections of the writers Neil Gaiman and his friend Terry Pratchett, entitled *The View from the Cheap Seats* and *A Slip of the Keyboard* respectively. Included in the latter work is *Shaking Hands with Death,* the 2010 Richard Dimbleby lecture, in which Pratchett discusses Alzheimer's disease, from which he suffered, and our relationship with death. *Shaking Hands with Death* is an astonishingly good piece of work.

For general books about public speaking, my baker's dozen of top recommendations goes like this:

- Chris Anderson – *TED Talks: The official TED guide to public speaking*
- Joey Asher – *15 Minutes Including Q&A: A plan to save the world from lousy presentations*
- Max Atkinson – *Lend Me Your Ears: All you need to know about making speeches and presentations*
- Scott Berkun – *Confessions of a Public Speaker*
- Carmine Gallo – *The Presentation Secrets of Steve*

Jobs: How to Be Insanely Great in Front of Any Audience

- James C Humes – *Speak Like Churchill, Stand Like Lincoln*
- Malcolm Kushner & Rob Yeung – *Public Speaking and Presentations For Dummies*
- Sam Leith – *You Talkin' to Me?: Rhetoric from Aristotle to Obama*
- Andy Lopata & Peter Roper – *… And Death Came Third! The Definitive Guide to Networking and Speaking in Public*
- Bob Monkhouse – *Bob Monkhouse's Complete Speaker's Handbook* (an earlier edition had the title *Just Say a Few Words*)
- Mitch Murray – *Mitch Murray's One-liners for Business: And How to Use Them in Your Speech*
- Simon Raybould – *Presentation Genius: 40 Insights From the Science of Presenting*
- Chris Steward & Mike Wilkinson – *The Bluffer's Guide to Public Speaking*

If you like following bloggers, my top recommendations at the time of writing are:

- Andrew Dlugan – *Six Minutes: Public Speaking and Presentation Skills Blog*
- Olivia Mitchell & Tony Burns – *Speaking about Presenting*
- Nick Morgan – *Public Words*
- John Zimmer – *Manner of Speaking*

Beyond these writers and bloggers, there is, of course, a vast body of writing about public speaking that has built up over the centuries. To me, the extracts from that writing incorporated into this book seem as relevant, fresh and thought-provoking as ever; I hope you feel the same.

A variety of other tips

Read widely, both from classic texts and from more popular works. That breadth of awareness is exceptionally helpful for a speaker.

Test your new material out on smaller audiences to start with, in situations where there is less pressure. This is a technique used by one of the world's most successful comedians, Jerry Seinfeld, so it will do for me.

There is a lot to learn from the best fictional oratory. On DVD, *The West Wing*, the American political drama, has some brilliant speeches, particularly in the first four series. The writer, Aaron Sorkin, gives Present Josiah 'Jed' Bartlet, played by Martin Sheen, some magnificent material which Sheen delivers with great skill.

Get a coach

Think about finding a trusted coach or mentor who can give you truthful feedback on both the dry runs of your presentations and the actual performances. We saw the value of coaching at the start of this chapter in the work required to become an outstanding performer, and it applies to the developing speaker as much as to the international expert. Your coach or mentor might be someone you work with or someone whose own speaking has impressed you.

It is important to find a coach who will be honest with you while being constructive and supportive. In particular, they must have a feeling for your personality. As Garry Kasparov, the former world chess champion and mentor to younger players, wisely puts it, in the context of the advice he gives to the people he coaches:

> "There's this conventional wisdom that it's possible to give universal advice – a tip. But we're all different. Something that works for you may be counter-productive for me... So make sure to play your own game."

Conclusion

Most important of all, do remember that the best way to get better at public speaking is to do more of it. There's a lot of truth in the maxim attributed (probably wrongly) to the Russian playwright Anton Chekhov: "Knowledge is of no value unless you put it into practice." So please do actively look out for opportunities to speak, and make it known among friends and colleagues that you are one of those rare individuals willing to stand up on a stage and talk. You will find the response hugely encouraging because there aren't many people like us around. Get out there and add yourself to the select ranks of decent speakers in the world! Just do it! Please!

Points to take from this chapter

- Getting effective feedback is the key to progressing as a speaker.
- Review your performance as soon as you can afterwards.
- Look for specific, detailed comments from audience members.
- Consider amateur dramatics or joining a local speaking club.

- Watch and listen critically to other speakers.
- Keep on reviewing your progress.
- Think about finding a constructive coach who will be honest with you.
- Do more public speaking!

Nothing now remains but for me to dot some i's, cross some t's, join up some loose connections and assert one more time why the effort we put into public speaking is so well justified. All that is coming up in the next, and final, chapter.

Notes

The Making of an Expert by K Anders Ericsson, Michael J Prietula and Edward T Cokely can be found in the July–August 2007 edition of the *Harvard Business Review*. The interview with Anders Ericsson comes from the 18 November, 2016 edition of *TES* magazine. More details on his research are available in his fascinating book written with Robert Pool, *Peak: How all of us can achieve extraordinary things*, Vintage, 2017. Jerry Seinfeld's practice of developing his material at small venues to start with can be seen in the fascinating documentary, *Comedian*. Garry Kasparov's comment is from an interview with him in the *Harvard Business Review* for April 2015.

CHAPTER 40

Put it all in context

Introduction

We've reached the point where I've told you more or less all I know about public speaking. If you've stuck with me so far, I would venture a guess that fruitful times as a speaker await you.

I now want to bring my themes together and round everything off. In this final chapter, I'll discuss how to work out whether any particular talk can be counted a success: it can't just be judged by the applause you get at the end. I'll explain why it's pointless worrying whether a speech will be regarded as a hit or a miss in the longer term. More generally, I'll argue that the future of public speaking remains rosy. I'll try (gently) to persuade you to be a force for good when you speak in public, and I'll remind you why all the hard work I've been asking you to undertake is so worthwhile. Then I'll stop.

How should you judge your success?

How do you judge the success of any speech or presentation you have given? Unless you have been speaking purely for entertainment, it must surely be judged by its results. It is not a question of whether, say, you produced some elegant gestures, or spoke with a musical voice. Rather, the fundamental issue follows on from our discussion in Chapter 4 about focusing on what you want to achieve. Quite simply, did you accomplish your purpose(s)?

In practice, some subsidiary questions may help answer that one big question:

- Could the audience hear you without straining?
- Did you convey your ideas clearly?
- Did they comprehend your message?
- Will they go ahead and act on it?

Sometimes it will be even more straightforward than this. In his book *The Delivery of a Speech*, Ray Keeslar Immel sets out the ultimate, no-nonsense, utilitarian approach:

> "A speech must be judged, not by any or all of its formal qualities of delivery, such as voice, gesture, position, etc, but by the results achieved. If two speeches are made to the same audience under the same conditions, both for the purpose of raising money for the Red Cross, and if one speech nets one hundred dollars and the other nets two hundred, the second is twice as good a speech as the first, regardless of any formal qualities of the two speeches."

How does history judge success?

It is fun to try to rank the great speeches and speakers, but I don't believe that the exercise can be much more than an entertaining game to play. Moreover, how do you set the criteria for greatness?

Was Adolf Hitler a great speaker? He was mesmerising as an orator, as we will see in a moment, but his views and actions were loathsome. Closer to home, how about Enoch Powell, an outstanding speaker in many respects but one who is today mainly remembered for his divisive 1968 'Rivers of Blood' speech criticising Commonwealth immigration?

The debate on the extent to which the quality of a speech depends on its truth and decency goes back through the millennia, at least to the time when the Greek philosopher Plato argued against the sophists, skilled teachers of rhetoric who seemed to him to live in a moral vacuum.

Beyond the ethical issues, sheer unadulterated luck plays a significant part in determining the views of history about a speech. The immediate reaction to Martin Luther King Jr's 'I have a dream' speech was mostly positive, but there were significant dissenting voices. He overran his allotted time by about ten minutes, which you will know from reading this book to be an unpardonable sin. He did not give much of a call to action: indeed, many civil rights activists were none too keen on the exposition of a wishy-washy dream as opposed to a plan of campaign. They would perhaps have been surprised to learn that the speech would later be voted the finest of the twentieth century.

Similarly, Abraham Lincoln's Gettysburg Address, perhaps the most famous speech from the nineteenth century, wasn't an immediate success either.

Here's what Henry Ketcham says in his *Life of Abraham Lincoln*:

> "The effect of this speech was not immediate. Colonel Lamon was on the platform when it was delivered and he says very decidedly that Everett, Seward, himself, and Lincoln were all of opinion that the speech was a failure. He

adds: 'I state it as a fact, and without fear of contradiction, that this famous Gettysburg speech was not regarded by the audience to whom it was addressed, or by the press or people of the United States, as a production of extraordinary merit.'"

However, after a few days, Ketcham adds, "The public awoke to the fact that Lincoln's 'few remarks' were immeasurably superior to Everett's brilliant and learned oration." (Everett was the main speaker.) And history has agreed: this was the speech which, above all others, helped heal the American nation after the disaster of the Civil War.

Even if a speech seems convincing today, will it endure in popular memory? Will it still seem good in a hundred years' time?

Well, of course, it all depends. Spencer Leigh Hughes, writing in 1913, commented that he had "a notion that some of the performances of the Parliamentary orators of other days have been much overrated, and that the action or gesticulation in which they indulged would be now regarded as extravagant even on a cart in Hyde Park." In practice, I don't think it's a question of previous performances being overrated so much as that styles change. Modern practice has increasingly favoured a more low-key approach.

In general, the reputation of any particular speech will change as public attitudes and opinions move on. Being on the winning side is, of course, hugely helpful in this process. We would not admire Winston Churchill's stirring oratory in the Second World War nearly as much if Britain and the Allies had been defeated. Margaret Thatcher's speeches would be no more than footnotes in scholarly texts if her political initiatives had failed.

In a fascinating book about Martin Luther King Jr's 'I have a dream' speech, *The Speech*, the journalist Gary Younge gives this excellent commentary on the way in which history reaches its capricious judgements:

"Not all great speeches are deemed historically significant. 'History' does not objectively sift through speeches, pick out the best on their merits, and then dedicate them faithfully to public memory. It commits itself to the task with great prejudice and fickle appreciation in a manner that tells us as much about historians and their times as the speech itself."

Is there a future for public speaking?

Throughout recorded history, it has been a commonplace among writers that oratory is in decline, that its great days lie in the past, that the era of eloquence and powerful speaking is gone. As long ago as 1742, the philosopher David Hume referred to the ancient orators in his essay *Of Eloquence* and commented that "the stile or species of their eloquence was infinitely more sublime than that which modern orators aspire to." In terms of American rhetoric, a scholar called Elvin T Lim devoted an entire book to showing that, as he put it in his very first sentence, "The state of presidential rhetoric today [his book was published in 2008] has taken a nosedive from our founding era."

Happily, there have always been contrary voices.

FE Smith, 1st Earl of Birkenhead, a politician and barrister who was an outstanding speaker himself, noted our tendency to idealise the speaking past. "Those who speak with pessimism of our modern orators," he said, "seem to me somewhat to ignore the tendency… of mankind to make heroes of their predecessors."

Over a century ago John P Altgeld got it spot on in his book *Oratory: Its Requirements and Its Rewards*:

"Is oratory dying? On the contrary, it is growing in favour and in importance. At no time in the history of the world did men listen as eagerly as they do in America today.

The newspapers, instead of destroying oratory, simply prepare the ground for a higher order of eloquence. They educate the public as to the facts, and thus partially relieve the speaker of dry detail, so that he can devote himself more largely to a discussion of principles than he otherwise could do. At the same time they multiply his audience by the thousand. Once the speaker reached only the people before him; now he reaches millions in addition, so that the orator can now wield an influence that heretofore was impossible. True, it increases his labour. He must charm not only his hearers, but also delight his readers.

The universal intelligence among the people, and the presence of cultivated women, have tended to give high character to public meetings and to place them far above the audiences of antiquity.

Neither Demosthenes nor Cicero ever saw such inspiring audiences as greet the modern orator."

John Altgeld's world had been enhanced by the bracing challenge of the press. Now we have an even greater enhancement, and challenge, in the form of the Internet and social media. In this new world, the power of a single voice is stronger than ever before, because modern information technology allows it to speak out to humanity so quickly and clearly. The most popular TED talks, for example, have each received over thirty million views.

A further development has been the return of the old-fashioned public meeting, a trend successfully exploited by Jeremy Corbyn and his allies in the UK and by Donald Trump in the United States. The presenter and columnist Steve Richards, writing perceptively in *The Guardian* in August 2016, noted that: "The glory of the public meeting is that there is no escape. A speaker must deliver. The audience is composed of real people. The speaker cannot hide away tweeting alone in a room."

These are days ripe for the development of public speaking.

Oratory must always change along with the world in which it functions. On 1 February 1867, John Stuart Mill, one of the leading philosophers of the nineteenth century, gave a well-received inaugural address as Lord Rector of the University of St Andrews. It was quite long (over fifty pages in the edition I own), and this was the first sentence:

> "In complying with the custom which prescribes that the person whom you have called by your suffrages to the honorary presidency of your University should embody in an address a few thoughts on the subjects which most nearly concern a seat of liberal education, let me begin by saying that this usage appears to me highly commendable."

That single sentence is nearly sixty words long, and I have to admit that it does not grab my attention. Its main significance, I think, is in showing that, with few exceptions, it is in the end unhelpful to ask whether oratory gets better or worse over the generations. It just changes, and changes almost beyond recognition.

John Stuart Mill gave his speech in an era when life proceeded more slowly. His leisurely style belongs to a bygone day. Life moves faster now, and the attention span of an audience is vastly shorter. If you compare that Mill sentence with the extract from Nick Clegg's speech in Chapter 11 (fifteen sentences averaging less than six words each), you'll see they have barely anything in common beyond being in a form of English. Public speaking must constantly develop and move on according to the spirit of the times.

Ultimately, the future of public speaking depends on what is taught in schools. We have recently seen, particularly in London, the beginnings of a movement to put more focus on teaching oracy in schools. Oracy, the ability to express oneself fluently and grammatically in speech and to comprehend the speech of others, is a term that was coined in the 1960s, and we must hope that it comes to be viewed as matching literacy and numeracy in importance in the classroom. There is a growing economic impetus for this to happen: employer organisations continue to complain about the lack of oral communication skills in their prospective workforce.

Be a force for good

At its essence, this book has been an instruction manual on how to speak successfully in public, and I have not commented much on the morality of what you say when you do that. Whether you are a force for good or a force for evil, the techniques we have discussed will usually work equally well. Adolf Hitler's speeches are perhaps the greatest proof of this.

Here, in November 1937, is the journalist Raymond Clapper writing about Hitler in his column *Between You and Me* for the *Washington Post:*

> "Soon after I arrived here in Berlin I saw Hitler in action before an audience of 20,000.
> … Hitler begins to speak. His voice has no arresting quality, none of the smooth resonance of Roosevelt's nor the sharply

penetrating huskiness of Al Smith – the two most effective
political speakers I have ever heard. But soon his tempo
increases until his words are pouring out in torrents, his neck
cords bulging. Interrupted by applause, he twists his neck
and rolls his eyes upward while waiting to resume.
I have observed countless audiences and never have I seen
more intense or more sustained attention. Not a head turns
away. Laughs and applause burst forth from all parts of
the hall with the bursting impact which comes only from
spontaneity, not from claque leaders. I have never seen an
audience more a unit. There were only two persons in the
hall – Hitler and the audience – completely meshed in their
mutual responsiveness. As he left, the crowd again surged to
the centre aisle to be near him."

Well, it worked for Hitler, in his speeches at least, but no sensible
speaker should want to follow the dark side. Apart from anything
else, it is hard to remember your lies from last time and to avoid
contradicting yourself. Yes, you can speak for either good or ill,
but I would recommend the former.

Surprisingly little practical work has yet been done on
effective ethical codes of conduct for public speakers. Much of
what does exist is either unwieldy or pompous. Far and away the
best code I have found is an American model. That is why in my
own speaking I adopt, to the best of my ability, the principles
of the *Credo for Ethical Communication,* approved by the US
National Communication Association in 1999.

They go like this:

- We advocate truthfulness, accuracy, honesty, and
  reason as essential to the integrity of communication.
- We endorse freedom of expression, diversity of
  perspective, and tolerance of dissent to achieve

the informed and responsible decision making fundamental to a civil society.

- We strive to understand and respect other communicators before evaluating and responding to their messages.
- We promote access to communication resources and opportunities as necessary to fulfil human potential and contribute to the well-being of families, communities, and society.
- We promote communication climates of caring and mutual understanding that respect the unique needs and characteristics of individual communicators.
- We condemn communication that degrades individuals and humanity through distortion, intimidation, coercion, and violence, and through the expression of intolerance and hatred.
- We are committed to the courageous expression of personal convictions in pursuit of fairness and justice.
- We advocate sharing information, opinions, and feelings when facing significant choices while also respecting privacy and confidentiality.
- We accept responsibility for the short- and long-term consequences for our own communication and expect the same of others.

If you take the view that any of this is self-evident and therefore barely worth saying, you might like to think back to the ethical standards displayed in the debates that led up to recent United Kingdom general elections and United States presidential elections. I say no more.

The book - summarised!

Remember that what I've said in this book represents rough guidelines together with tools for your speaking toolbox. None of it is written in stone: there are no fixed rules. As I warned you at the outset, nothing in this book has been rocket science.

Having said that, I leave you with the thoughts I hope you will take away with you:

- The secret of public speaking is, of course, that there is no secret, no cut and dried principles, no one formula for a great talk. Presenting is not an obscure or abstruse art. It's all rather straightforward, to be honest.
- Identify something worth saying to an audience, and then work out your individual style of saying it. It is as simple as that.
- It may be simple, but that doesn't make it easy. Though there are many routes to success, annoyingly none of them can be achieved without hard work on the part of the speaker.
- Good coaching helps, but beyond that you have to put the hours in and do the practice. It's worth persevering, because doing well at public speaking helps careers and provides tremendous personal satisfaction.
- Experience confirms that, if you can implement just those few ideas in this book that resonate with you and stick with them, you will significantly improve your performance as a speaker over time.
- You are more likely to achieve your aims if you enjoy yourself during the process. At the very least, you will have enjoyed yourself.

- However many presentations you give, however many speeches you make, you will still experience a degree of tension and discomfort in the process. And quite properly so: you need them to improve your performance. Otherwise, you will, at best, only be coasting. Public speaking is always a work in progress.
- When you get up to speak, forget the thousand and one details in this or any other book on the subject. Just look out at your audience and go for it.

Why it is all worth it

Some people are attracted into public speaking by the potential perks of the trade.

In April 2010, the speaking requirements of our friend Sarah Palin, the former governor of Alaska and famed, or infamous, public figure, were disclosed to a startled world. Her demands included:

- Two bottles of still water, unopened, beside a wooden lectern and accompanied by a 'bendable' straw (I swear I'm not making this up, and yes, I too thought most straws were bendy to start with).
- Three deluxe hotel rooms.
- A first-class flight or private aircraft that 'MUST BE a Lear 60 or larger'.

The contract did not mention Mrs Palin's actual fee as a speaker, but it was reckoned at the time that she regularly earned US$100,000 for a speech. Heaven knows what fees and perks she might have commanded if she were a better speaker.

Sadly, most of us will never reach the lofty heights of

remuneration and benefits enjoyed by Sarah Palin. We have a different form of compensation.

For me, an audience with smiles on their faces, or just paying attention, will be entirely sufficient, thank you. When things go well in your speech, you may get that amazing feeling that you have the audience in the palm of your hand or, even better, that you and the audience have joined to form a single unit. That is the ultimate experience for a speaker.

Conclusion

In finishing, I cannot do better than reproduce the final words of *The Art of Public Speaking* by my mentor, Spencer Leigh Hughes:

> "In looking back over the whole subject of public speaking, I am of opinion that, after all, the most important thing is to know how and when to stop, and have the courage and the good sense to stop when the right time has come. Nor does this remark apply only to speaking – it is of equal importance in regard to writing, and, that being so, it may be well that I, who have taken the liberty of giving so much advice to others, many of whom are very likely well qualified to instruct me, should act on my own precept – and cease."

As my end-of-speech notes would say, 'Ladies & gentlemen, I have nothing to add. Thank you for coming. [SIT DOWN]'

Points to take from this chapter

- Judge a speech on its results – in particular, did you accomplish your purpose?

- Luck is hugely important in determining history's view of a speech.
- There will always be a future for public speaking, as long as it moves with the times.
- Be a force for good when you speak.
- Those moments when you and the audience are as one make it all worthwhile.
- Stop when you have nothing more to say.

Notes

Elvin Lim's book is entitled *The Anti-Intellectual Presidency: The Decline of Presidential Rhetoric from George Washington to George W Bush*, OUP USA, 2008. Lord Birkenhead's words are from a piece by him on *Parliamentary Oratory* in Volume IV of *The Book of Public Speaking*. The extract from Raymond Clapper comes from *The Penguin Book of Columnists*, edited by Christopher Silvester, 1998. You can find the NCA Credo for Ethical Communication at https://www.natcom.org/sites/default/files/pages/1999_Public_Statements_NCA_Credo_for_Ethical_Communication_November.pdf.

About the author

Ian Nichol entered a public speaking competition at the age of thirteen and has been hooked ever since. He gained first class honours in Classics at Cambridge, where his studies in oratory and rhetoric gave further impetus to his speaking career.

Ian was a tax and training partner at the leading business advisory firm PricewaterhouseCoopers. He ended his career there in the specialist group which developed and ran training courses for clients in finance and management development. Ian went on to run his own training and management development business, focusing on leadership skills and executive coaching. He has also in his time been a commissioner of both the Criminal Cases Review Commission and the Press Complaints Commission.

This varied background means that Ian has gained extensive experience of successful speaking: as a business speaker, a careers lecturer, a technical trainer in tax and finance, a TV and radio performer, and a humorous after-dinner entertainer. In addition to his speaking work, he has coached individuals to give well-received presentations ranging from highly technical seminars to keynote speeches.

Ian lives in Warwickshire with his wife, Val. In his spare time he plays Scrabble, keeps fit and avoids gardening. He has previously been the author and editor of successful publications about tax; this is his first book on public speaking.

Please feel free to get in touch with Ian at ijnichol@btinternet.com.

Index

by Marian Aird